"In preparing for the international Synod of Bishops on 'The Word of God in the Life and Mission of the Church,' Pope Benedict XVI reminded the Church that a prayerful study of the Scriptures is at the heart of the Church's renewal. The new Catholic Commentary on Sacred Scripture promises to directly serve that purpose. Drawing on sound biblical scholarship, the commentaries present the reader with the rich harvest of that study, reflecting on the message of the biblical text and engaging the life of faith from a Catholic perspective."

—**Donald Senior, CP**, president, Catholic Theological Union

"This series promises to be spiritually and doctrinally informative, based on careful, solid biblical exegesis. The method and content of this work will be helpful to teachers of the faith at different levels and will provide a reliable guide to people seeking to deepen their knowledge and thereby nourish their faith. I strongly recommend the Catholic Commentary on Sacred Scripture."

—**Cormac Cardinal Murphy-O'Connor**, Archbishop of Westminster

"I welcome with great joy the launch of this new collection of commentaries on the Bible because the project corresponds perfectly to a pressing need in the Church. I am speaking about exegetical studies that are well grounded from a scholarly point of view but not overburdened with technical details, and at the same time related to the riches of ancient interpretation, nourishing for spiritual life, and useful for catechesis, preaching, evangelization, and other forms of pastoral ministry. This is the kind of commentary for which the majority of readers have a great desire."

—**Albert Cardinal Vanhoye, SJ**, Pontifical Biblical Institute, former secretary of the Pontifical Biblical Commission

"When the Scripture is read in the liturgy, it is heard as a living voice. But when expounded in a commentary, it is too often read as a document from the past. This fine new series unites the ancient and the contemporary by offering insight into the biblical text—verse by verse—as well as spiritual application to the lives of Christians today. I particularly like the sidebars inserted into the text called 'Living Tradition' that feature memorable sayings from great Christian teachers or brief explanations of puzzling terms and ideas."

—**Robert Louis Wilken**, University of Virginia

"This new Bible commentary series is based on solid scholarship and enriched by the church's long tradition of study and reflection. Enhanced by an attractive format, it provides an excellent resource for all who are serving in pastoral ministry and for the individual reader who searches the Scriptures for guidance in the Christian life."

—**Emil A. Wcela**, Auxiliary Bishop (retired), Diocese of Rockville Centre; past president, Catholic Biblical Association

"The Catholic Commentary on Sacred Scripture is an ideal tool for living our faith more deeply. This extraordinary resource combines superior scholarship and a vivid, accessible style that will serve the interested layperson and the serious scholar equally well. It feeds both the mind and the heart and should be on the shelf of every committed Catholic believer. I highly recommend it."

—**Charles J. Chaput, OFM Cap**, Archbishop of Denver

"This new commentary series appears to me to be a gift of the Holy Spirit to Catholic clergy, religious, and laity at this historic moment. Pope Benedict has effectively announced the rebirth of Catholic biblical theology, bringing together Scripture, tradition, and the teachings of the Church. This commentary reflects not only biblical criticism but also the unity of the Word of God as it applies to our lives. This is a marvelous and timely introduction."

—**Benedict J. Groeschel, CFR**, author and preacher

"This new commentary series should meet a need that has long been pointed out: a guide to Scripture that will be both historically responsible and shaped by the mind of the Church's tradition. It promises to be a milestone in the recovery of a distinctively Catholic approach to exegesis."

—**Aidan Nichols, OP**, University of Oxford; Fellow of Greyfriars, Oxford

"This series employs the Church's methodology of studying Sacred Scripture in a faithful, dynamic, and fruitful way. With interest in Catholic Bible studies growing rapidly, the repeated question has been, 'can you suggest a reliable commentary?' The Catholic Commentary on Sacred Scripture is now the go-to resource that I can enthusiastically recommend to all my students."

—**Jeff Cavins**, founder, The Great Adventure Catholic Bible Study System

Second
Corinthians

Catholic Commentary on Sacred Scripture

Series Editors
Peter S. Williamson
Mary Healy

Associate Editor
Kevin Perrotta

Consulting Editors
Scott Hahn, Franciscan University of Steubenville
†Daniel J. Harrington, SJ, Weston Jesuit School of Theology
William S. Kurz, SJ, Marquette University
†Francis Martin, Sacred Heart Major Seminary
Frank J. Matera, Catholic University of America
George Montague, SM, St. Mary's University
Terrence Prendergast, SJ, Archbishop of Ottawa

Second Corinthians

Thomas D. Stegman, SJ

Baker Academic
a division of Baker Publishing Group
Grand Rapids, Michigan

© 2009 by Thomas D. Stegman

Published by Baker Academic
a division of Baker Publishing Group
P.O. Box 6287, Grand Rapids, MI 49516-6287
www.bakeracademic.com

Printed in the United States of America

Library of Congress Cataloging-in-Publication Data

Stegman, Thomas.
    Second Corinthians / Thomas D. Stegman.
       p.   cm. — (Catholic commentary on sacred scripture)
    Includes bibliographical references and indexes.
    ISBN 978-0-8010-3583-8 (pbk.)
     1. Bible. N. T. Corinthians, 2nd—Commentaries. 2. Catholic Church—Doctrines. I. Title.
    BS2675.53.S75 2010
    227'.307—dc22
                                              2009031831

Imprimatur:
The Very Rev. G. Thomas Krettek, SJ
Provincial of the Wisconsin Province of the Society of Jesus

April 27, 2009

The *imprimatur* is an official declaration that a book or pamphlet is free of doctrinal or moral error. There is no implication that those who have granted the *imprimatur* agree with the content, opinions, or statements expressed therein.

Baker Publishing Group publications use paper produced from sustainable forestry practices and post-consumer waste whenever possible.

To my fellow Jesuits

Contents

Illustrations

Editors' Preface

The Church has always venerated the divine Scriptures just as she venerates the body of the Lord. . . . All the preaching of the Church should be nourished and governed by Sacred Scripture. For in the sacred books, the Father who is in heaven meets His children with great love and speaks with them; and the power and goodness in the word of God is so great that it stands as the support and energy of the Church, the strength of faith for her sons and daughters, the food of the soul, a pure and perennial fountain of spiritual life.

Second Vatican Council, *Dei Verbum* 21

Were not our hearts burning while he spoke to us on the way and opened the scriptures to us?

Luke 24:32

The Catholic Commentary on Sacred Scripture aims to serve the ministry of the Word of God in the life and mission of the Church. Since Vatican Council II, there has been an increasing hunger among Catholics to study Scripture in depth and in a way that reveals its relationship to liturgy, evangelization, catechesis, theology, and personal and communal life. This series responds to that desire by providing accessible yet substantive commentary on each book of the New Testament, drawn from the best of contemporary biblical scholarship as well as the rich treasury of the Church's tradition. These volumes seek to offer scholarship illumined by faith, in the conviction that the ultimate aim of biblical interpretation is to discover what God has revealed and is still speaking through the sacred text. Central to our approach are the principles taught by Vatican II: first, the use of historical and literary methods to discern what the biblical authors intended to express; second, prayerful theological reflection to understand the sacred text "in accord with the same Spirit by whom it was written"—that is, in light of the content and unity of the whole Scripture, the living tradition of the Church, and the analogy of faith (*Dei Verbum* 12).

The Catholic Commentary on Sacred Scripture is written for those engaged in or training for pastoral ministry and others interested in studying Scripture to understand their faith more deeply, to nourish their spiritual life, or to share the good news with others. With this in mind, the authors focus on the meaning of the text for faith and life rather than on the technical questions that occupy scholars, and they explain the Bible in ordinary language that does not require translation for preaching and catechesis. Although this series is written from the perspective of Catholic faith, its authors draw on the interpretation of Protestant and Orthodox scholars and hope these volumes will serve Christians of other traditions as well.

A variety of features are designed to make the commentary as useful as possible. Each volume includes the biblical text of the New American Bible (NAB), the translation approved for liturgical use in the United States. In order to serve readers who use other translations, the most important differences between the NAB and other widely used translations (RSV, NRSV, JB, NJB, and NIV) are noted and explained. Each unit of the biblical text is followed by a list of references to relevant Scripture passages, Catechism sections, and uses in the Roman Lectionary. The exegesis that follows aims to explain in a clear and engaging way the meaning of the text in its original historical context as well as its perennial meaning for Christians. Reflection and Application sections help readers apply Scripture to Christian life today by responding to questions that the text raises, offering spiritual interpretations drawn from Christian tradition or providing suggestions for the use of the biblical text in catechesis, preaching, or other forms of pastoral ministry.

Interspersed throughout the commentary are Biblical Background sidebars that present historical, literary, or theological information and Living Tradition sidebars that offer pertinent material from the postbiblical Christian tradition, including quotations from Church documents and from the writings of saints and Church Fathers. The Biblical Background sidebars are indicated by a photo of urns that were excavated in Jerusalem, signifying the importance of historical study in understanding the sacred text. The Living Tradition sidebars are indicated by an image of Eadwine, a twelfth-century monk and scribe, signifying the growth in the Church's understanding that comes by the grace of the Holy Spirit as believers study and ponder the word of God in their hearts (see *Dei Verbum* 8).

Maps and a Glossary are located in the back of each volume for easy reference. The glossary explains key terms from the biblical text as well as theological or exegetical terms, which are marked in the commentary with a cross (†). A list of Suggested Resources, an Index of Pastoral Topics, and an Index of Sidebars are included to enhance the usefulness of these volumes. Further resources, including questions for reflection or discussion, can be found at the series web site, www.CatholicScriptureCommentary.com.

It is our desire and prayer that these volumes be of service so that more and more "the word of the Lord may speed forward and be glorified" (2 Thess 3:1) in the Church and throughout the world.

Peter S. Williamson
Mary Healy
Kevin Perrotta

Note to Readers

The New American Bible differs slightly from most English translations in its verse numbering of the Psalms and certain other parts of the Old Testament. For instance, Ps 51:4 in the NAB is Ps 51:2 in other translations; Mal 3:19 in the NAB is Mal 4:1 in other translations. Readers who use different translations are advised to keep this in mind when looking up Old Testament cross-references given in the commentary.

Abbreviations

†	indicates that the definition of a term appears in the glossary
AB	Anchor Bible
ACCS	Ancient Christian Commentary on Scripture
AnBib	Analecta Biblica
Catechism	*Catechism of the Catholic Church* (Second Edition)
CBQ	*Catholic Biblical Quarterly*
CCSS	Catholic Commentary on Sacred Scripture
EBib	*Etudes bibliques*
Greg	*Gregorianum*
ICC	International Critical Commentary
JB	Jerusalem Bible
JSNTSup	Journal for the Study of the New Testament: Supplement Series
JTS	*Journal of Theological Studies*
Lectionary	*The Lectionary for Mass* (1998/2002 USA Edition)
NAB	New American Bible
NAC	New American Commentary
NEB	New English Bible
NIB	New Interpreter's Bible
NICNT	New International Commentary on the New Testament
NIGTC	New International Greek Testament Commentary
NIV	New International Version
NJB	New Jerusalem Bible
NRSV	New Revised Standard Version
NTL	New Testament Library
REB	Revised English Bible
RSV	Revised Standard Version
SBLDS	Society of Biblical Literature Dissertation Series
SBT	Studies in Biblical Theology
SP	Sacra Pagina
WBC	Word Biblical Commentary

Books of the Old Testament

Gen	Genesis	Deut	Deuteronomy	1 Sam	1 Samuel
Exod	Exodus	Josh	Joshua	2 Sam	2 Samuel
Lev	Leviticus	Judg	Judges	1 Kings	1 Kings
Num	Numbers	Ruth	Ruth	2 Kings	2 Kings

1 Chron	1 Chronicles	Eccles	Ecclesiastes	Amos	Amos
2 Chron	2 Chronicles	Song	Song of Songs	Obad	Obadiah
Ezra	Ezra	Wis	Wisdom	Jon	Jonah
Neh	Nehemiah	Sir	Sirach	Mic	Micah
Tob	Tobit	Isa	Isaiah	Nah	Nahum
Jdt	Judith	Jer	Jeremiah	Hab	Habakkuk
Esther	Esther	Lam	Lamentations	Zeph	Zephaniah
1 Macc	1 Maccabees	Bar	Baruch	Hag	Haggai
2 Macc	2 Maccabees	Ezek	Ezekiel	Zech	Zechariah
Job	Job	Dan	Daniel	Mal	Malachi
Ps	Psalms	Hosea	Hosea		
Prov	Proverbs	Joel	Joel		

Books of the New Testament

Matt	Matthew	1 Tim	1 Timothy
Mark	Mark	2 Tim	2 Timothy
Luke	Luke	Titus	Titus
John	John	Philem	Philemon
Acts	Acts of the Apostles	Heb	Hebrews
Rom	Romans	James	James
1 Cor	1 Corinthians	1 Pet	1 Peter
2 Cor	2 Corinthians	2 Pet	2 Peter
Gal	Galatians	1 John	1 John
Eph	Ephesians	2 John	2 John
Phil	Philippians	3 John	3 John
Col	Colossians	Jude	Jude
1 Thess	1 Thessalonians	Rev	Revelation
2 Thess	2 Thessalonians		

Introduction

Second Corinthians is chock-full of challenges and treasures. Victor Paul Furnish begins his magisterial commentary *II Corinthians* by remarking that no other letter attributed to Paul demands more study and effort than this one. At the same time, Furnish acknowledges the rich recompense that comes to the one who engages this text with care.[1] In this letter Paul opens to us a unique window into the way he understands his apostolic life and ministry as patterned after the example of Jesus. We see the Apostle's love and care for a church he has founded. We sense his joys and frustrations. We discover a fledgling community that struggles with many of the same issues that Christians face today, nearly twenty centuries later. And in the midst of all this, we catch glimpses of Paul's inspired—and inspiring—insight into who God is and how he has reached out in love to the world through the life, death, and resurrection of Jesus Christ and the gift of the Holy Spirit. Such insights into God's faithfulness and love demand an appropriate response, and Paul challenges the Corinthians—as well as us—to offer one.

I like to compare the study of 2 Corinthians to the story of Jacob wrestling with the angel of God (Gen 32:23–33). Just as Jacob struggled strenuously through an entire night in his contest with the mysterious heavenly figure, so the reader of 2 Corinthians must be willing to expend energy in hard work. But just as Jacob awakened from his struggle with the divine as a changed person, so the one who works carefully through this letter—a letter that communicates *God's* word—can experience transformation. In fact, Paul alludes to this transformation in 2 Cor 3:18, where he speaks of the Spirit's empowerment

1. Victor Paul Furnish, *II Corinthians: A New Translation with Introduction and Commentary*, AB 32A (New York: Doubleday, 1984), 3.

enabling us to grow more and more Christlike. It is my sincere hope and desire to facilitate the reader's fruitful engagement with this letter. Thus we begin with a brief discussion of its authorship, literary unity, historical context, theological themes, and relevance for today.

Authorship

No reputable scholar doubts that Paul is the author of 2 Corinthians. This epistle is one of the so-called authentic or undisputed Pauline letters.[2] But to say that Paul is the author of 2 Corinthians is not the same as claiming that he literally wrote the text itself. Paul's letters reveal a complex process of composition. Most (if not all) of his letters were likely dictated to a scribe, or amanuensis (see Rom 16:22). In some of his letters, Paul actually took pen in hand to write only the concluding remarks (1 Cor 16:21–24; Gal 6:11–18; Col 4:18; 2 Thess 3:17–18). Second Corinthians contains neither a reference to a secretary nor an explicit notice that Paul writes a note at the end. Does this indicate that this letter, which is personal in so many ways, is from Paul's own hand? Possibly, but not necessarily.[3]

Another indication of authorial complexity is found in the letter's opening line, where Paul identifies "Timothy our brother" as cosender of the letter. Timothy, along with Silvanus, ministered alongside Paul when Paul first brought the †gospel to Corinth (2 Cor 1:19). Some time later, he dispatched Timothy from Ephesus to Corinth to remind the community of what he had taught them (1 Cor 4:17; 16:10). How much, if any, of the content of 2 Corinthians is Timothy's contribution is not possible to determine. What cannot be disputed is that Paul's own personality and voice come through loud and clear. Indeed, the Apostle's voice is the predominant one.

Still, to say that Paul is the author of 2 Corinthians does not exhaust the question of authorship. According to *Dei Verbum*, Vatican II's Dogmatic Constitution on Divine Revelation, sacred Scripture is inspired by the Holy Spirit. Thus, in a very real sense, it is also proper to speak of God as the author of this letter, and this without denying Paul's own creativity and contribution (*Dei Verbum* 11).

2. The other undisputed letters are Romans, 1 Corinthians, Galatians, Philippians, 1 Thessalonians, and Philemon. Six other letters attributed to Paul—Ephesians, Colossians, 2 Thessalonians, 1 Timothy, 2 Timothy, and Titus—are regarded by many scholars as written in the Apostle's name after his death. Luke Timothy Johnson, however, offers plausible grounds for holding that all thirteen letters derive from Paul. See Luke Timothy Johnson, *The Writings of the New Testament: An Interpretation*, rev. ed. (Minneapolis: Fortress, 1999), 393–95, 407–12, and 423–28.

3. Galatians, like 2 Corinthians, includes several of Paul's personal revelations, but the final verses make clear that the letter itself was actually written by a secretary or scribe.

That is to say, we must take into account both the human and divine aspects of the letter's authorship. In connection with the human authorship, we must pay attention to how Paul expressed himself within the limits of a particular time and culture. This means that, among other things, we must be sensitive to the way he reads and interprets the Old Testament.[4] In connection with the divine authorship, we must examine 2 Corinthians within the wider context of the entire biblical canon, both Old and New Testaments, the content of the Church's tradition, and the †analogy of faith (*Dei Verbum* 12). It is my hope that in using this approach we will in some way do justice to both voices as they speak in this extraordinary letter.

Literary Unity

Several interpreters of 2 Corinthians have claimed that the canonical text as we have it today shows evidence of having one or more "seams." These are places in the text where juxtaposed material seems to lack logical coherence or reflects an improbable mood swing, at least in the minds of some. One example is found at 9:15–10:1. After working hard to facilitate reconciliation with the Corinthians following misunderstandings between himself and the community (7:5–16), and after asking them to be generous in contributing to the collection for the church in Jerusalem (8:1–9:15), why would Paul then harangue and threaten the Corinthians (10:1–13:10)? To some, this sudden shift suggests an unlikely mood swing—not to mention an ineffective way to raise funds!

Another seam is detected at 8:24–9:1. Given that Paul offers a lengthy exhortation for the collection in 8:1–24, why does he then speak about it in 9:1 as if he were raising a new topic? A third instance is 2:13–14. Why does Paul suddenly interrupt his report of his anxiety over not finding his coworker Titus (2:12–13) with an exclamation of thanksgiving that is followed by an extended discourse on †apostleship (2:14–7:4)? Yet another seam is discerned at 7:4–5. Why does Paul wait nearly five chapters to resume and finish the story concerning Titus (7:5–16)? Indeed, the resumption of the story at this point seems to some commentators to come from out of the blue. Finally, many interpreters of 2 Corinthians have been baffled by the unusual phrasing and imagery in 6:14–7:1, a passage that seems to interrupt two invitations from Paul to the community to open their hearts to him (6:13 and 7:2).

4. Of course, what we refer to today as the Old Testament was the only Scripture at the time when Paul composed his letters.

In addition to these literary seams, there are references to people and events that are difficult to reconcile in the text as it now stands. Paul's various references to Titus illustrate the difficulty. In 7:5–16 Paul recounts his reunion with Titus after the latter had undertaken a delicate mission to the Corinthians. Titus's task involved conveying to the community a letter from Paul, written in tears, at a critical moment in the Apostle's relationship with them. Titus's mission was apparently successful, as he was able to report back to Paul the Corinthians' desire to be reconciled with him.

Next, in 8:6 Paul alludes to Titus's having begun to facilitate the Corinthians' contribution to the collection for the church in Jerusalem. But when did Titus begin this work? At the time of his recent visit to the community? But was the occasion of that visit—to foster reconciliation between Paul and the Corinthians—an appropriate time to ask them for money? Or had Titus begun this work beforehand?

Then, in 8:16–24 Paul announces that he is sending Titus along with two un-named "brothers" in order to complete the administration of the collection. Finally, in 12:17–18 Paul refers to a previous visit made by Titus and one unnamed "brother," apparently in connection with their comportment while attempting to raise funds. How does one make sense of these various references?

In order to explain the presence of what may appear to be literary seams and the puzzling references to people and events, many commentators resort to partition theories. They claim that the text of 2 Corinthians as it presently stands is a composite of two or more letters, and they subdivide the text to cull out the original letters or parts thereof. According to these theories, a later editor arranged the text into its †canonical form. Partition theories range from the simple to the complex. One prominent hypothesis is that 2 Corinthians consists of two letters: Paul originally wrote what is now found in chapters 1–9, a letter in which he attempts to foster reconciliation between himself and the Corinthians. Later, when he learned of further problems in the community caused by intruding missionaries, he composed the angrily penned chapters 10–13. This theory claims to account for the mood swing between chapters 9 and 10. A more complex theory hypothesizes that 2 Corinthians is a composite of fragments from six different letters. This hypothesis pulls the text apart at all the literary seams and involves a detailed, complicated reconstruction of events between Paul and the community.

The very presence of partition theories attests to the challenge that any commentator on 2 Corinthians faces. There *are* places in the canonical text that present interpretive difficulties, and fine scholars disagree about how to resolve them. In my opinion, however, partition theories raise more questions and problems than they claim to solve.[5] Indeed, there is no manuscript evidence that any of the proposed partitioned letters or fragments of letters ever existed independently. Applying the principle of Occam's razor—namely, the simplest explanation that coherently explains the data is preferable—it is possible to make good sense of the text by reading it as a single, unified letter.[6] Readers may judge for themselves if the study presented in this commentary succeeds in offering a coherent way of resolving the aforementioned difficulties.

Whether 2 Corinthians was originally two or more letters, or a single letter, as I think, is ultimately not the most important question. I take as my responsibility to explain the inspired canonical text that the Church has handed on to us rather than what *might* lie behind it. The canonical form of 2 Corinthians is that of a single work, so in interpreting it for the life of the Church it makes the most sense to read it as such.

Historical Context

Second Corinthians is actually the fourth letter that Paul wrote to the community in Corinth after bringing the [†]gospel to them a few years earlier (1 Cor 2:1–5; 2 Cor 1:19). We can reconstruct the historical context of the letter according to stages, as follows.

Stage 1: Paul founds the church at Corinth, AD 50–51.[7] According to Acts 18:1–18, Paul spent eighteen months during his founding visit and succeeded in establishing a community of believers consisting of [†]Gentiles (the majority) and Jews.[8] The church in Corinth proved to be a vibrant but perplexing community, one that excelled in many things (2 Cor 8:7)—including its penchant for misunderstanding Paul!

Stage 2: Paul's first letter to Corinth between AD 51 and AD 53. From 1 Cor 5:9 we learn that Paul had written an earlier letter to the Corinthians. In this letter, now lost, he had urged them "not to associate with immoral people." Apparently

---

5. For a review and critique of the four main partition theories, see Thomas D. Stegman, *The Character of Jesus: The Linchpin to Paul's Argument in 2 Corinthians*, AnBib 158 (Rome: Pontifical Biblical Institute, 2005), 5–25.

6. Many of the recent commentaries and full-length studies of 2 Corinthians argue for the letter's unity.

7. Dates in this section are approximations. See figure 3 for a map of the [†]Aegean Sea.

8. For a helpful study of the city of Corinth at the time of Paul, see Jerome Murphy-O'Connor, *St. Paul's Corinth: Texts and Archaeology*, 3rd rev. and exp. ed. (Collegeville, MN: Liturgical Press, 2002). See also George T. Montague, "Corinth: A Cauldron of Cultures," in the introduction to *First Corinthians*, CCSS (Grand Rapids: Baker Academic, forthcoming).

some in the community misconstrued his words to mean that they were to avoid contact with *all* outsiders. (This may have been the source of the question about whether or not to divorce unbelievers; see 1 Cor 7:12–16.)

Stage 3: Paul sends 1 Corinthians from Ephesus via his delegate Timothy, spring AD 54. Some time later Paul wrote a second letter, what is presently known as †canonical 1 Corinthians. In this letter he responded to oral reports about divisions (1 Cor 1:11) and scandalous behavior in the community (5:1–6:20; 11:2–34), as well as to issues raised in a letter written to him by some of its members (see 7:1, 25; 8:1; 12:1; 16:1). Paul wrote 1 Corinthians from †Ephe-

Fig. 1. Paul first entered Corinth with "fear and much trembling" (1 Cor 2:3) ...

sus (16:8) in order to exhort the church in Corinth to strive for unity (1:10) as members of the one body of Christ (12:12–27). He also sent his coworker Timothy to Corinth to remind the community of all he had previously taught them (4:17; 16:10).

If Paul thought that his letter urging unity and his sending Timothy to Corinth would resolve all of the community's questions and problems, he was soon proven wrong. Most likely, Timothy returned quickly to Ephesus with some sobering news. The precise content of that news is impossible to reconstruct. Did the Corinthians reject the youthful Timothy in his role as Paul's envoy (see 1 Cor 16:11)? Did some persist in aberrant behavior as an expression of their freedom in the Spirit? Were some offended by Paul's use of irony and sarcasm (e.g., 4:8–13)? Were suspicions raised about Paul's proud insistence that he preaches the gospel free of charge (9:12–18) while collecting money for another church (16:1–4)? Had intruding missionaries arrived in Corinth, criticizing Paul's gospel and his manner of being an †apostle? Any one or combination of these is possible.

Stage 4: Paul makes an emergency visit, early summer AD 54. In response to the situation, Paul paid an emergency visit to Corinth during the summer of AD 54, a visit that he later confessed was "painful" (2 Cor 2:1). That this visit was urgent and unexpected is suggested by the fact that he changed the travel plans he had indicated in 1 Cor 16:5–7, deciding to go directly to Corinth from Ephesus. Paul's second visit to the Corinthians culminated in an unpleasant incident with a person

Jim Yancey

Fig. 2. ... and he resolved to preach nothing "except Jesus Christ, and him crucified" (1 Cor 2:2).

he later referred to as "the one who did the wrong" (2 Cor 7:12). Once again, we are left guessing as to what exactly happened.[9] The most common scholarly opinion is that a member of the community slandered Paul, calling his apostolic authority into question. Whatever happened, Paul apparently left Corinth abruptly and returned by sea directly to Ephesus. That his departure was abrupt is inferred from the fact that he deviated from his revised travel plans (1:15–17).

Stage 5: Paul sends a "†tearful letter" via his delegate Titus, late summer AD 54. Having returned to Ephesus, Paul decided to write another letter to the Corinthians, a letter penned "out of much affliction and anguish of heart" and "with many tears" (2 Cor 2:4; see 7:8). Like the lost letter alluded to in 1 Cor 5:9, this third piece of correspondence from Paul, known as the "tearful letter," is no longer extant.[10] Nevertheless, we know the gist of its contents from various references to it in 2 Corinthians. Paul wrote to express his love and concern for the community, as well as to convey his sense of pain: was he upset that the Corinthians had not come to his defense at the time of the nasty incident? He then entrusted delivery of the tearful letter to Titus, rather than Timothy. Titus

9. It is important to understand that Paul's letters leave much unsaid because recent events were common knowledge between him and the communities to which he wrote. In writing 2 Corinthians—in which he attempts to deepen and consolidate reconciliation between himself and the community—Paul discreetly chooses not to go into detail over the painful incidents that have transpired.

10. Some scholars claim that the "†tearful letter" is embedded in the †canonical text of 2 Corinthians. The usual candidate is 2 Cor 10:1–13:10. The problem with this hypothesis is that there is no reference in these chapters to the painful event alluded to in 2:5–11 and 7:8–13.

Fig. 3. The direct route (⟺) and the (mostly) land route (◄ - ➤) between Ephesus and Corinth.

was charged with gauging the community's response to it. Upon receiving the letter and hearing Paul's side of things, the Corinthians were cut to the heart. The majority of the community meted out a severe punishment, probably ostracism, to the person who had offended Paul (2 Cor 2:6; 7:11). Moreover, they grieved and expressed their desire to see the Apostle again (7:7).

By previous arrangement, Paul had instructed Titus to return to him via the circuitous land route north (probably because he had decided to leave Ephesus to proclaim the gospel to the north, in †Troas). But Paul was anxious to receive news from his envoy, and winter was approaching; so he left a promising missionary venture in Troas in order to cross over to †Macedonia to meet Titus along the way (2 Cor 2:12–13).[11] The two found each other somewhere in Macedonia, perhaps †Philippi, before the onset of winter (AD 54–55). There Titus relayed the Corinthians' heartfelt response to Paul's letter, which brought great joy and consolation to him (7:6–7, 13).

Stage 6: Titus reports new problems, winter AD 54–55. The report brought by Titus, however, was not all positive and sunny. A few ominous clouds still dotted the sky. Apparently not all the members of the community agreed with

---

11. According to Jerome Murphy-O'Connor, the land route to the north between Corinth and Ephesus (ca. 676 miles)—which still involved sailing between †Neapolis to †Troas—required on average six or seven weeks to complete. Sea travel across the Aegean took a fraction of that time, although travel across the eastern Mediterranean was viable only from April to mid-September or October. See Jerome Murphy-O'Connor, *Paul: A Critical Life* (New York: Oxford University Press, 1996), 20, 299.

the punishment imposed on "the offender" (see 2 Cor 2:6, where a "majority" is said to have punished him). In addition, Titus in all likelihood informed Paul of the arrival of other missionaries. Whether Timothy had known about them from his short visit is unclear.

These missionaries criticized Paul's appearance and lack of eloquence. They accused him of hiding behind the "severe and forceful" letters he wrote (2 Cor 10:10). They also claimed to have superior apostolic credentials, bringing with them "letters of recommendation" (3:1) while boasting of their pedigree (11:22) and spectacular exploits (11:23), such as visionary experiences (12:1–6). In contrast, Paul's way of life was marked by suffering, and his preaching focused on the cross (1 Cor 2:2). How, these missionaries demanded, do such a lifestyle and gospel show forth the power of the resurrection?[12]

Moreover, Titus reported to Paul that the community's participation in the collection for the Jerusalem church—an undertaking, we will see, that was most dear to his heart (Gal 2:10; compare Acts 11:29–30)—had come to a standstill (2 Cor 8:10). Indeed, it is easy to imagine that this was because the newly arrived missionaries planted seeds of doubt in the minds of some of the Corinthians: Isn't Paul just really lining his own pockets? Doesn't his constant change in travel plans reveal how untrustworthy his word really is? Doesn't his abrupt departure during his last visit expose a lack of strength and character? Lastly, Titus must have told Paul, there were still some cases of scandalous behavior in the community (12:20; 13:2).

Stage 7: Paul sends 2 Corinthians via Titus, spring AD 55. We are now in a position to understand why Paul wrote a fourth letter to the church in Corinth, the letter known as canonical 2 Corinthians. Having spent the winter of AD 54–55 in Macedonia, he was ready to come to Corinth for the third time (2 Cor 12:14; 13:1). In order to prepare for this visit, Paul needed to accomplish several things. Since doubts still existed about his character and the authenticity of his apostleship, Paul decided to clear the air over recent events by explaining his change in travel plans and his reasons for sending the tearful letter. He also sought to defend his way of being an apostle, a way marked by self-giving love patterned after the love embodied by Jesus. Also, Paul wanted to convey his joy over the Corinthians' response—at least the majority's response—to his third

---

12. The precise identity of these intruding missionaries—often referred to as "opponents"—has been the source of much scholarly debate. See Jerry L. Sumney, *Identifying Paul's Opponents: The Question of Method in 2 Corinthians*, JSNTSup 40 (Sheffield: JSOT Press, 1990). My method in the commentary is to offer a modest reconstruction based on the evidence given by Paul. As we will see, Paul's critique focuses on the behavior of the interlopers that, in his mind, betrays a faulty understanding of the centrality of the cross in the gospel.

letter. Real reconciliation was now possible between them, and he desired to consolidate it and promote further rapprochement. Toward this end, Paul offered to forgive the offending member and encouraged the community to reach out to this person and receive him back.

Then, because Paul felt confident about the Corinthians' renewed enthusiasm for him, he wanted them to recommit themselves to participate generously in the work of the collection for the Jerusalem church, which, as we will see, was another expression of reconciliation—here between Gentiles and Jews. Next Paul determined to go on the attack against the intruding missionaries, whom he dubbed "superapostles," by exposing the foolishness of their boasting. Finally, he wanted to warn those who persisted in their sinful ways that he would deal with them severely. By means of his various exhortations, the Apostle sought to have the members of the community attend to their own character rather than challenge his.

Thus, sometime in the spring of AD 55, Paul sent his fourth letter to the community via Titus and two unnamed brothers (2 Cor 8:16–24). As we will see in the following chapters, Paul bases his own self-defense—or better, †*commendation* of self—and his various exhortations on the character of Jesus, whose entire life was marked by faithful obedience to God in giving himself in love for the sake of others.

Theological Themes

Second Corinthians is a fertile source for theological reflection. To be sure, Paul was not what we would today call a systematic theologian. His letters are not theological treatises. Paul was a founder of local churches who, in the course of exercising pastoral care over them, wrote letters that dealt with practical matters and pressing concerns. Nevertheless, he tended to think theologically. In the course of handling even the most mundane affairs that arose, his strategy was to bring the realities of faith to bear on them. As we will see in our analysis of 2 Corinthians, Paul has much to say about God, Jesus, the Spirit, the Church, and salvation, but it may be helpful to provide here a few brief introductory comments about these themes.

God. Theology proper deals with the question "Who is God?" Throughout 2 Corinthians Paul names God in various ways: he is "our Father" (1:2) and the "Father of our Lord Jesus Christ" (1:3a), "the Father of compassion and God of all encouragement" (1:3b), the "living God" (3:3; 6:16). As the God of life, he is the one who "raises the dead" (1:9)—manifested in his raising Jesus from the dead (4:14)—and brings about a "new creation" (5:17; see 4:6).

Paul emphasizes that God, out of love, has taken the initiative to put an end to the enmity between himself and humanity—the enmity caused by human sin—by effecting reconciliation through Jesus' death (5:18–21). God desires to be "Father" to those willing to receive his mercy and become his "sons and daughters" (6:16–18). His character is thus revealed as marked by "love" and "peace" (13:11, 13), which he wishes to bestow on his children. God's character is also one of faithfulness (1:18), because through Jesus God has fulfilled *all* of his promises (1:20).

Moreover, Paul insists, God continues to express love and fidelity through the gift of the Spirit (1:21–22) and through the generous provision of blessings (9:8–11). As the one "who encourages the downcast" (7:6), God desires that those who have benefited from his bounty be generous in turn by giving themselves for others. It is through such self-giving that God's power continues to be at work in the world (4:7; 13:4).

Jesus. Paul's fundamental †gospel proclamation is "Jesus Christ [is] Lord" (4:5). Both titles—Christ and Lord—are important. For Paul, Jesus' lordship is intimately linked with the resurrection (4:14; see Phil 2:11), for it is the resurrection that reveals Jesus as Lord. Paul's reference to Jesus as *Kyrios* ("Lord") is striking when one realizes that the †Septuagint—the Greek translation of the Old Testament—uses *Kyrios* to translate the sacred name for God, †YHWH (a name so sacred it is not to be pronounced).

Jesus is also the †Messiah, a Hebrew term meaning the "anointed one." (The equivalent Greek term, *Christos*, gives us the English term *Christ*.)[13] As the Messiah, or Christ, Jesus fulfilled all God's promises. It was through Jesus, the one "who did not know sin" (5:21), that God has reconciled the world to himself (5:18–19). Jesus the Messiah is also the divine Son of God (1:3; 1:19). Jesus' filial relationship to the Father is exhibited most clearly in his faithfulness to God and his obedience to the Father's will (1:19). This obedience reached a climax in Jesus' giving his life "for all," a self-offering that declared the depths of his love (5:14–15).

Throughout 2 Corinthians Paul speaks of Jesus as the "†image of God" par excellence (4:4), the †new Adam who revealed how God intends human beings to live. In fact, one of the distinctive features of this letter is Paul's use of the unadorned name "Jesus" in 4:5–14, by which he focuses on Jesus' humanity. As we will see, Jesus' loving, self-giving character (e.g., 8:9; 10:1) plays an

---

13. Some commentators downplay or even deny that Paul's use of "Christ" is intended to signify Jesus' messiahship (rather, it is said to function, in effect, as part of Jesus' name). For a helpful explanation of the importance of Jesus' messiahship, see N. T. Wright, *Paul: In Fresh Perspective* (Minneapolis: Fortress, 2005), 46–49.

important role in the way Paul presents himself and in his exhortations to the Corinthians.

Spirit. The Spirit is a gift from God (1:22). Paul refers to the Spirit in different ways: "the Spirit of the living God" (3:3), "the Spirit of the Lord" (3:17), "the holy Spirit" (13:13; see 6:6). The Spirit's distinguishing trait is that he "gives life" (3:6). Twice Paul refers to the Spirit as *arrabōn* (1:22; 5:5), a term that signifies a "first installment," or "guarantee," of the eternal life that is to come to those who receive him.

The Spirit's outpouring into human hearts points to the arrival of the "†new covenant" (3:6) and produces wondrous effects in the present. The Spirit transforms human beings more and more into the likeness of Jesus (3:18; see also 1:21–22, where Paul makes a play on words to suggest as much), that is, the Spirit empowers his recipients to walk in the way of Jesus' faithfulness to God. Hence Paul refers to "the Spirit of faith" or of "faithfulness" (4:13, my translation). He acknowledges that it is the Spirit who enables him to exercise his ministry as a "servant" of God (6:4, 6 NRSV, NIV). Moreover, he reminds the Corinthians that it is the presence of the Spirit in their hearts that produces in their lives "a letter" of, or about, Christ for others to "read" (3:3, 2). Lastly, Paul mentions the *koinōnia*—"fellowship" or "communion"—of the Spirit (13:13), a reference to the reconciliation and unity that the Spirit produces in the Church.

Paul's references to Father, Son, and Spirit are striking. It can be natural for Christians today to read a developed understanding of the Holy Trinity back into his writings. We need to remind ourselves that trinitarian doctrine was not fully formulated and refined until the fourth century. Nevertheless, the Church's understanding of God as both one and triune makes explicit and unfolds what is implicit in 2 Corinthians as well as in other New Testament writings.

Church. Paul uses the word "church" (*ekklēsia*, from which the word †ecclesiology is derived) in 2 Corinthians to refer to local assemblies of Christians (1:1; 8:1). Nevertheless, such local churches are part of "the church of God" (1:1). The latter designation signifies both the divine origin of such assemblies and the fact that together they form a larger fellowship or communion. Paul calls members of the churches "holy ones" (1:1; 8:4; 9:1). They are already holy because, collectively (i.e., as local assemblies), they are "the temple of the living God" (6:16) in whom the Spirit dwells (3:3). Moreover, they are called to grow in holiness because, as *ekklēsia*, they are betrothed to Christ, whose character is marked by innocence and purity (11:2–3). According to Paul, God has entrusted the churches with the ministry of the new covenant (see 3:6), which is also "the ministry of reconciliation" (5:18–19).

26

One concrete manifestation of the ministry of reconciliation is the collection for the church in Jerusalem (8:4; 9:1). By means of this collection, material resources will be distributed to those in need, thereby fulfilling God's will (8:14–15) and giving tangible expression to the gospel (9:13). At the same time, the recipients will praise God and offer him petitions for their benefactors, thereby enhancing communion among the churches (9:13–15).

Salvation. An essential part of Paul's proclamation of the gospel is that "*now* is the day of salvation" (6:2, emphasis added). In fact, he understands the fruit of his ministry to be salvation (1:6).

Salvation (*sōtēria*, from which we get the word †*soteriology*) has both present and future ramifications. What does this salvation look like in the here and now? How are people's lives affected concretely? Paul reveals that God's outpouring of the Spirit has brought about a "new creation" (5:17), transforming those who receive him more and more into the likeness of Jesus (3:18). Moreover, the Apostle understands the ministry of reconciliation as an essential aspect of salvation in the present (see the following section). The fullness of salvation, however, awaits a future manifestation. Paul hopes to be raised along with the Corinthians into the presence of God, a hope that is founded on the resurrection of Jesus from the dead (4:14). He reminds the community to orient their lives in such a way that they may receive good at the final judgment, after which what is mortal will be swallowed up by life (5:1–10).

Relevance for Today

Although 2 Corinthians is almost two thousand years old, it speaks with uncanny relevance to us today. Discussion of the theological and pastoral implications of this letter will be the special purpose of the Reflection and Application sections that follow exegetical analyses throughout the commentary. However, I would like to prime the pump by suggesting some broad themes that speak to the Church today.

Paul sets forth a demanding model of Christian ministry. Although he is the founder of the community and exercises divinely given authority (10:8; 13:10), Paul refuses to "lord it over" the Corinthians (1:24). Instead, he regards them as a loving father does his children, always seeking what is best for them (12:14–15).

Even more, Paul views himself as the Corinthians' "slave" (*doulos*; 4:5), indicating that he has been called, first and foremost, to serve their needs. This is what it means to be a "servant" (*diakonos*) of God (6:4 NRSV, NIV). Paul has humbled himself (11:7) so that he might preach the †gospel free of charge. We know from his other letters that he labored with his hands in order to support himself so that he would not be a financial burden to his fledgling churches.[14] Thus we are not surprised when Paul describes his ministerial experience as follows: "in toil and hardship, through many sleepless nights, through hunger and thirst" (11:27; see also 6:5). He chooses to make sacrifices, to expend and empty himself, so that others might benefit (4:12; 6:10). And he does so for the sake of Jesus, whose example he follows (4:10–11). Indeed, Paul exemplifies Jesus' teaching that the one who desires to be great must become "the last of all and the servant of all" (Mark 9:35). To say the least, this is a challenging model for any ordained or lay minister to emulate!

But Paul knows that he is no "superman." He trusts that the power of God (2 Cor 4:7) will work through his weakness (12:9–10). Paul also recognizes that he is part of a team, and he relishes his coworkers' help and encouragement (7:5–7). In addition, although called to render selfless service to the communities he has founded, he acknowledges the importance of receiving love and support from those communities (2:2–4). This is an integral part of his understanding of the Church as the "body of Christ."

Second Corinthians offers a timely vision of one of the Church's primary ministries—namely, the "ministry of reconciliation" (5:18–19). Paul understands that the appropriate response to God's gift of reconciliation through Christ is to participate in the ongoing work of reconciliation (5:20). This work begins within the Christian community. In fact, one of Paul's main reasons for writing this letter is to continue healing old wounds in his relationship with the Corinthians (see, e.g., 6:11–7:4). Moreover, he seeks to foster the restoration of an ostracized community member (2:5–11). Given the situation of the early twenty-first-century Church—suffering from damaged credibility because of the misconduct of some clergy, from a lack of trust between parts of the hierarchy and laity, and from a lack of constructive dialogue between so-called traditionalists and progressives—the Apostle's vision of reconciliation *within* the Church is particularly relevant today.

Paul's understanding of the ministry of reconciliation, however, goes beyond intra-Church relationships. God's reconciling power is to reach out to the *world* (5:19). Paul's motive in promoting the collection for the church in Jerusalem is multifaceted. At one level, he advocates providing material or economic relief

---

14. See, e.g., 1 Thess 2:9: "You recall, brothers, our toil and drudgery. Working night and day in order not to burden any of you, we proclaimed to you the gospel of God." According to Acts 18:3, Paul plied the trade of tent making.

to those in need. Such social outreach is an essential part of proclaiming the gospel (9:13)—a tenet that echoes the teaching of Jesus (Matt 25:31–46; see also James 2:14–17) and that is as timely today as ever.

At a deeper level, the collection is an important way to express the reconciliation that God has brought about between †Gentiles and Jews. That predominantly Gentile churches would offer financial support to the Jewish-Christian community in Jerusalem would, in Paul's eyes, be a dramatic manifestation of how God, through Christ, has created the possibility of a new humanity no longer torn asunder by divisions (Eph 2:14–16). This vision of reconciliation certainly speaks with eloquence and hope to our world today—a world in which tribal, ethnic, nationalistic, economic, and religious differences are at the root of large-scale hatred and violence.

Second Corinthians also reminds us that cultural forces and values are often opposed to the message of the gospel. One of the ways the rival missionaries made inroads in the church in Corinth is by appeal to popular values—attractive physical appearance and rhetorical eloquence (2 Cor 10:10), pedigree (11:22), impressive exploits and experiences (11:23; 12:1), and financial remuneration as a sign of worth (11:7–12). These missionaries apparently criticized Paul for lacking some or all of these. In their view, his apostolic lifestyle seemed too preoccupied with suffering, a quality that held no place in their competition for acclaim (10:12). Paul counters by reminding the Corinthians that what is in one's heart is far more important than such externals (5:12). This is the case because the "heart"—signifying the inner core of one's existence—is where the Spirit resides (1:22; 4:6).

Moreover, the Spirit enables his recipients to live after the manner of Jesus, a manner marked by loving, self-giving service. Paul therefore insists that the way to resurrection leads through the cross. The powerful cultural values against which he struggles are similar to those we wrestle with today. While 2 Corinthians challenges the Church to exercise the ministry of reconciliation in the world, it makes it clear that core gospel values are not to be compromised.

This leads to a final observation. What 2 Corinthians offers to people today is a *spirituality*. By spirituality I mean a way of life that is inspired and empowered by the Holy Spirit. While Paul's vocation as †apostle and founder of churches has particular characteristics and responsibilities, he insists that *all* Christians are called to embody Jesus' loving, self-giving way of life in their own lives, within their own life circumstances. The †paschal mystery—God's bringing about new life through the life, death, and resurrection of Jesus—is at the center of Paul's understanding of life in the Spirit (1:3–7; 4:7–15). Christians participate in the paschal mystery by entering into the dynamic of Christ's self-offering for the sake of others, trusting in God to bring life—to others and to oneself—out of one's various "dyings." In these and so many other ways, 2 Corinthians—aptly called by a prominent commentator "the most extraordinary letter of the New Testament"[15]—is extremely relevant for Christian life today.

15. Murphy-O'Connor, *Paul: A Critical Life*, 309.

Outline of 2 Corinthians

I. Salutation (1:1–2)
II. Blessing of God (1:3–11)
III. Letter body (1:12–13:10)
    A. Paul's apostolic integrity (1:12–7:16)
        i. Narration of recent events (1:12–2:13)
        ii. Apostleship defined positively (2:14–7:4)
            a. Paul's role in the ministry of the new covenant (2:14–4:6)
            b. Paul's ministry as marked by suffering (4:7–5:10)
            c. Paul's role in the ministry of reconciliation (5:11–6:10)
            d. Paul's appeal to the Corinthians for reconciliation (6:11–7:4)
        iii. Resumption of narration of recent events (7:5–16)
    B. Paul's appeal for the collection (8:1–9:15)
    C. Preparations for Paul's third visit (10:1–13:10)
        i. Paul's integrity and missionary "boasting" (10:1–18)
        ii. Apostleship defined negatively ("foolish boasting") (11:1–12:13)
        iii. Warnings and final challenge (12:14–13:10)
IV. Letter closing and final benediction (13:11–13)

Setting the Stage

2 Corinthians 1:1–11

Paul begins his second †canonical epistle to the Corinthians with a formal greeting (1:1–2). He then offers a prayer of blessing to God for bringing encouragement in the face of affliction (1:3–7). In order to illustrate how God does this, Paul refers to a dramatic recent experience of being delivered from a grave danger—a deliverance that has resulted in his deeper trust in God (1:8–11). Throughout these verses he introduces themes and topics that he will take up in the letter.

Greeting (1:1–2)

---

¹Paul, an apostle of Christ Jesus by the will of God, and Timothy our brother, to the church of God that is in Corinth, with all the holy ones throughout Achaia: ²grace to you and peace from God our Father and the Lord Jesus Christ.

OT: Lev 19:2
NT: 1 Cor 9:1; 15:8–9; Gal 1:15–16; 1 Pet 1:13–16; 2:9
Catechism: Christian holiness, 2012–16

The standard form of a letter salutation in Paul's time was very simple, containing three elements: the name of the sender, the name of the addressee, and a simple greeting. Paul expands on each of these elements.

The first expansion concerns the sender, **Paul**. Observe that he refers to himself as **an apostle of Christ Jesus**. The term "†apostle" means one who is sent.

1:1

An essential characteristic of an apostle is to have seen the risen Lord (1 Cor 9:1; 15:8–9). In Gal 1:15–16 Paul narrates briefly his encounter with the risen Jesus, an encounter that was also a divine call to proclaim the †gospel to the †Gentiles (see Acts 9:1–19; 22:1–16; 26:1–18). Thus Paul's call to be an apostle derives ultimately from **the will of God.**

With these opening words, Paul sets forth a crucially important theme in 2 Corinthians: his way of being an apostle. At times in his letters, Paul's insistence that he is an apostle sounds defensive. Unlike the twelve apostles named in the canonical Gospels (Mark 3:16–19), he did not accompany Jesus during his earthly ministry. Not only that, at the time of his call Paul was persecuting the churches (1 Cor 15:9; Gal 1:13; 1 Tim 1:13). In the present context, he has come under attack from a group of missionaries whom he sarcastically calls "superapostles" (2 Cor 11:5; 12:11). The crucial issue, at least in Paul's mind, is *how* one's apostolic identity is put into action. According to him, the life of an apostle is to be patterned after the life of Jesus (4:10–11). Therefore, when Paul describes himself as "an apostle of Christ Jesus," he refers to Jesus as both the source of his call and the exemplar of how he lives out his calling. Just as Jesus' life was characterized by obedience to God (Phil 2:8), so Paul's life as an apostle is marked by fidelity to God's will.

Paul names **Timothy** as the cosender of the letter. Along with Silvanus, Timothy was Paul's coworker when he brought the gospel to Corinth (2 Cor 1:19; see Acts 18:5). When he wrote 1 Corinthians, Paul dispatched Timothy back to Corinth to remind the community of his ways in Christ (1 Cor 4:17). Timothy held a special place in the Apostle's heart. Paul handpicked him for ministry (Acts 16:1–3) and, in effect, ordained him for ministry (2 Tim 1:6–7). Not only was Timothy a trusted coworker, Paul also affectionately regarded him as a son (Phil 2:20–22). Here in the letter salutation, he refers to Timothy as **brother.** Throughout his letters, Paul uses familial language to describe members of the various churches. Despite differences in ethnicity, economic and social standing, gender, and age, Paul reminds us that Christians are first and foremost brothers and sisters in the Lord (see, e.g., 1 Cor 8:11; Philem 1–2).

The addressee of this letter is **the church of God that is in Corinth, with all the holy ones throughout Achaia.** Again, Paul's expansions are significant. The addition of the phrase "of God" to "church" serves to remind the Corinthians of their divine origin—they owe their very existence to God (1 Cor 1:26–31). Furthermore, it challenges them to realize that they belong to something much larger than themselves. Paul will later draw on this larger reality when he exhorts them to respond to the needs of the church in Jerusalem. This letter is

The Old Testament Background of *Ekklēsia*

BIBLICAL BACKGROUND

The word *ekklēsia*, normally translated "church" in the New Testament (as in 2 Cor 1:1), could refer, in the secular Greek of Paul's time, to any assembly or gathering of persons. Certain usages in the Greek Old Testament, however, gave the term more texture and specificity. For instance, Moses called the people who assembled at †Mount Sinai to hear God's words the *ekklēsia* (Deut 4:10: the mountain was also called Horeb). Similarly, the term was used to describe the people who gathered to hear the scribe Ezra read the law of Moses after the return from the exile (Neh 8:2). *Ekklēsia* was also employed to describe the whole community of Israel who assembled with Solomon to worship God at the dedication of the Temple in Jerusalem (1 Kings 8:2, 55; 2 Chron 6:3). Paul's use of *ekklēsia* draws on these uses in Scripture. Thus, for the Apostle, *ekklēsia* refers to the people who gather in the presence of the Lord to listen carefully to his word, who are formed by that word, and who offer praise and sacrifice to God.

also intended for Christians throughout †Achaia. Achaia (southern Greece today) was a Roman province of which Corinth was the capital. Paul's missionary strategy was to found churches in large urban areas (e.g., †Thessalonica, †Philippi, Corinth, and †Ephesus); his plan was that these local churches would then spread the gospel to the surrounding areas.[1]

Notice that he refers to the members of the church as "holy ones" (*hagioi*—see, e.g., Rom 16:15; Eph 1:1).[2] This designation both expresses a reality—the Holy Spirit has *already* sanctified us (2 Cor 6:16)—and implies a call—Christians are to *grow* in holiness (7:1). Paul expressed this double aspect in an earlier letter to the Corinthians: "to you who have been sanctified in Christ Jesus, called to be holy" (1 Cor 1:2).

Paul's salutation—**grace to you and peace from God our Father and the Lord Jesus Christ**—is a modification and expansion of the typical greeting of his time. He modifies the usual *chairein* ("hail," "greetings") to *charis*, "†grace." Grace is an extremely rich word for Paul, as we will see in our analysis of 8:1–9:15.

1:2

---

1. A comparison of 1 Cor 1:2 with 2 Cor 1:1 suggests that Paul's strategy is bearing fruit. In 1 Corinthians the addressee is "the church of God that is in Corinth"; in 2 Corinthians there are now Christians *beyond* the city.

2. Some translations (e.g., RSV, NRSV, and NIV) render *hagioi* as "saints." The NAB's use of "holy ones" precludes confusion with the Catholic Church's technical use of the term saint to designate a deceased member who has been canonized and declared both a model for Christian life and a heavenly intercessor.

Vatican II and the Universal Call to Holiness

LIVING TRADITION

Paul's salutation reminds us that *all* Christians are called to holiness, a call that the documents of the Second Vatican Council strongly reinforced: "All members of the Church, whether they belong to the hierarchy or are under its care, are called to holiness, according to the Apostle's saying: 'For this is the will of God, your sanctification' (1 Thess 4:3)" (*Lumen Gentium* 39). Indeed, the members of the Church constitute "a chosen race, a royal priesthood, a holy nation," a people that belongs to God (1 Pet 2:9). As such, we are to show forth his holiness (Lev 19:2). Catholics grow in holiness through faithful and active participation in the Church's liturgy and sacraments (*Sacrosanctum Concilium* 10). Growth in holiness by all her members is essential if the Church is to fulfill her fundamental vocation, namely, to be "the universal sacrament of salvation" (*Lumen Gentium* 48), called to manifest and actualize God's love in and for the world (*Gaudium et Spes* 45).

In its basic sense in Paul's writings, grace refers to God's redemptive love as manifested in the life, death, and resurrection of Jesus and is conferred on us by the Holy Spirit. Paul then adds "and peace," which was the typical greeting (*shalom*) among Jews.[3] With these alterations, Paul's salutation is more than a greeting; it is also a *prayer*, as he prays that God's grace and peace come upon the Corinthians. Implicit in his prayer is the requirement that the members of the community continue to open themselves to God's gift of reconciliation through Jesus (5:18–6:2), a gift that results in being at peace with God and with one another (13:11).

Note that the first reference to God in 2 Corinthians is as "Father," who is the bestower of grace and peace. Paul will later convey God's desire that the Corinthians base their lives on their identity as his "sons and daughters" (6:18) by shunning that which impedes their progress toward holiness. Here he teaches that God relates to us as a loving parent. The image of God as Father also influences the way Paul deals with the Corinthians. That is, as one called by God to bring the gospel to Corinth (1 Cor 4:15; 2 Cor 10:13–14), he exercises fatherly care for the community (12:14–15). Paul names "the Lord Jesus Christ" as the cogiver of grace and peace. Jesus is "Lord" (*kyrios*), according to Paul, by virtue of his resurrection and exaltation by the Father (Phil 2:11;

---

3. Raised as a Jew in the Greek-speaking city of Tarsus (in present day southeastern Turkey), it is not surprising that Paul mixes together Greco-Roman and Jewish elements.

see 2 Cor 4:14).[4] Christ is more than a surname for Jesus. The Greek word *Christos* means "†Messiah," Hebrew for "anointed one." As the Messiah, Jesus is the promised one through whom God has brought about reconciliation and salvation (5:14–21). Paul will allude to Jesus' anointing and its continuing effects in 1:18–22.

Reflection and Application (1:1–2)

Identity and vocation. The greeting in 2 Corinthians highlights the issues of Christian identity and vocation. Paul models what it means to respond faithfully to God's call. A cursory reading of 1–2 Corinthians reveals that he encountered several difficulties in his ministry to the church in Corinth. The young community struggled to understand the implications of the gospel. Some began to question the authenticity of his ministry. More broadly, Paul endured several hardships in his apostolic labors (1 Cor 4:9–13; 2 Cor 4:7–12; 6:4–10; 11:23–33). How was he able to persevere in the face of such frustrations, opposition, and rigors? Why was he so long-suffering with the Corinthians? The answer is that he was convinced of his call and identity as "an apostle of Christ Jesus by the will of God" (2 Cor 1:1). To be sure, Paul's call was dramatic and his vocation unique. Nevertheless, his example is relevant for all Christians. It is not easy to be a devoted spouse, a loving parent, a faithful priest or religious, or a person of integrity who attempts to bring Christian values to the workplace. Popular media and prevalent cultural values often militate against such commitments. Paul exemplifies the importance of starting every endeavor—indeed, starting every day—by reminding ourselves and others of who we are and how God is calling us to live.

Peace—and joy. One has only to visit the departments in a bookstore marked Self Help, Psychology/Counseling, or New Age Spirituality to find numerous books that claim to hold the keys to peace and joy. The number and popularity of such books reflect people's desire to find happiness and peace. Paul's prayer for the Corinthians teaches us a crucially fundamental truth in this connection. True peace, along with joy, is a gift from God. We do not find peace and joy; they find us when we open ourselves to receive God's grace and live according to his plan for us (Rom 15:13). Indeed, peace and joy are among the Spirit's gifts (Gal 5:22).

---

4. For further significance of calling Jesus *kyrios*, see the section Theological Themes in the introduction. To be sure, Paul also alludes to Jesus' pre-existence (i.e., his eternal existence with the Father before taking flesh) in 2 Cor 8:9 (see also 1 Cor 8:6 and Col 1:15–17). It is important to keep in mind that Paul's writings predate the full development of christological doctrine.

Lectio divina. It may seem as though I have offered much commentary on only two verses. Most of us tend to lead busy, hurried lives and it is all too easy to bring this same sense of haste to our reading of Scripture. There is, however, an ancient form of Christian prayer that offers a healthy alternative—*lectio divina* (a phrase that literally means "divine reading"). *Lectio divina* is a meditative, prayerful way of reading the Bible. Practitioners of this method read the text slowly, savoring each word or phrase for what it truly is, the word of God. Such careful, contemplative reading can produce much spiritual fruit and insight.

Blessing the God of All Encouragement (1:3–7)

[3]Blessed be the God and Father of our Lord Jesus Christ, the Father of compassion and God of all encouragement, [4]who encourages us in our every affliction, so that we may be able to encourage those who are in any affliction with the encouragement with which we ourselves are encouraged by God. [5]For as Christ's sufferings overflow to us, so through Christ does our encouragement also overflow. [6]If we are afflicted, it is for your encouragement and salvation; if we are encouraged, it is for your encouragement, which enables you to endure the same sufferings that we suffer. [7]Our hope for you is firm, for we know that as you share in the sufferings, you also share in the encouragement.

OT: 1 Kings 19; Ps 66
NT: Luke 22:31–32; Eph 1:3–14; 1 Pet 1:3–9
Catechism: prayer of blessing, 2626

Paul usually follows the greeting by reporting a prayer of thanksgiving he offers to God for the church to whom he is writing. A good example is 1 Cor 1:4–9, which begins, "I give thanks to my God always on your account for the †grace of God bestowed on you in Christ Jesus."[5]

1:3   In 2 Corinthians, however, Paul does not say "I give thanks to God." Instead, he offers a prayer of †blessing, a *berakah*, to God: **Blessed be** God. This type of prayer is found throughout the Bible[6] and is characteristic of Jewish piety and liturgy. To be sure, the distinction between blessing God and offering thanks to him ought not to be pressed too far. But rather than focus on what God has done for the Corinthians, Paul emphasizes how God has blessed and encour-

5. See Rom 1:8–15; Phil 1:3–11; Col 1:3–8; 1 Thess 1:2–10; 2 Thess 1:3–4.
6. See, e.g., Gen 14:20; Ps 66:20; 68:36; 2 Macc 1:17. In addition, see Luke 1:68–79; Eph 1:3–14; 1 Pet 1:3–9.

aged him in his apostolic ministry, which will be dramatically illustrated in verses 8–11. In doing so, he sets the stage for his appeals to the community to recognize that God is working through him, even though his ministry is marked by affliction.

Paul blesses God as **the God and Father of our Lord Jesus Christ** (see Eph 1:3). God, who was called "our Father" in verse 2, is now described as the Father of Jesus. The phraseology here signifies two key points. First, Paul—who from his youth had worshiped the one true God as a pious Jew—now understands that God cannot be fully known apart from Jesus, the †Messiah and Lord. Second, he reveals that Jesus' relationship with God is best understood in filial terms. That is, Jesus is "the Son of God" (2 Cor 1:19) whose life and ministry were marked by obedience and faithfulness in carrying out the Father's will.

Paul also blesses God as **the Father of compassion**. Compassion is one of God's distinctive characteristics (see, e.g., Ps 145:8–9). Because he is merciful and compassionate, God is concerned about the suffering of his creatures. Moreover, Paul names him as **God of all encouragement**. The term translated "encouragement" can also be rendered "comfort" or "consolation."[7] The NAB's choice of "encouragement"—its etymology connotes "putting into one's heart"[8]—is particularly apt because, as we will see, Paul insists that one essential way God encourages us is by bestowing the Holy Spirit in our hearts (2 Cor 1:22).

The normal formulation of a blessing is "Blessed be God, who . . ." The clause beginning with "who" then offers a reason why God is blessed. For instance, the psalmist exults, "Blessed be God, who did not refuse me the kindness I sought in prayer" (Ps 66:20). Paul blesses God because he **encourages** him in his **every affliction**. The Apostle makes an important claim here, namely, that God has a track record of strengthening and sustaining him in his ministry, especially when he experiences hardships. Paul goes on to make clear that God does so for a purpose: **so that** Paul is **able to encourage those who are in any affliction with the encouragement with which** he himself is **encouraged by God**. In other words, God gives gifts in order that they be shared with others. Paul can only give what he himself has received. A major aspect of his ministry is to offer encouragement to others (see 2 Cor 10:8, where he writes of the authority given to him by God for "building up" the Corinthians).

A quick glance at verses 3–7 reveals the prevalence of the words encouragement/encourage, affliction/afflict, and suffering/suffer. Similar to his thanksgivings, Paul's blessing in 2 Corinthians prefigures important topics; thus, as

1:4

1:5

---

7. Greek *paraklēsis*. The RSV and NIV have "comfort"; the NRSV has "consolation."
8. This etymology pertains to the English word "encouragement," not the Greek *paraklēsis*.

with the greeting, it is important to pay close attention here for clues that foreshadow significant themes. He will insist throughout this letter that God brings encouragement in the midst of suffering and affliction (e.g., 4:8; 7:6). Another important theme is introduced in verse 5, where he refers to **Christ's sufferings**. Paul will expound on the role Christ's suffering and death played in God's act of reconciling the world to himself (5:14–21).

Note Paul's claim that Christ's sufferings **overflow to us**. One of Paul's boldest convictions is that the story of Jesus continues in the lives of his faithful followers. We will see that he interprets his own afflictions and sufferings in light of Jesus' passion and death (4:10–11). But suffering and death do not have the last word. Paul also insists that it is **through Christ** that his **encouragement also overflows**. The expression "through Christ" refers to the power unleashed because of Jesus' resurrection from the dead. This power enables Paul's self-giving ministry to bring life to others (4:12).

1:6 Paul then applies the principles established in verses 3–5 to the Corinthians. He reveals that his afflictions are **for your encouragement and salvation**. How can this be? Paul is keenly aware that his ministry of proclaiming the †gospel necessarily involves him in suffering and persecution (4:7–12). Nevertheless, his service as an ambassador of Christ Jesus, in which he announces God's work of reconciliation, has brought salvation to the community (5:20–6:2). Moreover, when the Corinthians observe that God *continues* to preserve and encourage Paul in his ministry, they will be strengthened **to endure the same sufferings** that he suffers. What are the sufferings that the Corinthians endure? Paul knows that Christians can face misunderstanding, even opposition, from family, kin, friends, and associates (e.g., 1 Thess 2:14; see Matt 10:34–39; Mark 13:12–13). In addition, he realizes that the gospel calls us to learn to imitate Jesus' way of life, which demands sacrifice and self-denial.

1:7 Finally, Paul expresses his **hope** that the Corinthians will be steadfast as they **share in the sufferings** he encounters as an †apostle of Christ Jesus. By persevering in the face of misunderstanding and opposition for the sake of the gospel and entering into Jesus' self-giving love (as Paul will encourage them to do, e.g., in 8:1–9:15), the community will **also share in the encouragement** and sustaining power that come from God. The Apostle's own life bears witness to this assurance.

Reflection and Application (1:3–7)

Participating in the paschal mystery. The †paschal mystery is God's work of redemption through the life, suffering, death, resurrection, and glorification of

Jesus. This mystery teaches us the extent of the Father's love and power to give life: even suffering and death are subject to his transformative power. Paul's opening benediction reveals that Christians are called to participate in the dynamics of God's bringing about life through affliction. It teaches us that "the Father of compassion" is present to us in our suffering, giving us courage and strength. God works through our sacrifice and self-denial to bring encouragement and life to others. Indeed, it is important to appreciate that our sufferings and difficulties equip us both to grow in compassion and to help others.

Blessing God. Paul's prayer of blessing makes clear that *God* is the main character in the drama of life. It also communicates that the appropriate response to this reality is to offer praise for what he has done and is doing in our lives: "Bless the LORD, my soul; / all my being, bless his holy name! / Bless the LORD, my soul; / do not forget all the gifts of God" (Ps 103:1–2). The psalms are a treasure trove of beautiful prayers that express praise and thanksgiving to God. They can serve as models for developing and personalizing our own prayers of blessing and praise. Such prayer is important because it inculcates a sense of *gratitude*. To grow in gratitude is to grow in the truth of our existence, namely, that we stand before God as receivers of life and blessings. As the Catechism notes, blessing God is "the basic movement of Christian prayer" (2626).

The eucharistic liturgy recognizes and enacts this truth. Following the Liturgy of the Word, the faithful in the assembly present bread and wine, representing "the work of human hands," to the priest, who in turn lifts them to God and prays, "Blessed are you, Lord, God of all creation. Through your goodness we have this bread . . . this wine to offer." The faithful respond, "Blessed be God forever!" Familiarity with these prayers ought not to dull our senses to this profound action and benediction that lead to the great Eucharistic Prayer (from the Greek *eucharistia*, meaning "thankfulness" or "gratitude").

Encouragement. We can all remember an experience when someone very important in our life—a parent, a teacher or mentor, a supervisor, a religious superior—spoke an encouraging word to us. I can recall how that encouragement made me feel. A word of support can make a big difference in our lives. Sadly, most of us have also had the opposite experience when a negative remark ripped the heart right out of us (the very etymology of *dis*couragement). Paul took his service of "the God of all encouragement" very seriously. He understood his ministry to entail building others up. All of us are capable of participating in the ministry of encouragement. Each of us can ask, Do my words and actions encourage others and build them up?

A Recent, Vivid Example of God's Power to Rescue (1:8–11)

---

⁸We do not want you to be unaware, brothers, of the affliction that came to us in the province of Asia; we were utterly weighed down beyond our strength, so that we despaired even of life. ⁹Indeed, we had accepted within ourselves the sentence of death, that we might trust not in ourselves but in God who raises the dead. ¹⁰He rescued us from such great danger of death, and he will continue to rescue us; in him we have put our hope [that] he will also rescue us again, ¹¹as you help us with prayer, so that thanks may be given by many on our behalf for the gift granted us through the prayers of many.

OT: Ps 3; 6; 31; Dan 3; 6
NT: Mark 8:34–35; Luke 23:46; Acts 16:16–34; 1 Thess 1:10
Catechism: belief in the resurrection, 988–91

This passage is a continuation of the blessing that began in verse 3. Paul now offers to the Corinthians a vivid example of how the "God of all encouragement" rescued him from a life-threatening situation. In these verses he continues to sound the notes of key themes to be developed in the letter.

1:8–9   Paul addresses the Corinthians as his **brothers**, a term that should be understood here to include *all* the members of the community, male and female.[9] It is striking that he refers to the Corinthians with the same term he used for Timothy in verse 1. For Paul, all Christians form one family as God's adopted sons and daughters in Christ (Rom 8:14–17). The use of familial language at the outset of 2 Corinthians is significant, as Paul subtly reminds the community that he is their brother too. He is already laying a foundation for further reconciliation with them.

The opening words—**we do not want you to be unaware**—serve to convey the importance of what follows, as Paul informs the Corinthians about something they do not yet know. He discloses an **affliction that came to** him **in the province of Asia**. Asia was a Roman province that lay east of Corinth, across the [†]Aegean Sea, in what is now western Turkey. Its capital was [†]Ephesus. We know from Acts 19 that Paul ministered there for over two years, after he had founded the community in Corinth. The affliction was so severe that he was **utterly weighed down beyond** his **strength, so that** he **despaired even of life**. The situation was so desperate that Paul felt as if he had been given a **sentence of death**.

9. The NRSV's translation "brothers and sisters" captures the inclusive meaning. While the NEB's choice of "friends" achieves inclusiveness, it does so at the expense of the familial terminology Paul uses to describe members of the Christian community.

What exactly happened to Paul that left him despairing of life? Unfortunately, while his description in these verses is dramatic, it is also opaque. Scholars have speculated for centuries about what he suffered. Some hypothesize that Paul contracted a life-threatening illness, others that he was imprisoned in Ephesus (see Phil 1:12–26). Still others find a clue in Acts 19:23–41, which describes a riot that broke out on account of the proclamation of the †gospel in Ephesus. What Paul wishes to emphasize is that he was overcome by a great misfortune, one that led to extreme emotional distress.

The essential purpose of Paul's disclosure is found in verse 9, as he reveals what he learned from the aftermath of his affliction—that he **might trust not in** himself **but in God**. Although the Apostle rarely gives autobiographical information, we can glean a portrait of him from his letters. The amount of traveling he did, much of it on foot, could only be accomplished by one who was physically robust. Paul's writing also gives evidence not only of good rhetorical training but also of an agile mind. He certainly was well-versed in Scripture. Moreover, he comments on his own great zeal (Gal 1:14) and work ethic (1 Cor 15:10). In short, Paul had several reasons for being self-confident, for relying on his own strength, talents, and abilities.

Nevertheless, the traumatic incident in Asia, whatever it was, caused him to radically *deepen* his reliance on God, whom he now describes as the one **who raises the dead**.[10] Note that this characterization of God reveals a significant theological truth. The God in whom Paul trusts is not only the Creator (2 Cor 4:6); he is also the one who has brought about a "new creation" (5:17) by raising Jesus from the dead (4:14) and bestowing "the Spirit of the living God" (3:3).

Paul goes on to explain his profound trust in God. The key word in this verse is "rescue." The Greek verb, which can also be translated "draw out of danger," appears three times in this verse. First, Paul testifies that God has already **rescued** him **from such great danger of death**. This refers to how God delivered him from the affliction that befell him in Asia. Second, Paul confidently states that God **will continue to rescue** him—thereby expressing his renewed and deepened trust in God. Third, Paul continues, **in him we have put our hope [that] he will also rescue us again**. This can be taken in two ways. The NAB's translation suggests that Paul is reiterating that God will *continue* to rescue him, while adding the nuance of hope. This is certainly a possible rendering. A second possibility, which I think is preferable, is that Paul now expresses his

1:10

---

10. In no way do I want to suggest that Paul heretofore had not trusted in God. His earlier letters (e.g., 1 Corinthians, Galatians, 1–2 Thessalonians) give ample evidence of such reliance.

hope that God will *ultimately* rescue him by raising him from the dead.[11] This second interpretation picks up on the theological truth raised in the previous verse, namely, that God brings the dead to life. In any event, Paul's apostolic ministry is firmly grounded in his renewed trust in God. Later, he will return both to this characterization of God as the one who rescues from death and to the importance of faith in the resurrection (4:7–5:10).

1:11   Finally, Paul asks for help from the Corinthians. The expression **as you help us with prayer** serves as an implicit request that they pray for him.[12] In light of the preceding verse, Paul is asking them to pray that God continue to rescue him from difficulties and afflictions. The Corinthians' prayers will join **the prayers of many**, that is, of others who pray for Paul and his ministry. This appeal for prayers is a concrete manifestation of his dependence upon God. Moreover, Paul's ultimate motive for requesting prayers is that **thanks may be given by many on our behalf for the gift granted us**. In other words, he believes that his ministry of proclaiming the gospel will result in more and more people praising and thanking God—a theme that recurs in 4:15 and 9:13–15.

Reflection and Application (1:8–11)

"God who raises the dead." Paul's description of God in verse 9 states the basis of all Christian hope: "We firmly believe, and hence we hope that, just as Christ is truly risen from the dead and lives for ever, so after death the righteous will live for ever with the risen Christ and he will raise them up on the last day" (Catechism, 989; cf. John 6:39–40). Hope in the resurrection sustains us in our vocation to heed Jesus' call to take up the cross and follow him, to offer our lives for the sake of the gospel (Mark 8:34–35). Hope in God who raises the dead gives special meaning and comfort to the elderly and terminally ill. And this hope strengthens and consoles those who mourn the loss of loved ones. Indeed, Catholics pray at the Funeral Mass, "Lord, for your faithful people life is changed, not ended" (Preface, Christian Death I).

Trust in God. People involved in ministry face a paradox. On one hand we are expected to acquire professional skills and grow in competence; on the other hand we are summoned to deepen our trust in God, whom we serve. Ministerial competence and success can be seductive, especially if they lead us to depend exclusively on our own wherewithal. Similarly, ample material resources can

---

11. See Paul J. Barnett, *The Second Epistle to the Corinthians*, NICNT (Grand Rapids: Eerdmans, 1997), 88.

12. Paul also requests prayers for himself in Rom 15:30–32; Phil 1:19; Col 4:3–4; 1 Thess 5:25; Philem 22.

tempt us into thinking and acting as if we are totally self-sufficient. What Paul writes to the Corinthians can serve as a healthy antidote to such tendencies. It is important to humbly recall our experience of struggle, failure, even despair in order to remind ourselves that we need to place our reliance and trust in God. It is God who has blessed us with talents and abilities; it is God who calls us to ministry; and it is God who will supply what is needed to carry out his will.

Prayer for ministry. The preceding point makes clear the importance of prayer for those who are called to ministry. Each one of us must be faithful to personal prayer. Moreover, like Paul, we depend on the prayers of others. The religious order to which I belong, the Society of Jesus (the Jesuits), annually lists the ministries of each member. One of the striking features of this listing is the number of men, primarily those who are elderly and infirm, whose principal ministry is described as "praying for the Church and the Society." This is no mere platitude. Those so called take seriously their call to prayer, while Jesuits in active ministry count on those prayers. *All* Christians, regardless of age, can participate in prayer for ministry, for the effective proclamation of God's word and conveyance of God's love to people everywhere.

Aligned with the "Yes" of Jesus

2 Corinthians 1:12–22

Having greeted the Corinthians and blessed the God of all encouragement (1:1–11), Paul opens the body of the letter with a brief statement about his apostolic integrity (1:12–14). He then begins to rehearse a series of recent events that has resulted in misunderstanding. The first issue concerns his revised travel plans, which have led some in the community to question the trustworthiness of his word (1:15–17). Paul takes the opportunity to make a profound theological statement about how God's faithfulness, which has been manifested first and foremost through Jesus' faithfulness, continues to be revealed in the faithfulness of those who have been anointed and sealed with the Spirit (1:18–22).

Opening Statement (1:12–14)

---

[12]For our boast is this, the testimony of our conscience that we have conducted ourselves in the world, and especially toward you, with the simplicity and sincerity of God, [and] not by human wisdom but by the grace of God. [13]For we write you nothing but what you can read and understand, and I hope that you will understand completely, [14]as you have come to understand us partially, that we are your boast as you also are ours, on the day of [our] Lord Jesus.

OT: Ps 1; Jer 9:22–23
NT: John 17:12; Acts 20:17–24; 1 Tim 1:5; 1 Pet 3:13–17
Catechism: conscience, 1776–94

Paul sets forth his reason for writing. He both explains that he has always conducted himself in a way that reflects God's empowerment and expresses his hope that the Corinthians will fully understand his proclamation.

Paul begins with a statement that explains to the Corinthians why he writes. 1:12
Today it might seem odd that he begins with a **boast**, something that might seem
to smack of arrogance. I will withhold comment on this term for a moment,
as it appears again in verse 14. Paul's main point here is that he appeals to **the
testimony** of his **conscience**, the inner tribunal of critical self-evaluation. Paul
insists that he has a clear conscience about the way he has **conducted** himself
both in general—the expression **in the world** refers here to the arena of typical,
daily affairs—and **especially toward** the Corinthians.[1]

He then explains his conduct in two ways. First, Paul asserts that he has acted
with the simplicity and sincerity of God. The word translated as "simplicity"[2]
will play a significant role later in this epistle (8:2; 9:11, 13; 11:3). It points
to singleness of mind and heart, in short, to integrity, and is aptly rendered
"single-hearted devotion."[3] Paul declares that his single-hearted devotion and
sincerity are "of God," that is, they derive from God and partake of God's own
single-heartedness and truthfulness. Second, Paul maintains that he conducts
himself **not by human wisdom but by the grace of God**. The phrase "human
wisdom" is, literally, "fleshly wisdom." Paul often employs the adjective *sarkikos*—
along with the related noun *sarx* ("†flesh")—to denote something that derives
from human beings and is not divinely influenced or empowered (see, e.g.,
1:17; 5:16; 10:2–4; 11:18). He maintains that, rather than comporting himself
in such a "fleshly" way, he acts "by the †grace of God"—by the inspiration and
help that come from God.

Paul asserts that he writes **nothing but what** the Corinthians **can read and** 1:13–14
understand. This claim is a specific application of his statement in verse 12
about his blameless conduct toward them. Why does he here defend the way he
writes? Perhaps a clue can be found in 4:3–4, where he alludes to criticism that
his †gospel is "veiled." In any event, Paul claims in his opening statement what
he will reiterate in 10:11, namely, that his behavior is congruent with his letters.
In both his life and his letters, he insists, he acts with godly devotion and sincerity toward the Corinthians. Paul expresses his hope that the community **will
understand completely**. Before stating what it is that he hopes they understand,
he acknowledges that they already **have come to understand** him **partially**. This
shows pastoral adroitness. Paul credits them for partial understanding while
implicitly encouraging them to arrive at a fuller comprehension.

---

1. Paul is not insisting, however, that he knows God's judgment (see 1 Cor 4:4). His point is that
he has peace vis-à-vis his own "inner tribunal"; i.e., he is not aware of wrongdoing.

2. The Greek term is *haplotēs*.

3. Frank J. Matera, *II Corinthians: A Commentary*, NTL (Louisville: Westminster John Knox,
2003), 46.

What the Corinthians are to understand is this: **we are your boast as you also are ours**. According to Paul, there is a good kind of †boasting and a bad kind.[4] The latter refers to boasting in the sense that we normally associate with the term, that is, the attempt to promote oneself and one's own accomplishments, often at the expense of others. Later in the letter, Paul will rail against (10:12) and mock (11:1–12:13) boasting of this kind. Here, however, he obviously uses the term "boast" in a positive sense. Paul's principle is simple: "Whoever boasts, should boast in the Lord" (1 Cor 1:31; 2 Cor 10:17; an allusion to Jer 9:22–23). It is legitimate to boast about what is being accomplished "by the grace of God" (v. 12). Paul's point is that he was God's chosen instrument to bring the gospel to Corinth (10:13–14). Therefore the Corinthians can rightly take pride in him, his coworkers, and his ministry.

But in order to "understand completely"—and thus in order to be authentically proud of what God is doing through him—they must learn to accept Paul's way of being an †apostle. This way, as "an apostle of Christ Jesus" (1:1), is marked by self-giving and involves affliction and suffering (1:3–7). By accepting Paul and his manner more fully—which entails *their* appropriating his self-giving lifestyle—the Corinthians will become *his* "boast," his source of pride (see Phil 2:15–16; 1 Thess 2:19). As we will see, Paul's exhortations throughout the letter are geared toward the Corinthians' accepting and appropriating this way of life, which has been revealed by Jesus. The reference to **the day of [our] Lord Jesus** points to the final judgment (5:10). In the presence of the risen Lord of glory (4:14), the Apostle and the Corinthians will ultimately be one another's "boast."

Reflection and Application (1:12–14)

Conscience. Paul is the champion of conscience.[5] He came to realize that God has put his law into the hearts of *all* people (Rom 2:15). While he was concerned with the proper formation of conscience among members of his fledgling communities, Paul demanded sensitivity toward those whose conscience was not fully formed (1 Cor 8:7–13; 10:28–29). He recognized that a "good conscience" is only authentically developed alongside a "pure heart" and "sincere faith"—and that it is out of these that love emerges (1 Tim 1:5). The Catholic Church insists on the dignity of all people, a dignity that is associated closely with conscience:

4. Over 90 percent of the occurrences of "boasting" (*kauch-*) terminology in the New Testament appear in Paul's writings. More than half of his usage is in 2 Corinthians.

5. Of the thirty times the word *syneidēsis* ("conscience") appears in the New Testament, twenty are found in Paul's writings.

"For every person has in his or her heart a law inscribed by God. One's dignity rests in observing this law, and by it each person will be judged. One's conscience is his or her most secret core and sanctuary. There he or she is alone with God, whose voice echoes deeply within" (*Gaudium et Spes* 16).

One of the primary tasks of every Christian is the ongoing formation of his or her conscience. In particular, we are called to turn to the word of God for light, assimilating this word through prayer and faith (Catechism, 1785). Paul's letters hold up the self-giving love of Jesus—a love that "impels" his followers to emulate him (2 Cor 5:14)—as *the* key criterion for moral decision making. Following this criterion, we are sure to grow in the single-hearted devotion to and sincerity of God that the Apostle exemplifies.

Appropriate "boasting." There is an old adage that goes, "It ain't bragging if it's true." Paul, I think, would agree with this statement, but with an important caveat, namely, it is true only when we acknowledge *God* as the source of our successes and accomplishments. If we seriously reflect on our lives, we will come to recognize that we can do nothing without God. On our better days, many of us recall and give thanks to God for our talents and opportunities. Less often do we confess our dependence on God for our health and well-being—unless we happen to get sick or injured or experience an economic setback. Indeed, the ability to be disciplined and to work hard is itself a gift. All of us know how off-putting the bragging of others can be. In fact, such bragging often masks an insecure sense of self-worth. Nevertheless, Jesus does invite us to talk about ourselves to family, friends, and others, but with a special emphasis: we are to share with them what the Lord in his great mercy and compassion has done for us (Mark 5:19; Luke 8:39). Even more, we are called to sing God's praises, proclaiming his marvelous deeds to all (Ps 96:3).

Revised Travel Plans (1:15–17)

[15]With this confidence I formerly intended to come to you so that you might receive a double favor, [16]namely, to go by way of you to Macedonia, and then to come to you again on my return from Macedonia, and have you send me on my way to Judea. [17]So when I intended this, did I act lightly? Or do I make my plans according to human considerations, so that with me it is "yes, yes," and "no, no"?

OT: 1 Sam 3:1–10
NT: Matt 5:37; Mark 14:32–36; James 5:12

Having set forth in verses 12–14 his purpose for writing, Paul begins to review some recent events that have fueled the fires of mistrust on the part of some of the Corinthians. He has just insisted on his blameless conduct toward the community. How, then, does he explain not following through on a promised visit?

1:15–16   In order to understand this passage, we need to look briefly at 1 Cor 16:5–7. Writing from †Ephesus, Paul told the Corinthians that he planned to visit them after passing through †Macedonia, the Roman province north of †Achaia. Earlier he had founded churches there, in †Philippi and in †Thessalonica. Paul's intention, presumably, was to visit those communities before coming to Corinth. He informed the Corinthians that he desired to stay with them more than just in passing. In fact, he told the community that he might spend the entire winter with them.

Paul soon felt the need to modify these travel plans, however. Troubling news from Corinth led to his paying an emergency visit to the Corinthians *before* he went to Macedonia.[6] At some point during this sudden visit, Paul must have informed the community of his modified plans. The new itinerary was to go on **to Macedonia, and then to come to** Corinth **again** on his **return from Macedonia** (v. 16). Thus, according to Paul, the Corinthians would **receive a double favor** (v. 15)—the present surprise visit, dealing with the problems that had been communicated to him, and then another visit after his return from Macedonia. (The reference to sending him on his **way to** †**Judea** refers to his plans to deliver the monies collected for the church in Jerusalem; see 8:1–9:15.)

But just as Paul did not execute his original travel plans in 1 Cor 16:5–7, neither did he follow through on his modified plans. After the painful incident with "the one who did the wrong" (2 Cor 7:12) and "caused pain" (2:5), Paul did *not* go directly to Macedonia but immediately returned to Ephesus. Moreover, at the time of his writing 2 Corinthians, approximately nine months after the surprise visit, he still had not made good the promise of "a double favor."

1:17   How did the Corinthians react to these developments? Paul himself offers two clues as to the opinions of at least some in the community. One opinion is that he has acted **lightly**, that is, his constant changes reveal a fickle character. Another opinion is that he has conducted himself **according to human considerations**. The latter phrase is a good translation of *kata sarka*, literally, "according to the flesh." As in verse 12, Paul uses the word †flesh here to denote human activity that lacks the inspiration and empowerment of God. Hence he is accused of acting according to self-interest. According to the NAB's translation,

---

6. See stage 4 under Historical Context in the introduction.

Paul summarizes the accusations of his supposedly fickle and "fleshly" behavior as follows: **with me it is "yes, yes," and "no, no."** This translation suggests, in effect, that he says yes and no at the same time.[7]

I submit, however, that with his second question—"Or do I make my plans according to human considerations, so that with me it is 'yes, yes,' and 'no, no'?"— Paul intends a different nuance. The Greek text is more complex and subtle than the NAB's reading might suggest.[8] It is possible to render Paul's words thus: "Or do I make my plans according to human considerations, so that yes being yes and no being no *should rest with me*?" Indeed, this is how St. John Chrysostom, the great fourth-century commentator on Paul and a native Greek speaker, understood the meaning. Chrysostom remarks: "The servant of the Spirit is led by the Spirit. He cannot just do what he likes. He is dependent on the Spirit's authority. Paul was not able to come to Corinth because it was not the Spirit's will for him to go there."[9] In other words, Paul suggests that the real issue concerns what *God's* will has been for him. He thus defends himself against the charges of fickleness and of acting according to human considerations by claiming that his changes in travel plans were in response to his following the promptings of God.

Reflection and Application (1:15–17)

Reserving judgment. The mistrust that some of the Corinthians felt toward Paul seems to have resulted from their jumping to conclusions and judgment rather than giving him the benefit of the doubt and awaiting his explanation. The rush to judge others frequently results in harm and has no place in the Christian community. Near the beginning of his *Spiritual Exercises* (22), St. Ignatius of Loyola encourages both the retreat director and the person making the retreat to be ready to give the best interpretation to what the other says and to seek clarification if something seems amiss, rather than presuming ill will or error. If correction of the other is necessary, it is then to be given with charity. Ignatius's advice applies well to all relationships, especially to those between ministers and the people whom they serve.

Doing God's will. The reading of verse 17 proposed above, which highlights the issue of doing God's will, invites us to consider something very familiar,

---

7. The NJB and NRSV make explicit the phrase "at the same time"; compare the NIV's "in the same breath."

8. Here I follow closely the reading set forth by Frances Young in "Note on 2 Corinthians 1:17b," *JTS* 37 (1986): 404–15.

9. *Homilies on 2 Corinthians* 3.3, quoted from Gerald Bray, ed., *1–2 Corinthians*, ACCS (Downers Grove, IL: InterVarsity, 1999), 201.

namely, the Lord's Prayer. At liturgical celebrations and in private devotions such as praying the rosary, we pray the words that Jesus taught us. The prayer is so familiar to us that we can easily go into automatic pilot when reciting it— saying the words without giving much thought to what we are praying. One of the petitions in this prayer is "Thy will be done." That is, we pray that God's will be accomplished more and more each day "on earth as it is in heaven." In order to say this prayer sincerely, we must grow in readiness that God's will be done more and more in our own lives. Indeed, Jesus not only taught us to pray the Our Father, he also modeled an unwavering devotion to doing the Father's will (to which Paul will refer in the following passage, vv. 19–20). This commitment was most evident in his prayer in the Garden of Gethsemane on the night before he died for us: "Abba, Father, all things are possible to you. Take this cup away from me, but not what I will but what you will" (Mark 14:36).

Anointed and Sealed to Walk in the Way of Jesus' "Yes" (1:18–22)

---

[18]As God is faithful, our word to you is not "yes" and "no." [19]For the Son of God, Jesus Christ, who was proclaimed to you by us, Silvanus and Timothy and me, was not "yes" and "no," but "yes" has been in him. [20]For however many are the promises of God, their Yes is in him; therefore, the Amen from us also goes through him to God for glory. [21]But the one who gives us security with you in Christ and who anointed us is God; [22]he has also put his seal upon us and given the Spirit in our hearts as a first installment.

OT: Exod 29:4–9, 21; 1 Sam 16:12–13; Ps 119:1–8

NT: Luke 4:16–21; Acts 10:38; Rom 6:1–11; Gal 3:27–29

Catechism: indelible spiritual mark bestowed at baptism (1272–74) and at confirmation and Holy Orders (698)

Paul recognized the implications of the doubts raised because of his changes in travel plans. Can his word really be trusted? What about the words spoken by him when he first brought the †gospel to Corinth? Are *they* trustworthy? Paul offers a theologically rich explanation of why the Corinthians can trust him. Because the language in this passage is dense, it is necessary to unpack it with care.

1:18 Paul begins by appealing to the faithfulness of God: **As God is faithful.**[10] That is, he grounds the trustworthiness of his word—**our word to you is not**

10. Paul also names God as faithful (*pistos*) in 1 Cor 1:9 and 10:13 and refers to God's faithfulness (*pistis*) in Rom 3:3.

"yes" and "no"—in *God's* faithfulness. Paul's "word" refers here to his use of words in general, that is, he says what he means and means what he says. But he refers especially to his proclamation of the gospel, as the following verse makes clear. His appeal to God as faithful is the foundation of his presentation in verses 18–22 for, as we will see, faithfulness is the key theme that runs through these verses.

God's faithfulness, according to Paul, has been manifested most clearly
through **the Son of God, Jesus Christ**. In fact, Jesus is the main content of the gospel that was **proclaimed** by Paul, along with **Silvanus and Timothy**, at the establishment of the church in Corinth. We have already been introduced to Timothy (see 1:1). Silvanus was another of Paul's coworkers. He is listed as a cosender of 1–2 Thessalonians. Identified as Silas in Acts of the Apostles 15–18, he accompanied Paul during his founding visits to †Philippi and †Thessalonica. Silvanus showed himself willing to suffer for the gospel, enduring both physical punishment and imprisonment with the Apostle (Acts 16:19–34).

Paul associates Jesus, who is identified as "Son of God" and "Christ" ("the anointed one," or "†Messiah"), with the word "yes." He says that Jesus **was not "yes" and "no"**; rather, he insists, **"yes" has been in him**. What does Paul signify by linking Jesus with "yes"? In order to understand the meaning here, it is helpful to look ahead to the first half of verse 20. There Paul asserts that all **the promises of God** have **their Yes** in Christ. His point is that Jesus is the fulfillment of the promises God made to Abraham (Gal 3:15–18) and to Israel through the prophets and Scripture (Rom 1:2). Jesus, God's Son and the "anointed one," fulfilled God's promises through his life, ministry, death, and resurrection, thereby revealing God's faithfulness and love (Rom 5:8; see also John 3:16). That is, Jesus fulfilled God's promises through his own filial love and obedience to the Father's will.[11]

We are now in position to understand better the association of Jesus with "yes" in verse 19. In proclaiming that Jesus was not "yes" and "no," Paul refers to Christ's unwavering faithfulness, to his unconditional "yes" to God during his earthly ministry. Jesus' "yes" culminated with his giving his life on the cross (Phil 2:8), a self-offering that expressed his love for all people (2 Cor 5:14; Gal 2:20). Paul thereby anticipates his later allusions to Jesus as the †new Adam (2 Cor 3:18; 4:4) who reveals how human beings were intended to live—in obedience to the designs of God their Father (Rom 5:12–21; 1 Cor 15:12–22; see Gen 1–3). Moreover, Paul makes an important point at the end of verse 19, one that is not obvious from English translations. By employing a perfect tense verb

---

11. Paul alludes to Jesus' will and agency with the phrase "in him."

(literally, "has come to be"), he indicates that Jesus' "yes" has *ongoing* implications for the present—even to us today.[12]

Paul picks up on the ongoing implications of Jesus' "yes": **the Amen from us also goes through him to God**. The phrase "through him" refers to Jesus. Through Christ a new possibility has been opened up for human beings.[13] Paul refers to this new possibility as "the Amen." This word is a transliteration (i.e., spelling a word in the letters of another alphabet) of a Hebrew term that means "steadfastness" and "faithfulness." With the phrase "the Amen from us," Paul alludes to his own steadfast fidelity and that of his coworkers, a fidelity that is directed "to God." The Amen is thus Paul's shorthand expression for living in faithfulness to the will of God, whose own character is marked by faithfulness (v. 18). The "yes" of Jesus, which is at the heart of the gospel proclamation, is, in effect, his "Amen" to the Father. And one of the fruits of Christ's faithfulness is that we are empowered to walk in faithfulness to God's will—something that Paul claims for himself here as he proclaims the gospel to the Corinthians in word and actions.[14] (Recall too from v. 17 that he intimates that he has heeded God's promptings in connection with his travel plans.)

Finally, Paul adds that living in fidelity to God's will is **for glory**. By submitting ourselves to God's design we give him glory and praise. At the same time, human beings, who are created in the †image of God (Gen 1:26–27), reflect God's greatness and glory when they live as he intends, as revealed in Jesus' self-offering in love.

1:21–22   Paul now describes *how* human beings are empowered to walk in the way of faithfulness after the manner of Jesus. It is critically important to note that the subject of all of the verbs in these verses is **God**. God is **the one who gives us security with you in Christ**. The verb translated "gives security" also has the sense of making a person strong in his or her commitment. Paul claims that God is strengthening him (the verb is in the present tense) along with the Corinthians. Moreover, God strengthens them "in Christ." The Greek phrase means, literally, "into Christ." Paul's language here suggests a *process* in which God is empowering him to become more like Jesus by taking on his character, a character marked by faithfulness to God and self-giving love for others.

The process whereby God continues to strengthen Paul stems from the fact that God has already **given the Spirit in our hearts**, a gift that is first conferred

---

12. In Greek the perfect tense signifies something that happened in the past that continues to have ramifications in the present.

13. In the Greek text, the phrase "through him" is at the *beginning* of the second half of v. 20.

14. Interpreting "the Amen" as referring to the conclusion of a prayer (e.g., the RSV's "that is why we utter the Amen") misses Paul's nuance. The key theme in these verses is *faithfulness*.

Anointing in the Old Testament

Two special groups of people were anointed in the Old Testament: priests and kings. God directed Moses to anoint Aaron and his sons to be priests (Exod 29:7, 21). Their anointing functioned both as an act of consecration, setting them apart for God, and as an ordination, empowering them to perform their sacred duties (Exod 28:41). Subsequent high priests, following Aaron, were also anointed (Lev 21:10). In addition, God commanded Samuel to anoint Saul as king to deliver Israel from her enemies and to rule over her (1 Sam 9:16; 10:1). David and later kings were similarly anointed (e.g., 1 Sam 16:12–13; 1 Kings 1:39). Their kingly charge was first and foremost to shepherd God's people with care (2 Sam 5:2) and to govern them with justice (Ps 72:2). (According to 1 Kings 19:16, the prophet Elisha was also anointed.)

Jesus takes up the royal and priestly offices in a manner par excellence. Jesus not only inaugurated the kingdom of God (Mark 1:15) through his ministry, death, and resurrection; as risen and exalted Lord, he now reigns as "King of kings" (Rev 19:16). And, after offering his own body and blood on the cross (Mark 14:22–25), Jesus has entered the heavenly tabernacle (Heb 9:11–12) as the great and merciful high priest (Heb 4:14–16). Jesus' royal and priestly identity is celebrated on the Feast of Christ the King.

---

in baptism (see Acts 9:17–18). He describes this initial empowerment by God's Spirit through two powerful images. First, he states that God **anointed** him. It is from the verb "anoint," *chriō*, that we get the word *Christ* (*Christos*, the "anointed one").[15] Paul's single use of the verb occurs here. In fact, *chriō* is employed only four other times in the New Testament, each case in connection with Jesus. The description in Acts 10:38 is particularly relevant in this context: "God anointed Jesus of Nazareth with the holy Spirit and power. He went about doing good and healing all those oppressed by the devil, for God was with him."[16] Paul's claim to be "anointed," which follows his statement that God is strengthening him "into Christ," indicates that the same Spirit who anointed Jesus now empowers Paul. The Apostle's testimonial teaches us that *all* Christians are "little Christs" who share in his identity and destiny.

The second dramatic image is found in verse 22: God **has also put his seal upon us**. This is another allusion to baptism. The verb "seal" has rich

---

15. In fact, Paul creates a wordplay in the Greek text of v. 21: *eis Christon kai chrisas*.

16. In Luke 4:18 Jesus himself describes his anointing with the Spirit and the resulting empowerment in similar terms. See also Acts 4:27 and Heb 1:9.

St. Augustine on the Anointing of Baptism

In his *Sermon on Psalm 26*, St. Augustine points to the anointing of kings and priests in the Old Testament as a prefiguration of Christ. He then sets forth how Jesus' anointing is linked with Christian baptism: "Not only has our head [i.e., Christ] been anointed, but we, his body, have been anointed too. . . . We are the body of Christ because we have been 'anointed' with him and are 'christs,' that is, 'anointed ones,' as well as Christ himself, who is 'the Anointed One.' . . . It therefore happens that with head and body the whole Christ is formed" (2.2).

connotations. It can refer to marking or branding as a means of identification. For example, Rev 7:3 relates the marking of the "servants" (literally, "slaves") of God. In this instance, the marking provides both identity as belonging to God and protection to those so marked. Indeed, Paul refers to himself elsewhere as "a slave of God" (Titus 1:1). We will see that he employs this imagery of being God's slave later in this letter (2:14; 4:13). In doing so he intimates that, having been "sealed" by God, he now belongs to God and enjoys his protection. The verb "seal" also pertains to the use of a signet or seal to make an impression on malleable material such as wax or clay (1 Kings 21:8; see 2 Tim 2:19). This sense applies here as well. That is, Paul alludes here to being "impressed" or "imprinted," an action that has left an indelible impression on him. But imprinted with what? The preceding context suggests that he refers to having been imprinted with the character of Christ Jesus, an imprinting shared by all Christians.

Paul concludes with a reference to the Spirit as a **first installment**. Although God's gift has already produced wondrous effects in him, the presence of the Spirit is also the divine pledge of the fullness of life to come, when what is mortal will be swallowed up by life (2 Cor 5:1–10; Eph 4:30).

Reflection and Application (1:18–22)

Participating in the story of Jesus. If our New Testament contained only the letters of Paul, we would know very little about Jesus' earthly life and ministry. Paul does not tell the story of Jesus as do Matthew, Mark, Luke, and John. Nevertheless, the story of Jesus is important to Paul, often lying just beneath the surface of his writings. He does not have to rehearse this story in his letters because he has already proclaimed to his communities the good news about what God has done in and through Christ. Thus Paul merely needs to allude to this story—and to the character and attributes of its protagonist, Jesus. His readers know what Paul is referring to by such allusions. That is what is going on in 2 Cor 1:19–20.

Paul teaches us, moreover, that the story of Jesus is not just a thing of the past. Rather, the story of what God has done through Jesus continues into the present. The story continues because God has poured out on us the gift of the Holy Spirit (Rom 5:5), the Spirit of Christ Jesus (see Rom 8:9; Phil 1:19). Anointed and sealed with the Spirit, *all* Christians are called and empowered to participate in the story (see Eph 1:13; 4:30). We do so by becoming more and more "conformed" to Jesus—the ultimate Yes man—and to his self-giving love (Rom 8:29). This leads to the next point.

Baptism and confirmation. Christians receive the Spirit's anointing and sealing in the sacrament of baptism, a gift that is strengthened in the sacrament of confirmation. It is worth paying close attention to the celebration of these sacraments in order to appreciate the awesome gift we have received. Immediately following the baptism proper in the Catholic liturgy, the priest or deacon anoints the baptized with special oil called Sacred Chrism (from the same Greek word, *chriō*, from which "Christ" is derived, as is the term "christening," another word for baptism). During this anointing the priest or deacon prays, "[God the Father] now anoints you with the chrism of salvation. As Christ was anointed Priest, Prophet, and King, so may you live always as a member of his body" (Rite of Baptism). At the Catholic celebration of confirmation, the bishop lays hands on the ones being confirmed while praying that God will "anoint them to be more like Christ the Son of God." The bishop then anoints with the Sacred Chrism, saying, "Be sealed with the Gift of the Holy Spirit" (Rite of Confirmation).

Clearing the Air

2 Corinthians 1:23–2:13

Having expressed his purpose in writing (1:12–14) and explained his change in travel plans (1:15–17), which led to the dense theological statement in which he aligned himself with the "yes" of Jesus (1:18–22), Paul now resumes his rehearsal of recent events. He explains why he has not yet returned to Corinth and chose instead to write a letter to the community (1:23–2:4). Paul then discreetly alludes to his prior, painful visit and exhorts the Corinthians to forgive the person who "caused pain" (2:5–11). Finally, he informs them that he left a promising missionary opportunity out of love and concern for them (2:12–13). Throughout this passage Paul's goal is to clear the air between himself and the community.

Why a Letter Was Preferable to a Visit (1:23–2:4)

²³But I call upon God as witness, on my life, that it is to spare you that I have not yet gone to Corinth. ²⁴Not that we lord it over your faith; rather, we work together for your joy, for you stand firm in the faith.

²:¹For I decided not to come to you again in painful circumstances. ²For if I inflict pain upon you, then who is there to cheer me except the one pained by me? ³And I wrote as I did so that when I came I might not be pained by those in whom I should have rejoiced, confident about all of you that my joy is that of all of you. ⁴For out of much affliction and anguish of heart I wrote to you with many tears, not that you might be pained but that you might know the abundant love I have for you.

OT: Ezek 18:21–32; Hosea 11:8–9
NT: Mark 10:42–45; John 15:11–17; Rom 15:13; Gal 5:22
Catechism: swearing oaths, 2154

Swearing Oaths

Largely because of Paul's use of oaths (2 Cor 1:23; see Gal 2:10), the Catholic Church has understood that Jesus' prohibition against swearing oaths (Matt 5:33–37) does not include those "made for grave and right reasons (for example, in court)" (2154). The Catechism cites Roman Canon Law (1199 §1): "An oath, that is the invocation of the divine name as a witness to truth, cannot be taken unless in truth, in judgment, and in justice."

Paul suggested in 1:17 that he had changed his travel plans because he follows the promptings of God. Nevertheless, he feels obligated to give to the community a full explanation for why he has not yet returned to Corinth. In addition, he explains his reason for writing a letter to them in lieu of making a visit.

Paul begins by calling on **God as witness**. Whereas he appealed to the "testimony" of his own conscience in 1:12, he now summons God as witness to affirm the truth of what he is about to say.[1] The importance of what Paul is about to say is made clear by his calling divine punishment on himself if what he says is not true—this is the significance of the phrase **on my life**. He thus solemnly swears that he has not yet returned **to Corinth** because he wanted **to spare** the community. Paul refers here to the situation that resulted from his second, emergency visit to the Corinthians. During that visit, someone "caused pain" to Paul (2:5), probably by insolently challenging his authority. Moreover, it seems that the community did not immediately come to his defense.[2] In the aftermath of that visit, Paul decided he could not return to Corinth for a fruitful visit until the community addressed what had taken place. Had Paul returned as he had planned (1:15–16), he would have been forced to bring the "rod" of punishment (see 1 Cor 4:21).

As we will see below (2:3–4), Paul opted instead to write a letter that conveyed his side of things; perhaps he also hoped that the Corinthians themselves would take appropriate action against the wrongdoer. Hence, when he explains that he refrained from returning in order "to spare" the community, he expresses his preference to forgo the option of discipline.

1:23

---

1. Paul evokes God's witness and presence throughout 2 Corinthians in order to reinforce the truthfulness of his statements and claims (2:17; 11:31; 12:19). See also Rom 1:9; Phil 1:8; 1 Thess 2:5, 10.
2. See stage 4 under Historical Context in the introduction.

1:24   Paul claims that he does not **lord it over** the Corinthians' **faith**. While he was convinced that he had a God-given authority over the communities he founded, this authority was primarily for "building up," not for "tearing down" (2 Cor 10:8). Paul strives to exercise authority and leadership after the manner of Jesus—as one who came to serve, not to be served (Mark 10:42–45). In fact, he will soon refer to himself as the Corinthians' *slave* (4:5). Paul's preference is to use his authority "with love and a gentle spirit" (1 Cor 4:21) instead of with a rod. Rather than "lord it over" them, he insists, he works for the community's **joy**. When Paul claims that he labors for the "joy" of the Corinthians, he does not mean that he toils for their emotional happiness. Rather, he alludes here to the joy that is bestowed by the Holy Spirit (Gal 5:22) and is a consequence of the coming of God's kingdom (Rom 14:17). Thus Paul claims that he serves the Corinthians in order that they might receive the gift of joy that is a sure sign of their living in the truth of the †gospel. His final statement—**you stand firm in the faith**—is an acknowledgment that the community has *already* received the gospel faith. It also recognizes that the Corinthians have walked in the way of faithfulness by punishing "the one who did the wrong" (2 Cor 2:6; 7:12) and by lamenting their own role in the painful incident (7:7).

2:1–2   Paul continues to explain his reasons for not visiting earlier:[3] he **decided not to come** to the community because a visit at that point would have been **in painful circumstances**. He foresaw that, were he to return to Corinth as planned, the result would have been painful for both parties. Feelings were too raw for reconciliation. Sometimes the prudent thing to do is to let matters cool off. Paul's unspoken premise is that a visit from the founding †apostle should be an occasion of joy for all. The opening words of verse 2—**For if I inflict pain upon you**—refer to the possibility of his coming with the rod of discipline and punishment. If that had happened, he explains, there would have been no one among the Corinthians **to cheer** him up. (The expression **the one pained by me** refers generically to each member of the community.) Note how Paul presumes here a strong sense of mutuality between himself and the Corinthians. Not only does he work for their joy (1:24), he also looks to them for support and encouragement.

2:3–4   Paul next explains why he sent a letter—written **out of much affliction and anguish of heart** and **with many tears**—to the community in lieu of making an immediate return visit. This letter is no longer extant.[4] His description of his

3. 2 Cor 2:1 belongs with the paragraph beginning at 1:23. The New Testament was divided into chapters in the thirteenth century and into verses in the sixteenth. Paragraph divisions and subheadings—as well as all punctuation marks—in our Bibles are editorial decisions of translators. While helpful, they are not part of the inspired text itself.

4. See stage 5 under Historical Context in the introduction.

experience conveys how heart-wrenching it was for him to compose the letter. Paul wrote with an eye toward returning to Corinth. His desire, upon returning to the Corinthians, was **not** to **be pained by those in whom** he **should have rejoiced**. The letter was meant to facilitate this desire.

Indeed, Paul reminds the community that his **joy** and theirs are intimately connected. To some ears, his words may sound self-serving, as if the real issue were *his* joy. Verse 3, however, must be interpreted in light of Paul's opening statement. Recall that in 1:14 he reminded the Corinthians that they are to be his boast and vice versa. That is, both parties can justly take pride and rejoice before God in what God is accomplishing, namely that, through Paul's apostolic labors of laying a foundation, the church in Corinth has become a temple of God, a people in whom the Holy Spirit dwells (1 Cor 3:10–16).

What was the actual content of Paul's †tearful letter? One can hazard an educated guess based on the reaction of the Corinthians, who lamented (2 Cor 7:7), punished the wrongdoer (2:6; 7:11), and renewed their zeal for their founding apostle (7:7). He must have communicated his deep hurt over what had happened during his second visit. What we *do* know is that Paul's motivation in writing was to convey his **abundant love** for the community. In fact, the word order of the Greek text gives special emphasis to Paul's expression of love.[5] His love for the Corinthians arises, as we will see, from the wellspring of "the love of Christ" (5:14). Paul's reference to "affliction" echoes the opening benediction, in which he blessed God for bringing encouragement to those who are afflicted (1:3–7). Where is the divine encouragement in this instance? We will have to wait until Paul concludes his rehearsal of recent events—interrupted by a lengthy discourse on apostleship—in 7:6–7.

Reflection and Application (1:23–2:4)

Exercise of authority. Second Corinthians has much to say about ministry and the proper attitude and comportment of ministers. The present passage raises the issue of the exercise of authority—an issue that pertains not only to the life of the Church but also to many other areas of life (e.g., the workplace and the home). Paul insists that those in positions of authority are not to "lord it over" those in their charge. In this he alludes to the teaching of Jesus (Mark 10:42–45). While Paul recognizes that discipline and punishment are necessary at times,

---

5. The word "love" is given the prominent first position. Because Greek uses different endings for nouns depending on their grammatical function, it has greater flexibility in word order than English does.

they are not to be the leader's first option in dealing with difficult persons and situations. The exercise of authority by those who are ordained or empowered to minister in the name of Jesus is to be marked, first and foremost, by gentleness and love. To say the least, authority exercised with gentleness and love is regarded as anomalous, if not downright laughable, in many quarters today. The word of God communicated through Paul challenges ministers and all Christians who hold positions of authority to ask themselves how they exercise that authority.

The minister's needs. We will come to some passages where Paul holds the minister to heroic standards. People enter into ministry because they feel called to serve. Yet no one, not even the great Apostle himself, is above the need for support and encouragement from others. The key issue is: Where does the minister seek his or her support? Paul's words in 2:3 can easily be misconstrued. The point is *not* that he ministers to the Corinthians in order to meet his own needs. As we noted, Paul refers in this verse to the *God*-given joy that the Christian community and their leaders experience when all are faithful to living the gospel.

A red flag for any minister is the need to be needed. To engage in ministry in order to receive from those ministered to is a distortion of authentic ministry and a road that leads to disaster. While it is nice, even important, to receive encouragement and gratitude from those to whom we minister, our main human support must come from elsewhere, such as from colleagues, family, and friends. Our primary support, however, has to come from God through prayer and the sacraments, because even the best human support has its limits.

"I love you." These words are both the most sublime and the most abused in the English language. They are subject to two extremes. One extreme is their overuse by people whose emotional immaturity and actions betray the very meaning of love, understood as the commitment to act on another's behalf for his or her well-being. The other extreme is found, tragically, among people who actually *do* love one another but never verbalize it. Too many spouses, parents, children, intimate friends, and colleagues pass through life without expressing in words their love for one another. Such expressions of love are crucially important when, as in the case of Paul and the Corinthians, the relationship becomes strained, as any close relationship is bound to become at times.

Summons to Offer Forgiveness (2:5–11)

⁵If anyone has caused pain, he has caused it not to me, but in some measure (not to exaggerate) to all of you. ⁶This punishment by the majority is enough for such a person, ⁷so that on the contrary you should

forgive and encourage him instead, or else the person may be overwhelmed by excessive pain. ⁸Therefore, I urge you to reaffirm your love for
him. ⁹For this is why I wrote, to know your proven character, whether you
were obedient in everything. ¹⁰Whomever you forgive anything, so do I.
For indeed what I have forgiven, if I have forgiven anything, has been for
you in the presence of Christ, ¹¹so that we might not be taken advantage of
by Satan, for we are not unaware of his purposes.

OT: 1 Sam 24; Ps 133
NT: Matt 6:14–15; 18:15–20, 21–35; Luke 6:37; 15:11–32; Col 3:12–13
Catechism: Satan, 391–95; "Deliver us from evil," 2850–54

Paul now moves on to address the painful incident that occurred during
his second visit to the Corinthians. Specifically, he deals with the *aftermath*
of the incident—the punishment of "the one who did the wrong" (7:12)—that
followed the community's reception of the †tearful letter. Paul's concern in this
passage is not to open old wounds but to encourage the community to forgive
and receive back the offender.

The way the passage begins reveals Paul's pastoral sensitivity—**If anyone has**   2:5
caused pain. Note that Paul neither identifies the wrongdoer nor discusses the
offense. There is no need to do so, because all the parties concerned already
know what happened. Paul proceeds with circumspection because he desires to
facilitate the ministry of reconciliation within the community. He emphasizes
here that he was not the only victim in the nasty incident in which, it is commonly thought, one of the members of the community challenged his authority.[6]
Paul insists that the wrongdoer "caused pain" to the *entire* community—**in some**
measure (not to exaggerate) to all of you. How can he make such a claim?
Paul holds that the Church, although it consists of many individual members,
is "the body of Christ" (Rom 12:4–5; 1 Cor 12:12–27). As such, if one part
suffers, "all the parts suffer with it" (1 Cor 12:26). Moreover, Paul considers
his relationship with the Corinthians in intimate, familial terms. As founding
†apostle, he is their "father" (1 Cor 4:15; 2 Cor 12:14–15) who regards them
affectionately as "children" (2 Cor 6:13). Just as tension, disaffection, and rifts
between individual family members adversely affect the entire family, so the
painful incident left its mark on all. The sin of one member negatively affects
the whole body of Christ.

Paul mentions the **punishment** meted out by the community against the of-   2:6–8
fender. This action was part of the community's response to the †tearful letter

---

6. See stage 4 under Historical Context in the introduction.

(vv. 3–4). In all likelihood, the punishment took some form of social exclusion.[7] Paul notes that **the majority** of the Corinthians concurred with the penalty. What about those who did not? Did this minority oppose the punishment because they were sympathetic with what the wrongdoer had said? Or did they advocate an even more severe penalty because they sought to show their support for Paul? It is impossible to say. In any event, this detail gives evidence that the incident caused even more division within the community than the exclusion of one member.

Paul declares that the imposed punishment **is enough**. Then he exhorts the Corinthians to **forgive and encourage** the wrongdoer. Notice his compassionate concern for "the one who did the wrong": he does not want the person to be **overwhelmed by excessive pain**. Later in the letter Paul will refer to himself as "an ambassador for Christ" entrusted with the message and ministry of reconciliation (5:18–20). He engages in this ministry here as he urges the community to extend forgiveness to the offender (see Gal 6:1; Eph 4:32; Col 3:13). Paul also wants them to offer encouragement to the offender. In doing so, they will be instruments of God's work of bringing encouragement to those who are afflicted (2 Cor 1:3–7). Moreover, Paul makes clear that by extending forgiveness to the offender the Corinthians will **reaffirm** their **love for him**. Just as Paul has declared his love for the community (2:4) even in the midst of difficult circumstances, so now he exhorts them to express their love for the one who has caused pain. He thus reveals to us that the ministry of reconciliation "involves more than simply explaining to others what God has done in Christ. It requires that one become an active reconciler oneself."[8]

2:9   Most commentators understand verse 9 to be a parenthetical statement, as Paul offers another explanation for why he **wrote** the tearful letter, namely, to ascertain whether the Corinthians **were obedient in everything**. That is, he explains that he wrote the letter to test the community's obedience by ordering them to punish the offender. While this command might seem to be in tension with Paul's insistence that he does not "lord it over" the Corinthians' faith (1:24), we know that he has already exercised his authority to punish another member of the community (1 Cor 4:18–5:5). This additional reason for writing the tearful letter might also seem to be at odds with the claim above (2:4) that he wrote to express his "abundant love" for the community. But as any parent

---

7. Furnish points out that this likely entailed exclusion from the eucharistic celebration. See Victor Paul Furnish, *II Corinthians: A New Translation with Introduction and Commentary*, AB 32A (New York: Doubleday, 1984), 161.

8. David E. Garland, *2 Corinthians*, NAC (Nashville: Broadman and Holman, 1999), 291.

can testify, the exercise of love entails showing the tough love of discipline when a child acts disrespectfully or in any inappropriate manner.

There is much to commend this interpretation, but another possibility, one I think is preferable because it better maintains the flow of verses 7–10, is that Paul here gives an explanation for why he is writing *in the present* (i.e., for why he is writing 2 Corinthians). Admittedly, the verb—"I wrote"—is in the past tense. But we should understand that there is a literary convention in Greek[9] in which the author self-consciously describes events from the perspective of the audience's time frame. In this case the Corinthians, upon receiving this letter some time after Paul sent it, would regard Paul's action of writing it as a past event. Thus I propose rendering the beginning of this verse as follows: "For this is why *I have written*."[10] If this is the case, then Paul writes for the purpose of ascertaining, here and now, whether or not the community is "obedient" in the matter of forgiving and receiving back in love the wrongdoer. Their obedience would then be directed, ultimately, to *God*, who through Christ Jesus has bestowed on the Church the gift and ministry of reconciliation (5:18–6:2).

There is another important detail to point out. Paul tells the Corinthians that he is writing in order **to know** their **proven character**. The phrase "proven character" is an apt translation of the single Greek word *dokimē*. Paul employs this noun, along with its verbal and adjectival forms, throughout the letter, especially in the climactic final chapter.[11] The term denotes the process of testing one's character; it also refers to the tried and true quality of character ascertained by such testing. Here Paul offers an important clue as to why he writes 2 Corinthians. In addition to defending his apostolic integrity—in part because his own character has been called into question—he challenges the community to attend to their own character. In accord with the second interpretation offered in the preceding paragraph, Paul exhorts them to obey God's call to be reconciled. By heeding the will of God, the Corinthians will align themselves with the "yes" of Jesus, whose own character was marked by obedience to God (1:19–20).

Paul then makes it clear that he has already forgiven the offender. To be sure, **2:10–11** he could hardly ask the community to do so if he himself withheld mercy and love. Note once again his pastoral skillfulness, shown by his opening words: **Whomever you forgive anything, so do I.** As St. John Chrysostom astutely perceived, "Paul lets the Corinthians take the lead and tells them that he will

---

9. The convention is called the †epistolary aorist.

10. Epistolary aorists also appear in 8:17, 18, 22; and 9:3, where the NAB translates them as such.

11. See 8:2, 8, 22; 9:13; 10:18; 13:3, 5–7. Over half of Paul's use of the noun *dokimē* and cognates is found in 2 Corinthians.

follow. This is the best way to soften an exasperated and contentious spirit."[12] Paul, although he has forgiven the man in his heart, gives the community the opportunity to take the initiative to forgive; he will then follow *their* lead in extending forgiveness, in effect ratifying their decision. He thus shows himself true to his word in 1:24 about not lording it over their faith. Paul adds that his action of offering forgiveness is **in the presence of Christ**. He acts with Christ Jesus as his witness, who looks on with approval.[13] It was Jesus who taught that the true measure of having received God's mercy and compassion is the willingness to forgive one's brother or sister from one's heart (Matt 18:23–35).

Finally, Paul states that by enacting the ministry of reconciliation, he and the Corinthians will **not be taken advantage of by Satan**. Paul refers to Satan in various ways throughout this letter. He is "the god of this age" who blinds the hearts of those who fail to heed the message of the †gospel (4:4); the liar who is opposed to Christ (6:15); the "serpent" who deceived Eve (11:3) and continues to deceive by masquerading as "an angel of light" (11:14). Moreover, it is "an angel of Satan" who continually afflicts Paul (12:7). The Apostle has no doubt about the existence of the power of evil in the world, a power that seeks to thwart the spread of the gospel and to ensnare Christians whose faith is weak.[14] Indeed, Paul is **not unaware** of Satan's **purposes**. Here Satan's purpose would be to plunder the Corinthian church of one of its members and to leave the community in division and discord. Paul strives diligently to prevent this from happening.

Reflection and Application (2:5–11)

The body of Christ. One of the distinguishing characteristics of Western culture, especially since the time of the Enlightenment, is its pronounced emphasis on the individual over the community. People today tend to focus on their own individual uniqueness and autonomy, emphasizing their own interests and concerns over those of the community or group to which they belong. One manifestation of the priority of the individual is that many people today identify themselves as spiritual or as having a personal relationship with God without belonging to a particular church or congregation.

This stress on the individual, however, is foreign to the biblical worldview. In the Old Testament, to be a child of Abraham was to be first and foremost

---

12. *Homilies on 2 Corinthians* 4.5, quoted from Gerald Bray, ed., *1–2 Corinthians*, ACCS (Downers Grove, IL: InterVarsity, 1999), 207.

13. See E. Bernard Allo, *Seconde épître aux Corinthiens*, EBib (Paris: J. Gabalda, 1956), 41.

14. Paul also refers to "Satan" in Rom 16:20; 1 Cor 5:5; 7:5; 1 Thess 2:18; 2 Thess 2:9; 1 Tim 1:20; 5:15. He mentions the "devil" in Eph 4:27; 6:11; 1 Tim 3:6, 7; 2 Tim 2:26.

a member of "the people of God." In the New Testament, to be a follower of Christ Jesus meant joining an assembly (*ekklēsia*), or belonging to the fellowship (*koinōnia*) of believers. We have just seen how Paul insists that the actions of one community member have a profound spiritual effect, for good or evil, on the whole group. This is a practical consequence of his famous teaching that Christians are members of "the body of Christ." The communal aspect of our religious identity has challenging ramifications. It means that our horizons of concern must extend beyond ourselves and our immediate circle of relationships such as our family, friends, or colleagues at work. Catholics believe themselves to be "linked to one another, especially to those who are suffering, to the poor and persecuted" (Catechism, 806). Such linkage entails the responsibility to be sensitive and responsive to those in need of mercy and compassion.

The power of evil. "The devil made me do it." These words usually evoke laughter, not fear. The existence and power of Satan are doubted in many quarters today. His status is similar to that of the proverbial bogey man—not to be believed in or feared by anyone with maturity and reason. On the contrary, Paul gives witness, along with the rest of the New Testament, to the reality of Satan, "the Evil One, the angel who opposes God. The devil (*dia-bolos*) is the one who 'throws himself across' God's plan and his work of salvation accomplished in Christ" (Catechism, 2851). To be sure, when Jesus inaugurated the coming of God's kingdom through his ministry, passion, death, and resurrection, he defeated Satan's stranglehold over humankind and the world (see, e.g., Mark 3:27; Heb 2:14–15).

Nevertheless, until the Father puts all enemies under Jesus' feet (1 Cor 15:25), the devil exerts power, although "he cannot prevent the building up of God's reign" (Catechism, 395). Christians find themselves in a battlefield and thus "have to struggle to do what is right, and it is at great cost to themselves, aided by God's †grace, that they succeed in achieving their own inner integrity" (*Gaudium et Spes* 37). It is little wonder that, in teaching us to pray, Jesus offered as the final petition "deliver us from evil."

Reconciliation begins at home. One of the works of Satan is the breakdown of relationships. All of us are familiar with the saying "Charity begins at home"—a saying that is easy to understand but challenging to enact. The same is true with reconciliation. If the Church is to become more authentically "the universal sacrament of salvation" (*Lumen Gentium* 48), and if it is to carry with credibility the message and ministry of reconciliation to the world (2 Cor 5:18–19), then it needs to practice reconciliation at home. On the night before he died, Jesus prayed for his future followers—including us, here and now!—"that they may all be one, as you, Father, are in me and I in you, that they also may be one in us, . . . that they may be brought to perfection as one, that the world may know that you sent me" (John 17:21–23).

The greatest scandal in Christianity at large remains its splintering into different denominations and sects. Sadly, the spirit of ecumenism, so robust in the wake of Vatican II, seems to be diminishing. Within the Catholic Church itself, there is increased polarization between progressives and conservatives, both of whom can seem eager at times to exclude the other. The sexual abuse of children by a small number of priests and religious has caused unspeakable pain and suffering. One of the many tragic consequences of the scandal has been a breakdown of trust between laity and hierarchy—not to mention, a breakdown in trust, in some places, between bishops and their priests. Moreover, the closing and consolidation of parishes have resulted, at times, in splintering groups and cliques. In short, the need for in-house reconciliation is great. Paul's actions and exhortations in 2 Cor 2:5–11 are as timely now as ever.

Taking the first step. The preceding point is somber and challenging. Reconciliation, whether between individuals or groups, is very difficult. Some years back, Elton John recorded a song that included the lyrics, "Sorry seems to be the hardest word." All of us can relate to this sentiment. I submit, however, that it is even more difficult to say the words, "I forgive you." Indeed, this is a profound statement and one not to be lightly pronounced or received. Prayer is the necessary prelude to being able to genuinely offer forgiveness. Tragically, many relationships that were once life-giving but have since broken down—usually a dynamic that involves fault on both sides—remain broken because neither party is willing to take the initiative to seek reconciliation. Paul's example offers a different way, one that is life-giving.

A Sign of Paul's Love for the Corinthians (2:12–13)

[12]When I went to Troas for the gospel of Christ, although a door was opened for me in the Lord, [13]I had no relief in my spirit because I did not find my brother Titus. So I took leave of them and went on to Macedonia.

OT: Mic 6:8
NT: Matt 21:28–32; Luke 8:21; James 1:22–25

After urging the Corinthians to forgive and receive back the offender, Paul informs them of his restlessness as he waited for news about how they had

In the Liturgy

Paul's reference to his "spirit"—that dimension of human existence wherein the divine Spirit communicates with and inspires us—can help Catholics understand the new translation coming to the Church's liturgy. Following the priest's invocation "The Lord be with you," the congregation will respond, "And *with your spirit*." This dialogue both recognizes the special Spirit-endowed gifts of the priest and reminds the community that it is God's Spirit who has gathered them together for worship and praise, and who empowers them to go forth to do the work of transforming the world.

---

received and reacted to the †tearful letter. His purpose here is to convey his love and concern for the community.

Paul now reports that, after writing the tearful letter, he **went to Troas**. He left †Ephesus, where he had been ministering (Acts 19:1–41), and traveled one hundred fifty miles north to †Troas, an important port city on the coast of the †Aegean Sea in northwest Asia Minor (in present-day Turkey). Paul's intention was to proclaim the †**gospel of Christ** there. Indeed, he comments that **a door was opened for** him **in the Lord**; that is, by God's †grace, there were people in Troas receptive to the good news.[15]

    2:12

Paul goes on to tell the Corinthians that, although he was engaged in promising and fruitful missionary work, he **had no relief** because he **did not find** his **brother Titus**. Note that Paul says that he found no relief in his **spirit**. According to the Apostle, the spirit is the interior "place" of contact with or sensitivity to the Spirit of God. Thus he implies that his unrest was instigated by God.

    2:13

Paul refers for the first time in this letter to Titus, someone who will figure prominently later on, especially in chapters 7 and 8. Titus was an exemplary †Gentile convert whom Paul had taken to the so-called Council in Jerusalem as a demonstration of the fruit of his gospel ministry among the Gentiles (Gal 2:1–10). Paul will later call him "my partner and co-worker for you," that is, for the Corinthians (8:23). The context here strongly suggests that Titus was the bearer of the tearful letter and that he was charged with clarifying Paul's position to the Corinthians and gauging the community's reaction to the letter. That Titus was entrusted with such a delicate mission shows how much Paul trusted him, as well as how much he was respected and trusted by the Corinthians (see

---

15. Cf. 1 Cor 16:8–9, in reference to Paul's earlier ministry in Ephesus: "I shall stay in Ephesus until Pentecost, because a door has opened for me wide and productive for work."

12:18, where it is presumed that his integrity was unquestioned). Paul apparently had arranged for Titus to return to him via the land route that went north from Corinth through †Macedonia.[16] When he did not hear from Titus—and because he felt a divine stirring within—he **took leave of** the Christians in Troas **and went on to Macedonia** in order to find his "brother" en route.

Why does Paul give this information to the Corinthians? He desires that they know his love and concern for them. Indeed, so great is his affection and care that he left behind a promising missionary opportunity in order to learn how the community had reacted to his previous letter. Verses 12–13 therefore form the climax of the crescendo that has been building since 1:23. In clearing the air between himself and the Corinthians, Paul has attempted to convey his love and concern for them—by sparing them pain (1:23–2:2), by writing a letter out of love (2:3–4), by offering to forgive (2:5–11), and, most tellingly, by foregoing fruitful apostolic ministry for their sake.

Reflection and Application (2:12–13)

Love is best expressed in deeds. As important as the words "I love you" are, they are most effectively communicated by deeds, as Paul does here. His actions also give flesh to Jesus' teaching in Matt 5:23–24 that reconciliation with one's brother or sister has high priority, even over offering a gift on the altar.

---

16. See stage 5 under Historical Context in the introduction.

Minister of the New Covenant

2 Corinthians 2:14–3:11

Having rehearsed recent events between himself and the Corinthians in order to clear the air and to demonstrate his love and concern for them (1:23–2:13), Paul now dramatically shifts gears. Beginning at 2:14 he embarks on a long, four-part discourse on apostleship that continues through 7:4. The first part of this discourse (2:14–4:6) pertains to Paul's role in the ministry of the †new covenant. He introduces his ministry through two striking metaphors (2:14–17). Then, apparently in response to criticism that he lacks proper credentials, Paul argues that the church in Corinth is his letter of recommendation (3:1–3) and insists that it is God who has made him a minister of the new covenant (3:4–6). Finally, in order to highlight the greatness of the new covenant ministry, he compares it to that of the †Mosaic covenant (3:7–11).

Paul as God's Slave and as the Aroma of Christ (2:14–17)

[14]But thanks be to God, who always leads us in triumph in Christ and manifests through us the odor of the knowledge of him in every place. [15]For we are the aroma of Christ for God among those who are being saved and among those who are perishing, [16]to the latter an odor of death that leads to death, to the former an odor of life that leads to life. Who is qualified for this? [17]For we are not like the many who trade on the word of God; but as out of sincerity, indeed as from God and in the presence of God, we speak in Christ.

OT: 2 Sam 6:12–19; Isa 52:13–53:12
NT: Rom 12:1–2; 1 Cor 5:7–8; Eph 4:8–10; 1 Pet 2:9

Paul has reached the point in his rehearsal of recent events where the Corinthians would expect to learn how he reacted to Titus's report that the community had responded favorably to the †tearful letter. But Paul leaves his readers hanging until 7:6! Now that he has their full interest and attention, he sets forth what he really wants to communicate,[1] namely, the true meaning of †apostleship. Apostleship, Paul insists, is marked not by renown or power or glamour but by conformity to the passion of Christ Jesus. Paul's hope is to persuade the Corinthians, some of whom have misunderstood and criticized him, to realize that he is faithful to the way God has called him to exercise his apostolic vocation.

2:14–15a   Paul begins his exposition with a note of thanksgiving—**thanks be to God.** "Thanks" translates the word *charis*, a term that is normally rendered "†grace."[2] Paul's point is to emphasize from the very outset the primacy of God's grace. He then employs two metaphors to illustrate how God has called him to be an apostle. The first, signaled by the expression "being led **in triumph**," involves a well-known phenomenon of the time, the †triumphal procession. This was a spectacle held in Rome to celebrate a great military victory. The victorious army showed off the spoils of war and paraded their defeated enemies, some of whom were led to execution. What is surprising, if not shocking, is how Paul uses this metaphor. He portrays God as the conquering general and himself as a captured prisoner being led to death!

How are we to understand this depiction of Paul as God's captured slave? It conveys, at least in part, his awareness that, prior to his call to be an apostle, he had been acting as an enemy of God because he persecuted the Church. But God "captured" Paul and enlisted him into his service (Gal 1:15–16). Indeed, recall from the analysis of 1:22 that he has described himself as "sealed" by God. As one so sealed, Paul has been marked or branded like a slave, as one who now belongs to God. In addition, our passage offers two further clues to Paul's meaning. Note that he says that he is being led in triumph **in Christ,** that is, in close association with Jesus (Gal 2:20; Phil 3:9). Moreover, he asserts that this happens **always**. Paul here anticipates what he will claim a little later in the letter: that he "always" carries about in the body "the dying of Jesus" (4:10) and that he is "constantly being given up to death for the sake of Jesus" (4:11). As we will discover when treating these verses, Paul employs this graphic language to indicate that he aligns himself with the way of life revealed by Christ Jesus, a way characterized by love and self-giving—as well as by suffering—in

---

1. I am indebted to Frank J. Matera, *II Corinthians: A Commentary*, NTL (Louisville: Westminster John Knox, 2003), 31–32, for this insight.

2. See 8:1–9:15 for Paul's rich use of the term *charis*.

Fig. 4. Detail from the Arch of Titus that depicts the triumphal procession following the Roman conquest of Jerusalem.

obedience to God. Such a way of life, paradoxically, is the way God's kingdom triumphs over the way of self-assertion and violence.

The second striking metaphor, that of "odor," or fragrance (*osmē*), being spread, appears at the end of verse 14. The image of fragrance here conveys the wafting of incense. Paul claims that God **manifests through** him (i.e., Paul) **the odor of the knowledge of** Christ **in every place**.[3] This image works in tandem with the first metaphor. That is, Paul suggests that his manner of giving himself in love for the sake of others reveals Jesus. Paul reiterates this point by stating that he is **the aroma** (*euōdia*) **of Christ for God**. With this second metaphor Paul intimates that, just as Jesus faithfully obeyed God's will (1:19–20, the Son's "yes"), so now his life is a sacrificial offering to God (1:20, the Amen to God[4]— note once more the use of liturgical imagery to describe faithful human existence). This interpretation is confirmed by Paul's use of the words "odor" and "aroma" elsewhere. In Phil 4:18 he juxtaposes these terms as "a fragrant aroma," that is, "an acceptable sacrifice, pleasing to God." More tellingly, in Eph 5:2

3. Although many commentators take the pronoun in the phrase "knowledge of him" as referring to God, the preceding phrase "in Christ" and the following phrase "of Christ" suggest that the referent is Jesus.

4. The NAB's rendering of 2:15—"the aroma of Christ *for* God"—loses the echo from 1:20, "the Amen . . . *to* God." In both instances the prepositional phrase is the same, *tō theō* ("to God").

Paul employs this same expression in connection with Jesus: the †Messiah is a fragrant offering and sacrifice to God because he gave himself in love for the sake of others (see Gal 2:20).

With the metaphors of being led as God's captured slave and being a fragrance of Christ, Paul explains that he participates in and embodies Jesus' self-giving love, a way of life that entails suffering and sacrifice. In doing so, he makes Christ known to others. Paul, and by extension all Christians, are like crushed, burning grains of incense; they make Jesus present in the world such that others can sense him and be attracted to him. This is the case because the risen Jesus is actually present within them.

2:15b–16   The revelation of the †gospel through Paul's apostolic ministry evokes two opposite responses. On the one hand, **among those who are perishing** his manner of being an apostle wafts like **an odor of death**. That is, they interpret Paul's self-giving way as folly and weakness. In short, they fail to recognize the significance of the cross of Jesus (see 1 Cor 1:23), and their rejection of the gospel **leads to** (eternal) **death**. On the other hand, **among those who are being saved** Paul's embodied proclamation wafts like **an odor of life**. In other words, they understand that his way of living manifests the paradoxical "life" and "power of Christ" (2 Cor 4:10–11; 12:9). They comprehend that receiving the gospel with faith involves choosing to walk through "the narrow gate" of Jesus (Matt 7:13–14; Luke 13:24), the way that **leads to** (eternal) **life**.[5]

At the end of verse 16, Paul steps back and asks, **Who is qualified for this?** How can any human being become "the aroma of Christ" to God? The answer to this question is forthcoming in 3:5–6, but the opening words in verse 14—"thanks be to God"—already point to the answer.

2:17   Paul goes on to contrast his apostolic behavior with the behavior of those **who trade on the word of God**. He refers here, in all likelihood, to a group of missionaries who had arrived in Corinth and questioned his credentials and manner of exercising ministry.[6] Paul alludes to this group throughout chapters 1–9 before launching an offensive against them in chapters 10–12, where he dubs them "superapostles" (11:5; 12:11). What does he mean when he says that these missionaries "trade on," or peddle, God's word? In a previous letter to the community (1 Cor 9:6–14), Paul defended the right of Christian missionaries to receive financial support for their labors. Thus it does not seem that he criticizes the intruding missionaries for taking in money. Rather, their offense is having too much pride in their status as paid professionals. The verb

---

5. We will look at Paul's understanding of eternal life when we arrive at 5:1–10.
6. See stage 6 under Historical Context in the introduction.

translated "trade on" can also mean "dilute."[7] Thus it is also possible that Paul's criticism is that the interlopers dilute the message of the gospel—most likely through their behavior, a behavior that does not reflect the centrality of the cross (see 2 Cor 11:20).

On the contrary, Paul acts **out of sincerity**—a claim that reiterates his opening statement (1:12). As was the case there, his sincerity is grounded in the fact that his mission derives **from God**. Hence it is **in the presence of God,** that is, with God as witness (1:23), that the Apostle speaks **in Christ**. As the letter unfolds, we will see that to "speak in Christ" entails not only proclaiming the gospel in words but also, and especially, embodying Jesus' manner of living and dying for others.

Reflection and Application (2:14–17)

The importance of liturgy. Paul uses liturgical imagery to express how he lives his apostolic call. We have analyzed his references to the Amen (1:20) and "the aroma of Christ" (2:15). Elsewhere he describes his self-giving way of living as a "libation" (Phil 2:17; see 2 Tim 4:6) and refers to his "priestly service" that involves "the offering up of the Gentiles" as an "acceptable" sacrifice to God (Rom 15:16).

Such allusions suggest the connection between liturgical celebration and what might be called "the liturgy of life." According to *Sacrosanctum Concilium,* the "liturgy is the summit toward which the activity of the church is directed; it is also the source from which all its power flows" (10.1). We are called to worship in order to give glory to God as well as to be made holy. Attentive openness to the proclamation of God's word and devout reception of the Eucharist are "supremely effective in enabling the faithful to express in their lives and portray to others the mystery of Christ" (*Sacrosanctum Concilium* 2). The liturgy makes present the act of love in which Christ died, thus empowering us to conform our whole lives to that sacrifice and make Jesus present in the world, thereby extending our worship into the liturgy of life (Rom 12:1–2). Paul's cultic language, though subtle, helps make clear that, in Christ, *all* Christians, ordained and lay, are called to participate in the new covenant ministry through their priestly service. We do so, empowered by liturgical celebration, by offering our whole lives in worship to God.

Call to decision. Over the course of a day, we hear various words that are easy to ignore or forget. There are words, however, that demand a response,

---

7. The NJB and REB follow this line of interpretation, translating the verb *kapēleuō* as "adulterate."

especially when spoken by certain persons. The words "I love you," expressed for the first time in a relationship, raise the ante of that relationship. The recipient of these words cannot pretend they have not been uttered. A child's desperate cry for help simply cannot be ignored. Even more, God's message of love communicated in the sending of his Son (John 3:16–17; Rom 5:8) demands a response. In fact, Jesus himself declared that his coming would necessarily create a division between those who heeded him and his kingdom proclamation and those who rejected him (Matt 10:34–36; Luke 12:49–53). Paul's statement in 2 Cor 2:15–16 is a reminder that the gospel does not permit a position of neutrality. In this case, indifference is tantamount to rejection. And note Paul's use of present tense verbs in verse 15: "are being saved" and "are perishing." These indicate an ongoing process. Deciding for the gospel is not just a once-and-for-all decision. It is one that needs to be ratified *every* day.

The dangers of peddling and diluting God's word. Paul's criticism of the intruding missionaries for peddling and diluting the gospel serves as a caution to ministers. We can at times be tempted to preach only what people want to hear, leaving out inconvenient, unpopular, or challenging aspects of God's word or the Church's teaching. Ulterior motives such as ambition, success, and popularity can distort the way we engage in ministry. Paul's words challenge us to reflect on whether our motives, words, and actions cohere with the ways revealed by Jesus.

Minister of the New Covenant (3:1–6)

¹Are we beginning to commend ourselves again? Or do we need, as some do, letters of recommendation to you or from you? ²You are our letter, written on our hearts, known and read by all, ³shown to be a letter of Christ administered by us, written not in ink but by the Spirit of the living God, not on tablets of stone but on tablets that are hearts of flesh.

⁴Such confidence we have through Christ toward God. ⁵Not that of ourselves we are qualified to take credit for anything as coming from us; rather, our qualification comes from God, ⁶who has indeed qualified us as ministers of a new covenant, not of letter but of spirit; for the letter brings death, but the Spirit gives life.

OT: Exod 31:18; Ezek 11:19–20; 36:24–28; Jer 31:31–34
NT: Luke 22:20; Rom 5:5; 1 Cor 11:25; Heb 8:7–13
Lectionary: Common of Pastors

Paul's Use of Self-Commendation in 2 Corinthians

BIBLICAL BACKGROUND

The issue of self-commendation occurs frequently in 2 Corinthians. Curiously, Paul seems to be of two minds about it. There are places where he denies that he commends himself (3:1; 5:12), and he distances himself from missionaries who commend themselves (10:12). Thus self-commendation has a negative sense. There are other places, however, where Paul *does* commend himself (4:2; 6:4). In these instances, self-commendation is intended as something positive.

Paul indicates a subtle distinction in his usage that is not apparent in English translations.[a] When he refers negatively to self-commendation, he places the reflexive pronoun *before* the verb "commend." A helpful literal translation would be "†*self*-commend," with the emphasis on *self*. Self-commending is marked by measuring and comparing oneself with others at their expense, seeking one's own interests and glory, and boasting of one's own accomplishments (10:12–17). Paul considers such self-commendation as foolish and untruthful because it fails to acknowledge what *God* has accomplished.

Conversely, when Paul speaks positively of self-commendation, he inserts the reflexive pronoun *after* the verb. A good translation is "†*commend* oneself," with the accent on "commend" rather than "self." That which commends a person is living in accord with the truth of the gospel (4:2). More specifically, God's ministers commend themselves when they bear hardships; when they manifest qualities such as purity, patience, and genuine love; when they speak the truth; and when they live for the sake of others (6:4–10)—in short, when they take on the characteristics of Jesus, the "†image of God" (4:4). According to Paul, *self*-commendation counts for nothing; what matters is the one whom the Lord commends (10:18).

a. John T. Fitzgerald flags these syntactical points in *Cracks in an Earthen Vessel: An Examination of the Catalogue of Hardships in the Corinthian Correspondence*, SBLDS (Atlanta: Scholars Press, 1988), 187.

Having employed the images of triumph and fragrance to describe his own ministry, Paul uses another metaphor—a letter of recommendation—to remind the Corinthians of his role as their founding †apostle and of their own identity and call. He then refers to "†a new covenant," marked by God's pouring forth his life-giving Spirit. Paul maintains that God has made him a minister of this new covenant.

Paul asks two rhetorical questions, both of which expect a negative answer. **3:1** He denies that he is **beginning to commend** himself. His bold claims in 2:14–17 are not to be construed as self-praise but rather as pointing to God's †grace. In addition, Paul denies that he is in need of **letters of recommendation**. Such letters were very important in the early church. They were the means by which a local church introduced and vouched for missionaries who wanted to minister, or were sent to minister, in communities to whom they were strangers (see Acts 18:27). Paul's letters contain such recommendations. In Rom 16:1–2 he commends the deacon Phoebe to the church in Rome. As we will see, he commends Titus and two "brothers" to the church in Corinth for the purpose of facilitating the collection for the church in Jerusalem (2 Cor 8:18–23).

Here in verse 1, however, Paul insists that, unlike **some**—an allusion to the intruding missionaries—he has no need of a letter of recommendation to the Corinthians. The issue has arisen because the missionaries, in all likelihood, had brought recommendation letters with them (**to you**) when they arrived in Corinth. And they may have planted seeds of doubt concerning Paul by asking whether *he* had ever brought such a letter to the community. Notice the mention of letters of recommendation written by the Corinthians (**from you**). This may suggest that the interlopers were seeking such letters as a way of adding credentials to their own prestige. Asking the Corinthians for letters would also serve to flatter the community.

3:2–3 Paul asserts that the Corinthians themselves serve as his letter of recommendation: **You are our letter**. That is, the very existence of a Christian community in Corinth constitutes his apostolic credentials (1 Cor 9:2), as it was he who first brought the †gospel to them (2 Cor 10:14). The next two phrases—**written on our hearts** and **known and read by all**—are, at first glance, difficult to reconcile with one another. How can something in one's heart be available for all to see? Paul is trying to make two different points at once. First, he reminds the Corinthians of his love for them, that is, he holds them close to his heart. Once again, Paul shows his pastoral astuteness, as he lets the community know that he loves them even as he attempts to adjust their attitudes. Second, he reminds them that their existence as a church and their manner of living are readily available for others to observe (see Rom 1:8; 1 Thess 1:8).

The community is Paul's recommendation letter because, as he says in verse 3, they are **a letter of Christ**. While most interpreters understand this phrase to mean that Christ is the "letter's" author, it is equally possible to interpret the statement as referring to a letter *about* Christ. In fact, Paul tells us later in this verse who the author is: the church in Corinth has been "written" **by the Spirit of the living God**. Just as the Apostle has been anointed and sealed with the Holy Spirit and thereby empowered to be the Amen to God (2 Cor

1:20–22)—enabled to walk in the way of Jesus' faithfulness and obedience—so too are the Corinthians anointed and sealed. Through the gift of the Spirit in their "hearts," the church in Corinth, both in its individual members and collectively, is empowered to manifest the character of Jesus. In doing so, they are a "letter about Christ" (my translation) for others to "read." Paul's words serve both as a reminder to the Corinthians of their dignity and as a subtle exhortation to mature so that Christ is fully formed in them (Gal 4:19).

It is necessary to linger over verses 2–3, because they contain allusions to important Old Testament passages. Paul makes clear in verse 3 that the Spirit's writing has not taken place on **tablets of stone**. The latter phrase is an allusion to Exod 31:18, where God gives Moses the two stone tablets with the Ten Commandments "inscribed by God's own finger." Paul insists that the Spirit has now "written" **on tablets that are hearts of flesh**. The activity of "the Spirit of the living God" and the phrase "hearts of flesh" recall two passages from Ezekiel. In Ezek 11:19 and 36:26–27 God promises his people to remove their "stony heart," to replace it with a "heart of flesh" (literal translation), and to place "a new spirit" within them. In addition, reference in verse 2 to a letter "written on our hearts" echoes Jer 31:33, where God indicates that the days are coming when he will place his law within his people and "write it upon their hearts." What is striking about this last passage is that God's action will be an expression of "a new covenant" that he intends to make with his people (Jer 31:31).

These Old Testament allusions form the background for what Paul will say in 3:4–4:6. He draws on the growing recognition in the Israelite prophetic tradition that human beings are incapable of fulfilling God's law on their own. In fact, Jeremiah wrote his prophecy of a new covenant at a critical juncture in Israel's history, just as the people of Jerusalem were about to be taken into exile to Babylon as punishment for their persistent covenant breaking. Ezekiel wrote his promise of hearts of flesh a little later, while in exile in Babylon. Their message about God placing his spirit within people and writing his law on their hearts pointed to a new hope, namely, that God himself would provide a new, interior principle of obedience. By bestowing "hearts of flesh" on his people, God would bless them with the wherewithal to live according to his way—and to delight in doing so.

Paul expresses his **confidence**, the confidence that derives in part from the fruit of his apostolic labors. Lest he be mistaken for engaging in †*self*-commendation, however, he stresses that his confidence is ultimately **through Christ toward God**. The phrase "through Christ" refers to the centrality of Jesus' life, death, and resurrection in God's salvific activity, an activity that now extends through

The Meaning and Importance of Covenant

BIBLICAL
BACKGROUND

"Covenant" in the ancient world referred, in the first place, to a solemn agreement between two parties that established a relationship between them and spelled out the obligations assumed by them. A covenant could also add further definition to an already established relationship. The story of the Old Testament is a story of covenant. God entered into covenant with Abraham by promising him countless descendants and a prosperous land (Gen 15; 17). The critical moment, however, arrived with God's act of mercy bestowed on the Israelites enslaved in Egypt. God decided to take them as his special people; he, in turn, would be their God (Exod 6:7). After the exodus event, the people of Israel assembled at †Mount Sinai. There God declared them to be his "special possession"—the privileged recipients of his blessings and protection—and declared that they would be "a holy nation" (Exod 19:1–7).

After Israel agreed to be God's people, he gave to them, through Moses, the law (Exod 19–24). Israel was to live out their covenantal relationship by obeying God's commandments; they would thereby fulfill their vocation to show forth God's holiness (Lev 19:2) to the nations (i.e., †Gentiles). But Israel's history, as recorded in Scripture, reveals a pattern of infidelity and disobedience that resulted in God's punishment, which was in turn mitigated by acts of mercy, including the promise to "make a new covenant" (Jer 31:31).

Paul understands that God has fulfilled his promise to establish a new covenant through the coming of Messiah Jesus and the outpouring of the Holy Spirit, the gift that empowers obedience to the divine commands. Furthermore, he recognizes that the reception of the gospel by the Gentiles was the full realization of the promise made to Abraham: "Through you shall all the nations be blessed" (Gal 3:8). Thus through Christ God has created a single people from Jews and Gentiles who respond to the gospel (Eph 2:14–16).

the apostolic ministry. Paul thus keeps his gaze "toward God," who has called and empowered him to proclaim the gospel. For this reason, he acknowledges that he is **not . . . qualified to take credit for anything as coming from** himself. Instead, his **qualification comes from God**. Note that Paul here answers the question raised above in 2:16: Who is qualified to be God's slave and the "aroma of Christ"? It is only God who can accomplish his purposes through ministers like Paul—an important point for all in pastoral ministry to remember. This is why he insists that one should only boast "in the Lord" (10:17).

Paul goes on to make the main claim of this part of the letter: God has **qualified us as ministers of a new covenant**. The phrase "new covenant"

LIVING
TRADITION

St. Augustine on Law and Grace

St. Augustine, who thoroughly studied and reflected on Paul's writings, clearly understood the relationship between law and grace: "The law was given in order that grace might be sought; grace was given in order that the law might be fulfilled." The Doctor of Grace also explained the significance of the law written on human hearts: "What are God's laws written by God himself on hearts but the very presence of the Holy Spirit, who is 'the finger of God,' by whose presence love is diffused in our hearts, which is the fulfillment of the law?" (*On the Spirit and the Letter* 34, 36).

is crucial.[8] We have just noted the allusions to prophecies in Jeremiah and Ezekiel about "a new covenant" in which God would confer "a new spirit" on his people and inscribe his law in "new hearts." Paul, in effect, proclaims that *these prophecies are now being fulfilled*. Earlier in the letter he referred to the fulfillment of all of God's promises through the faithfulness of Jesus the †Messiah, whose "yes" to God climaxed in the offering of his life on the cross (1:20). It was certainly no accident that Paul then immediately described God's gift of the Holy Spirit (1:21–22). God's promises continue to be fulfilled by the proclamation of the gospel, through which believers are enabled to "fulfill the law of Christ" (Gal 6:2) because they have the Spirit in their hearts (2 Cor 1:22). Christians participate in Christ's own love and obedience to the Father by loving God with their whole being and their neighbors as themselves (Mark 12:28–34, the "great commandment").

Paul makes clear that God's "new covenant" is **not of letter but of spirit**. Given the thrust of his argument—that a distinguishing characteristic of the new covenant is the conferral of the gift of the Holy Spirit—"spirit" should be spelled here with a capital *S*.[9] Paul then offers an explanation: **the letter brings death, but the Spirit gives life**. What does this mean? Undoubtedly, "the letter" is associated with what was written on the "tablets of stone," in other words, the law (see v. 3—we will see an allusion to Moses receiving the law in the verses that follow). Paul makes a careful distinction here. Notice that he does not say that the law itself brings death. In fact, elsewhere he claims that the law

8. Elsewhere in the New Testament the phrase "new covenant" appears in Luke 22:20; 1 Cor 11:25; Heb 8:8 (which quotes the text in Jeremiah); 8:13; 9:15; 12:24. The first two instances refer to Jesus' words over the cup in the eucharistic narrative. The references in Hebrews are to Jesus as mediator of a new covenant.

9. As is done in the RSV, NJB, and NIV.

is "holy" and "spiritual" (Rom 7:12, 14), for it still remains God's revelation. What the law lacks, however, is the power on its own to give life (see Gal 3:21). That is, the law merely reveals sin for what it is. The law is something external and does nothing to remove our deeply ingrained selfishness and pride. Thus by "the letter" that "brings death" Paul means "the law without the power of God's life-giving Spirit."[10] The Spirit alone gives life (Rom 8:11) and enables his recipients to fulfill the just requirement of the law (Rom 8:4).

Reflection and Application (3:1–6)

Letters of recommendation. Résumés and curricula vitae are part of the world we live in today. So too are letters of recommendation. Whether applying for a job or for admission to a program, academic or otherwise, we seek to promote ourselves and to have others vouch for our qualifications. All of this is necessary. However, Paul's use of the recommendation letter in verses 2–3 challenges the conventional form of self-promotion. I confess that I have neither written nor read a recommendation that contained any of the following statements: "This person is poor in spirit." "She is merciful." "He hungers and thirsts for righteousness." "She is a peacemaker." Yet these are the qualities that Jesus values (Matt 5:3–10). By embodying the qualities of the Beatitudes, we become letters about Christ for others to read. In fact, we will see that Paul offers a résumé in 2 Cor 6:4–10 that is a good example of †*commending* oneself by showing forth the character of Christ.

Spiritual exegesis and the unity of Scripture. Paul's statement in verse 6, that "the letter brings death, but the Spirit gives life," has played a significant role in how the Church has interpreted Scripture. Since the time of Origen, who died in 254, this passage has been used to explain the Church's practice of going beyond the literal sense of texts, especially those of the Old Testament, in order to uncover their deeper, spiritual meaning. Two centuries later, St. Augustine famously remarked that the New Testament lies hidden in the Old while the Old Testament is made fully manifest in the New.[11] In other words, the whole of Scripture, despite all its variety, tells a *unified* story that finds its climax and fullest meaning in Jesus the Messiah. While it is important to study the Old Testament on its own terms, Catholics read it in the eucharistic liturgy in light of the gospel because the key to understanding Scripture lies therein. In fact, Sunday liturgical readings from the Old Testament are chosen on the principle

10. Matera, *II Corinthians*, 81–82.
11. See *Questions on the Heptateuch* 2.73.

of harmony, that is, they are selected in order to correspond with the gospel reading of the day (see Introduction to the Lectionary, paragraphs 66–67). We will see in the next chapter that Paul himself offers a daring interpretation of Exod 34, the story of Moses and the veil, by reading it anew in light of the revelation of Christ (3:12–16).

Comparison of Two Ministries (3:7–11)

[7]Now if the ministry of death, carved in letters on stone, was so glorious that the Israelites could not look intently at the face of Moses because of its glory that was going to fade, [8]how much more will the ministry of the Spirit be glorious? [9]For if the ministry of condemnation was glorious, the ministry of righteousness will abound much more in glory. [10]Indeed, what was endowed with glory has come to have no glory in this respect because of the glory that surpasses it. [11]For if what was going to fade was glorious, how much more will what endures be glorious.

OT: Exod 34:27–35; Deut 27:26
NT: Rom 3:20–22; 7:7–12; Gal 3:23–25

Having explained that God has made him a minister of a †new covenant, Paul now contrasts and compares the new covenant and its ministry with the †Mosaic covenant and its ministry. His intent is to show the surpassing glory of the new covenant ministry.

In Paul's treatment, the point of comparison with the new covenant is the covenant given to Moses on †Mount Sinai. This is evident both from the expression **carved in letters on stone**, which recalls the "tablets of stone" mentioned in verse 3, and the reference to **the face of Moses**, an allusion to Exod 34:27–35. There we are told that, after being in the presence of God on Mount Sinai for forty days and nights, Moses' face shone with glory as he descended from the mountain with the two stone tablets. 3:7–11

Paul contrasts the ministry (*diakonia*) of the new covenant with that of the Old in three ways.[12] First, whereas the Mosaic covenant resulted in a **ministry of death** (v. 7), the new covenant ministry is empowered by **the Spirit** (v. 8). This contrast reiterates the point just made in verse 6, namely, that only the Spirit enables us to obey the just requirements of the law, thereby giving *life.*

---

12. Although Paul speaks of "ministry" and not "covenant" in vv. 7–11, the two concepts are closely linked. As Murray J. Harris remarks, "it is a 'covenant' that is 'administered'" (*Second Epistle to the Corinthians*, NIGTC [Grand Rapids: Eerdmans, 2005], 280).

The Glory of God in the Old Testament

BIBLICAL BACKGROUND

God's glory refers to the awesome splendor of his presence and the radiant manifestation of his holiness and love. The Hebrew word *kabod* and the Greek translation *doxa* convey majestic radiance and brightness, magnificence, as well as honor and prestige. God's majestic glory, as revealed visibly to Israel, is portrayed variously as a thick cloud, lightning (and thunder), and a devouring fire (Exod 19:16–18; 1 Kings 8:10–11; Ezek 1:4–28). God's glory was manifested when he brought about Israel's salvation (Exod 14:19–20); when he revealed himself to Moses as the God of mercy, kindness, graciousness, and fidelity (Exod 33:18; 34:6–7); and when he came to his people in judgment (Num 16:42–50). It also will appear when God brings about the fullness of salvation in the future (Isa 60:1–2). The appropriate human response to God's majesty is to stand in awe and ascribe glory to him (Ps 22:23).

Paul links the glory of God, first and foremost, with Jesus, who reveals God's glory (2 Cor 4:6—"the glory of God on the face of [Jesus] Christ"). Moreover, in prayerfully contemplating Jesus and opening themselves to the power of the Spirit, Christians are transformed into the same glory (3:18).

Conversely, the law that promised life actually led to death because it was co-opted by the power of sin (Rom 7:7–12).

Second, whereas the †old covenant resulted in a **ministry of condemnation**, the new covenant enacts **the ministry of righteousness** (v. 9). The law given to Moses concluded with the pronouncement of a curse on whoever "fails to fulfill any of the provisions of this law" (Deut 27:26). Moreover, according to Paul, the law failed to bring about righteousness but rather led to the "consciousness of sin" (Rom 3:20). Now, however, God has definitively revealed his own righteousness through the faithfulness of Christ[13] (Rom 3:21–22; see 2 Cor 1:19–20), thereby bringing about for us the possibility of living in right relationship with God and growing in righteousness. Indeed, as we will see later in the letter, God's righteousness continues to be revealed through those who, like Paul, are reconciled with God and empowered to walk in Jesus' way of self-giving love (5:21).

Third, whereas the Mosaic covenant was temporary (vv. 10–11; see Gal 3:23–25), the new covenant **endures** forever (v. 11). A key verb in this passage and the following verses is *katargeō* (vv. 7, 11, 13, 14—all in the passive voice).

---

13. With many other scholars, I hold that the phrase *pistis Iēsou Christou* in Rom 3:22 should be rendered the "faithfulness of Jesus Christ," rather than humans' "faith in Jesus Christ."

Although many translations, including the NAB, render *katargeō* as "fade" in verses 7, 11, and 13, this meaning does not correspond to Paul's usage elsewhere. Rather, he uses this verb to explain that the old covenant ministry "has been set aside" or "rendered inoperative."[14] Because God has now acted once for all through the life, death, and resurrection of Jesus and through the sending of the Spirit, the new covenant ministry is marked by permanence.

Paul does not just *contrast* the old covenant ministry with that of the new. He also *compares* them in a form of argument called "from the lesser to the greater." An example of this form of argument is: if love and loyalty are due to parents, who bring forth and care for their children, then how much more are love and loyalty due to God, who brings all things, including one's parents, into existence and sustains them? Just as there were three contrasts, Paul uses the lesser-to-greater comparison three times (vv. 7–8, 9, 11) to make the same basic point. Paul acknowledges that the covenant given to Moses *was* **glorious**—so much so that his fellow **Israelites could not look intently at** his **face** (v. 7; see Exod 34:33–35). It was God's gift to guide his people in the way of holiness. Even so, in light of what God has now accomplished through Christ Jesus, Paul insists that it is as though the Mosaic covenant **has come to have no glory** . . . **because of the glory that surpasses it** (v. 10). In short, if the old covenant came with glory, then how much more glory does the new covenant possess—the enduring covenant of the Spirit and righteousness?

Paul's treatment here, as we will see in 3:16–4:15, involves a paradox. Moses' face literally shone with glory; the Apostle's does not. In fact, Paul's life seems anything but glorious—as his opponents were only too quick to point out! Nevertheless, those whose lives are transformed by the †gospel *do* manifest God's glory—his love and power—through lives of self-giving after the manner of Jesus.

Paul's lesser-to-greater comparisons make another important point. Notice that the verbs associated with the new covenant ministry are in the future tense: **will . . . be** (v. 8), **will abound** (v. 9), **will . . . be** (v. 11). Paul thereby intimates the glory to be realized in eternal life. It is in the presence of God in heavenly glory that the *fullness* of the blessings of the new covenant will be enjoyed (see 2 Cor 5:1–10).

In conclusion: As a minister of the new covenant, Paul's concern in these verses is to highlight the surpassing glory of its ministry, a ministry exercised through his proclamation of the gospel. Through this ministry God bestows

---

14. See John M. McDermott, "II Corinthians 3: The Old and New Covenants," *Greg* 87 (2006): 25–63, esp. 34–35. The NRSV's "set aside" captures well Paul's sense.

his promised gift of the Spirit, empowering people to walk in the way of righteousness, in the way that leads to life. As such, the new covenant ministry is
marked by its enduring character. Paul's primary purpose here is not to denigrate
the Mosaic covenant; in fact, he goes out of his way to acknowledge its glory.
Yet he undeniably uses some harsh terms—"ministry of death" and "ministry
of condemnation"—to describe it. How does Paul understand the relationship
between the covenants? How does he understand Moses, whom he associates
both with glory and with what has been set aside? These questions are to be
taken up in the analysis of 3:12–16.

Transformed into "the Image of God"

2 Corinthians 3:12–4:6

Paul continues his treatment of the new covenant ministry and of his role in it, introduced in 2:14–3:11. He resumes the comparison of his ministry with that of Moses by offering an interpretation and application of Moses' veil (3:12–16). Next, Paul describes the Spirit's ongoing work of transforming Christians into the †image of God, the image that has been restored by Jesus (3:17–18). He then commends his own ministerial conduct to the Corinthians by insisting that he proclaims the †gospel openly through his spoken word and humble service (4:1–6). Paul thereby completes the first part of his extended discourse on †apostleship (2:14–7:4), in which he explains to the community his manner of being "an apostle of Christ Jesus by the will of God" (1:1).

Moses and the Veil (3:12–16)

¹²Therefore, since we have such hope, we act very boldly ¹³and not like Moses, who put a veil over his face so that the Israelites could not look intently at the cessation of what was fading. ¹⁴Rather, their thoughts were rendered dull, for to this present day the same veil remains unlifted when they read the old covenant, because through Christ it is taken away. ¹⁵To this day, in fact, whenever Moses is read, a veil lies over their hearts, ¹⁶but whenever a person turns to the Lord the veil is removed.

OT: Exod 34:27–35; Sir 17:19–21
NT: Rom 9:1–5; 10:1–4; 2 Tim 4:2

Paul takes up from 3:7 the allusion to Moses' face. He employs this allusion in order to make two points. First, he contrasts his apostolic behavior—the way he openly proclaims the †gospel—with the act of veiling or concealing. Second, he applies the veil to Israel in order to explain why the followers of the †Mosaic covenant have failed to understand that their Scriptures point to Jesus as the †Messiah.

Paul begins with a reference to hope. His hope is grounded in his conviction that the †new covenant will never pass away (3:11). This conviction also allows readers, then and now, to share in his hope. Because Paul has **such hope**, he acts **very boldly** (literally, "with much boldness"). He courageously brings the message of salvation to people, especially in those places where the gospel has not yet been proclaimed (10:15–16; Rom 15:20–21).[1] The word *parrēsia*, in addition to meaning "with courage or boldness," can also signify "with frankness or open speech." As we will see shortly, Paul responds to charges that his gospel is veiled (4:3) by asserting that, to the contrary, he acts and speaks openly (4:2). Thus he probably intends the connotation of frankness as well as boldness.

Paul contrasts his openness with **Moses, who put a veil over his face**. At one level, the reference to Moses simply serves as a foil: Paul's open comportment as a minister of the new covenant is all the more striking when compared with Moses' concealing action. But as is so often the case with Paul, his point is more complex. In order to understand what he is saying in this and the following verses, it is necessary to familiarize ourselves with the content of Exod 34:27–35. In this passage Moses descended from †Mount Sinai where God had given him the words of the Ten Commandments, written on two stone tablets. Because he had been in the presence of God, the appearance of Moses' face was altered; it now radiated God's glory. At first the people of Israel were afraid to approach Moses on account of his shining face. After communicating God's commandments to them, Moses put a veil over his face. Although no reason is given, it can be inferred from the story that he covered his face because the people were unnerved at seeing its radiance. The last two verses of the text then recount what Moses adopted as his typical practice: whenever he went before God in the †meeting tent, he would remove the veil; and upon leaving the tent, Moses would convey God's words to the people and then cover his face until he returned to encounter the Lord in the tent.

Returning to 2 Cor 3:13, observe that Paul ascribes to Moses a *different* motive for the veiling. Whereas the story in Exodus gives the impression that the people of Israel did not want to look at Moses' face, Paul states that Moses veiled himself **so that the Israelites could not look intently**, as if they desired to stare

---

1. Indeed, Paul will shortly announce his goal of proclaiming the gospel in Spain (Rom 15:22–29), which in his mind was the (western) end of the world.

at or fixate on something—
the sense of the Greek verb.
Hence, according to Paul,
Moses' action was a *preven-
tative* measure rather than a
response to the people's fear.
In his retelling, Moses did
not want the people to stare
at or fixate on the **cessation**
"of what was being set aside"
(my translation).[2]

What does this mean?
This passage has vexed interpreters for centuries, up
to our own day. Indeed,
several interpretations have
been offered.[3] In my opinion, Paul means this: Moses
veiled himself so that the
Israelites would not fixate
on that which was bound to
be set aside. In other words,
Moses wanted to prevent the
people from so focusing on

Fig. 5. A traditional depiction of the glory of the Lord as rays of light
emanating from Moses after his encounter with God on Mount Sinai.
(*Moses Coming Down from Mount Sinai* by Gustave Doré, in *The Doré
Bible Illustrations*, Dover)

the ministry given to him that they would fail to see that, ultimately, it would
be rendered inoperative at the coming of Christ Jesus. To be sure, Paul's interpretation of the Exodus text is innovative and peculiar. But we must remember
his starting point: God has now acted definitively through the life, death, and
resurrection of Jesus and the sending of the Spirit (Gal 4:1–7). From this perspective, Paul now looks back to the story of Moses' veiling and understands
that Moses somehow recognized that the covenant and law given to him were
only temporary and provisional, and that God would one day bring them to
their definitive completion.[4]

2. See the exegesis of 3:7–11 for translating the passive form of *katargeō* as "be set aside" or "rendered inoperative," rather than as "fade" (as in the NAB).
3. For a list of interpretations, see Margaret E. Thrall, *A Critical and Exegetical Commentary on the
Second Epistle to the Corinthians*, ICC, 2 vols. (Edinburgh: T&T Clark, 1994–2000), 1:259–61.
4. Compare Gal 3:8, where Paul states, remarkably, that Abraham was foretold the gospel! While
Paul's interpretive moves might strike some as idiosyncratic, Jewish methods of biblical interpretation
in his time exhibited much freedom and creativity.

3:14   Although, according to Paul's interpretation, Moses tried by veiling his face
to prevent the Israelites from fixating on that which was destined to be set
aside, the people's **thoughts were rendered dull**. The verb translated "rendered
dull" means "petrify" or "harden." Paul draws here on the image of hearts of
stone in Ezek 11:19 and 36:26, which he alluded to back in 3:3. In fact, he will
refer to veiled *hearts* in the very next verse. Paul is more concerned, however,
with his Jewish contemporaries—with those who did not believe that Jesus is
the †Messiah—than with the Israelites of Moses' time (notice the transitional
phrase **for to this present day**). According to Paul, when Jews of his day **read
the †old covenant**[5]—that is, when in their synagogue services they read their
Scriptures—**the same veil remains unlifted**. He thus takes the image of the
veil covering Moses' face and adapts it metaphorically to describe his Jewish
contemporaries' inability to fully understand God's revealed Word. The proper
understanding of Scripture is possible only **through** (literally, "in") **Christ**: it
is only when one recognizes that the Old Testament points to and is fulfilled
by Jesus that the veil **is taken away**.[6]

3:15–16   Paul reiterates these points as he focuses again on the unbelief of Israel in
his **day**. The phrase **whenever Moses is read** refers primarily to the Pentateuch,
the first five books of the Bible that were traditionally ascribed to Moses and are
called Torah by Jews (see Rom 10:5, 19). The Apostle again asserts that when the
Jews of his time read Scripture **a veil lies over their hearts**. Note that he now
mentions "a veil" rather than Moses' veil. With this subtle change, Paul suggests
that a pervasive spiritual blindness has descended on the people, one that has
resulted in hardened "hearts." The logic is this: if the new covenant ministry that
proclaims "the Son of God, Messiah Jesus" (2 Cor 1:19, my translation) brings
about the gift of "hearts of flesh" and the bestowal of the Spirit in them (3:3),
then those who reject the gospel message remain in the condition of having
"stony hearts" (Ezek 36:26).

Finally, Paul offers the remedy for such blindness: **whenever a person turns
to the Lord the veil is removed**. He alludes here to Exod 34:34, which reads,
"Whenever Moses entered the presence of the LORD . . . he removed the veil."
The reference is to Moses' practice when he went into the meeting tent to
discourse with God. Note that Paul makes some interesting changes as he applies the Exodus text. First, he removes "Moses" as the subject of the opening
clause, thereby leaving open to *anyone* the possibility of encountering "the

---

5. This verse is the only place in the entire Bible where the phrase "old covenant" appears.

6. The subject of "is taken away" (the passive of *katargeō*) at the end of v. 14 is unnamed. Gram-
matically, the subject could be either "the old covenant" or "the same veil." Here the context calls for an
explanation of how the veil is removed, as the reiteration of v. 14 in vv. 15–16 makes clear.

Lord." Second, Paul replaces "entered" (past tense) with "turns to" (present tense). Paul's text thus serves as a perennial invitation to us to "turn" to the Lord. The notion of "turning" involves both turning toward God and turning away from sin, and thus conversion and repentance. Third, the passive verb— the veil is "removed"—suggests that it is the Lord who removes the veil, that is, those obstacles that prevent us from receiving his mercy and love.[7] In short, Paul's interpretation of Exod 34:34 explains that God now offers to *all* people the possibility of encountering him in his glory. *This is the fruit of the new covenant ministry.* Paul will offer a further description of this encounter in verses 17–18. Before analyzing these verses, however, it will be helpful to step back from the text to consider a few questions.

Why does Paul take up the issue of Jewish unbelief in the gospel at this point? St. John Chrysostom suggested that he responds here to a concern raised by some of the Corinthians. They are asking, Why don't more Jews, the people to whom God's promises were initially given, respond favorably to the gospel?[8] Indeed, it is pertinent to note that Paul treats this question at great length in his letter to the Romans (9:1–11:36), which he wrote from Corinth during his third visit there (and thus shortly after composing 2 Corinthians). It could simply be, however, that he took up the issue in the course of comparing his new covenant ministry with the covenant given to Moses. In any event, we do know that Paul anguished over the unbelief of those whom he still regarded with love as his "kin according to the flesh" (Rom 9:3).

Another question pertains to the relationship between "the old covenant" and "the new covenant." As we saw in the analysis of 3:7–11, Paul's assessment of the Mosaic covenant is not entirely negative; in fact, he acknowledges that it was "glorious." He claims elsewhere that the definitive revelation of God's righteousness, manifested through Jesus the Messiah, was "testified to by the law and the prophets" (Rom 3:21–22). That is, after his encounter with the risen Lord (Gal 1:15–16), Paul came to appreciate that Israel's Scriptures point to God's work of redemption through Christ, who himself is the fulfillment of all the promises contained therein (2 Cor 1:20; see Rom 1:2). Thus, according to Paul, the old covenant, rightly understood, unfolds into the new covenant with the coming of Jesus and the gift of the Spirit. In this sense there is one overarching covenant of God. Yet, Paul at times employs negative terms and imagery in connection with the old covenant (e.g., "condemnation" and "death") and its people, whom he characterizes as having hearts of stone. Indeed, in the passage from Romans

---

7. This use of the passive voice is called the †divine passive.

8. *Homilies on 2 Corinthians* 7.2.

Jewish-Christian Relations

Paul's characterization of the Jews of his time as having hardened hearts must be handled with great care. Sadly, anti-Semitism is one of the truly dark marks on the history of Christianity. Over the centuries some Christians have persecuted Jews, who were viewed not only as having rejected God's revelation through Jesus but also as being implicated, on the basis of texts like Matt 27:25, in the killing of Jesus. It is important to understand that 2 Cor 3:12–16 does not exhaust Paul's thoughts on the people he still regarded as his kin. In Rom 11:26–29 he states that the Jewish people *remain* beloved by God, that his call and gifts to them are irrevocable, and that "all Israel will be saved."

In an important document, *Nostra Aetate* (*Declaration on the Relation of the Church to non-Christian Religions*), the bishops at Vatican II recalled the "common spiritual heritage" shared by Jews and Christians. The council fathers declared that "Jews should not be spoken of as rejected or accursed as if this followed from Scripture." And condemning all forms of anti-Semitism, they encouraged "mutual understanding and appreciation" between Jews and Christians, especially in the arenas of theology and Scripture (4).

A recent fruit of such reflection and dialogue is the Pontifical Biblical Commission's 2002 document *The Jewish People and Their Sacred Scriptures in the Christian Bible*. In the course of discussing fundamental themes in the Jewish Scriptures and their appropriation by Christianity, the Commission writes: "Jewish messianic expectation is not in vain. It can become for us Christians a powerful stimulant to keep alive the †eschatological dimension of our faith. Like them, we too live in expectation" (II.A.5). Theological reflection of this type can serve as a model for promoting healthy Jewish-Christian relations today.

---

referred to above, he also says that the righteousness of God has been revealed "*apart* from the law" (Rom 3:21)! How does one reconcile these two views of the law? This is a complex question, to which I can attempt only a brief answer.

Paul's former zeal for the law led him to persecute the church (Gal 1:13–14; Phil 3:3–6) because he had failed to recognize that Jesus was the Messiah (2 Cor 5:16), through whom God had reconciled the world to himself (5:18–19). It is likely that Paul had opposed the early church in part because of the way he regarded Jesus as cursed by God, on the basis of Deut 21:23—"God's curse rests on him who hangs on a tree" (see Gal 3:13). Moreover, he had been blind to the fact that God was now calling *all* peoples, Jews *and* †Gentiles, to form a single people on the basis of faith—first and foremost, on the basis of Jesus' faithfulness, and then on the basis of people's response of faith to the salvation offered by God through Christ (Rom 3:21–31).

But Paul came to understand that God had rendered inoperative and had set aside several aspects of Paul's former existence, such as his way of understanding Scripture and his focus on those aspects of Judaism—for example, circumcision, the observance of Sabbath, food laws, and other regulations—that kept him from seeing how God was now calling *all* peoples to be "in Christ" (Gal 3:28). Even more, Paul came to realize that his "old self" had been enslaved under the power of sin and that the law was powerless to reverse the human condition of enmity with God and spiritual death (Rom 6:6; 7:7–25). He now came to appreciate that the way to forgiveness and right relationship with God—indeed, the way to life—is through Christ (Rom 5:6–11) and that it is only by the power of the Spirit that people can fulfill the just requirement of the law (Rom 8:4) by loving one's neighbor as oneself (Rom 13:8–10; see Lev 19:18). In this, Paul is in full agreement with Jesus (Mark 12:28–34).

Transformed by the Spirit into "the Image of God" (3:17–18)

[17]Now the Lord is the Spirit, and where the Spirit of the Lord is, there is freedom. [18]All of us, gazing with unveiled face on the glory of the Lord, are being transformed into the same image from glory to glory, as from the Lord who is the Spirit.

OT: 1 Sam 16:12–13; Isa 6:1–8
NT: Matt 17:1–2; Rom 8:28–30; 12:1–2; Gal 5:22–23
Catechism: dignity of the human person as the image of God, 1700–1709

Paul has employed the account of Moses and the veil as a foil to the openness that characterizes the †new covenant ministry and as a metaphor to explain Israel's blindness. Now, through the image of unveiled faces, he describes the transformation brought about by the life-giving Spirit. He teaches that the Spirit empowers his recipients to take on the character and likeness of Christ Jesus.

The opening words—**Now the Lord is the Spirit**—have caused the spilling of much ink by exegetes and theologians. As one prominent commentator remarks, "Few sentences in the New Testament have prompted more debate than this linguistically simple statement."[9] Some of the early Church Fathers took these

3:17

9. Murray J. Harris, *Second Epistle to the Corinthians*, NIGTC (Grand Rapids: Eerdmans, 2005), 309–10.

The Old Testament Concept of "Turning, or Returning, to God"

The verb *epistrephō* ("turn"), used by Paul in 2 Cor 3:16, is one of the Greek words used in the †Septuagint to translate the Hebrew word *shuv* ("turn," "return"). In particular, *epistrephō* renders *shuv* when the latter has the connotation of repenting of one's sins and turning, or returning, to God. The twin themes of *turning away* from sin and of *returning to* God and his covenant are especially prominent with the prophet Hosea. Hosea's climactic exhortation illustrates well this sense of *shuv*: "*Return*, O Israel, to the LORD, your God; / you have collapsed through your guilt. / Take with you words, / and *return* to the LORD; / Say to him, 'Forgive all iniquity, / and receive what is good'" (Hosea 14:2–3).

words as affirming the divinity of the Holy Spirit. While that is not Paul's intent here, their later theological reflection does make explicit what is implicit in the text. Many commentators understand "the Lord" as referring here to the risen Christ. They take Paul's claim as touching on the intimate relationship between the risen Christ and the Spirit (e.g., it is the Spirit who mediates the presence and power of the risen Christ to the Church). A better interpretation, in my opinion, is to understand Paul's words as an exegetical gloss or explanation of his adaptation of Exod 34:34 in the previous verse. Recall that he has just said, "whenever a person turns to the Lord the veil is removed." In the Exodus passage, "the Lord" refers to God (i.e., to †YHWH; see Exod 3:14). Now, in contemporizing this passage, Paul explains that "the Lord" in the Exodus text *stands for the Spirit*.[10] His meaning, therefore, is best conveyed by punctuating the text as follows: "Now the 'Lord' is the Spirit" (my translation).

If this is the case, what does it mean to "turn to the Spirit"? Turning to the Spirit is, in effect, the equivalent of *receiving the Holy Spirit*, the fruit of the new covenant ministry.[11] But such a turning toward and receiving are only one side of the coin. The other side of that coin involves another turning, the turning *away* from sin. To be sure, the call to repentance and conversion remain implicit in Paul's text. But they are the necessary concomitants of turning to the Lord.

10. The NEB and REB capture this sense well: "Now the Lord of whom this passage speaks is the Spirit."

11. See J. D. G. Dunn, *Baptism in the Holy Spirit: A Re-Examination of the New Testament Teaching on the Gift of the Spirit in Relation to Pentecostalism Today*, SBT (Naperville, IL: Alec R. Allenson, 1970), 136.

Paul goes on to say that **where the Spirit of the Lord is, there is freedom**. This is the only place where he uses the phrase "the Spirit of the Lord," which here signifies *God's* Spirit (see, e.g., 1 Sam 16:13; Isa 11:2). Paul claims that a distinguishing mark of the Spirit's presence is "freedom." Given the immediate context of his adaptation of the Exodus passage, Paul's point here is that the Spirit liberates people from the veil that prevents them from recognizing God's revelation through Christ Jesus. In addition, he teaches elsewhere that the Spirit's gift of freedom is even more profound. For example, in Gal 5:1 Paul states, "For freedom Christ set us free."

This succinct statement points to two realities. First, the enslaving dominion of sin and death—those cosmic forces unleashed at the first Adam's disobedience—has been broken (Rom 5:12–14) through the life, death, and resurrection of Jesus, the †new, or second, Adam. Second, because they are no longer shackled, Christians can walk in the Spirit (Gal 5:16) by offering themselves freely in self-giving love for others. In fact, Paul has a paradoxical way of describing this Spirit-driven exercise of freedom: "*become slaves* of one another through love" (Gal 5:13, my translation; see 2 Cor 4:5).

Paul now dramatically describes what happens when a person "turns to the Lord," that is, when he or she turns away from sin and receives the Spirit. Like Moses, **with unveiled face** that person looks **on the glory of the Lord**. Note that Paul makes clear that this experience is not limited to him; *all* Christians receive it (**All of us**). What does he mean by "the glory of the Lord" here? The referent of "the Lord" is God the Father. But, as Paul will make clear in the next passage, "the glory of God" has been made manifest "on the face of [Jesus] Christ" (4:6). Indeed, Christ is "†the image of God" (4:4). In other words, "the glory of the Lord" refers to God's glory as it has been revealed through Jesus. Paul himself saw this glory when the risen Christ appeared to him on the road to †Damascus (Acts 26:13). When he saw the glorious †Messiah, he knew that he had encountered God.

3:18

One of the keys to understanding Paul's meaning involves the notion of **gazing**. The Greek verb, which appears in the Bible only in this verse, connotes beholding or contemplating something as in a mirror. Paul draws on the experience of gazing intently. But his concern is not self-contemplation in a mirror. Rather, he refers to "gazing" closely at "the glory of the Lord." And because "the glory of the Lord" is God's glory as reflected in Jesus, what Paul indicates here is the attentive contemplation of Christ the new Adam, whose self-giving love showed in an unsurpassable manner how human beings ought to reflect God's image and likeness. As Moses once gazed "with unveiled face" on God in his glory, so those who, through the ministry of the new covenant, receive the Holy Spirit are enabled to behold God's glory reflected in Jesus.[12]

Paul then states that those who behold God's glory in Christ **are being transformed into the same image.** The phrase "the same image" refers to Jesus, "the image of God" (4:4). The verb translated "being transformed" is *metamorphoō*. Interestingly, this is the same verb used to describe what happened to Jesus at his transfiguration, when his face shone like the sun and his garments became white as light, reflecting the glory of God (Matt 17:2). How does Paul use the verb *metamorphoō* in the present passage? The first thing to notice is the passive voice of "being transformed." The passive voice signifies the action of another—in this case, the Spirit.[13]

Further light is shed on Paul's meaning when we look at other passages where he employs *morph* terminology (the root *morph* indicates form or shape). In discussing the work of the Spirit in Romans, he speaks of people being "conformed to the image of God's Son" (Rom 8:29, my translation). The word "conformed" translates the related term *symmorphos*. Paul uses *metamorphoō* in Rom 12:2: "Be *transformed* by the renewal of your mind, that you may discern what is the will of God." Notice that Paul's use of *morph* terminology brings together the following elements: the Spirit's action, the renewal of minds (e.g., the attentive contemplation of Jesus discussed above), the discernment of God's will, and the conforming of people to the likeness of Christ. Returning to 2 Cor 3:18: Paul refers here to a *process* whereby the Spirit transforms those who receive him to become more like Jesus, who himself lived in faithful obedience to God. Spirit-empowered contemplation of Christ therefore leads to transformation into his likeness.

We are now in a position to appreciate what Paul means when he says that the Spirit transforms people **from glory to glory.** Note that all of the verbs in verse 18 are in the present tense. Paul is not talking about a future reality but something that takes place here and now. Recall, from the analysis of 1:20, the reference to the Amen to God, which was the Apostle's shorthand expression for human faithfulness in imitation of Jesus' obedient "yes" to the Father. We saw that, according to Paul, this obedience to God's will is "for *glory.*" In addition, recall that Paul then asserted (1:21–22) that it is the Spirit who empowers such faithfulness and obedience to God. These same dynamics are also at work in 3:18. Transformation into the likeness of Jesus empowers greater fidelity to God's intention for humanity, a fidelity marked by love and self-giving. When

---

12. See the Reflection and Application below for *how* this Spirit-driven encounter takes place.
13. This is another instance of the †divine passive.

St. Irenaeus on Human Beings and the Glory of God

The Church Father St. Irenaeus, who died around 200, famously declared that "the glory of God is a living human being" (*Against Heresies* 4.20.7). This popular quotation can be subject to misunderstanding, in large part because the remainder of the sentence is usually omitted. Irenaeus goes on to say "... and the life of a human being consists in beholding God." In order to be fully alive and thus reflect the glory of God in our present lives, we must be in intimate relationship with Jesus, the Son who fully reveals God's glory (John 1:14), and be conformed to his likeness through the Spirit. The second part of Irenaeus's teaching is illuminated in part by Paul's reference to the Spirit-empowered contemplation of Christ in 2 Cor 3:17–18. Irenaeus's statement also pertains to the future fullness of salvation, when eternal life will be experienced by those who dwell in the presence of God and behold his glory (1 John 3:2).

people live in this manner, they too reflect aspects of the glory and holiness of God in whose image they are created. They also thereby render glory and praise to him.

Throughout the preceding discussion, I have been referring to the action of the Spirit. Paul makes this action explicit in the final words of verse 18: **as from the Lord who is the Spirit**. These words also function as a restatement of the opening words of verse 17—"The 'Lord' is the Spirit" (my translation). They are an appropriate conclusion to Paul's profound statement concerning the transforming power of the Spirit, the fruit of the new covenant ministry.

Reflection and Application (3:17–18)

The "how" of transformation. While Paul describes the process and effect of the Holy Spirit's transforming power, he does not explain *how* such transformation occurs. Nevertheless, he provides an important clue. Paul's use of a verb that connotes "contemplate" suggests the importance of *prayer,* especially reverent, attentive listening to God's revelation in Christ as set forth in Scripture, both in private devotion and in the liturgical assembly. For Catholics, another privileged arena for contemplating Jesus and his self-giving love is the Eucharist. Frequent reception of Holy Communion, prayer before the Blessed Sacrament, and eucharistic adoration facilitate the intense encounter and transformation that Paul portrays. The transforming power of the Spirit is at work in every eucharistic liturgy. Just before the words of consecration, the presiding priest extends his hands over the gifts of bread and wine while praying that the Spirit make them holy so "that they may become the body and blood" of Jesus Christ. After the consecration, the priest prays that those who receive Jesus' body and blood "may be filled with his Holy Spirit, and become one body, one spirit in Christ" (Eucharistic Prayer 3). Through the prayerful and frequent reception of Holy Communion, Catholics are empowered to become that which they receive—the body of Christ.

Paul's Commendation of His Apostolic Conduct (4:1–6)

> ¹Therefore, since we have this ministry through the mercy shown us, we are not discouraged. ²Rather, we have renounced shameful, hidden things; not acting deceitfully or falsifying the word of God, but by the open declaration of the truth we commend ourselves to everyone's conscience in the sight of God. ³And even though our gospel is veiled, it is veiled for those who are perishing, ⁴in whose case the god of this age has blinded the minds of the unbelievers, so that they may not see the light of the gospel of the glory of Christ, who is the image of God. ⁵For we do not preach ourselves but Jesus Christ as Lord, and ourselves as your slaves for the sake of Jesus. ⁶For God who said, "Let light shine out of darkness," has shone in our hearts to bring to light the knowledge of the glory of God on the face of [Jesus] Christ.

OT: Gen 1:3–4; Isa 43:19–21; Jer 20:10–11
NT: John 1:1–5; 1 Cor 2:2; Phil 2:6–11
Lectionary: Common of Pastors; Holy Orders

After his lengthy discourse on the †new covenant ministry, Paul now offers a positive commendation of his apostolic behavior. He then explains why some people do not respond favorably to the proclamation of the †gospel. Finally, he sets forth the content of his preaching. In doing so, he responds to criticism of his way of being an †apostle.

4:1–2   Paul insists that he is **not discouraged**, because the "God of all encouragement" (1:3) has bestowed on him **this ministry**, that is, the ministry of the new covenant. The phrase **through the mercy shown** is an allusion to Paul's call to be a minister of the gospel (Acts 9:1–19). He never forgot that, because he had previously persecuted the Church, he is "the least of the apostles, not fit to be called an apostle" (1 Cor 15:9). But he also took great heart in the fact that he was "mercifully treated" by God (1 Tim 1:12–16). What might lead Paul to discouragement? First, recall the apostolic hardships alluded to in 2:14–15—a topic that will emerge again in 4:7–15. Second, Paul has become aware of criticism that he preaches a "veiled" gospel (v. 3). But despite such hardships and criticism, he is not discouraged as he takes consolation in his divine calling.

Paul then †*commends* himself:[14] **we commend ourselves to everyone's conscience in the sight of God**. His steadfast denial of **shameful, hidden things** seems to be made with the rival missionaries in mind, as the following verbal connections suggest. The phrase translated **acting deceitfully** means, literally, "walking in craftiness." We will see that Paul later rebuts the charge, likely instigated or abetted by the interlopers, that he has acted craftily with regard to the collection for the church in Jerusalem (12:16). The expression **falsifying the word of God** recalls his criticism of those who trade on or dilute God's word by offering a watered-down version of the gospel (2:17)—in large part, by behaving in a manner that fails to express the way of the cross through self-giving love (11:20). Paul then distinguishes himself from these other missionaries by commending himself. He does so by means of **the open declaration of the truth**, a declaration that is both verbal and enacted. I will treat the content of this declaration when we come to verse 5, where Paul makes it explicit. For the time being, it is sufficient to point out his repeated emphasis on the openness of his ministerial conduct (3:12). Whereas in 1:12 Paul appeals to his own conscience, here he commends his conduct "to everyone's conscience." That is, he asserts that he acts in such a way that no fair-minded person would find fault with him. Even more, he insists that his conduct lies open "in the sight of God," thereby once more calling on God as his witness (1:23; 2:17).

Paul now alludes to the criticism that the **gospel** he preaches **is veiled**. Note that he picks up the image of veiling and the theme of unbelief from 3:12–16. Paul declares that the gospel **is veiled** only **for those who are perishing**. This evokes what he said in 2:15–16, that his embodied proclamation of the gospel wafts like "an odor of death that leads to death" for those who view his suffering and humble service as foolishness and weakness. In verse 4 Paul adds that **the god of this age has blinded the minds of the unbelievers**. The "god of this age" is Satan. Admittedly paradoxical, referring to Satan as a "god" coheres with Paul's worldview and terminology elsewhere.[15] According to him, the world

4:3–4

---

14. For the significance of positive †self-commendation, see the sidebar on p. 77.

15. See 1 Cor 2:6, 8 ("the rulers of this age") and Eph 2:2 ("the ruler of the power of the air, the spirit that is now at work in the disobedient"). See also John 12:31; 14:30; 16:11 ("the ruler of this world").

presently stands at the juncture of two ages. Although Christ Jesus has ushered in the new age marked by the gift of the life-giving Spirit, Christians await the complete manifestation of God's kingdom, when all of Christ's enemies, including death, will be fully defeated (1 Cor 15:24–28). In the meantime, even though the enslaving reign of sin and death (Rom 5:12–14) has been broken, Satan still exercises power as he attempts to foil the spread of the gospel (see 1 Thess 2:18). Paul thus acknowledges the malignant influence of Satan in the present. Nevertheless, he insists on people's ability to choose for or against the gospel.[16]

Notice how Paul describes this gospel at the end of verse 4. The **gospel** is the "good news" concerning **Christ,** that is, concerning Jesus the †Messiah. Jesus is the Son of God, in whom all of God's promises have been fulfilled (2 Cor 1:19–20) and through whose death God has reconciled the world to himself (5:18–19). Because he is the eternal †**image of God** who reflects divine **glory,** Jesus has revealed God's intention for human existence, an existence characterized by self-giving love, which is the way of life that leads to being raised up, body and soul, in communion with the Triune God.

4:5–6   Paul returns to his positive self-commendation. Here he fills in what he meant by the phrase "the open declaration of the truth" (v. 2). To begin with, he makes clear that **we do not preach ourselves,** that is, he does not use his status as an apostle to promote himself or seek his own advantage. Nor does he direct attention to himself as a savior figure. Rather, Paul preaches **Jesus Christ as Lord.** A quick glance at Phil 2:6–11 sheds light on his meaning. This passage, known as the "Christ hymn," sets forth in poetic terms the highlights of the "good news" concerning Jesus: his incarnation, his ministry of humble service ("taking the form of a slave"), his obedience unto death, and his resurrection (implied) and exaltation by God. At the climax of the hymn is the exclamation: "Jesus Christ is Lord!" (Phil 2:11). Hence the Apostle's statement that he preaches "Jesus Christ as Lord" serves as a summary of his proclamation of the gospel.

But notice that Paul says that he *does* preach himself in a certain manner, as **your slaves for the sake of Jesus.** To be a "slave" means to belong to someone else and to live one's life in humble service. Recall that Paul has already declared that he is *God's* slave (2:14). As such, he has been called to give of himself in love for the Corinthians.[17] When Paul says that he is a slave to the Corinthians "for the sake of Jesus" (*dia Iēsoun*), he means two things. First, he serves the

16. See the second point in the Reflection and Application section for 2:5–11.
17. We can now better appreciate Paul's claim in 1:24 that he does not "lord it over" the Corinthians' faith.

community in response to Jesus' call to him to be an apostle (1:1). Second, he imitates Jesus, who in "taking the form of a slave / . . . humbled himself" (Phil 2:7–8), and who declared that he came "not to be served but to serve" (Mark 10:45). Therefore, in addition to preaching the gospel with words, Paul proclaims it existentially through his self-giving service rendered in love after the manner of Jesus. He understands himself to be Christ's "ambassador" (2 Cor 5:20) and herald, who not only has an important announcement to make but also embodies the message, thereby giving it greater credibility.

The passage concludes as it began, with a reference to Paul's call. He speaks of **God** as the one **who said, "Let light shine out of darkness."** This is an allusion to Gen 1:3–4. Paul refers here to God in his role as creator. God, whose activity of creating the world involved separating light from darkness, has now brought a new light, "the light of the gospel of the glory of Christ" (v. 4). Indeed, Paul will shortly discuss the "new creation" that results for anyone who is "in Christ" (5:17). The new creation comes about because God **has shone in our hearts to bring to light the knowledge of the glory of God on the face of [Jesus] Christ**. This is, first and foremost, a reference to Paul's encounter with the risen Lord (see Gal 1:15–16, where he says that God revealed his Son, literally, "in me"), an encounter through which he was called to preach the gospel to the †Gentiles. But Paul's words at the end of verse 6 also point back to 3:18, where he describes the Spirit-empowered transformation that takes place within all Christians as they contemplate the image of God reflected in Jesus, the †new Adam. That is, we see the face of Jesus with the eyes of faith, and in seeing his face we recognize the divine majesty revealed in him.

Reflection and Application (4:1–6)

Living icons. The word translated "image" in 3:18 and 4:4 is *eikōn*. From this Greek term comes the word *icon*. In Eastern Christianity there is a rich tradition of depicting Jesus, Mary, and various saints through sacred icons. Because they make present the persons portrayed, icons are venerated in Orthodox liturgical celebrations and private devotion.

Paul's reference to Jesus as the "image of God" par excellence (4:4) along with his teaching that all Christians are being transformed "into the same image" (3:18)—that is, into the image of God as restored by Christ—reveals that we are called to be *living* icons. By becoming more and more Christlike, we give powerful witness to the presence of God within us. This reality is both ennobling and challenging. It is ennobling because to be bearers of God's image

In the Liturgy

Second Corinthians 4:1–2, 5–7 is, most appropriately, a recommended reading in the Common of Pastors and for liturgies that celebrate Holy Orders—the ordination of deacons, priests, or bishops. It encourages and challenges those called to pastoral leadership and ordained ministry to courageous proclamation of the gospel and to radical service.

is to possess an awesome gift. It is challenging because with the privilege also comes the responsibility to grow, with the Spirit's help, in holiness, faithfulness, compassion, forbearance, and love. Moreover, we are challenged to treat others, who are likewise bearers of God's image, with greater dignity and respect. Indeed, the Orthodox liturgy beautifully reinforces this point. In addition to incensing the sacred icons, the priest or deacon incenses the people assembled for worship.

St. Peter Claver. Paul's commitment to be a slave to the Corinthians "for the sake of Jesus" is a dramatic instance of taking to heart Jesus' example of humble, selfless service to others (John 13:1–20). Another heroic incarnation of Jesus' example is the Spanish Jesuit St. Peter Claver. For over forty years in the first half of the seventeenth century, Claver labored in the port city of Cartagena, in present day Colombia, which at that time was a major center of the slave trade. He tended to the physical and spiritual needs of tens of thousands of slaves as they disembarked from the deplorable conditions of the ships that had unmercifully transported them from Africa. Upon writing out the formula of his final solemn vows, this saint humbly signed his name, "Peter Claver, the slave of the slaves."

Suffering as a Mark of Apostleship

2 Corinthians 4:7–15

Having set forth the †new covenant ministry and its principal fruit—the Spirit-empowered transformation of Christians into the †image of God after the likeness of Jesus—Paul moves on to the second part (4:7–5:10) of his extended discourse on †apostleship (2:14–7:4). As he continues to explain the way God has called him to proclaim the †gospel, he sets forth the paradox that the new covenant ministry, which leads to glory, also entails suffering. Paul depicts this suffering in general terms (4:7–9), then interprets it in light of Jesus' suffering and self-giving (4:10–12). Paul insists that he has been given "the same Spirit of faithfulness" (my translation) that animated Christ Jesus (4:13–15).

Treasure in Earthen Vessels (4:7–9)

---

⁷But we hold this treasure in earthen vessels, that the surpassing power may be of God and not from us. ⁸We are afflicted in every way, but not constrained; perplexed, but not driven to despair; ⁹persecuted, but not abandoned; struck down, but not destroyed;

OT: Gen 28:10–22; Ps 16; Jer 18:1–6
NT: Matt 13:44–46; Acts 16:16–40

The immediately preceding verses have already intimated the paradoxical nature of Paul's apostolic ministry. On the one hand, his call involved the revelation of God's glory (4:6), and the †gospel he proclaimed concerns the

4:7

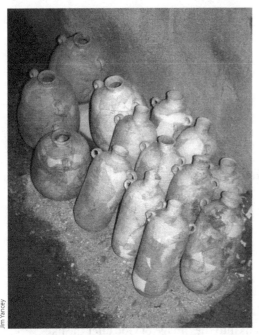

Fig. 6. The type of earthen vessels that Paul's phrase in 2 Cor 4:7 would have evoked for the Corinthians.

glory of Christ (4:4). On the other hand, an integral part of Paul's gospel proclamation to the Corinthians is his humble, self-giving service for their benefit (4:5). He expresses the paradox even more succinctly here: **we hold this treasure in earthen vessels**. What is *this treasure*? The context suggests three possibilities: "the knowledge of the glory of God on the face of [Jesus] Christ" (4:6); "the gospel of the glory of Christ" (4:4); and "this ministry" (4:1), referring to the †new covenant ministry. It is not necessary to limit the reference to any one of these possibilities, because they are interrelated. Like the discoverer in Jesus' parable of the treasure (Matt 13:44), Paul has committed his whole life to "this treasure," that is, to proclaiming the good news concerning Christ.

His emphasis, however, is on the metaphor of "earthen vessels." The image recalls Jeremiah's oracle of the clay vessel in the potter's hands (Jer 18:1–6). It evokes a container that is cheap, ordinary, and fragile (see Lev 11:33; Lam 4:2). Paul uses this imagery to signify his precarious embodied existence, as his references below to "our body" (v. 10) and "our mortal flesh" (v. 11) make clear. It is important to appreciate how he uses body language throughout this passage. Paul shows that his lived experience and actions proclaim the gospel. The paradox is that glory is revealed through suffering.

The second half of verse 7 presents the crucial insight that Paul has come to appreciate, namely, **that the surpassing power may be of God and not from us**. Reflecting on his divine call as well as his own fragility, Paul lives by the conviction that it is only through *God's* empowerment that he can exercise the new covenant ministry. This insight echoes both 1:9, where Paul says that he has learned to place his trust in God, and 3:5–6, where he declares that God is the one who has qualified him as a minister of the new covenant. The reference to the divine "power" (*dynamis*) looks back to the transforming "Spirit of the Lord" in 3:17 and anticipates the "Spirit of faithfulness" in 4:13 (my translation).

Paul then lists four pairs of participles that illustrate the point just made: even **4:8–9** though he is like an easily broken "earthen vessel," God's "surpassing power" sustains him through various sufferings. In each pair, the first participle refers to hardships that Paul endures; the second indicates that God has delivered him from such hardships. Note the phrase **in every way**, which in the Greek text is given the prominent first position. He thereby indicates that the sufferings named here are typical and ongoing.[1]

The initial pair—**afflicted in every way, but not constrained**—serves as an introduction or heading to the list. The reference to being "afflicted" recalls the opening benediction (1:3–7), where Paul blesses God as the one "who encourages us in our every affliction." It is therefore not surprising that, in this passage, he immediately adds that, although he is constantly afflicted, he is not left without the means of deliverance or escape.[2]

The second pair—**perplexed, but not driven to despair**—homes in on the psychological effect of suffering hardships. Interestingly, Paul confessed earlier that, in connection with the affliction in Asia, he "despaired even of life" (1:8). The discrepancy is more apparent than real, however, and reflects a common experience. It is sometimes only in retrospect, through the eyes of faith, that we come to appreciate how God was indeed present to us in our sufferings and gave us his assistance. Paul's repeated experience of God's deliverance has taught him that there is no reason to despair.

The third pair—**persecuted, but not abandoned**—highlights the opposition he has endured in his ministry. Here Paul alludes to the biblical tenet that God does not abandon those who are righteous.[3] And the fourth pair—**struck down, but not destroyed**—functions as a summary statement. While sufferings and hardships for the sake of the gospel are a reality, the Apostle knows that it is only the rejection of this gospel that leads to destruction (2:15–16; 4:3).

Paul's list of sufferings here is the first of four "†hardship catalogs" in this letter (6:4–10; 11:23–33; 12:10).[4] The second and third lists, as we will see, describe his hardships with greater specificity. A quick glance at verses 8–9 could give the impression that Paul's sole concern is with the *passive* endurance of suffering, that is, dealing with what is inflicted on him by others. The longer lists reveal a more complex view, as they include hardships that he has

---

1. This observation is reinforced by the present tense participles in vv. 8–9 and by the adverbs "always" and "constantly" in vv. 10–11.

2. See the NEB ("never hemmed in") and the REB ("never cornered").

3. See, e.g., Gen 28:15; Deut 31:6; Josh 1:5; Ps 16:10; 37:25, 28, 33. We will see at 4:13–15 how Paul takes up and transforms the Old Testament theme of God's deliverance of the righteous sufferer.

4. See the sidebar on hardship catalogs on p. 152.

imposed on himself in the course of bringing the gospel to others. For instance, Paul later refers to his commitment to labor with his hands and to forgo meals and sleep (6:5; 11:27). He makes these sacrifices so that he can proclaim the gospel without becoming a financial burden to his communities (1 Thess 2:9; see 1 Cor 4:11–12). Recall, moreover, that Paul describes himself as a "slave" to the Corinthians "for the sake of Jesus" (4:5). It is therefore necessary to keep in mind both aspects of his hardships—those that he passively endures as well as those that he willingly takes on—as we work through 4:7–15.

Reflection and Application (4:7–9)

Earthen vessels. Many people in pastoral ministry can easily relate to Paul's self-description as a fragile clay pot. Pastors and associates are often overwhelmed by the sheer number of tasks and needs to which they are called to respond. Youth ministers and people involved in religious education can at times wonder if their efforts in reaching our young people are succeeding. It is easy to doubt ourselves in moments of discouragement and failure, real or apparent. Paul, however, reminds us that we *do* have a precious treasure, the treasure of the gospel. Moreover, we *do* have the Spirit's power at work within us. Rather than despair, we are invited to rely even more on God's †grace so that we can share with others the treasure we have received.

Physical appearance. Paul's reference to earthen vessels also challenges a feature of contemporary society, namely, the obsession with physical appearance. Our society tends to glamorize youth and beauty. People today spend millions on the latest fashions, not to mention body piercings and tattoos, as they attempt to express themselves. In large part, these are attempts to live up to cultural expectations—or, in some cases, rebel against them. Because of the bias for youth and beauty, it is understandable that, as we become older, many people seek to counter the physical ravages of aging and mortality. Ageism has joined other "isms" (for example, racism, sexism) as a pernicious and prevalent reality. This is especially true in the workplace, where age discrimination is rampant. It thus should come as little surprise that stores abound with skin and hair products that promise to produce a "younger, healthier look," or that cosmetic surgery has become a routine medical procedure, even among the young.

Paul's image of earthen vessels invites us to engage in some critical reflection in this regard. He recognized the fragility and vulnerability of embodied human existence. Rather than despair, however, Paul turned in trust to God as the giver of life, the sustainer of life—and as the one "who gives life to the dead" (Rom 4:17). In chapter 5 we will look at Paul's teaching on the resurrection body (5:1–5). For the time being, it is sufficient to reflect on our present flesh-and-blood existence. Undoubtedly, we are called to be good stewards of our bodies and our health. Such stewardship, however, should be wary of cultural obsessions with youth and beauty, and should be on guard against all forms of vanity. What might happen if we took some of the energy and money we expend on bodily appearance and redirected it toward those who have *real* bodily needs?

Aligned with the Story of Jesus (4:10–12)

---

¹⁰**always carrying about in the body the dying of Jesus, so that the life of Jesus may also be manifested in our body. ¹¹For we who live are constantly being given up to death for the sake of Jesus, so that the life of Jesus may be manifested in our mortal flesh.**

   ¹²**So death is at work in us, but life in you.**

OT: Isa 42:1–4; 49:1–7; 50:4–11; 52:13–53:12
NT: Mark 8:34–38; John 12:24–26; Phil 3:8–11
Catechism: suffering as participation in Jesus' work of salvation, 1508, 1521

After listing his sufferings in general terms in verses 8–9, Paul now makes a   **4:10** bold move. In this verse—which, in the Greek text, is the continuation of the sentence that began in verse 7—he offers an interpretation of his constant endurance of suffering and hardships. He aligns his experience of being afflicted, perplexed, persecuted, and struck down with what happened to Jesus: **always carrying about in the body the dying of Jesus**.

With that in mind, there are several important observations to make with respect to this text. First, Paul is talking about an *ongoing* process, as evidenced by the adverb "always" and the present tense of the participle "carrying." Second, he emphasizes the *embodied* or *incarnate* nature of this process—it is something that occurs "in the body." Third, Paul refers to a graphic aspect of the story of Jesus, his *nekrōsis*. While this term can denote the state of "deadness" (i.e., the result of dying),[5] the NAB appropriately stresses a slightly different nuance, namely, the process or action that results in death. That is, Paul's point is that he always carries in his embodied existence "the dying of Jesus," or even "the putting

---

5. The RSV, NRSV, and NJB render the term as "the *death* of Jesus."

to death of Jesus" (my translation). A fourth notable feature is his concentrated use of the unadorned name "Jesus" here and in verses 11 and 14.[6]

What does it mean to *always* bear in one's body the *nekrōsis* of Jesus? Paul's stress on ongoing experience only makes sense if the expression "the dying," or putting to death, "of Jesus" refers to more than the actual crucifixion itself, although that is certainly included. Paul's language suggests that he is referring more broadly to Jesus' *entire* way of life, one that was marked by suffering and privation (e.g., Luke 9:58).[7] It is important to appreciate that Paul connects his ongoing experience of enduring hardships with the story of Jesus (see Rom 8:36; 1 Cor 15:31; Phil 3:10). He boldly claims to walk in the way of Christ. Even more, as will be made explicit momentarily, Paul reveals that Jesus is living within him. In fact, Jesus' union with him is so intimate that he says elsewhere that he is completing what is lacking in the sufferings of Christ (Col 1:24). Paul's constant "carrying about in the body the dying of Jesus" is his appropriation of Jesus' teaching to take up one's cross each day and follow him (Luke 9:23). The wording in this verse also reminds us that Jesus identifies himself with his suffering and persecuted followers (Acts 9:4; 22:8; 26:14). Before commenting on the remainder of this verse—**so that the life of Jesus may also be manifested in our body**—it will be helpful to look first at the beginning of the next verse.

4:11   Here Paul sets forth the reason for what he has asserted in verses 7–10: **For we who live are constantly being given up to death for the sake of Jesus**. Note that, with the adverb "constantly," he once again underlines the notion of an ongoing process. His phraseology also brings out the paradox of his apostolic existence—though *living*, he is continually being given up to *death*. Paul continues to refer here to his endurance of suffering on account of proclaiming the †gospel (vv. 8–9). In fact, he picks up on a theme from the opening benediction (1:5), namely that "Christ's sufferings overflow to us."

But the passage here alludes to more than the passive endurance of hardships. A key to understanding this passage is the verb *paradidōmi* ("give up"; "hand over") and its close association with Jesus.[8] Whereas Paul applies *paradidōmi* to himself in verse 11—it is he, the Apostle, who is "being given up to death"—he elsewhere applies this verb to Jesus. In 1 Cor 11:23 Paul recalls Jesus' words

6. Paul's use of the unadorned name Jesus in vv. 10–14 represents nearly one-third of all the instances in his writings (Rom 3:26; 8:11; 10:9; 1 Cor 12:3; 2 Cor 11:4; Gal 6:17; Eph 4:21; Phil 2:10; 1 Thess 1:10; 4:14). By using Jesus' unadorned name (i.e., without the title Christ and/or Lord), he gives special emphasis to Jesus' *human* identity and character.

7. See Victor Paul Furnish, *II Corinthians: A New Translation with Introduction and Commentary*, AB 32A (New York: Doubleday, 1984), 283: "the whole course of Jesus' life" can be construed as a "dying."

8. In the Greek text, the verb "being given up" is directly juxtaposed to the phrase *dia Iēsoun* ("for the sake of Jesus").

over the bread and cup "on the night he *was handed over*." And in Rom 4:25 he adverts to the tradition that Jesus "*was handed over* for our transgressions." Paul emphasizes that Jesus' being handed over was part of God's plan of salvation and an expression of God's love for humanity (Rom 8:32).

Christ's "being handed over" or "given up to death" does not tell the whole story, however. According to Paul, Jesus plays more than a passive role in the divine plan of salvation. Indeed, Paul speaks of Jesus' active role in this plan in two other passages where Jesus is the subject of the active form of *paradidōmi*. In Eph 5:2 Paul writes, "Christ loved us and *handed* himself *over* for us." Notice that Paul here links Jesus' love with his giving himself up for the sake of humankind. Similarly, in Gal 2:20 he portrays "the Son of God" as the one "who has loved me and *given* himself *up* for me." Jesus' "yes" to God (2 Cor 1:19–20) was manifested throughout his earthly life, and especially at his death, by his self-giving love. Hence the verb *paradidōmi* evokes not only Jesus' passive being handed over but also his active giving himself in love for the sake of others.

Returning to 2 Cor 4:11, we are now able to grasp Paul's full meaning. In saying that he is "constantly being given up to death for the sake of Jesus," he not only refers to his endurance of suffering on account of the gospel but also implies that he is more than a passive victim. That is, the flip side of "being handed over" is Paul's own choice to give himself in love for others. Indeed, observe that he adds the phrase "for the sake of Jesus" (*dia Iēsoun*). This is the same phrase used in 4:5, where he stated that he is a "slave" to the Corinthians. As was the case there, the phrase connotes that Paul is loyal in his service to Jesus, whose †apostle he is (1:1), and that he follows the pattern of Christ's self-giving love and endurance of suffering for the sake of others.

Paul goes on to say that his alignment with the story of Jesus serves a special purpose: **so that the life of Jesus may be manifested in our mortal flesh**. This statement—which basically repeats the second half of verse 10—refers to the revelation of "the life of Jesus" in Paul's enfleshed existence. That is, he points here to the presence of the risen Christ within him (Gal 2:20). This presence is another way of expressing the "surpassing power" of God on which he relies (v. 7). It is only by means of the risen Jesus dwelling within him that Paul can both endure sufferings and embody Christ's self-giving love. Consequently, by walking in the way of the cross, he bears witness to the power of the risen Christ within him. We too are enabled to manifest this power because the risen Lord is actually present within us, revealing himself anew.

Finally, Paul sets forth the effect of his apostolic existence: **So death is at work** 4:12 **in us, but life in you**. This sentence is best taken as belonging to the paragraph beginning in verse 7 (rather than, as the NAB renders it, beginning a new paragraph). Paul concludes that through his sufferings the Corinthians benefit. How? At an obvious level, the community benefits from his commitment to actively enter into the dynamic of Christ's self-giving love for them, a commitment that makes him their "slave" (4:5). But Paul also speaks at a deeper level. Because he aligns his suffering with Jesus' redemptive suffering, his suffering has *redemptive* value for the Corinthians. Indeed, it is consoling and ennobling to know that we, like Paul, can align our sufferings with "the dying of Jesus," thereby entering into the †paschal mystery in which God brings life out of our dyings. In the eyes of the Corinthians, it may seem that Paul merely suffers one blow after another and that his humble service is unbecoming of an apostle. Nevertheless, he insists, divine life is being sacramentally mediated through him, as God's †grace comes to the community through "the life of Jesus" within him.

Reflection and Application (4:10–12)

Christ's whole life as redemptive. In discussing God's work of redemption, Paul stresses the centrality of Jesus' death and resurrection (e.g., Rom 4:25). According to some scholars, this is his exclusive focus. It is certainly appropriate to emphasize Jesus' suffering and death when reflecting on the mystery of redemption since "redemption comes to us above all through the blood of his cross" (Catechism, 517; Eph 1:7; Col 1:13–14; 1 Pet 1:18–19). Nevertheless, it is crucial to recognize that Jesus' life as a whole is "a mystery of *redemption*" and that "this mystery is at work throughout Christ's entire life" (Catechism, 517). Christ's love and self-giving, which culminates at the cross, marked his *entire* human existence. As we have seen, Paul draws on Jesus' manner of living and dying in setting forth his own role as a minister of the †new covenant. He will continue to draw on the example of Christ in his exhortations to the community because all Christians are called, within their particular circumstances of life, to imitate Christ (1 Cor 11:1).

The mystery of suffering. Human suffering is a complex issue and the object of much deep questioning. Limitations of space allow for only four brief observations. First, suffering ought not to be glorified or trivialized. Indeed, much of the ministry of the Church is intended to *alleviate* the sufferings of others (e.g., the ministries of providing food, shelter, and healing). Second, Scripture makes clear that when God brings about the fullness of the kingdom there will be no more suffering (Rev 21:3–5). In the present, however, there is much unavoidable suffering (e.g., sickness, physical and mental decline, anxiety for the well-being of loved ones, etc.). The good news is that we can align our sufferings with those

John Paul II on Sharing in Christ's Sufferings

In his 1984 apostolic letter *Salvifici Dolores*, Pope John Paul II taught that Paul's words in Col 1:24 and 2 Cor 4:8–11 have validity for all Christians. Because our redemption has been accomplished through the passion and death of Christ—the passion that so eloquently expresses divine love—all human suffering now finds itself in a new situation. That is, Jesus' cross has not only brought about redemption through suffering, it also redeems human suffering itself. Every person is called to "become a sharer in the redemptive suffering of Christ" (*Salvifici Dolores* 19). Jesus, who invites us to share in his sufferings, becomes an intimate sharer in our sufferings. Thus, while from one vantage point the work of redemption has *already* been completed by Christ, John Paul II insisted, it is also "constantly being accomplished" by the Church, the body of Christ. For this reason we can say that the Church, in its continual development in space and time, is "the dimension in which Christ's redemptive suffering can be constantly completed by the suffering" of her members (24).

of Jesus, who invites us to participate in his suffering and also shares in ours. In union with Christ, we can offer up to God our sufferings and afflictions with trust and hope in the ongoing work of the paschal mystery. Third, to follow in the footsteps of Jesus is to invite opposition, even persecution, from others. The way of the gospel and the way of the world are often in conflict. Anyone who has worked or demonstrated for the right to life, for peace, or against systemic economic injustice can vouch for this. In fact, if I find that I encounter little or no opposition on account of my faith, it may be that I am compromising gospel values. Fourth, heeding the call of Jesus entails, at times, sacrificing one's well-being, rights, and needs for the sake of others. It is with respect to the second, third, and fourth points that Paul proclaims: "Now I rejoice in my sufferings for your sake, and in my flesh I am filling up what is lacking in the afflictions of Christ on behalf of his body, which is the church" (Col 1:24).

Blessed Teresa of Calcutta. A contemporary figure who exemplifies Paul's teaching in 2 Cor 4:7–12 is Mother Teresa. Her work—and that of the order she founded, the Missionaries of Charity—among the poorest of the poor is well known and admired. Blessed Teresa's driving motivation was to bring Christ's love to people, to make manifest "the life of Jesus" through selfless love and service. As we have learned from her spiritual journals, in her mystical prayer life she profoundly experienced the passion of Christ and the misery of the poor, which led her all the more to rely on God's power. God certainly worked wonders through this fragile earthen vessel. Countless people have experienced life through her participation in the "dying of Jesus."

The "Same Spirit of Faithfulness" (4:13–15)

[13]Since, then, we have the same spirit of faith, according to what is written, "I believed, therefore I spoke," we too believe and therefore speak, [14]knowing that the one who raised the Lord Jesus will raise us also with Jesus and place us with you in his presence. [15]Everything indeed is for you, so that the grace bestowed in abundance on more and more people may cause the thanksgiving to overflow for the glory of God.

OT: Ps 116
NT: Rom 15:1–6; 1 Cor 15:20–28; Phil 2:6–11
Lectionary: Common of Martyrs

4:13   Paul now connects his experience of suffering hardships with words from Scripture, as signified by the phrase **according to what is written**. He asserts that, as the psalmist who declared, **"I believed, therefore I spoke,"** so too does he **believe and therefore speak**. Many translations and commentaries render this verse as beginning a new line of thought. Whereas in verses 7–12 Paul focused on his experience of suffering and hardships, he now explains that he perseveres in proclaiming the [†]gospel (v. 13) because of his faith in the resurrection (v. 14). This standard interpretation, which has much to commend it, understands the formulation **the same spirit of faith** to refer to the disposition of faith expressed in the line cited from Scripture.[9]

I propose a different reading, however, one that takes account of [†]intertextuality and treats the present passage as continuing the presentation begun in verse 7.[10] In order to appreciate what Paul is saying here, it is necessary to briefly consider the entire context of the verse he quotes.

The cited words—translated by the NAB as "I believed, therefore I spoke"—are from Ps 116:10. This line appears at the heart of a psalm in which a righteous sufferer tells his story. It is important to understand that Paul used the *Greek* text of this psalm[11]—not the Hebrew, from which English translations of the

9. As in the NJB: "we have the same spirit of faith as is described in scripture."
10. For a more thorough and technical explanation, see Thomas D. Stegman, "*Episteusa, dio elalēsa* (2 Cor 4:13): Paul's Christological Reading of LXX Ps 115:1a," *CBQ* 69 (2007): 725–45.
11. Ps 116 in English translations is found in the [†]Septuagint as two psalms: Ps 114–115.

Old Testament are derived. There are thus nuances of the †Septuagint that the English translation of Ps 116 does not make apparent. In the Septuagint, the psalmist identifies himself as God's "slave" (Ps 116:16). He refers twice to an event in which he was "brought low" (116:6, 10). He depicts his affliction and suffering in vivid terms: he was caught in "the cords of death," and the "snares of Sheol" seized him (116:3). In the throes of death, he cried out, "O Lord, save my life!" (116:4), and then bears witness that he has been delivered "from death" (116:8). Finally, near the end of the psalm, the righteous sufferer professes, "Precious before the Lord is the death of his holy ones" (116:15). Hence, according to the story told in the Greek version of Ps 116, the psalmist speaks as one who has been faithful to God—he confesses that he has served as God's *slave*—and who has trusted in God to save him from death. In citing the central words of Ps 116, Paul evokes the *entire* story of this faithful, righteous sufferer.

Significantly, the story of Ps 116 closely resembles the story of Jesus as told in Phil 2:6–11. That hymn portrays Jesus as one who emptied himself and took on the form of a "slave" (Phil 2:7),[12] "humbled," or lowered, himself,[13] and became obedient unto "death" (2:8). And it goes on to declare that God regarded Jesus' death as precious and thus vindicated him (*"Because of this,* God greatly exalted him"—2:9).

Paul evokes the story of Ps 116 because *it resembles the story of Jesus.* Thus it is Jesus whom Paul has in mind in quoting the psalm. In Paul's mind, Jesus is the protagonist of the story told there; he is the one who took on the form of a slave, who humbled himself even more, who gave himself for others, suffered, and offered his life in obedience to God, and who was vindicated and exalted. Thus in Paul's reading of the psalm, it is Christ who speaks the cited words, which can be rendered: "I have been faithful, therefore I have spoken."[14] These words are the testimony of Jesus, now raised from the dead (v. 14), to his own faithfulness, which was grounded in his trust in God to vindicate him. They also point to Jesus' *love.*[15]

We are now properly positioned to interpret verse 13. Paul continues to allude here to the story of Jesus' faithfulness in order to explain how he, Paul, a mere "earthen vessel," is able to endure sufferings and give himself in love after the manner of Christ. Paul can do so because he has "the same Spirit of faithfulness" that Jesus had (my translation). The Greek word *pneuma*, "spirit,"

---

12. The word here for slave, *doulos,* occurs twice in the Greek version of Ps 116:16.

13. The verb is *tapeinoō,* the same verb found in the Greek version of Ps 116:6, 10.

14. The Greek verb *pisteuō,* usually rendered "believe" or "trust," can also mean "be faithful," a faithfulness that is manifested holistically in mind, heart, will, and action.

15. The first word of the Greek text of Ps 116 is *ēgapēsa* ("I have loved").

Jesus and the Psalms in the New Testament

The gospels relate that Jesus himself prayed the Psalms (Luke 23:46—"Father, into your hands I commend my spirit," from Ps 31:6; see Mark 14:26). Jesus also made some of their words his own (Mark 14:34—"My soul is sorrowful even to death," from Ps 42:6, 12; 43:5). The author of the letter to the Hebrews twice describes Jesus as speaking the words of psalms (Ps 22:23 in Heb 2:12; Ps 40:7–9 in Heb 10:5–7).

Second Corinthians 4:13 is not the only text in which Paul interprets a psalm as expressing the words of Jesus. In Rom 15:3 he evokes the story of Ps 69 to communicate the thoughts of Christ, who did not seek to please himself but suffered for his zeal for God.

For the authors of the New Testament, linking the Psalms to Jesus was no exegetical whim. The New Testament writers considered the author of these sacred texts to be David. To David, who was anointed king of Israel, was promised a descendant who would be the †Messiah—*the* anointed one. In light of the life, death, resurrection, and exaltation of Jesus, early Christians took the step of interpreting some of the Psalms (e.g., Ps 2; 16; 110) as biblical prophecies by David concerning his descendant, Christ Jesus (see Acts 2:22–36).

here refers to the *Holy* Spirit—the "Spirit of the Lord" referred to in 3:17–18. This is the Spirit who filled and led Jesus throughout his earthly ministry (Luke 4:18–21). And this is the Spirit who now mediates to us the presence and power of the risen Christ ("the life of Jesus," vv. 10–11). He is the one who enables us to walk in the way of Jesus' faithfulness to God. Verse 13 can therefore be rendered as follows: "Because we have the same Spirit of faithfulness according to what has been written—'I have been faithful, therefore I have spoken'—so also are we faithful, and therefore we also speak."

What then does Paul, empowered by the Spirit, *speak*? The answer is found in 4:5: he proclaims in words that †Messiah Jesus is "Lord." And even more, he proclaims *in action* that he is a slave who ministers to the Corinthians. In doing so, Paul shows that his most eloquent proclamation of the gospel is the way he incarnates the love of Jesus, who took on the form of a slave, suffered, offered his life for us in obedience to God, and was raised from the dead.

Before proceeding to verse 14, it is worth pausing to note how this interpretation reinforces and expands on earlier parts of the letter. We saw in 1:18–22 that, after referring to Jesus' "yes" to God, Paul revealed that God has anointed and sealed him, the Apostle, with the gift of the Spirit, who empowers his fidelity to

---

In the Liturgy

LIVING
TRADITION

Second Corinthians 4:7–15 is read on the Feast of St. James (July 25). This is a fitting selection, as James was the first of the twelve apostles to suffer martyrdom (Acts 12:2). In doing so, he showed himself willing to drink from the same cup of suffering from which Jesus drank (Mark 10:38).

This passage is also proposed as a reading in the Common of Martyrs. The word *martyr* comes from the Greek *martys*, meaning "witness." Martyrs bear witness to the love and power of God working through weak "earthen vessels" (see the Preface for Martyrs). They fearlessly proclaim God's way in the face of opposition and follow in the footsteps of Jesus by giving their lives for the sake of the gospel. Paul's discourse on suffering in 2 Cor 4:7–15 reminds us that all Christians, filled with "the Spirit of faithfulness," are called to bear witness to the gospel and to endure daily dyings so that others might have life—and, if the occasion arises, to be actual martyrs.

God's will (i.e., his Amen to God). These are the very same dynamics set forth in our passage here. Recall too how, in 2:14, Paul employed the metaphor of the Roman †triumphal procession to explain that he is God's slave "in Christ," that is, in close association with Jesus, who is named as God's faithful slave in the christological reading of Ps 116. Now, in the passage here, Paul explains how the Spirit enables him to be a "slave" after the manner of Jesus. Earlier, in calling attention to the calamity that befell him in Asia in 1:8–10, Paul referred three times to God's power to "rescue" him. Paul uses the same verb found in the Greek text of Ps 116 when the righteous sufferer cries out, "O Lord, save my life!" (116:4). Finally, back in 1:9 Paul named God—the one who has rescued him and will continue to rescue him—as the one "who raises the dead." Not surprisingly, because he alludes here in verse 13 to the story of Christ, he now refers to God as "the one who raised the Lord Jesus."

In referring to the resurrection of Jesus, Paul points to his own trust in the power of God: **knowing that the one who raised the Lord Jesus will raise us also with Jesus**. Paul's faithfulness, manifested by his suffering and his giving himself in love for others, is grounded in his profound faith and hope in God to vindicate him. God's "surpassing power" (v. 7) has been revealed first and foremost through the resurrection of Jesus from the dead. Indeed, Christ is "the firstfruits" of the resurrection (1 Cor 15:23). Paul now declares his hope that God will ultimately vindicate all of his dyings after he has physically passed

4:14–15

away. He hopes to dwell forever in the divine presence. Notice, moreover, how Paul includes the Corinthians in this hope, as he claims that God will **place him with you in his presence**. This echoes his opening statement, where he expressed his hope that he and the community will be justly proud of one another "on the day of [our] Lord Jesus" (1:14).

Finally, Paul reiterates for the Corinthians what he asserted in verse 12: **Everything indeed is for you**. His proclamation of the gospel in word and deed and his endurance of suffering are for their building up and benefit. But Paul's concern goes beyond Corinth. His desire is that [†]**grace** be **bestowed in abundance on more and more people**. That is, he wants the gospel to be preached to and received by all (10:15–16). Paul's ultimate goal is that **thanksgiving** might **overflow for the glory of God**. Thanksgiving and praise to God will issue from the reception and appropriation of the gospel by "more and more people."

Resurrection Hope

2 Corinthians 4:16–5:10

Near the end of the previous section, on his suffering after the likeness of Jesus (4:7–15), Paul referred to the resurrection of Jesus and to his hope of being raised up with him. As he continues to explain to the Corinthians his way of being an †apostle, Paul now expounds on the hope that underlies his commitment to bear "the dying of Jesus." First, he makes clear that the present life is not the whole story; we await a glory that is beyond comparison (4:16–18). He then affirms the reality of the resurrection body (5:1–5) and describes how he prepares for his heavenly "home" (5:6–10).

Looking to What Is Unseen (4:16–18)

---

[16]Therefore, we are not discouraged; rather, although our outer self is wasting away, our inner self is being renewed day by day. [17]For this momentary light affliction is producing for us an eternal weight of glory beyond all comparison, [18]as we look not to what is seen but to what is unseen; for what is seen is transitory, but what is unseen is eternal.

OT: 2 Macc 7:20–23
NT: Rom 8:18–25; 1 Cor 2:9–10; Eph 3:14–21; Heb 11:8–16

In the previous passage Paul insisted that, although he is like a fragile clay jar, he is empowered to persevere through suffering to reveal Jesus' self-giving love. He takes up this theme again, but now points to the †eschatological hope that sustains him.

4:16   Paul reiterates what he said in 4:1—he is **not discouraged**. Despite much suffering and opposition (4:9), he does not lose heart. He previously stated that he derives encouragement from God's call to him to be a minister of the †new covenant. Now Paul stresses that he is bolstered by the hope of eternal life that God is preparing for him. That is, through faith he is able to keep the big picture in view, recognizing that his apostolic life is a pilgrimage toward a "better homeland, a heavenly one" (Heb 11:16). When Paul makes a distinction between **our outer self** and **our inner self** he is not simply referring to the division of the human person into body and soul.[1] The "outer self" denotes embodied human existence that is subject to aging, weakness, affliction, sickness, and ultimately physical death; in short, it is a synonym for human beings as "earthen vessels" (2 Cor 4:7). Paul does not deny that, from this perspective, he **is wasting away**. Nevertheless, he is not discouraged, because his "inner self" **is being renewed day by day**. The "inner self" refers to human existence that is transformed and strengthened by the indwelling of God's Spirit (Eph 3:16); it is equivalent to "the 'I' of Gal 2:20 who by faith has grasped the reality of new life in Christ."[2]

According to Paul, Christians are "being renewed day by day": What does this mean? Recall, from the analysis of 3:18, his teaching that the Holy Spirit transforms us more and more into the divine image after the likeness of Christ Jesus. Paul alludes to this same dynamic here. As the next verse and following passage (5:1–5) indicate, this transformation ultimately leads to the Spirit's work of raising our bodies to resurrected glory.

4:17   Paul goes on to compare **this momentary light affliction** with the **eternal weight of glory**. The reference to "affliction" echoes a key theme of the letter, namely, that God brings encouragement to us in our afflictions (1:3–4). Paul's description of present afflictions as "momentary" and "light" is striking. How can he say such a thing, especially after his vivid portrayal of his sufferings in the previous passage (4:7–15)? Indeed, when describing his affliction in Asia in 1:8, he said "we were utterly weighed down beyond our strength" (using the same expression, *kath' hyperbolēn*, that he now employs to help convey the "glory" **beyond all comparison**). Paul's point is that, compared with the wondrous glory that will be revealed to us, our present sufferings are as nothing (Rom 8:18). He does not negate the difficulty and pain of our hardships and afflictions; rather,

---

1. For a list of the different ways commentators have defined "outer self" and "inner self," see Margaret E. Thrall, *A Critical and Exegetical Commentary on the Second Epistle to the Corinthians*, ICC, 2 vols. (Edinburgh: T&T Clark, 1994–2000), 1:348–51.

2. Victor Paul Furnish, *II Corinthians: A New Translation with Introduction and Commentary*, AB 32A (New York: Doubleday, 1984), 289.

he relativizes them in light of what God has prepared for those who love him (1 Cor 2:9). These temporary afflictions, moreover, prepare us to experience the fullness of God's glory as they deepen our capacity for love, compassion, and self-sacrifice. That Paul refers here to the fullness of *future* glory is evident from his use of the adjective "eternal."[3] In addition, recall from the exegesis of 3:7–11 that he signaled there the future aspect of glory—"how much more will what endures be glorious" (3:11).

Paul makes explicit the vantage point from which he lives—**we look not**   **4:18**
to what is seen but to what is unseen. The verb translated "look" means "pay careful attention to" or "focus on." Paul's vision derives from faith. Through the eyes of faith he focuses on "what is unseen," such as the Spirit's transforming presence in human hearts and the exaltation of the Lord Jesus. His attention is on the "inner self" as well as on "what is above, where Christ is seated at the right hand of God" (Col 3:1). Paul knows well, as conveyed through the image of fragile earthen vessels, that **what is seen is transitory**, or temporary. He also believes that **what is unseen is eternal**, as was just noted in connection with divine "glory." His vision, therefore, is also characterized by hope.

In fact, Paul writes in Rom 8:24–25: "For in hope we are saved. Now hope that sees for itself is not hope. For who hopes for what one sees? But if we hope for what we do not see, we wait with endurance." As we will discover in the following passage, what he waits for is the glory of the resurrection. Like the farmer who labors strenuously because he keeps his eye focused on the expected harvest, Paul conducts himself as one whose destiny is to be raised up to heavenly glory.

Reflection and Application (4:16–18)

Proper perspective. One mark of wisdom is the ability to maintain proper perspective, to recognize what is truly important in life. Our contemporary culture suffers from an immature nearsightedness. Marketers and advertisers have done an effective job of leading people to think they have several "needs"—the need to have the latest and best technology, the most recent clothing fashions, and so on. The very speed at which things become outmoded and out of style dramatically illustrates Paul's point about the transitory quality of "what is seen." Christian wisdom recognizes that our present life is a pilgrimage to a heavenly homeland. The Apostle's teaching here can help us discern properly

---

3. See the sidebar on God's glory on p. 84. The Hebrew word for "glory," *kabod*, denotes both weightiness and importance, which Paul draws on here with the phrase "eternal weight of glory."

between what is truly needed for the journey and what, in actuality, diverts and encumbers us, such as "worldly anxiety, the lure of riches, and the craving for other things" (Mark 4:19).

Heeding the Spirit. Our lives are filled with many sounds. Some sounds are imposed on us—phones, traffic, sirens, construction projects, to name but a few. However, many people also routinely seek and invite constant noise into their lives, for instance, by unreflectively turning on entertainment devices immediately upon entering a room or a car and by constantly choosing to be at the beck and call of various means of communication.

When the prophet Elijah was invited to encounter God on Mount Horeb, he recognized the divine presence in "a tiny whispering sound" (1 Kings 19:12). Because love does not coerce, God moves gently within us. In order to mature in Christian wisdom, it is necessary to spend time in silence so that we can heed the divine presence in what Paul calls here the "inner self." Setting aside quiet time for prayer each day enables us to sense the holy desires that God's Spirit elicits within us and to keep the eyes of faith focused on "what is unseen." Silent retreats are a great aid in honing our ability to listen to God as well as to sharpen our spiritual focus. How am I attending to the transforming invitations of the Spirit within me? To my spiritual eyesight?

Resurrection Body (5:1–5)

---

¹For we know that if our earthly dwelling, a tent, should be destroyed, we have a building from God, a dwelling not made with hands, eternal in heaven. ²For in this tent we groan, longing to be further clothed with our heavenly habitation ³if indeed, when we have taken it off, we shall not be found naked. ⁴For while we are in this tent we groan and are weighed down, because we do not wish to be unclothed but to be further clothed, so that what is mortal may be swallowed up by life. ⁵Now the one who has prepared us for this very thing is God, who has given us the Spirit as a first installment.

OT: Dan 12:2–3; 2 Macc 7:9–14; 12:43–46
NT: Mark 12:18–27; Rom 8:11; 1 Cor 15; Phil 3:20–21
Catechism: Christ's resurrection and ours, 997–1004; Christian death, 1010–14

Paul's focus on things not seen leads him to a discussion of the resurrection of the body. He employs two metaphors—building and clothing—to express the Christian belief that God will bring his faithful people to share in the fullness

Resurrection in the Old Testament

The resurrection of the dead is not a frequent theme in the Old Testament. Several texts speak of Sheol, a gloomy and comfortless place in the underworld where the dead are separated from God and from all that is living (see Gen 37:35; 2 Sam 22:6; Job 7:9; Ps 6:6; 49:15). But God is portrayed as having power over Sheol (Job 12:22) and as delivering from Sheol (Ps 49:16). At the time of the exile, the prophets spoke of the return and restoration of God's people Israel in terms of resurrection (Ezek 37:13–14; see Isa 26:19). The first unambiguous declaration of belief in the resurrection—the raising of individuals, body and soul, from the dead—does not occur, however, until the second century BC (see Dan 12:2–3; 2 Macc 7:9–14; 12:43–46).

When confronted by the Sadducees, who did not believe in the resurrection, on the question of whether the dead are raised, Jesus responded that they did not understand the Scriptures. Jesus then interpreted God's self-revelation to Moses in Exod 3:6 ("I am the God of Abraham, the God of Isaac, the God of Jacob"—all of whom had died long ago) as evidence that the dead are raised (see Mark 12:18–27). After his death and resurrection, Jesus explained to the apostles all the Old Testament passages that pointed to him (Luke 24:44–47). In all likelihood, one of these was Ps 16:8–11, which Peter interpreted as a prophecy of Jesus' resurrection from the dead in Acts 2:22–32. Indeed, in light of Jesus' resurrection Christians now read passages like Ezek 37:13–14 ("when I open your graves and have you rise from them, O my people! I will put my spirit in you that you may live") as pointing to the future resurrection.

of Christ's resurrection. Paul reveals that the gift of the Spirit is God's pledge of our future glory.

Paul begins by discussing **our earthly dwelling**, a reference to our present embodied human existence that is subject to suffering, breakdown, and eventually death. "Our earthly dwelling" is a synonym of "earthen vessels" (4:7) and the "outer self" that is wasting away (4:16). He also tellingly refers to "our earthly dwelling" as **a tent**. It is important to appreciate that, as a tent maker (Acts 18:3), Paul knew firsthand that "tent" is an apt metaphor for human existence as nomadic, precarious, and always on the move—thereby evoking the notion of pilgrimage.[4] The tent metaphor calls to mind Isaiah's vivid description of human life being "struck down and borne away" (Isa 38:12; see 2 Pet 1:13–14).

5:1

4. See Murray J. Harris, *Second Epistle to the Corinthians*, NIGTC (Grand Rapids: Eerdmans, 2005), 370.

Indeed, Paul acknowledges that when we die our bodies—our "earthly dwell-ing" or "tent"—will **be destroyed**.

Nevertheless, he does not despair, because **we have a building from God**. That is, God is preparing for us a glorious resurrection body that is not subject to death and decay, as indicated by the image of a building, which is much more substantial and permanent than a tent. Paul describes this "building" as **a dwelling not made with hands**. This phrase echoes the words Jesus used to point to his own resurrected existence in the new creation (John 2:19). As Paul observes elsewhere, the risen Jesus is the "firstfruits" of the resurrection (1 Cor 15:20), of the life that is **eternal in heaven**.

5:2   Paul states that, while **in this tent**, human beings **groan**. Although the Greek verb can convey a sense of discontent (e.g., "groan against"), here it has a more positive connotation. That is, despite our present sufferings and hardships, our groaning expresses hopeful longing for the fullness of redemption (see Rom 8:18–25). In fact, Paul makes clear that our **longing** is **to be further clothed with our heavenly habitation**. Notice that he now introduces a second meta-phor, the metaphor of putting clothes over a body. In an earlier letter to the Corinthians he employed the clothing metaphor to describe the resurrection of the dead: "For this which is corruptible must clothe itself with incorruptibility, and this which is mortal must clothe itself with immortality" (1 Cor 15:53). Although Paul's mixing of metaphors creates a clumsy image—being clothed with a habitation!—it makes two important points. First, the phrase "heavenly habitation" picks up from the previous verse the imagery of "a dwelling not made with hands," signifying the glorious resurrection body. Second, Paul ap-peals here to a deep human instinct that is manifested in the action of clothing ourselves. The act of putting clothes over our bodies expresses a deep longing that we have as human beings—the longing to share in a fuller, more glorious life than our present mortal existence.[5]

5:3   Verse 3 presents a difficulty, for two reasons. First, while some Greek manu-scripts have the verb *ekdysamenoi* ("unclothed"; "stripped"), others have the verb *endysamenoi* ("clothed"). These two words differ only in their second let-ter. The NAB chooses the first option—**when we have taken it off**. The other option, however, has better textual attestation. Hence a preferable translation of verse 3 is: "(if indeed when we are clothed, we shall not be found naked)" (my translation, including parentheses).[6] What does Paul mean by this? The key

---

5. See N. T. Wright, *Paul for Everyone: 2 Corinthians* (Louisville: Westminster John Knox, 2004), 54.

6. The RSV and NIV translate *endysamenoi* ("clothed").

is determining the correct meaning of the expression **we shall not be found naked**. The thrust of his presentation suggests that it is best to interpret being "found naked" as "overcome by death."[7] Paul contrasts the image of being clothed (having a resurrection body for eternity) with being naked (remaining in a permanent state of death).

But now the second difficulty emerges. Why does Paul say "*if* indeed we are clothed . . ."? It is best to take the conditional "if" as a real condition, as something that will in fact happen. Verse 3 is thus a parenthetical comment, as Paul reinforces why he groans in hope (v. 2). While acknowledging that the "earthen vessel" will inevitably be shattered, he also insists that death will not have the final say, because God will clothe those who respond favorably to the †gospel with a glorified body (see Phil 3:20–21). The Catholic Funeral Mass captures well the teaching here: "Lord, for your faithful people life is changed, not ended" (Preface, Christian Death 1).

Paul then reiterates what he expressed in verse 2. He repeats that **while we are in this tent** and **are weighed down**—while we live in the present with our various burdens and sufferings—**we groan**. Paul now conveys the object of this groaning in both negative and positive terms. Negatively, **we do not wish to be unclothed**, that is, we do not want to be overcome by death once and for all. Positively, we long **to be further clothed**, to receive the fullness of life in the resurrection from the dead.

5:4

Paul then expresses the purpose of our groaning—**that what is mortal may be swallowed up by life**. That is, our groan is actually a prayer (see Rom 8:26–27), for it is directed to God, who alone can bring the dead to life. Although God has not been explicitly named as the subject of any verbs in verses 1–4, he has been present throughout the passage. God is the one who brings into being what is "not made with hands" (v. 1). Moreover, God is the implied subject of the action of clothing further (vv. 2, 4). Now, at the end of our verse here, God is the one who makes what is mortal have eternal life. Indeed, throughout his extended explanation for his way of being an †apostle (beginning in 2:14), Paul has alluded to God's action, through the Spirit's empowerment, of transforming us into the divine image as revealed by Jesus (2:14–15; 3:3, 18; 4:4, 6, 14). The process of "Christification," of causing us to take on Jesus' character and way of living, will not be complete, however, until God fully "clothes" us with

---

7. As suggested by Frank J. Matera, *II Corinthians: A Commentary*, NTL (Louisville: Westminster John Knox, 2003), 122. I follow Matera's reading of the entire verse. The term "naked" is often used in Scripture as a metaphor of shame—e.g., Gen 3:10; Isa 32:11; Ezek 16:39; 23:29; Hosea 2:5. But Paul's concern in our passage here is different.

Benedict XVI on "Faith-Based Hope"

LIVING TRADITION

In his 2007 encyclical *Spe Salvi* (*Saved in Hope*), Pope Benedict XVI observed that a distinguishing mark of Christians is "the fact that they have a future" (2). Commenting on the concept of faith-based hope in the New Testament and drawing on the work of St. Thomas Aquinas, he taught that through faith "there are already present in us the things for which we hope: the whole, true life" (7). That is, faith-based hope does not consist merely in reaching out for things not possessed; rather, it also "gives us even now something of the reality for which we are waiting" (7). In Christ, God "has already communicated to us the 'substance' of things to come" (9). Benedict's teaching on faith-based hope complements the point Paul makes in 2 Cor 5:5, concerning God's gift of the Spirit as "a first installment" of the fullness of life to come. That is, we groan with hope-filled longing because we *already* possess the Spirit. Indeed, according to Paul, it is the Spirit who intercedes for us "with inexpressible groanings" (Rom 8:26).

a glorious resurrection body. It is then that we will most closely resemble the risen and glorified Christ.[8]

5:5   This interpretation is confirmed as Paul explicitly names **God** as the subject: he is **the one who has prepared us for this very thing**. The phrase "this very thing" refers to being clothed with a resurrection body. God—who has already been named as "God who raises the dead" (1:9) and as "the one who raised the Lord Jesus" (4:14)—has prepared us through our suffering (4:17), as well as through his gift of **the Spirit** within us. Paul describes this bestowal of the Spirit as **a first installment**. He has already employed this term at the end of his description of the Spirit's activity in 1:21–22. But while the emphasis there was on the Spirit's having already "anointed" and "sealed" us to walk in the way of Jesus' faithfulness, the focus here is on the Spirit's *future* work of transformation. As Paul says elsewhere, "If the Spirit of the one who raised Jesus from the dead dwells in you, the one who raised Christ from the dead will give life to your mortal bodies also, through his Spirit that dwells in you" (Rom 8:11). In other words, the gift of the Spirit, who already empowers us to take on Jesus' loving and self-giving way of life, is God's pledge of an *even more* glorious transformation, namely, raising us from the dead with a glori-

8. See Murray J. Harris, who reads the end of v. 4 in a similar manner (*Second Epistle to the Corinthians*, 360). The expression "Christification" is his.

ous resurrected body.[9] The metaphor of "first installment" teaches us that God will not hold back in "paying" the rest. No wonder the Apostle declares that he is not discouraged (4:16) and, in a moment, proclaims that he is "always courageous" (5:6)!

Reflection and Application (5:1–5)

"*We believe in the resurrection of the body and life everlasting.*" Both the Nicene and Apostles' Creeds culminate in this proclamation. Belief in the resurrection of the dead and in everlasting life is thus an essential element of our faith.[10]

The how and when of resurrection. Second Corinthians 5:1–5 can be supplemented by other passages in which Paul discusses death and the resurrection of the body in order to fill out the picture of his teaching on these subjects. In 1 Thess 4:13–18 and 1 Cor 15:51–55, he makes clear that it is at the parousia, at Jesus' coming again in glory at the end of time, that the dead will be raised. Nevertheless, Paul was also convinced that at his death he would "be with Christ" (Phil 1:23). What the Apostle leaves unstated is what happens between one's death and the resurrection on the last day. The Catholic Church teaches that at the moment of death the soul is separated from the body. Although the body is subject to decay, the soul goes to meet God. Moreover, at the appointed time, "God, in his almighty power, will definitively grant incorruptible life to our bodies by reuniting them with our souls, through the power of Jesus' Resurrection" (Catechism, 997).

The dignity of the body. The belief in the resurrection of the body has ramifications for the present. Christianity does not despise the body; it does not, for instance, consider it a "prison of the soul," as in Platonism. To the contrary, the Church upholds the dignity of the body. By virtue of our baptism and our participation in other sacraments, Christians belong—body and soul—to the body of Christ. Indeed, Paul reminded the Corinthians of this in a prior letter: "Do you not know that your bodies are members of Christ?" (1 Cor 6:15). In addition, Paul taught them that "your body is a temple of the holy Spirit within you" (6:19) and that the appropriate response to these awesome gifts is to "glorify God in your body" (6:20). We glorify God by treating our own bodies, and the bodies of others, with great respect. Such respect should influence the way we eat and drink, care for ourselves, and relate to others. It should also affect the

---

9. Indeed, Paul speaks of this body as a "spiritual body" (1 Cor 15:44), as fully transformed by God's Spirit.

10. I refer the reader to the first entry under Reflection and Application (1:8–11) for comments on the importance of the hope generated by this belief.

way we extend care to those who suffer from infirmities and the lack of necessary bodily needs, such as clothing, food, and shelter (see Matt 25:31–46).

Preparing for the Heavenly Home (5:6–10)

**⁶So we are always courageous, although we know that while we are at
home in the body we are away from the Lord, ⁷for we walk by faith, not
by sight. ⁸Yet we are courageous, and we would rather leave the body and
go home to the Lord. ⁹Therefore, we aspire to please him, whether we are
at home or away. ¹⁰For we must all appear before the judgment seat of
Christ, so that each one may receive recompense, according to what he did
in the body, whether good or evil.**

OT: Ps 50:1–6
NT: Matt 25:31–46; Rom 14:10–12; Phil 1:20–26; 3:12–16; Col 1:9–12
Catechism: particular judgment (following death), 1021–22; Last judgment, 1038–41
Lectionary: Mass for the Dead

Paul's teaching on the resurrection leads him to resume his confession of confidence and trust in God. He explains how he conducts himself, as "an †apostle
of Christ Jesus by the will of God" (1:1), in the present life on the journey to
his true "home" in heaven. Conduct pleasing to God is necessary, because all
of us will appear "before the judgment seat of Christ."

5:6   Paul once again emphasizes that he is **always courageous** (see 4:1; 4:16).
Even though he is presently **at home in the body**—in an "earthen vessel" (4:7),
a tent-like "earthly dwelling" (5:1) that "is wasting away" (4:16)—he presses on
in his apostolic way of life that is patterned after the self-giving love of Jesus.
He does so because of his faith and hope in the resurrection. At first glance,
Paul's statement that he is, here and now, **away from the Lord** is surprising.
Has he not insisted all along that God's Spirit is within him? And does he not
write elsewhere of Christ dwelling in him (see Gal 2:20)? To be sure, Paul is not
denying the divine presence within him. His point is that, in our present lives,
we have not yet entered into the heavenly, glorious presence of God where the
Lord Jesus is exalted (see 2 Cor 4:14; Phil 2:9–11). Now our lives are "hidden
with Christ" (Col 3:3). Although Jesus is truly present to us, we still await the
full realization of the promises we have received.

5:7   Paul explains the appropriate way to live for those presently "at home in the
body": we are to **walk by faith**. The verb translated "walk" refers broadly to

the conduct of one's life; hence it can aptly be rendered "behave," even "live." The verb also evokes the connotation of being on pilgrimage.[11] We are to live in this life by means of "faith." Paul has already made clear what this means in 4:13. To live by faith entails both trusting in God and conducting oneself after the manner of Jesus' "yes" to God, that is, in self-giving love. Paul adds emphasis to the phrase "by faith" by placing it in the prominent first position in the Greek text. The opposite of faithful existence is living **by sight**, that is, "by appearance." Paul thus reiterates what he said in 4:18, namely, that Christians are to keep their focus on what is unseen, for example, the "inner self" and the exalted Lord Jesus, rather than on what is visible and transitory.

What is visible is often very misleading, for instance, that Paul seems to be of no account, that the church in Corinth is tiny and fragile. Another nuance, as we will see in 5:13, is that, in relating to other people, we are to value what is in their hearts rather than their external appearances.

The NAB's rendering of the beginning of verse 8—**Yet we are courageous**— **5:8–9**
suggests a contrast with verse 7. However, the particle translated "yet" serves to pick up the thought from verse 6. A better translation is "Indeed, we are courageous."[12] Paul continues to confess his God-given courage to persevere in his labors despite suffering and hardship. He then reverses the "home" and "away" imagery from verse 6. That is, Paul recognizes that our true home, the place where we were created to belong, is actually in the presence of the Father and his risen Son (4:14). Therefore he now expresses his desire to **leave the body and go home to the Lord**. Nevertheless, because it is not up to him when he will pass on from this life, he sets forth in verse 9 his fundamental attitude in the here and now: **we aspire to please him**. The verb translated "aspire" is particularly strong; it denotes having much zeal and eagerness. Paul eagerly aspires to do everything that is according to the divine will. The expression **whether we are at home or away** conveys, with rhetorical flourish, his powerful desire to please God in *all* things.[13]

Finally, Paul offers a crucial reason why it is important to "walk by faith" **5:10**
and to seek constantly to "please" the Lord: **For we must all appear before the judgment seat of Christ**. The word for "judgment seat" (*bēma*) refers to a raised platform on which a magistrate was seated to hear cases and pronounce judgment. In fact, Paul himself had appeared before such a judgment seat dur-

---

11. See Harris, *Second Epistle to the Corinthians*, 396.
12. See the NRSV: "Yes, we do have confidence"; see also the NIV.
13. That is, Paul is not suggesting here that moral choice still exists after death. The theme of pleasing God appears throughout the Apostle's writings (e.g., Rom 12:1–2; 14:18; 1 Cor 7:32; Col 1:10; 1 Thess 4:1).

Fig. 7. The place of judgment, or the *bēma*, where Paul appeared before the proconsul Gallio in Corinth.

ing his first stay in Corinth. He had been charged with contravening Roman law, a charge that the proconsul Gallio summarily dismissed (Acts 18:12–17). In the present passage, Paul speaks of the heavenly judgment seat, where the exalted Christ is seated in judgment.[14] He reveals that judgment has universal and particular aspects. It is universal in the sense that *everyone* will be judged; it is particular in the sense that *each individual* will be judged **according to what he did in the body, whether good or evil**. Observe that, once more, Paul emphasizes the importance of embodied human existence. Bodily human existence is the arena of all moral activity, and God's judgment of each person will be based on what he or she has done in this arena.

Reflection and Application (5:6–10)

Preaching about God's and Christ's judgment. It is rare to hear a homily today about divine judgment—about either the judgment that immediately follows

14. At times Paul speaks of Christ as judge (e.g., 1 Cor 4:4); at other times of God as judge (e.g., Rom 14:10); at still other times of God judging *through* Christ (e.g., Rom 2:16).

The Catechism on Death and Judgment

The Catechism teaches that, immediately following death, each person will receive eternal retribution in his or her immortal *soul*—either "the blessedness of heaven" or "everlasting damnation" (1022) in accordance with his or her "works and faith" (1021). This judgment is alluded to in the parable of the rich man and Lazarus (Luke 16:19–31) and in Jesus' words from the cross to the repentant criminal: "Amen, I say to you, today you will be with me in Paradise" (Luke 23:43).

The Catechism also sets forth the Church's teaching on the *last*, or final, judgment. Paul's teaching about judgment in 2 Cor 5:10—with both its particular and universal aspects—refers to this judgment. The last judgment will follow upon Christ's glorious second coming, when all the dead will be bodily raised (1038). In the presence of Christ, "the truth of each" person's "relationship with God will be laid bare," revealing "the good each person has done or failed to do" during his or her earthly life (1039; cf. John 12:49). The saved will then be separated from the damned (see Matt 25:31–46). The last judgment will make manifest that "God's justice triumphs over all the injustices committed by his creatures and that God's love is stronger than death" (1040; cf. Song 8:6).

one's death or the last judgment that will mark the consummation of human history (see the sidebar). In part this absence is an understandable reaction to the overemphasized and distasteful "fire and brimstone" approach to preaching. While such preaching has biblical foundations, it frequently distorts God's concern for justice by downplaying his love and mercy. Indeed, it is crucially important *not* to present God as punitive and vindictive, because he is always ready to extend mercy to the repentant sinner (Luke 15:11–32) and derives no pleasure in the death of the wicked (Ezek 18:23).

Nevertheless, to fail to preach about judgment when the occasion is appropriate (e.g., at the end of the Church's liturgical year) is to err in the opposite direction. As we will see in the next chapter, Paul speaks of a salutary "fear of the Lord." His teaching in 2 Cor 5:10 makes clear that each one of us will have to give an account of our lives to Christ. This reality ought to motivate us to commit ourselves more zealously, each day, to follow in the ways set forth by Jesus. It can also serve as a beneficial warning when we are tempted to choose the pathway of sin.

Preparing for death. Back in the fifteenth century, in the wake of the bubonic plague and wars that produced unthinkable carnage throughout Europe, there arose a body of Christian literature called the *Ars Moriendi* ("Art of Dying"). All too aware of the fragility of human existence and the prospect of individual judgment, these writings prepared people in their final days for a good death. In our own times the outbreak of epidemics (e.g., AIDS and viral influenzas); the massive destruction wrought by natural disasters; and the escalation of violence, terrorism, and warfare are all dramatic reminders of the vulnerability of human existence. Paul's vision of Christian living is as timely now as ever: the best way to prepare for a good death is to lead lives of faithfulness and integrity, after the manner of Jesus. The Apostle's energetic response to Christ's call exemplifies the wisdom of living each day as if it were one's last. The point is not to inculcate a feverish pace of life, but to live in such a way that we would be happy to offer this day to God as our *final* offering were our lives to be suddenly taken away.

The relationship between faith and works. Paul's statement that works provide the criteria for judgment seems to be in tension with his teaching that human beings are brought into right relationship with God and are saved *through faith* (e.g., Gal 2:16; Rom 10:9–10). The tension, however, is more apparent than real. A careful reading of Romans and Galatians reveals that God has redeemed us *through the faithfulness of* †*Messiah Jesus*—the faithfulness that culminated in giving his life on the cross. God's offer of salvation, then, must be received in faith. This human response of faith, which itself is possible only through †grace, entails not only believing in what God has accomplished through the sending of his Son but also what Paul describes in Gal 5:6 as "faith *working* through love," that is, faith expressing itself through acts of love. Indeed, Paul uses the striking expression "the work of faith" (1 Thess 1:3). He is thus in complete agreement with the teaching of James that faith is useless without works; instead, faith is completed and fully expressed by works (James 2:14–26). The apparent tension in Paul's writings concerning the role of faith and works is resolved when we understand that, according to him, although we are saved by faith, we are judged by our works.

Christ's Compelling Love and God's Gift of Reconciliation

2 Corinthians 5:11–21

Having explained the role that suffering plays in his ministry as well as his hope in the resurrection, Paul moves on to the third section of his lengthy discourse on apostleship (5:11–6:10), as he continues to describe to the Corinthians how God has called him to minister. He explains that the †new covenant ministry entails the ministry of reconciliation. After setting forth the implications of a proper "fear of the Lord" (vv. 11–13), Paul discusses the compelling love of Christ Jesus and the far-reaching implications of his death and resurrection (vv. 14–17). One of these implications is God's gift of reconciliation (vv. 18–21).

"Fear of the Lord" and Apostolic Integrity (5:11–13)

---

¹¹Therefore, since we know the fear of the Lord, we try to persuade others; but we are clearly apparent to God, and I hope we are also apparent to your consciousness. ¹²We are not commending ourselves to you again but giving you an opportunity to boast of us, so that you may have something to say to those who boast of external appearance rather than of the heart. ¹³For if we are out of our minds, it is for God; if we are rational, it is for you.

OT: Deut 4:9–14; 1 Sam 16:1–13; Ps 34:12–16
NT: Matt 5:8; Luke 6:43–45; Acts 9:31; 1 Thess 2:1–12; Rev 14:6–7

Once again Paul offers a defense of his apostolic integrity as he reiterates themes from the letter's opening statement (1:12–14). He exhorts the Corinthians

"Fear of the Lord" in the Old Testament

BIBLICAL BACKGROUND

While God's presence and impending judgment should evoke dread and terror among those who turn from his way (e.g., Gen 3:10; Jer 5:22), "fear of the Lord" most often refers, in the Old Testament, to proper worship and conduct before God. Fundamentally, fear of the Lord conveys awe and reverence before God's holiness and might, as described, for example, in Exod 19:16–19 and Deut 4:9–12. The Wisdom literature insists that fear of the Lord be translated into an entire way of life: keeping God's law (Sir 21:11) and all the commandments (Eccles 12:13); pursuing truth, justice, and peace (Ps 34:12–16); making friends with righteous people (Sir 9:16); spurning the company of the proud (Sir 19:20); and hating the way of evil (Prov 8:13). Understood thus, fear of the Lord is truly the beginning of wisdom (Sir 1:12) and knowledge (Prov 1:7). The way of life to which it leads produces great joy (Ps 34:13). Scripture thus reveals that the element of *fear* involved in fear of the Lord refers to the horror of displeasing God, not because of the threat of punishment, but out of love and reverence for him.

to judge not by appearances but by character. He also alludes to differences between himself and the intruding missionaries.

5:11   The opening word, **Therefore**, links this passage with the preceding verse. Recall that Paul has just referred to appearing "before the judgment seat of Christ" (5:10). He now explains how this reality motivates him. The prospect of judgment evokes in him **the fear of the Lord**. What is meant by this phrase? Paul is alluding here to the sense of reverence and awe that the glorious risen Jesus stirs within him. This reverential awe spurs him to commit himself wholeheartedly to the service of proclaiming to others what God has done through Jesus—**we try to persuade others**. As we have seen throughout the letter, Paul's strategy of persuasion involves more than verbal proclamation; it also entails his *manner* of living out his call to be an †apostle. He twice employs the verb "be apparent" at the end of verse 11. This is the same Greek root used in 2:14; 4:2; and 4:10–11, where he indicated how he demonstrates the †gospel through a self-giving way of life patterned after that of Christ. He insists that his ways are **clearly apparent to God**, that is, he conducts himself with the awareness that he is in the presence of God (see 2:17). Moreover, Paul expresses his **hope** that his apostolic conduct is **apparent** to the conscience[1] of every member of

---

1. The NAB renders *syneidēsis* as "consciousness" here. As it is in 1:12 and 4:2, this word should be translated "conscience" (as in the RSV, NRSV, NJB, and NIV).

the Corinthian church (see 4:2). Whereas he appealed to his own conscience in 1:12, he now appeals to the Corinthians' consciences. His hope is that their inner tribunal will attest to the authenticity of his manner of making Christ known (2:14). Paul comports himself with transparency, offering himself as an example for others to follow (1 Cor 11:1). In doing so, he reminds all who are called to proclaim the gospel to be mindful that in the eyes of their congregations their behavior speaks about Jesus. He also reminds *all* Christians that *all* our actions bear witness to Christ.

Paul quickly denies that he is **commending** himself (in the negative sense of †*self*-commendation that focuses on one's own accomplishments and glory; see 3:1).[2] His purpose in referring to his apostolic conduct is to give the Corinthians **an opportunity to boast of** him. This echoes Paul's statement in 1:14 that he seeks to be their "boast." Recall that, for him, †boasting has both a positive and a negative sense. In the first part of verse 12 Paul uses the word in a positive sense. Since he is faithful to God's way, the Corinthians can "boast" of him, because in doing so they are really giving praise to God, whose power is at work in him. In the second part of the verse, Paul refers to boasting in the negative sense, that is, self-promotion. Here he alludes to the intruding missionaries (see 2:17–3:1; 4:2), **those who boast of external appearance rather than of the heart**.

5:12

Paul's meaning is illuminated by the story of the prophet Samuel and the sons of Jesse (1 Sam 16:1–13). God sent Samuel to Bethlehem to anoint one of Jesse's sons as king. Impressed by the appearance and stature of the oldest son, Eliab, Samuel presumed that he must be God's chosen one. However, God revealed to Samuel that he was mistaken: "Not as man sees does God see, because man sees the appearance but the LORD looks into the heart" (16:7). Samuel was then led to anoint Jesse's youngest son, David.

Returning to our passage, Paul intimates that the missionaries who arrived in Corinth placed much stock in externals. As we will see, they valued impressive physical appearance and eloquence (2 Cor 10:10), as well as distinguished lineage, heroic exploits, and dramatic religious experiences (11:22–12:10). Paul, on the contrary, asserts that the heart is what is important, that one's *character* is what matters most in the eyes of God. Indeed, the heart is where God has placed his Spirit within us (1:22; 3:3), the Spirit who empowers us to take on the character of Jesus. Hence Paul desires that the Corinthians value his loving, humble, self-giving ways so that they can reject the false values of the intruding missionaries.

2. See the sidebar "Paul's Use of Self-Commendation in 2 Corinthians" on p. 77.

The issue of the missionaries' boasting provides the background for interpreting verse 13. When Paul says **if we are out of our minds**, he likely refers to ecstatic religious experiences, such as receiving special visions (12:1–6). Apparently the intruding missionaries boasted of having such experiences and, moreover, criticized Paul for not having them. The Apostle intimates that he *has* had ecstatic experiences. These experiences, however, are special gifts from God and are only for the benefit of the one to whom they are given (see 12:4). As such, they ought not to be a source of bragging to others, as the intruders have made them. Paul informs the Corinthians that when he ministers to them he communicates God's word in a **rational** manner, in ways that can be clearly understood, so that it is *they* who benefit (1:13–14): **it is for you**. Such "rational" communication appeals to human intelligence in a way that makes sense to people.

Reflection and Application (5:11–13)

Proper fear of the Lord. Paul illustrates well how fear of the Lord serves as a basis for Christian living. In doing so, he avoids two pitfalls. One pitfall is a scrupulosity that is so afraid of offending God that life becomes burdensome and joyless. Another pitfall is a laissez-faire attitude that overlooks God's demands and casually presumes upon his mercy. Paul knew well the mercy of the Lord (see 4:1), but he also recognized that he would have to give an account of himself before the heavenly tribunal. Proper fear of the Lord entails placing ourselves each day in reverent awe before God, in whose presence we always are. This reverent awe should then energize and inform all our decisions and actions as we strive to please God in all things. The flip side of such striving to please such a loving and generous God is that we want to avoid offending him.

The danger of valuing appearance. A long-running ad campaign for a popular camera employed the slogan "Image is everything." The importance of image in our culture cannot be overstated. It is sobering to realize how much money is spent on trying to project a certain appearance. While young people are particularly susceptible to the "need" to have the right image, advertisers know only too well that the appeal to appearance works with people of all ages. We are constantly encouraged to drive the best car or have the elite credit card or belong to the right group—all geared toward projecting an air of success. People too easily allow themselves to become enslaved to obtaining markers of popularity and success, markers that are, in reality, shallow and hollow.

Other, more subtle, forms of this dynamic also exist. For instance, the anxious concern behind the question "How will this course of action look to others?"

can lead us to compromise our values in the face of difficult decisions. Paul's teaching in verses 11–13 challenges us to reflect on whether we have our priorities straight. He reminds us that life in the Spirit and the development of a Christlike character are of true value in winning others over to Christ and attaining eternal life.

Christ's Compelling Love (5:14–17)

¹⁴For the love of Christ impels us, once we have come to the conviction that one died for all; therefore, all have died. ¹⁵He indeed died for all, so that those who live might no longer live for themselves but for him who for their sake died and was raised.

¹⁶Consequently, from now on we regard no one according to the flesh; even if we once knew Christ according to the flesh, yet now we know him so no longer. ¹⁷So whoever is in Christ is a new creation: the old things have passed away; behold, new things have come.

OT: Gen 1–2; Isa 42:9; 43:18–19
NT: Mark 10:42–45; Rom 5:1–6:11; 1 Cor 8:11; Gal 6:14–15
Catechism: Christ's redemptive death, 601–5; Christ's unique sacrifice, 613–17; baptism, 1265–70

Paul declares that his ministry is energized and directed by Jesus' love, the love made manifest by his death on the cross. After explaining the universal implications of Jesus' death, Paul sets forth two consequences for those who are "in Christ."

Having raised the issue of his apostolic conduct in verses 11–13, Paul now   **5:14** identifies its ultimate source of power: **the love of Christ**. While the phrase "the love of Christ" could signify Paul's love for Jesus, most exegetes agree that it refers here to Christ's love for him—and, by extension, for us. Jesus' love is such that it *compels*[3] or drives Paul to proclaim the †gospel. In addition, because the Greek verb also has the connotation of "control" or "direct," he suggests that Christ's love likewise "'controls' or 'directs' all that he does, even if his behavior may appear to be abnormal to others."[4]

Paul refers to the most dramatic expression of Jesus' love—**one died for all** (see Gal 2:20; Eph 5:2).[5] This compact statement requires unpacking. First,

3. As aptly translated by the NIV.
4. Frank J. Matera, *II Corinthians: A Commentary*, NTL (Louisville: Westminster John Knox, 2003), 135. The RSV and REB render *synechō* as "control."
5. Paul also insists that Jesus' death is an expression of *God's* love for us. See Rom 5:6–8; 8:31–39.

observe that Christ's death is for all. Jesus willingly gave up his life in love for each and every person, even those who least deserve it, for God desires that all people be saved (1 Tim 2:4). Second, the meaning of the preposition translated "for" is inherently rich. Elsewhere Paul proclaims that Jesus died, or gave himself, "*for* the ungodly" (Rom 5:6), "*for* our sins" (1 Cor 15:3; Gal 1:4), and, most typically, "*for* us" (e.g., Rom 5:8; 1 Thess 5:10).

But what precisely does it mean that Christ died *for* us? Jesus' death was *substitutionary* in the sense that he died "in the place of" sinful humanity. Although he remained sinless, Jesus joined himself in solidarity with us in the human condition and bore the punishment we merited because of our sins (see Gal 3:13). It is in this sense that Paul describes Christ's death as sacrificial, or †expiatory (Rom 3:25; see also Rom 8:3; 1 Cor 5:7); in fact, he will do so in the very next passage (5:21). Moreover, he understands Jesus as a *representative* figure, as one who died "on behalf of" or "for the sake of" humanity. That is, Christ—the †new Adam, whose entire life was marked by obedience to God's will unto death (Rom 5:15–19; Phil 2:8)—is the head of the whole human race. In a mysterious way, what happened to him affects all, just as the first Adam's sin affected all.

At the end of verse 14, Paul sets forth a †soteriological implication of Jesus' redemptive death: **therefore, all have died**. What does he mean by this provocative statement? Wouldn't we expect him to say that because Christ died in the place of sinful humanity therefore all now *live*? Paul's statement "all have died" has deeply perplexed commentators. He seems to be expressing two things: first, that Jesus' death has universal significance ("all"); second, that everyone is *potentially* dead in the sense that Christ's death has brought about the possibility of dying to oneself and receiving the gift of new life.

However, while offered to everyone, this gift of salvation must be received and appropriated in faith. Paul teaches that this gift is first received in baptism (Rom 6:1–11). In baptism we are baptized into Christ's death (Rom 6:3–4); "our old self was crucified with him" (Rom 6:6) so that we are now "dead to sin" (Rom 6:11). Jesus' death has thus created a new possibility for human beings, the possibility of being freed from the enslaving and death-dealing power of sin unleashed by the first Adam's sin (Rom 5:12–14). By being incorporated into the risen Christ as the new Adam, we have died to self, to all the attachments and self-seeking that are deeply rooted in our fallen nature. Such things no longer have power over us. Instead, we now live for Christ, as the next verse makes clear.

5:15   Paul repeats the central claim of the previous verse: **He** (Christ Jesus) **indeed died for all**. The Apostle then explains that Christ died for a particular purpose.

The Impact of 2 Corinthians 5:15 on St. Augustine

LIVING TRADITION

After his baptism and conversion, St. Augustine desired to live a quiet life of Christian contemplation. However, the bishop of Hippo, recognizing the new convert's enormous gifts and abilities, called him to ordination so that he could serve the people as a priest. Recalling this moment later in life, Augustine acknowledged that he was seized with great fear as he thought of his past sins. This fear tempted him to avoid ordination by fleeing to the desert. But then Augustine wrote that God "prohibited me from doing so and confirmed me in strength" (*Confessions* 10.43.70). In fact, God confirmed him through the very words of 2 Cor 5:15. As Pope Benedict XVI commented, Augustine came to appreciate that living for Christ "means allowing oneself to be drawn into" Jesus' way of "being for others" (*Spe Salvi* 28). Augustine's tireless expenditure of energy as theologian and pastor (he became bishop of Hippo five years later) bears eloquent testimony to his desire to live for the one who died and was raised for him.

Expressed negatively, Jesus died **so that those who live might no longer live for themselves**. Here we learn how Paul understands human existence under the enslavement of sin: it is marked by egocentrism and self-seeking. The good news is that Christ died so that we would now live **for him**. In other words, to be truly free is to live for him whom Paul refers to here as the one who **died and was raised** for us.

What does it mean to "live for" the crucified and risen Christ? Living for Christ means, in the first place, to commit our lives wholeheartedly to his service. Even more, because we have been incorporated into Christ through baptism, it means living as Jesus, the new Adam, lived—in faithful obedience to God and in giving himself in love for others. Elsewhere Paul describes this self-giving love as "not seeking my own benefit but that of the many" (1 Cor 10:33) and as striving to "please our neighbor for the good, for building up" (Rom 15:2). Indeed, he insists throughout his writings that love for Christ cannot be separated from loving and serving the members of his body (e.g., Rom 14:1–15:13). Notice how Paul marks out a circle of love: Jesus' love, revealed most powerfully in his dying for us, has created the possibility of our walking in the way of self-giving love for the sake of others, and it is through such loving service to others that we express our love for him.

Paul spells out two specific consequences of Jesus' compelling love, indicated by the words **consequently** and **so** at the beginning of verses 16 and 17. The first consequence is the transformation of our knowledge, especially as it pertains to how we evaluate other people. Paul states that **from now on**—in the new age inaugurated by Christ's death and resurrection that is actualized for us at the moment of our baptism—we are to **regard no one according to the flesh**. The phrase "according to the †flesh," as we saw in 1:17, denotes activity that lacks the inspiration and empowerment of God. To regard others in a fleshly way is to look at them from a merely human perspective or, worse, through lenses scratched and distorted by selfishness and falsehood.

Paul then alludes to the time when he **knew Christ according to the flesh**. This statement has led to much speculation, as scholars have asked whether Paul had met Jesus during his earthly ministry. However, "according to the flesh" is adverbial, modifying the verb "knew," not adjectival, modifying Christ.[6] That is, Paul refers to how, in his days as a †Pharisee zealous for the Jewish law, he regarded Jesus as a troublemaker, as one who played fast and loose with the law and whose end was an accursed death (Gal 3:13; see Deut 21:23). But in light of his encounter with the risen Jesus, Paul no longer regards him in this manner.

How can the transformation of knowledge referred to in verse 16 be expressed positively? We can start with Paul's experience of seeing the risen Lord (1 Cor 9:1; see Acts 9:3–6; 22:6–11; 26:12–18). Upon perceiving the glorified Jesus, Paul could **no longer** regard him as a cursed lawbreaker; rather, he came to recognize Jesus as the †Messiah and Lord. Moreover, the risen Jesus' words to him—"Saul, Saul, why are you persecuting *me*?"—showed Paul that Christ identifies himself with the members of the Church, whom Paul was persecuting as heretics. This led him to recognize that Christians are members of the body of Christ (Rom 12:3–8; 1 Cor 12:12–27). Paul also came to see that Jesus has formed a new family (Mark 3:31–35). Thus he now regards his coworkers and those to whom he ministers as his brothers and sisters. Distinctions that in the "old" age divided people—such as ethnicity, economic standing, gender—have now been relativized for those who "belong to Christ" (Gal 3:28; Col 3:11). Fundamentally, Paul has come to view every person as one "for whom Christ died"[7] (Rom 14:15; 1 Cor 8:11), as having an unspeakable and inviolable value. Therefore the transformed knowledge of others is an essential feature

---

6. Paul consistently employs the phrase *kata sarka* adverbially in 2 Corinthians. See 1:17; 10:2, 3; 11:18.

7. See J. Paul Sampley, "Second Letter to the Corinthians: Introduction, Commentary, and Reflections," in *The New Interpreter's Bible: A Commentary in Twelve Volumes*, ed. L. E. Keck et al. (Nashville: Abingdon, 2000), 11:98.

of walking by faith and not by appearance (2 Cor 5:7) and of valuing what is in the heart (5:12).

Paul describes a second, more overarching, consequence of Christ's compelling love: **So whoever is in Christ is a new creation**. The creator God has established a new order through the coming of Jesus, the new Adam (2 Cor 4:6; Gal 6:15). Because the obedient Messiah has defeated the enslaving powers of sin and death (see Rom 5:18–19), new life exists for those who are "in Christ," who are in personal union with Christ and incorporated into his body through baptism. God has brought about "new things" in the baptized that exceed anything we could achieve on our own—a new heart, a new ability to love God and others, a new capacity to participate in the actualization of God's kingdom on earth, inaugurated by Jesus' ministry. Paul refers to this divine work within us when he states that **the old things have passed away; behold new things have come**. These words evoke several passages from the book of Isaiah (e.g., 42:9; 43:18–19; 48:6). Just as the †new covenant ministry, through which God's Spirit now transforms hearts, fulfills Jeremiah's and Ezekiel's prophecies (see 2 Cor 3:1–6), so also Isaiah's promises of "new things" to come are being fulfilled following the world-changing death and resurrection of Christ Jesus.

Reflection and Application (5:14–17)

Being open to the compelling love of Jesus. The sidebar above noted the powerful effect that verse 15 had on St. Augustine. Jesus' compelling love continues to call and empower people today, especially the young who are at the age of making life decisions. St. Ignatius of Loyola offers a practical way to prayerfully reflect on Christ's love for us. During the First Week of Ignatius's *Spiritual Exercises*—when one meditates on God's immense love for us, on the truth about one's sinfulness, and on the profound gift of forgiveness God offers through the death of his Son—Ignatius invites the retreatant to kneel before a crucifix and meditate on the extent of Jesus' love for him or her. The meditation culminates with consideration of the following three questions: What have I done for Christ? What am I doing now for Christ? What ought I to do for Christ? (*Spiritual Exercises* 53). That is, in the face of such self-giving love—a love that we can truly *experience*—what is an appropriate response?

Ignatius knew well the transforming power of Jesus' compelling love and desired to share the *Spiritual Exercises* with young people, such as Francis Xavier. Xavier's encounter with Christ's love led him to join the group that became the Society of Jesus—the Jesuits. Moreover, it led him to go all the way to India

In the Liturgy

Second Corinthians 5:14–17 is an optional first reading for the Memorial of St. Mary Magdalene (July 22). It is appropriate because Mary's life was compelled by Jesus' love. She accompanied him during his Galilean ministry, ministering and providing financial support. Mary's devotion to Christ was so strong that she followed him to Calvary, where she witnessed his death and burial. And it was Mary who was summoned by the risen Lord to proclaim his resurrection to the male apostles (John 20:17–18). Hence she is properly called the "apostle of the apostles."

and Japan, where he brought the gospel to and baptized thousands of people. Today St. Francis Xavier is a patron saint of missionaries and a great example of what can happen when young people open their hearts to the compelling love of Jesus.

Educating "men and women for others." Paul's insistence that living for Jesus in the "new creation" entails loving service of others has been taken seriously in Catholic education. Over the past few decades, several Catholic high schools, colleges, and universities have incorporated into their mission statements the express intent to educate their students to become "men and women for others." Among the ways they do so are offering courses on Scripture and Catholic social teaching, engaging in critical analysis of economic systems and social structures, and promoting participation in service projects, many of which expose students to unjust consequences of those systems and structures. This pedagogic strategy of sensitizing our young people to the world's needs and of inspiring them to respond with compassionate service is laudable.

Of course, Christian formation is a *lifelong* task. The way par excellence that deepens our commitment to live for Christ is faithful participation in the Eucharist, whereby we are illumined and strengthened to grow in becoming people "for others." There we partake in the sacrifice of Jesus, whose body is broken and whose blood is poured forth "for us." Moreover, the same Spirit who consecrates the bread and wine is also bestowed on us by Christ so "that we might live no longer for ourselves but for him" (Eucharistic Prayer 4, drawing from 2 Cor 5:15).

Putting on new lenses. Those of us who wear glasses or contact lenses know well the powerful effect that corrective lenses have on our vision. Paul's teaching in verse 16 challenges us to put on new glasses in order to see one another in a totally new light—as brothers and sisters, as people whom Christ loves and for whom he died. What would our world be like if we started wearing these glasses and accorded to *everyone* we encounter the respect that is theirs as people for whom Jesus laid down his life?

The Ministry of Reconciliation (5:18–21)

[18]And all this is from God, who has reconciled us to himself through Christ and given us the ministry of reconciliation, [19]namely, God was reconciling the world to himself in Christ, not counting their trespasses against them and entrusting to us the message of reconciliation. [20]So we are ambassadors for Christ, as if God were appealing through us. We implore you on behalf of Christ, be reconciled to God. [21]For our sake he made him to be sin who did not know sin, so that we might become the righteousness of God in him.

OT: Exod 34:5–7; Lev 4:1–5:13; Ps 103; Isa 52:13–53:12
NT: Matt 11:28–30; Luke 15; Rom 3:21–26; 5:6–11; 1 Pet 2:21–25; 1 John 4:9–10
Catechism: Sacrament of Reconciliation, 1440–70, 1480–84; Christ died for our sins, 606–18
Lectionary: Fourth Sunday of Lent (Year C); Common of Pastors; Holy Orders; Mass for priestly vocations

Paul introduces a new way of understanding the mystery of redemption in Christ: it is a work of *reconciliation*. As Christ's ambassador, he is a minister of reconciliation. In addition to explaining that Jesus' sacrificial death has brought about the forgiveness of sins, Paul sets forth the new possibility of our manifesting God's righteousness to others.

Paul begins with a summarizing statement: **And all this is from God**. The **5:18–19** phrase "all this" refers to the new creation that has come about through the death and resurrection of Jesus, the [†]new Adam (v. 17). Paul makes explicit that *God* is the source of our redemption, a redemption he here describes as reconciliation: God **has reconciled us to himself through Christ**. The language of reconciliation is one of Paul's unique contributions to the New Testament.[8] It conveys the restoration of a relationship broken by enmity. In this case, the enmity resulted from human sin (Rom 5:12). Because all humanity was entrapped by the power of sin (Rom 1:18–3:20), only God could bring about reconciliation. And God,

8. The verb *(apo)katallassō* ("reconcile") appears in Rom 5:10; 1 Cor 7:11; 2 Cor 5:18, 19, 20; Eph 2:16; Col 1:20, 22; the noun *katallagē* ("reconciliation") in Rom 5:11; 11:15; 2 Cor 5:18, 19.

who was the offended party,[9] demonstrated his love by magnanimously reaching out to us through the death of Jesus (Rom 5:6–11).

Paul reveals that God has **given us the ministry of reconciliation**. Note that he uses the same word, "ministry" (*diakonia*), that he used in 3:7–11 to describe the †new covenant ministry. He thereby suggests that proclaiming and enacting the message of reconciliation are essential components of the new covenant ministry. Commentators are divided over the referent of the pronoun "us": Does it refer to *all* Christians or to particular figures like Paul and his coworkers who have a special role in the ministry of reconciliation? The following verses (especially v. 20) suggest the latter.

Verse 19 amplifies what Paul has just declared. He reiterates that **God was reconciling the world to himself in Christ**. Because the word order in the Greek text is "God was in Christ [the] world reconciling . . . ," this verse has been interpreted as indicating the divine presence *in* Christ (e.g., Catechism, 433). While this is a legitimate understanding of the passage, especially in light of the Church's teaching that Jesus is "true God and true man," the NAB captures the Apostle's emphasis on the *role* that Christ played in God's work of reconciliation. When Paul asserts that God was reconciling "the world," he refers specifically to human beings. He goes on to make explicit what reconciliation involves: **not counting their trespasses against them**. The Greek verb for "count" or "reckon" is an accounting term. Paul employs it to signify that through Christ's death "for all" God has wiped clear from the debit ledger the transgressions of those who have availed themselves of his gift of reconciliation. Paul's words here are the closest thing we have to a definition of forgiveness of sins in the New Testament.[10] Notice that Paul once again suggests that the ministry of the new covenant entails the ministry of reconciliation. According to Jer 31:34, an important feature of the new covenant is God's promise to forgive evildoing and to no longer remember his people's sins. Paul reveals that this promise is now being fulfilled through Christ (see 2 Cor 1:19–20). He concludes by speaking again of God **entrusting to us the message of reconciliation**. The proclamation of reconciliation is necessary for people to receive God's gift.

5:20   Paul explains his own role in God's work of reconciliation: he is an **ambassador** for Christ. An ambassador, like an †apostle, is commissioned by someone

9. As Chrysostom (*Homilies on 2 Corinthians* 11.5) aptly observes. It is important to note that the New Testament never speaks of God as our enemy; rather, it is we who rebelled and became his enemies. God in himself is pure love; he is never hostile toward human beings, even those who rebel against him.

10. See Murray J. Harris, *Second Epistle to the Corinthians*, NIGTC (Grand Rapids: Eerdmans, 2005), 444.

to represent him or her. Here Paul asserts that he represents Jesus, a point he emphasizes by twice deploying the phrase *hypēr Christou* (translated **for Christ** and **on behalf of Christ**). And just as God worked through Jesus in his earthly ministry, so now **God** is **appealing through** Paul. Thus it is *God's* word—and not mere human words (see 1 Thess 2:13)—that he proclaims when he **implores** people,[11] **be reconciled to God**! Paul emphasizes here the vertical dimension of reconciliation, that is, his primary focus is on God's invitation to people to be brought into right relationship with him. The ministry of reconciliation also entails a horizontal dimension—the reconciliation between people who are at enmity with one another (see Eph 2:14–16). We already saw Paul enacting this horizontal dimension of reconciliation in connection with the member of the Corinthian church who had offended him (2:5–11). In addition, he is about to exhort the *entire* community to be fully reconciled with him (i.e., with the Apostle; 6:11–13; 7:2–4).

We now arrive at a verse that "invites us to tread on sacred ground."[12] Because **5:21** there is a great deal of theology packed into a single sentence here, it is necessary to analyze it carefully. Paul declares that **he made him to be sin who did not know sin**. The subject of the clause, "he," refers to God, while "him" refers to Jesus. Note how Paul describes Christ as the one who "did not know sin." The Greek verb refers to knowing that is derived from experience. Hence, by describing Jesus as not knowing sin, Paul affirms Christ's sinlessness, a theme found throughout the New Testament.[13] Christ's *entire* life was marked by faithfulness and obedience, by his "yes" to God (1:19–20), a "yes" that led to the cross (Phil 2:8). Indeed, Jesus' willingness to offer himself in love "for us" (Eph 5:2; see Gal 2:20) illuminates Paul's enigmatic statement that God "made" the sinless one "to be sin." He refers to Christ's suffering and sacrificial death on the cross, a death that was **for our sake**.

The key to understanding Paul's meaning is to appreciate that he uses the word "sin" (*hamartia*) in two different senses here. In saying that Jesus did not know "sin," he intends the typical meaning of the word: Jesus was never guilty of deliberate infidelity to God's will. At the same time, Paul draws on a technical use of *hamartia* in the †Septuagint to refer to the "sin offering." As described in Lev 4:1–5:13, the sin offering involved the sacrifice of an *unblemished* animal in reparation for transgressions that broke one's relationship with God. Paul thus

---

11. The NAB's insertion of "you"—referring to the Corinthians—is not supported in the Greek text. In v. 20 Paul sets forth his *general* proclamation.

12. Harris, *Second Epistle to the Corinthians*, 456.

13. Elsewhere in the New Testament Christ's sinlessness is alluded or referred to in Matt 3:13–15; John 7:18; 8:46; Acts 3:14; Heb 4:15; 7:26; 1 Pet 1:19; 2:22; 3:18; 1 John 3:5.

alludes to the sinless Christ's death as a sacrifice for our sins,[14] which is how Jesus himself interpreted his death at the Last Supper (Matt 26:26–28). Recall the statement in verse 19 that through Christ a new reality exists for those who have accepted God's offer of reconciliation: their sins are no longer counted against them. This is because of Christ's sacrificial death.

In addition to the sin offering set forth in Leviticus, Paul's statement that God made Christ to be sin likely has Isaiah's suffering servant songs in the background, especially the fourth song (Isa 52:13–53:12). This passage portrays an innocent, suffering person who bore the sins of others and was led to death. The servant is described as bearing people's "guilt" (53:11) and as having "the guilt of us all" laid on him (53:6). Because of the lawlessness of God's people, the servant was "taken away" and "cut off from the land of the living" (53:8). And as one who alone was innocent and without deceit (53:9), he was an "offering for sin" (53:10). It therefore appears that just as Jesus understood his passion and death as a fulfillment of Isaiah 53 (Mark 10:45; Luke 22:37), so does Paul.[15]

The fourth Isaian servant song contains a line in the Septuagint—"the righteous one (*dikaios*), my good servant, will make many righteous" (Isa 53:11, my translation)—that sheds light on the second half of verse 21: **so that we might become the righteousness of God in him**. Here Paul explains that, in addition to the forgiveness of sins, God has a purpose ("so that") in reconciling the world to himself through Christ. In order to understand his meaning, we must first look at what he denotes by the phrase "righteousness of God" (*dikaiosynē theou*), a phrase that has been the source of much theological debate. Does it refer to God's own righteousness, expressed by his actions that accord with his covenant promises? Or to the righteousness God bestows on human beings, so that they are able to conduct themselves in accord with the divine will? As we will see, Paul in fact draws on both senses of "righteousness of God."

Throughout Paul's letter to the Romans, where "righteousness of God" is a central theme, the phrase refers primarily to *God's* righteousness, especially to his covenant faithfulness (see Rom 1:17; 3:5; 3:21–22; 10:3). Paul states that God's covenant faithfulness was revealed, first and foremost, through Christ's faithfulness (Rom 3:21–22). In fact, Paul pointed to this same dynamic in 2 Cor 1:18–20 when he spoke of God's faithfulness and of Jesus as the "yes," the fulfillment, of all God's promises. Recall that Christ's "yes" to God was manifested in his giving

---

14. As captured well by the NJB: "For our sake he made the sinless one a victim for sin."

15. Paul J. Barnett remarks that Paul's expression "he made him to be sin" is an apt summary of the fourth Isaian servant song (*The Second Epistle to the Corinthians*, NICNT [Grand Rapids: Eerdmans, 1997], 313n61).

himself in love for others. Moreover, we saw that, through the anointing and sealing action of God's Spirit, *we* are empowered to incarnate Jesus' self-giving love, a way of life that Paul calls our Amen to God (1:20–22).

We are now in position to understand what Paul means by the expression "we might become the righteousness of God." Through Christ's saving death on the cross, we are enabled to "live for him" (v. 15), to offer ourselves in self-giving love for the sake of others. Our Spirit-empowered transformation becomes the visible manifestation of the ongoing fulfillment of God's promises (3:1–6; see Jer 31:31–33; Ezek 11:19; 36:26–27). Thus God's covenant faithfulness—his righteousness—*continues* to be revealed through us in the here and now. This is an essential manifestation of the "new creation" (v. 17). It is no accident that Paul uses the same Greek verb, "become," that he employed in 1:19–20 in connection with Jesus' becoming "yes" and our becoming the Amen. By saying that we "become the righteousness of God," he signifies that we who have been reconciled to God have been made righteous, empowered to walk in the way of Jesus. Indeed, we have been made righteous "in him," that is, through our baptismal incorporation into Christ, the "righteous one" (see Isa 53:11), whose life was marked by faithfulness to God.

Reflection and Application (5:18–21)

The Sacrament of Reconciliation. For Catholics, the ministry of reconciliation is enacted in a privileged and unsurpassed manner in the Sacrament of Reconciliation. In fact, the opening words of the prayer of absolution make the connection explicit: "God, the Father of mercies, through the death and resurrection of his Son has reconciled the world to himself" (employing words from 2 Cor 5:18–19). Because sin damages our relationship with God and others, it is necessary to seek reconciliation with God and the Church. Penitents confess their sins to a priest or bishop, who is an instrument of God's merciful love and forgiveness. The priest or bishop also represents the community, whose witness to Christ and fraternal bonds are weakened by the sin of its members. The words of absolution—which are prayed by the priest or bishop after the penitent's confession of sins, act of contrition, and resolution to do penance—are extremely powerful, for by means of them God brings about what he intended through the sacrificial death of Christ. Priests and bishops thus have the awesome privilege and responsibility of continuing the work of Jesus the Good Shepherd. Their demeanor and comportment in the confessional, especially when marked by patience and compassion, can have

In the Liturgy

On the fourth Sunday of Lent (Year C), 2 Cor 5:17–21 is read along-side Luke 15:11–32, the parable of the Prodigal Son. The parable dramatically portrays in narrative form what Paul sets forth: namely, God's mercy and desire to reconcile sinners to himself. In particular, Jesus' description of the father—who races to embrace and receive back his humiliated, bedraggled, repentant son—illuminates Paul's description of God. In short, the two passages together reveal that God is a loving Father who magnanimously offers us forgiveness and restoration to his family when we acknowledge our sinfulness.

life-changing consequences. I have found that intimacy with Jesus' Sacred Heart and recognition of my own sinfulness are essential aids to celebrating this beautiful sacrament.

Ambassadors of [†] *Messiah Jesus.* Because Christ conferred the power to forgive sins on his apostles (Matt 16:19; John 20:21–23), bishops and priests represent and speak for him in a unique manner, as when celebrating the Sacrament of Reconciliation. Nevertheless, by virtue of their baptism and confirmation *all* Christians participate in the priesthood of Jesus (e.g., *Lumen Gentium* 30–31) and thereby in his mission. That is, every one of us is called to be an ambassador of Jesus, a person who bears witness to him by living out gospel values, by building up the community of faith, by advocating for justice, and by working for peace. Christ "willed that . . . his whole Church should be the sign and instrument of the forgiveness and reconciliation that he acquired for us at the price of his blood" (Catechism, 1442). One way that Catholics can participate in the ministry of reconciliation is to frequent the Sacrament of Reconciliation. It is only when we appropriate God's mercy and love in our own lives that we are able to be conduits of that mercy and love for others. Like all his gifts, God's gift of reconciliation is bestowed on us in order to be shared.

Résumé of the Minister of Reconciliation

2 Corinthians 6:1–10

Following his introduction of the ministry of reconciliation and of his role as Christ's ambassador (5:18–21), Paul begins to appeal to the Corinthians for further reconciliation with him. He exhorts the community to recognize that "now" is the time for such reconciliation (6:1–2). He then sets forth his credentials as God's minister (6:3–7a), as well as the paradox of his apostolic existence (6:7b–10).

The "Acceptable Time" (6:1–2)

¹Working together, then, we appeal to you not to receive the grace of God in vain. ²For he says:

"In an acceptable time I heard you,
and on the day of salvation I helped you."

Behold, now is a very acceptable time; behold, now is the day of salvation.

OT: Isa 49:1–13
NT: Mark 1:14–15; Luke 19:1–10; Rom 10:14–15
Lectionary: Ash Wednesday

As a coworker of Christ Jesus, Paul begins to exhort the Corinthians to be reconciled to him. He actualizes a passage from Isaiah to encourage the community to see that *now* is the "acceptable time" to respond to his appeal.

147

6:1   In connection with the opening words, **working together**, Paul's text does not make explicit with whom he is working. Most commentators understand him to be saying that he works together with God. They point to 5:20, where he explained that it is God who appeals through him when he proclaims, "Be reconciled to God." So now in 6:1 Paul "appeals"—using the same Greek verb—directly to the Corinthians. It is also possible that he alludes here to being a coworker of Jesus. In my opinion, this is the preferable option. Paul has just insisted that he is an ambassador for Christ, one who represents and speaks for him. Moreover, the immediate antecedent of the word translated "working together" is "in him" (5:21), which refers to Jesus.[1] Whether God or Jesus is intended, the important point is that Paul aligns his authority with one of the divine Persons. This does not mean that, as "coworker," he places himself on the same level as God or Christ. He is acutely aware that his qualification comes from above (see 3:5).

What does Paul mean when he appeals to the Corinthians **not to receive the grace of God in vain**? In its most basic sense, "†grace" (*charis*) refers to a gift or expression of favor. Here, in light of 5:18–21, "the grace of God" refers to God's gracious act of reconciling the world to himself through the death and resurrection of Jesus.[2] The expression "in vain" denotes "without meaningful effect or result" (see Gal 2:2; Phil 2:16; 1 Thess 3:5). Paul does not deny that the Corinthians have received grace. Indeed, the existence of the church in Corinth speaks of their initial acceptance of the †gospel and their being reconciled with God. Paul's exhortation not to receive God's grace in vain is an appeal to deeper conversion, that is, to avoid becoming partners with evil and to continue to purify themselves in mind and body (see 2 Cor 6:14–7:1).

In addition, he challenges them to see the connection between being reconciled with God and being reconciled with their founding †apostle. Paul is under attack and has been compelled to defend his integrity and comportment. Yet, as we have seen throughout the letter, his humble, self-giving way of exercising his apostleship, a way that involves suffering, is itself a proclamation of the gospel (4:5, 7–15). To reject Paul is tantamount to abandoning the gospel he proclaims. If the Corinthians break off their relationship with the one whom God sent to them, they are in danger of abandoning the condition of being reconciled with God. Thus Paul's appeal not to receive the grace of God in vain is a call to be reconciled with him as Jesus' ambassador and coworker.

1. Another clue is Paul's reference to "the grace of *God*." If God were the clear referent as coworker, we would expect Paul to write "*his* grace."
2. We will look more extensively at Paul's use of the term *charis* in the analysis of 8:1–9:15, below.

Paul conveys the urgency of his appeal by citing a biblical passage. Notice   **6:2**
how he introduces the citation with **he says,** a reference to *God,* the ultimate
author of Scripture. The passage cited is Isa 49:8: **"In an acceptable time I
heard you, / and on the day of salvation I helped you."** Many commentators
argue that Paul cites this text as pointing to Christ in order to actualize its significance for the present situation. That is, the "acceptable time" and "the day
of salvation" point to the "new creation" that God has now brought about by
reconciling the world to himself through Jesus (5:17–19). Because of what God
has done through Christ, Paul insists, the Corinthians should respond fittingly:
Behold, now is a very acceptable time; behold, now is the day of salvation.
They ought to recognize that Paul speaks for Christ and heed his call *now* to be
fully reconciled with him. In doing so, the community will appropriate God's
gift of reconciliation more completely and authentically.

While this interpretation has much to commend it, I propose that Paul
intends a different nuance in citing Isa 49:8. The two instances of the pronoun "you" in this passage are *singular,* making it problematic to apply them
to a plural referent (i.e., the Corinthians). The text itself is from the second
Isaian servant song (Isa 49:1–13), where one who is designated as God's
"slave" is commissioned to bring Israel back to God and, furthermore, to be
a light to the †Gentiles. At a time of discouragement, the slave hears God's
words of encouragement that Paul cites here. Now, recall that the Apostle
has earlier presented himself as God's slave (2:14; see also 4:13). Moreover,
in Gal 1:15–16 he alludes to Isa 49:1, 5 in describing his call—"from my
mother's womb" God "had set me apart and called me"—a call that involves
proclaiming the gospel to the Gentiles. Therefore, in citing Isa 49:8, I suggest that Paul understands his call as similar to that of the Isaian slave.[3]
Like that slave, he has a crucial role to play in God's work of reconciliation
(2 Cor 5:20). Like the Isaian figure, he receives God's consolation in the face
of discouragement (see 1:3–4).

But the words from Isaiah are not only for Paul's benefit; he cites them here
to remind the Corinthians that he is *God's* chosen instrument in bringing the
gospel to them. Indeed, he now turns to the Corinthians in the second half of
verse 2. Just as in the traditional interpretation, Paul exhorts them to see that
now is a very acceptable time to deepen their initial conversion and, more
specifically, to be reconciled with him as God's slave and Jesus' coworker. The

---

3. See Rom 10:15 for another Isaian passage (52:7) that Paul appropriates for himself. There is,
however, a significant difference between Isaiah and Paul in that the latter proclaims what God has done
in and through Jesus the †Messiah.

In the Liturgy

LIVING TRADITION

Second Corinthians 5:20–6:2 is proclaimed on Ash Wednesday, the beginning of the great penitential season of Lent. This reading summons us "not to receive the grace of God in vain." We are invited to "return to the LORD" by rending our hearts (Joel 2:13), recognizing that *now* is "the very acceptable" time to respond to God's offer of mercy. Through almsgiving, prayer, and fasting we prepare ourselves for forty days to celebrate Easter—"the day of salvation" that has come about through the passion, death, and resurrection of Jesus and the sending of the Spirit.

"now" proclaimed here is also a perennial call to us to grow in faith and deepen our commitment to live for Christ (5:15).

Reflection and Application (6:1–2)

Reconciliation between ministers and parishioners. Misunderstandings, tensions, and hurt can easily arise for any number of reasons between pastoral leaders and the people to whom they minister. Paul's words in verses 1–2 challenge both ministers and parishioners in such situations. On the one hand, those of us who exercise ministerial authority, whether lay or ordained, are challenged to honestly examine ourselves to see whether or not the point at issue is, at least in part, due to our failure to conduct ourselves as ambassadors and coworkers of Jesus. While Paul could rightly insist on his fidelity to living after the manner of Christ, many of us at times fall short of this standard. On the other hand, parishioners are challenged to recognize and respect the special role and authority of those who have been commissioned to lead them. In my experience, breakdowns happen too frequently because of personality clashes or differing opinions over matters that, while they may seem important to the parties involved, do not pertain to essential issues of faith and morals or the overall well-being of the community. Whatever the cause of division, Paul highlights the urgency with which we should seek reconciliation—"*now* is a very acceptable time."

Letting the Bible speak to us "now." For Paul, Scripture was not a relic of the past, as his actualization of the words of Isa 49:8 in verse 2 makes clear. Rather, it was the "living and effective" word of God (Heb 4:12) that spoke to him afresh within his life circumstances. We too are invited to allow this living word to communicate to us within our own situations. In fact, this is the principal responsibility of the homilist at eucharistic celebrations. Through the practice of *lectio divina*,[4] individuals and prayer groups can also experience the biblical revelation as speaking to them words of encouragement or of prophetic challenge in the here and now. To be sure, the danger exists that I might try to force Scripture to say what I want it to say. However, there is a safeguard against this danger: the commitment to humbly *listen* to what the Holy Spirit is saying while reading Scripture in light of the Church's teaching and tradition.

Credentials of the Minister of God (6:3–7a)

> [3]We cause no one to stumble in anything, in order that no fault may be found with our ministry; [4]on the contrary, in everything we commend ourselves as ministers of God, through much endurance, in afflictions, hardships, constraints, [5]beatings, imprisonments, riots, labors, vigils, fasts; [6]by purity, knowledge, patience, kindness, in a holy spirit, in unfeigned love, [7]in truthful speech, in the power of God;

OT: Ps 16; 27
NT: Mark 9:42–48; 13:9–13; Gal 5:22–23

After his initial appeal to the community to be fully reconciled with him, Paul once again emphasizes his apostolic integrity by providing an extensive list of his credentials. In doing so, he gives the Corinthians several reasons to be reconciled with him. He presents his résumé as a minister of reconciliation in four parts. In this section we will look at the first two.

By listing his apostolic credentials, does Paul contradict his earlier claim that he does not need a letter of recommendation? No, because the concern in 3:1–3 was whether he needed a recommendation *to the Corinthians*. Here the issue is different. Recall from 5:12 that Paul wants to provide the community with "something to say to those who boast of external appearance," that is, to the intruding missionaries. He now presents the Corinthians with plenty of talking points.

Paul begins by insisting that he causes **no one to stumble in anything**. That is, he denies that his conduct has been a source of offense or scandal. He assiduously avoids giving offense **in order that no fault may be found with** the **ministry**. The "ministry"[5] (*diakonia*) refers to the ministry of the [†]new covenant

6:3–4a

---

4. See the third entry under Reflection and Application (1:1–2), above.
5. The word *our* is not present in the Greek text.

Paul's Use of Hardship Catalogs
BIBLICAL BACKGROUND

The lists of sufferings found in 2 Cor 4:8–9; 6:4–10; 11:23–33; and 12:10 bear a resemblance to the catalogs of hardship produced by a number of Greco-Roman philosophers and moralists who lived during the first century AD. Especially among Stoics these hardship catalogs, which listed various sufferings that the author had overcome, functioned to demonstrate the author's wisdom and strength. Adversity brought with it the opportunity for the truly wise person to overcome difficult circumstances and to rise above the vicissitudes of life. The Stoics emphasized the importance of courage in the face of suffering, of resignation over what was beyond one's control, and the ideal of self-sufficiency.

Although Paul's hardship catalogs are similar to those of his †pagan contemporaries, there is also a crucial difference. He lists personal hardships not in order to promote his own bravery and merit but to highlight the power of *God* at work within him. Paul thus adapts a known philosophical convention in order to make one of his central claims in 2 Corinthians, namely, that true power is made perfect in weakness (12:9). Rather than strive for self-sufficiency, he has learned that God's †grace is sufficient for him.

(3:7–11), which is exercised in large part through the ministry of reconciliation (5:18). Paul's overriding concern is for the work that *God* is doing through him and other ministers. Therefore, at the beginning of verse 4, he expresses the same point, now in positive terms: **on the contrary, in everything we commend ourselves**. Here he employs the positive notion of †self-commendation.[6] Paul asserts that it is *because* he is a faithful "minister" (*diakonos*) **of God** that he †*commends* himself. As we will see, the following list points, in many places, to divine empowerment. For this reason Paul can engage in positive self-commendation. His list of credentials includes three groups of three hardships suffered (vv. 4b–5), two series of four items that explain how he endures and overcomes such hardships (vv. 6–7a), three transitional phrases (vv. 7b–8a), and a series of seven antitheses that illustrate the paradoxes of his apostolic ministry (vv. 8b–10).

6:4b–5   Paul opens his list of credentials with the phrase **through much endurance**. This phrase serves not only as an introduction to the nine hardships that immediately follow but also as a heading for the entire list. Generally speaking, "endurance" refers to the ability to withstand difficulties and hardships. While

6. See the sidebar on "Paul's Use of Self-Commendation in 2 Corinthians" on p. 77.

Paul undoubtedly draws on this broad notion of the term, his usage elsewhere indicates a more particular understanding. In Rom 5:3–4 he declares that "affliction produces endurance, and endurance produces proven character, and proven character produces hope" (my translation). Observe that Paul links endurance with the formation of character. The following list indicates how he embodies—and is empowered to embody—the character of Jesus. Notice too that Paul connects the endurance that builds character with "hope" (see 1 Thess 1:3). We have already seen that it is his hope in the resurrection that bolsters him in his suffering and self-giving in love after the likeness of Christ (4:7–5:10).

The first set of sufferings—**afflictions, hardships, constraints**—is, in effect, a list of three synonymous terms. They express in a general manner the difficulties Paul faces as a minister of God. As with the brief †hardship catalog in 4:8–9, he begins with "afflictions." The reference to his being afflicted summons the Corinthians to recall what was proclaimed in the opening blessing (1:3–7). There Paul blessed God for encouraging him in his "every affliction" (1:4). He thereby sets the present list of sufferings within the wider context of divine support, something that is important for all ministers to keep in mind. In addition, Paul revealed that his afflictions are for the community's "encouragement and salvation" (1:6). We will see how this is the case, particularly when we come to the third set of trials below.

The second set of three hardships—**beatings, imprisonments, riots**—offers specific examples of how Paul has suffered at the hands of others. To what does his reference to "beatings" allude? Later in the letter (11:24–25) he will disclose that he has been scourged five times by synagogue officials and beaten with wooden rods three times by Roman officials (see Acts 16:22–23). It is interesting to note that Paul uses the plural "imprisonments," because Acts records, up to this point in his career, only one occasion when he was imprisoned—during his first visit to †Philippi (16:23–40).[7] However, many scholars hypothesize, correctly in my opinion, that he was confined at some point during his ministry in †Ephesus, during which he wrote some of the so-called †captivity epistles. Paul's mention of "riots" alludes to various frightening disturbances and violent mob uprisings provoked by his ministry, including one that took place in Corinth (Acts 18:12–17).[8]

---

7. According to Acts, Paul will *later* be imprisoned in Caesarea (23:23–26:32) and Rome (28:16–31).

8. Acts lists a number of tumults precipitated by Paul's proclamation of the gospel: in Pisidian †Antioch (13:50), †Iconium (14:5), †Lystra (14:19), Philippi (16:22), †Thessalonica (17:5–9), †Beroea (17:13), and Ephesus (19:23–40).

The third set of three sufferings—**labors, vigils, fasts**—depicts those hardships that Paul has willingly imposed on himself in order to proclaim the †gospel. The term "labors" refers to his work as a tent maker (Acts 18:3). Paul often labored with his own hands (1 Cor 4:12) so that he would not be a financial burden to his fledgling churches. He was committed to proclaiming the gospel without remuneration (1 Cor 9:18; 2 Cor 11:7). What does Paul mean by "vigils"? Because he spent so many hours at manual labor, it was often necessary for him to forgo sleep. He sometimes worked both day and night (1 Thess 2:9; 2 Thess 3:8), proclaiming the gospel at every opportunity. At other times he preached and taught deep into the night (see Acts 20:7–11). Not only did Paul lose sleep because of his commitment not to charge for his missionary work, but his hectic schedule also meant that at times he had to deprive himself of regular meals; thus, his reference to "fasts."

6:6–7a   How is Paul able to endure these hardships? The second part of his list explains. Here Paul reveals to all who are called to ministry what is needed to persevere in fidelity. First, he offers a list of three virtues and the knowledge that buttress his comportment: **purity, knowledge, patience, kindness**. "Purity" signifies moral probity, innocence, and integrity. Paul insists that he always conducts himself honorably and honestly. We will see that he associates this quality with Jesus (11:3). Paul's reference to "knowledge" recalls "the knowledge of the glory of God on the face of [Jesus] Christ" that was bestowed on him (4:6). It is this gift that enables the Apostle to spread "the knowledge of him in every place" through his proclamation and way of life (2:14–15). "Patience" denotes forbearance, the exercise of restraint in the face of provocation, while "kindness" refers to goodness and generosity extended to others. Paul attributes the latter two characteristics to God (Rom 2:4),[9] while he associates "patience" with Christ (1 Tim 1:16). Hence Paul insists that he has been endowed with *divine qualities* that enable him not only to be long-suffering but also to be merciful and kind to others. Indeed, we have seen that he exhibited these qualities in his dealings with the person who offended him (2:6–8). Significantly, he reveals elsewhere that knowledge, patience, and kindness are gifts conferred by the Holy Spirit (see 1 Cor 12:8; Gal 5:22).

The latter observation leads to another set of four sources of Paul's ability to endure hardships: **in a holy spirit, in unfeigned love, in truthful speech, in the power of God**. The NAB's translation "in a holy spirit," which seems to refer to Paul's spirit of holiness, misses the connections he has been making to divine empowerment. It is better to render this phrase as referring to the *Holy*

9. See also Rom 9:22; 11:22; Eph 2:7; Titus 3:4.

St. Ignatius and the Standard of Christ

LIVING TRADITION

At the heart of the *Spiritual Exercises* of St. Ignatius of Loyola is The Meditation on the Two Standards. Here the two standards refer to the military banners of Lucifer (Satan) and Christ. Ignatius, like Paul (see Rom 13:12; Eph 6:11–17; 1 Thess 5:8), viewed the spiritual life in military terms. Each person must choose to belong to one of two warring camps. Lucifer's strategy is to lure people under his standard by inducing them to seek wealth and worldly renown, both of which lead to pride. His goal is to enslave people to sin. On the contrary, Jesus invites his followers to embrace spiritual poverty—and, in the case of some, actual poverty. Moreover, Jesus cautions them that they must be willing to be held in low esteem and even contempt by the world. Jesus' purpose is ultimately to inculcate humility, the virtue from which arise all other virtues, such as purity, patience, and kindness. The person engaged in the *Spiritual Exercises* is called to prayerfully consider the way of Christ, the supreme commander in chief, and then to pray for the grace to be received under his standard, that is, the "standard of the cross" (*Spiritual Exercises* 136–48). Paul's list of credentials makes clear that he is a soldier of Christ who walks under the banner of the cross. Indeed, he alludes to his weaponry in the very next passage.

Spirit, the one who empowers Paul's Amen, his walking in the way of Jesus' faithfulness to God (see 1:20–22; 3:17–18; 4:13).[10] The next phrase, "unfeigned love," literally means love "without hypocrisy," that is, genuine love. This "love" alludes to the compelling love of Jesus (5:14) that energizes and directs all of Paul's activities, including his earlier letter to the Corinthians (now lost) that tearfully expressed his love for them (2:4). The phrase "truthful speech," which can be rendered "message of truth," is a synonym for "the gospel of salvation" (Eph 1:13; see Col 1:5). Thus he refers here to the gospel he has received and now proclaims.

Finally, Paul names "the power of God," the same "power" he indicated when he described himself as a fragile "earthen vessel" who nevertheless is empowered by God to faithfully proclaim the good news of salvation (4:7). He thus sets forth in different ways the divine empowerment that enables him to withstand suffering and opposition as well as to manifest the way of Christ to others. It is this divine empowerment that continues to support those whom God calls to minister in the Church today.

10. The RSV, NIV, and NJB render it as "Holy Spirit."

Reflection and Application (6:3–7a)

Acquiring the heart of Jesus. Paul sets a very high standard for those involved in pastoral ministry. That is because his standard is the standard of Jesus. Notice how, in his apostolic résumé, Paul highlights characteristics that Christ himself embodied in an unsurpassable manner: purity, loving-kindness, and forbearance. Paul also alludes at the end of verse 6 to Jesus' love as a source of his ability to offer himself in love through labors, vigils, and fasts.

Devotion to the Sacred Heart of Jesus is a wonderful way to open ourselves to the empowering and compelling love that energized Paul in his ministry (5:14). We deepen our understanding of his love that knew no bounds (John 13:1) through daily, prayerful reflection on Jesus' life as portrayed in the Gospels, especially the way he manifested compassion; through eucharistic adoration and frequent reception of the Eucharist; and through active participation in special liturgical celebrations such as First Fridays and the Solemnity of the Most Sacred Heart of Jesus. In these ways we open ourselves to receive this love that transforms our hearts so that we can offer "love-filled service to our brothers and sisters" (Alternative Opening Prayer of the Solemnity of the Sacred Heart).

Paradoxes of Apostolic Existence (6:7b–10)

... with weapons of righteousness at the right and at the left; [8]through glory and dishonor, insult and praise. We are treated as deceivers and yet are truthful; [9]as unrecognized and yet acknowledged; as dying and behold we live; as chastised and yet not put to death; [10]as sorrowful yet always rejoicing; as poor yet enriching many; as having nothing and yet possessing all things.

OT: Ps 118:17–18; Prov 3:11–12
NT: Rom 6:13; 1 Cor 4:9–13; 1 Tim 4:11–12; Heb 12:1–11
Lectionary: Common of Martyrs

Paul continues the résumé of his credentials as a minister of reconciliation. After insisting that he manifests God's righteousness in all circumstances, he sets forth a series of antitheses that vividly portray the paradoxes of his life and that, in some way, characterize the life of every minister of the gospel.

6:7b–8a   The third part of Paul's list of credentials has a transitional function. He declares that he conducts himself **with weapons of righteousness at the right and at the left**. Paul's use of military imagery conveys that Christian life in general and the apostolic life in particular are opposed by powerful forces—sin (Rom 7:22–23), the †flesh (Gal 5:17), and Satan (e.g., 2 Cor 2:11; 4:4; 6:15; 11:13–15). He uses such imagery later in this letter (10:3–6) and throughout his writings.[11] What are the "weapons of righteousness"? Paul himself offers a clue in Rom 6:13, when he exhorts the members of the churches in Rome: "present yourselves to God . . . and the parts of your bodies to God as weapons of righteousness." In other words, the expression "with weapons of righteousness" refers to our ability to show forth the goodness and fidelity of God through our bodily actions.

We saw in 5:21 that God's righteousness, which was revealed preeminently through Christ, *continues* to be manifested by our love and self-giving after the manner of Jesus. Our ability to "become the righteousness of God" (5:21) is due to the empowerment of the Spirit (see 1:21–22; 3:17–18; 4:13). It is no accident, then, that Paul earlier called the †new covenant ministry "the ministry of the Spirit" (3:8) and "the ministry of righteousness" (3:9). Thus he presents himself as outfitted by God to manifest righteousness. He is like a soldier equipped with a sword in his right hand and a shield in his left.

Paul insists at the beginning of verse 8 that he faithfully proclaims the gospel **through glory and dishonor** and through **insult and praise**. Here he alludes to the various reactions his ministry has provoked. He knows human fickleness well. Once, after healing a man crippled from birth, Paul—to his horror—was acclaimed as a "god" by the people of †Lystra, only to be stoned and dragged out of the city moments later (Acts 14:8–19; see also Gal 4:13–16). His point is that, whether he is highly regarded or despised by those to whom he ministers, he is faithful in his vocation. Paul does not play to the crowds or allow how they perceive him to get in the way of the work God has called him to do. He persistently proclaims the †gospel, "whether it is convenient or inconvenient" (2 Tim 4:2), whether he is honored or reviled.

The fourth and final part of Paul's résumé is a series of seven antitheses. In **6:8b–10** each case the first half of the phrase conveys how he is perceived from a human or fleshly point of view (see 5:16). The second half then sets forth the true reality of his existence, seen with the eyes of faith (4:18). Thus Paul is regarded in some quarters as a **deceiver**. Recall how his change in travel plans (1:15–17) raised questions about the reliability of his word. We will also see that he is accused of deceiving the Corinthians in regard to the collection for the church in Jerusalem (12:16–18). But the reality is that Paul is **truthful**. He openly manifests the truth (4:2) because he proclaims the gospel, the "message of truth" (see 6:7), in word

---

11. See Rom 6:13; 13:12; Eph 6:11–17; 1 Thess 5:8.

and deed. As one in whom "the truth of Christ" resides (11:10), he "cannot do anything against the truth, but only for the truth" (13:8).

The second antithesis involves the issue of being recognized by others. In the eyes of the world, Paul is **unrecognized**, that is, he does not have fame, fortune, or success as they are popularly understood. He concedes that he has "become like the world's rubbish, the scum of all" (1 Cor 4:13). Nevertheless, he insists, he is **acknowledged**. Paul is fully known by God (1 Cor 13:12) and conducts himself in a transparent manner before him (2 Cor 2:17). Moreover, he and his ministry have been recognized by other prominent church leaders (Gal 2:9) and his integrity has been made apparent to the Corinthians' consciences (2 Cor 5:11).

The wording of the third and fourth antitheses derives from Ps 118:17–18. Like the psalmist who confesses, "I shall not die but live / and declare the deeds of the LORD" (v. 17), Paul declares that, while his "outer self" (2 Cor 4:16) is **dying**, even so **we live**. In this way he adapts Ps 118:17 so that it speaks to his circumstances. In effect, Paul offers here a summary of 4:7–15, where he revealed that the power of God enabled him not only to survive sufferings and hardships but also to continually offer himself in love after the manner of Christ. Self-giving love is an essential aspect of his proclaiming "the deeds of the LORD."

The fourth antithesis then draws on Ps 118:18: "The LORD chastised me harshly, / but did not hand me over to death." Paul again actualizes the text, acknowledging that he is **chastised**—for instance, by the sufferings inflicted on him by others. But he does not interpret this as others do, namely, as God's punishment. Rather, Paul interprets his chastisements in light of the divine discipline bestowed on those whom God loves (see Prov 3:11–12).[12] He understands that "at the time, all discipline seems a cause not for joy but for pain, yet later it brings the peaceful fruit of righteousness to those who are trained by it" (Heb 12:11). And as was the case with the psalmist, although he is chastised the Apostle is **yet not put to death**.

At the beginning of verse 10 Paul reports that he is seen by others as **sorrowful**, as one whose life seems to offer no grounds for happiness. Yet, while he does refer to his sorrow over recent events with the Corinthians (2:4–5), his ministry is marked by constant **rejoicing**. The joy to which he refers here is both a gift of the Spirit (Gal 5:22) and the result of the coming of God's kingdom (Rom 14:17). Along with peace, joy is the fruit of living in fidelity to the gospel. For

---

12. See Victor Paul Furnish, *II Corinthians: A New Translation with Introduction and Commentary,* AB 32A (New York: Doubleday, 1984), 347.

this reason Paul can encourage his communities to "rejoice in the Lord" (Phil 3:1) and to do so "always" (Phil 4:4). He works with the Corinthians for their joy (2 Cor 1:24) and rejoices when they heed him as God's minister (7:6–16).

The sixth and seventh antitheses are expressed in economic terms. Paul allows that he is economically **poor**—hungry, thirsty, poorly clad, homeless (1 Cor 4:11)—yet, paradoxically, he is capable of **enriching many**. As we will see, he has committed himself to facilitating a collection for the church in Jerusalem, one that would provide economic relief to people in great need (8:1–9:15). Paul's main way of enriching others, however, is by proclaiming the gospel. As Jesus' coworker, he dispenses *spiritual* enrichment, "the inscrutable riches of Christ" (Eph 3:8). Whether Paul enriches others materially or spiritually, he imitates Jesus, who became poor so that others might be enriched (2 Cor 8:9). Hence, although in the eyes of the world Paul is regarded as **having nothing,** he is actually **possessing all things**—including the "treasure" (4:7) of "the gospel of the glory of Christ" (4:4), which he preaches by word and, even more eloquently, by self-giving love.

We can now step back and see the progression of Paul's résumé as a minister of reconciliation. He †*commends* himself as God's minister by enduring many sufferings—both those inflicted by others and those self-imposed—with divine assistance. This heavenly aid empowers him to take on the character of Jesus. Paul thereby shows forth God's righteousness in all situations. His existence is indeed paradoxical: while his life does involve poverty, sorrow, and dying, nevertheless he is wealthy beyond telling and has great joy because of the life he has already entered into.

Reflection and Application (6:7b–10)

Perseverance in ministry. Two phrases in the middle of Paul's dizzying list of credentials—"through glory and dishonor" and through "insult and praise" (v. 8)—ought not to be passed over too quickly. They speak of the need to persevere in pastoral ministry in the face of suffering, opposition, and rejection. While pastoral ministry is seldom easy, its burdens are greatly lightened when we see positive results from our labors, when we have a good support system, and when those to whom we minister show us appreciation. But what happens—as it eventually does—when our ministry seems to bear no tangible fruit? When we feel alone in our work? When no one bothers to say thanks? When we are criticized and second-guessed? When we are misunderstood? Paul teaches that we are called to transcend the vicissitudes of ministerial circumstances. While no one is called to work in an impossible situation, we should not err on the side of running away at the first signs of discouragement. More importantly, Paul emphasizes that it is *God* who provides the wherewithal to persevere in ministry. This is why daily prayer and regular sacramental nourishment are basic necessities of pastoral ministers.

"Open Your Hearts"

2 Corinthians 6:11–7:4

Having set forth his credentials as a minister of reconciliation, Paul moves on to the fourth and last section of his lengthy discourse on †apostleship (6:11–7:4). Picking up from what he started in 6:1–2, he now enacts the ministry of reconciliation he spoke about (5:18) by calling the Corinthians to be reconciled with him. Paul begins with a direct appeal to the community to open their hearts to him (6:11–13). He then reminds them of their identity as the temple of God and exhorts them to grow in holiness—a process that entails separation from everything that prevents them from living out of their identity as the temple of God and as God's children (6:14–7:1). Finally, he pleads once more for reconciliation with him (7:2–4).

Appeal to the Corinthians for Reconciliation (6:11–13)

---

[11]We have spoken frankly to you, Corinthians; our heart is open wide. [12]You are not constrained by us; you are constrained by your own affections. [13]As recompense in kind (I speak as to my children), be open yourselves.

OT: 1 Sam 24:9–16
NT: Mark 10:17–22; 1 Cor 4:14–16; Gal 4:12–20

Although the word *reconcile* does not appear in these verses, Paul's strategy is to encourage the Corinthians to be reconciled with him as the ambassador of Christ Jesus. The purpose of setting forth his apostolic résumé (vv. 4–10) was to dispose the community to listen favorably to his appeal. Now, employing the language of the heart, he expresses his unhindered love for them and encourages them to reciprocate his love.

6:11–12   Paul reminds the Corinthians of his candor and his love for them. He asserts that he has **spoken frankly** to them, a reference to everything he has spoken and written up to this point, as well as to what he is presently going to say. Paul has been transparent and forthright in his dealings with the community. Note that he refers to them directly as **you, Corinthians**. Paul rarely addresses his communities directly by name. When he does, it is to personalize what he wishes to express.[1] Here the direct address serves to communicate his affection. Paul makes this affection explicit at the end of the verse: his **heart is open wide** to the Corinthians. The verb translated "is open wide" means "enlarge." The image of an enlarged heart conveys warm affection and love. St. John Chrysostom explains that, as heat causes things to expand, so does Paul's love for the community cause his heart to expand.[2] A commentator of our day fittingly remarks: "In medical terms, an enlarged heart is a dangerous liability; in spiritual terms, an enlarged heart is a productive asset,"[3] something that is essential for growth in the spiritual life. The Apostle thus grounds his appeal to reconcile with an assurance of his love.

Paul then reiterates his love for the Corinthians by informing them that they **are not constrained** in his affections. The verb for "constrain," or "confine to a narrow place," is the opposite of the previous verb, "enlarge," or "open wide." Paul insists that there is no restraining or holding back of love on his part. It is the Corinthians, or at least some of them, who are holding back their **affections** from him. The word translated "affections" refers to the seat of the emotions, especially to compassion and love; it is a synonym of "heart." We saw in 1:15–2:13 how Paul attempted to clear the air over the misunderstandings that arose on account of recent events between himself and the community. Here he puts the onus on the Corinthians: it is they who have closed their hearts to him, not vice versa.

6:13   Paul goes on to make his appeal for reconciliation. (Recall from 6:1–2 his underlying logic: if the community is not fully reconciled with him as God's minister of reconciliation, they cannot be fully reconciled with God.) It is important to

---

1. The only other instances are Gal 3:1, where Paul expresses his frustration; and Phil 4:15, where he conveys his gratitude.

2. See *Homilies on 2 Corinthians* 13.1.

3. Murray J. Harris, *The Second Epistle to the Corinthians*, NIGTC (Grand Rapids: Eerdmans, 2005), 490.

note that he now addresses the Corinthians with another term of endearment: **children**.[4] Paul is their spiritual father (1 Cor 4:14; see 2 Cor 11:2; 12:14–15), the one who brought the †gospel to them. It is as their father that he makes his appeal: **be open yourselves** (employing the same verb translated "open wide" in v. 11). In other words, Paul exhorts his spiritual children to enlarge *their* hearts—to open their hearts to his love and affection for them and be magnanimous, greathearted, as he is. By doing so they will give a proper **recompense in kind** to him.

It is worth lingering for a moment over Paul's focus on the heart in this passage. By emphasizing the importance of the heart, he reminds the Corinthians of the presence of the Spirit in their hearts—the Spirit who enables them to become "a letter of Christ" (3:2–3; see 1:21–22). Paul thus subtly challenges them to heed the Spirit's power. Moreover, the theme of hearts calls to mind the †new covenant promises that God would remove people's stony hearts and replace them with hearts of flesh, hearts amenable to the Spirit's promptings (3:3). Paul thereby exhorts the community to bear in their relationship with him the fruit of the new covenant ministry. In fact, we will see that new covenant themes pervade the passage that follows.

Reflection and Application (6:11–13)

An open heart. All of us at one time or another have been encouraged to keep an open mind about a person, a situation, an idea. As important as it is to be open-minded, Paul teaches us that it is even more important to be open-hearted, especially when it comes to our dealings with other people. As long as we hold others within our hearts, regarding them with affection, compassion, and magnanimity, we are able to overlook their foibles and shortcomings with mercy and even a sense of humor. We can be patient and generous with them, choosing to focus on their good qualities. Genuine openheartedness is rooted in humility, as I recognize my own faults and limitations. Failure to maintain an open heart—that is, closing one's heart to others—is symptomatic of a hardened heart, one in need of the Spirit's cleansing and replenishing of life.

Call to Holiness (6:14–7:1)

[14]**Do not be yoked with those who are different, with unbelievers. For what partnership do righteousness and lawlessness have? Or what**

---

4. See also 1 Cor 4:14; Gal 4:19; 1 Thess 2:7, 11.

fellowship does light have with darkness? ¹⁵What accord has Christ with Beliar? Or what has a believer in common with an unbeliever? ¹⁶What agreement has the temple of God with idols? For we are the temple of the living God; as God said:

> "I will live with them and move among them,
>> and I will be their God
>> and they shall be my people.
> ¹⁷Therefore, come forth from them
>> and be separate," says the Lord,
> "and touch nothing unclean;
>> then I will receive you
> ¹⁸and I will be a father to you,
>> and you shall be sons and daughters to me,
> says the Lord Almighty."

⁷:¹Since we have these promises, beloved, let us cleanse ourselves from every defilement of flesh and spirit, making holiness perfect in the fear of God.

OT: Lev 19:1–2; 26:11–12; 2 Sam 7:12–16; Isa 52:11–12; Ezek 20:33–34; 37:23–28
NT: Matt 6:24; John 3:20–21; 1 Cor 6:19–20; Eph 2:19–22; 1 Pet 2:1–10
Catechism: Church as the temple of the Holy Spirit, 797–98

Paul's call for the Corinthians to be reconciled to him as Jesus' ambassador entails their repudiating anyone or anything that prevents them from walking in the way of Christ. Part of the problem in Corinth is that some in the community have not fully repented of their former way of life (12:20–21; 13:2). Paul reminds the community of their identity as the temple of God and as God's children. He exhorts them to be cleansed of all immorality and to strive to grow in holiness.

6:14 Paul begins by admonishing the Corinthians **not to be yoked with those who are different**. What is meant by being "yoked" with someone who is "different"? Paul draws on two passages from the Old Testament: the prohibition in Deut 22:10 against harnessing an ox and ass together for the purpose of plowing a field and the prohibition in Lev 19:19 against crossbreeding animals. His point is that there are persons with whom Christians ought not to associate, with whom a relationship is essentially incompatible with their relationship with Christ. Paul refers here to the dangers of relating too closely with those **unbelievers**, or "faithless ones," whose values and way of life differ greatly from Christian life and values. In particular, he is concerned with the ongoing danger of idolatry (see v. 16). Indeed, he had warned the Corinthians in an earlier letter about the perils of associating too closely with their †pagan neighbors because of the prevalence of the latter's idolatrous practices (see 1 Cor 10:14–22).

Paul follows his initial admonition with a series of rhetorical questions that take the general form: What does X have in common with Y? The answer expected for each of the five questions is "Absolutely nothing!" Paul's point is to make clear that there are ways of behaving that are irreconcilable with Christian life. Thus the first question opposes **righteousness** to **lawlessness** (see Rom 6:19). At the most basic level, Paul points to the contrast between a Christian lifestyle that keeps God's law and a pagan lifestyle that does not. But there is a deeper meaning as well. Paul has taught that because of the impelling love of Jesus—the love that led him to die "for all" (5:14–15)—Christians have "become the righteousness of God" (5:21). That is, through the Spirit's empowerment, we are enabled to incarnate Christ's self-giving love (1:21–22). Because such a loving existence for others is the fulfillment of the law (Rom 13:10; Gal 5:14), it is utterly incompatible with any form of lawlessness, of not living in accord with God's will.

Similarly, Paul's second question contrasts **light** with **darkness**. He insists that Christians are "children of light" (Eph 5:8; see 1 Thess 5:5) in whose hearts God has shone "the light of the gospel of the glory of Christ" (2 Cor 4:4, 6). We who belong to "the day" (1 Thess 5:8) are to conduct ourselves openly so that others can see that our works are "done in God" (John 3:21; see Matt 5:16). On the contrary, the mark of the lawless is to act under the cover of darkness so that their works are not exposed (John 3:20).

The third question draws the most fundamental distinction, that between **6:15–16a**
Christ and **Beliar**. Recall that, following his opening statement (1:12–14), Paul's first reference to Christ Jesus was in connection with his "yes" (1:19–20), with his filial obedience to the Father that led him to offer his life on the cross (Phil 2:8). Jesus' faithful obedience to God is in stark contrast to Satan, known in some noncanonical Jewish works by the name "†Beliar," meaning "wickedness." Beliar's disobedience resulted in his becoming God's archenemy. As the enemy of God, he attempts to lure people into disobedience and sin.[5] Because there is absolutely no compatibility between Christ and Beliar, there ought to be no mutual fellowship between their adherents. The one who belongs to Christ is a **believer**, or "faithful one"; the one who belongs to Beliar is an **unbeliever**, or "faithless one." Christians are distinguished by heeding Jesus' invitation to take only his "yoke" upon them (Matt 11:28–30), that is, the way of humility, gentleness, and self-giving love. While obedience to "the law of Christ" (Gal 6:2) leads

5. See, e.g., *Testament of Dan* 5.11.

Fig. 8. The ruins of the Temple of Apollo, one of the many pagan temples found in Corinth in Paul's day.

us to freedom (see Gal 5:1), adherents of Beliar become slaves to disobedience and sin (Rom 6:16).

The series of rhetorical questions reaches its climax at the beginning of verse 16: **What agreement has the temple of God with idols?** Paul's evangelization was directed, in large part, to pagans who worshiped a number of different gods. (Archaeologists have unearthed remains of several temples in Corinth that existed during the first century AD.[6]) Paul exhorted his †Gentile listeners to turn away from idols and turn instead to "the living and true God" and serve him alone (1 Thess 1:9). There is only one God; the gods represented by idols are as dead as the materials from which their likenesses are made (see Isa 44:6–20; 46:1–13).

Paul's fifth question also serves to set up the statement that follows, as he now reminds the Corinthians of their fundamental identity: **we are the temple of the living God**. The community has been established by the †new covenant ministry, in fulfillment of the promises found in Jeremiah and Ezekiel that spoke of God's pouring his Spirit into hearts of flesh. The Church is the place where God now dwells. Indeed, Paul's reference to the "living God" echoes 3:2–3, where he alluded to these prophetic promises by describing "the Spirit of the living God" writing on the Corinthians' hearts. Note that it is first and foremost the *community* that he identifies as the temple of God (1 Cor 3:16–17; Eph 2:21). While it is true that every Christian is a temple of God because God's

6. See Victor Paul Furnish, *II Corinthians: A New Translation with Introduction and Commentary*, AB 32A (New York: Doubleday, 1984), 15–19; Jerome Murphy-O'Connor, *St. Paul's Corinth: Texts and Archaeology*, 3rd rev. and exp. ed. (Collegeville, MN: Liturgical Press, 2002), 186–91.

Temple in the Old Testament

BIBLICAL BACKGROUND

When †YHWH chose Israel as his special people, he instructed Moses to build the †ark of the covenant and an elaborate, portable tent-tabernacle in which to house the ark (Exod 25:1–31:18). The Exodus account concludes with God's glory filling the tabernacle (40:34–38). As Israel journeyed through the wilderness, God was present among his people.

When Israel eventually settled in the promised land, King David desired to construct a grander edifice for God (2 Sam 7:1–2). However, it was his son Solomon who built the temple in Jerusalem in the tenth century BC (1 Kings 6). The inner sanctuary, called the "holy of holies," where the ark of the covenant was placed, was filled with God's glory at the dedication of the temple (1 Kings 8:10–11)—as was the entire temple. Although the heavens cannot contain God, he condescended to dwell in the temple and promised to be attentive to the prayers and sacrifices offered there (8:27–30).

Solomon's temple was destroyed by the Babylonians early in the sixth century BC, a result of Israel's sin. Within a hundred years a second temple was built on the same site, which was later enlarged by Herod the Great. Described by Jesus as his "Father's house" (Luke 2:49), this is the temple he "cleansed" in the days leading up to his death (Mark 11:15–17). This second temple was destroyed by the Romans in AD 70.

Jesus transformed the reality of "temple" when he revealed that, in and through his person, God was dwelling among his people in an unsurpassable manner (John 2:19; see 1:14). Paul continues this new understanding of temple. He teaches that, following Jesus' death and resurrection, the new covenant promises have been fulfilled through the gift of the Holy Spirit bestowed in human hearts. The entire Church, the "body of Christ," is now God's temple (see Eph 2:19–22).

Spirit is present within him or her (1 Cor 6:19; 12:7–11), Paul's emphasis is on the Spirit's presence within the collective body of Christ (1 Cor 12:12–27). It is because the Church is God's temple that we are warned to "not be yoked with" unbelievers or faithless ones (v. 14).

Paul turns to Scripture to substantiate his claim that the Church is the temple **6:16b** of God. The words cited—beginning in the middle of this verse and continuing through verse 18—have the appearance of being a single quotation. In reality, Paul has strung together a number of different passages, and it is illuminating to look at his biblical sources in order to appreciate what he attempts to communicate. Before doing so, it is important to point out once again that the ultimate author of biblical revelation is God. Paul emphasizes this point by naming God three times as the speaker of the cited words—at the beginning (**as God said**, v. 16), the middle ("says the Lord," v. 17), and the end ("says the Lord Almighty," v. 18).

The first part of the scriptural quotation, found at the end of verse 16, combines Lev 26:11–12 and Ezek 37:27. The context of the Leviticus passage is the blessings God promised to bestow on Israel if they obeyed the divine commandments. Such obedience would distinguish them as God's holy people. The final and most important blessing promised is that God would **live with them and move among them** on their journey to the promised land (as well as after they settled there). While both passages have the covenant formula[7]—**I will be their God / and they shall be my people**—the Ezekiel passage is set in the context of the promise of an everlasting "covenant of peace" (Ezek 37:26). So what does Paul mean by combining these two texts? The quoted words point to the fulfillment of the new covenant promises through the death and resurrection of Jesus the †Messiah and through the outpouring of God's Spirit in the hearts of the Corinthians (see 3:2–3). Paul wants the church at Corinth to fully appreciate that God now lives with—indeed, *within*—them (and, by extension, within the entire Church).

6:17–18 Paul next cites a combination of words from Isa 52:11 and Ezek 20:34. The Isaiah passage exhorts the Israelites, including the priests bearing the sacred vessels, to return from exile (**come forth from them / and be separate**) and to avoid impurity (**touch nothing unclean**). The Ezekiel passage—**I will receive you**—likewise is set in the context of God's calling Israel to return from exile. How does Paul adapt these words for the Corinthians? They are to separate themselves from all who would endanger their identity as God's people, especially from pagan associates who would lead them to idolatry. They are also to avoid immorality in all its forms. In addition, Paul exhorts the community to separate themselves from the intruding missionaries who would undermine the authentic †gospel he preaches.[8] The Apostle's words here challenge us to separate ourselves from anyone or anything that jeopardizes our Christian identity and vocation—to avoid all occasions of sin. His citation of the words of Ezekiel ("I will receive you") reminds the Corinthians once more that the new covenant promises concerning the Spirit-empowered transformation of human hearts are now fulfilled. Like Jesus in his parable of the Prodigal Son (Luke 15:11–32), Paul portrays God as eager to "receive" those who repent and return to him.

---

7. See the sidebar on "The Meaning and Importance of Covenant" on p. 80.

8. Recall that Paul has been alluding to these interlopers all along—2:17; 3:1; 4:2; 5:12—and implying that the Corinthians be wary of their influence. He makes similar use of Scripture in Gal 4:30.

St. Augustine on God's Intimacy with the Church

LIVING
TRADITION

St. Augustine famously stated, "What the soul is to the body of a human being, the Holy Spirit is to the body of Christ, which is the Church" (Sermon 267). Commenting on this passage in his 1986 apostolic letter *Augustine of Hippo*—a letter that commemorated the sixteenth centenary of Augustine's conversion—Pope John Paul II observed that the Spirit is "the principle of community," the principle by which the faithful are not only united to one another but also "to the Trinity itself" (2.3). Elaborating on the latter point, John Paul cited Augustine's teaching that the Father and Son have shared the very bond of love between them—that is, the Spirit—with the Church because they willed that the members of the Church be in intimate communion with them (Sermon 71).

The third part of Paul's quotation, in verse 18, is comprised of 2 Sam 7:14 and Isa 43:6. The passage from 2 Samuel is set in the context of God's promise to David that God would raise an heir after David and make the heir's throne last forever. God's relationship with this heir would be special, as the cited words, **I will be a father to you**, make clear.[9] Paul reads this text messianically. That is, Jesus—who is †Son of David and Son of God (Rom 1:3–4)—is the one who reigns on an eternal throne. And through their incorporation in Christ, Christians are **sons and daughters** of God (the words "sons" and "daughters" come from Isa 43:6). Paul thus teaches that God relates to members of the Church as a loving father to his children (Rom 8:14–17; Gal 4:4–7). He also emphasizes that men and women are equally children of God (Gal 3:28; see Gen 1:27). It is also worth observing the transition in Paul's description of the Church from verse 16 to verse 18: the Christian community is not only the "place" where God is present (the temple of God), it is also the *family* of God. The notion of family communicates even more effectively God's intimacy and closeness to his people. Paul thereby reminds the Corinthians—and us—of our most fundamental identity: we are children of God.

Finally, Paul concludes this section with an exhortation to take appropriate action. He addresses the Corinthians as **beloved**, as fellow members of the family of God. The reference to **these promises** points to the biblical passages just cited, promises that have been fulfilled through Christ Jesus and the bestowal of the

7:1

9. In its original context, Solomon was understood as the referent of the promise.

Spirit (1:20–22). Given the community's identity as God's temple and as God's children, Paul sets forth the ethical implication: **let us cleanse ourselves from every defilement of flesh and spirit**. Note that he continues to use language associated with worship and sacrifice (see 2:14–15). In doing so, he reminds Christians that we are to extend our worship of God into *all* the circumstances and dealings of our lives. We do so in part by repudiating and avoiding anyone or anything that leads to sin. Paul's use of the phrase "flesh and spirit" signifies that the *whole* person is affected adversely by sin (1 Cor 6:12–20).

Paul then states positively what all Christians are called to do: make **holiness perfect in the fear of God**. This expresses in a nutshell what Christian life entails. We who have been filled with the Holy Spirit are called to continually strive toward growth in holiness (Phil 3:14). This growth involves embodying more and more the character of Jesus (Gal 4:19; Col 1:28), which is the very thing the Spirit empowers us to do (Eph 3:16–19). And just as Paul conducts his ministry in "the fear of the Lord" (2 Cor 5:11), so ought we who are God's family to strive for holiness "in the fear of God," that is, out of reverence and awe of the one who has called us to be holy because he is holy (Lev 19:2).[10]

Reflection and Application (6:14–7:1)

The Church's call to holiness and mutual responsibility. We have already reflected on how the Church's call to holiness is integral to her vocation as "the universal sacrament of salvation" (*Lumen Gentium* 48).[11] Paul's teaching and exhortation in 6:14–7:1 challenges us to consider our own responsibilities in fulfilling this vocation. Each one of us is responsible, first and foremost, for our own growth in holiness. We cannot just leave it up to the "saints" among us to be holy. The only way the Church becomes holier is for her individual members to strive for greater holiness.

However, Paul's image of the Church as the family of God entails something more: we are mutually responsible to help one another to grow in holiness. In my opinion, this is where we sell one another short. We encourage our young people to become better students; we dole out helpful advice to friends; we assist our colleagues at work. These are good and important things to do. But how much more important is it for us, as fellow members of God's family, to help one another become better Christians. To pray and worship together. To

10. See the sidebar on "'Fear of the Lord' in the Old Testament" on p. 132.
11. See the sidebar "Vatican II and the Universal Call to Holiness" on p. 36.

encourage one another to use our talents and gifts in service to others. To support someone who is attempting to change a sinful pattern of behavior. To be there for others when they are struggling with their faith. To work together in volunteer and service projects that give witness to our faith. Like any family, the family of God is called to mutually support one another.

Getting rid of idols. It is easy to quickly pass over Paul's warning about idols in verse 16. We tend to relegate the practice of idolatry to times and places more primitive than our own. Nevertheless, idols continue to be as prominent as they ever have been. They go by names like "wealth," "prestige," "power," "success," and "pleasure." We must all ask ourselves, Is there anything—or even anyone—in my life that I seek more than I seek to love and serve God? Has that become my most important pursuit and goal? It is easy to deceive ourselves in this regard. One way to examine the priorities in our lives is to reflect on the way we use our discretionary time. If idols have in fact crept into our lives, we need to hear and heed Paul's admonition: "Come forth from them / and be separate" (v. 17).

"*Be separate.*" To be sure, the call to separation in verse 17 does *not* exclude normal interaction with the surrounding society and culture. There are people of good will and values from traditions different from our own. Moreover, we are called to participate in the Church's work of evangelization by bearing witness to the gospel, which cannot be done unless we engage society and culture. Paul's warning, however, makes clear that we must exercise great care to recognize and reject values and behavior that contradict the teaching of Christ and the Church. Young people in particular are susceptible to peer and social pressure that can lead to great harm. It is important for parents, teachers, and ministers to help and support young people to make good, life-giving choices, such as in the selection of their friends, in the cultivation of their interests and abilities, and in their vocational decisions. More broadly, Paul's call to be separate challenges each one of us to critically assess our relationships, our work commitments, and our choices for recreation—and to "come forth from" those people and things that draw us away from the path to life.

Resumption of Paul's Appeal (7:2–4)

²Make room for us; we have not wronged anyone, or ruined anyone, or taken advantage of anyone. ³I do not say this in condemnation, for I have already said that you are in our hearts, that we may die together and live together. ⁴I have great confidence in you, I have great pride in you; I am

filled with encouragement, I am overflowing with joy all the more because of all our affliction.

OT: Job 23:10–12; Ps 26
NT: Acts 20:17–38; Phil 1:3–11

Paul resumes his appeal to the Corinthians to open their hearts to him. After briefly defending his conduct among them, he again declares his love for them. He then expresses his pride in the community in anticipation of the report about his reunion with Titus (7:5–16).

7:2   Paul begins by exhorting the Corinthians to **make room for** him in their hearts. He thereby reiterates the request made in 6:13 that they enlarge their hearts in love and affection for him. Paul wants the community to be fully reconciled to him as their spiritual father. Hence he declares, once more, that his conduct among them has been blameless—he has **not wronged anyone, or ruined anyone, or taken advantage of anyone**. He is responding to lingering suspicions about him or perhaps to specific charges some have raised against him. In saying he did not "wrong" anyone, Paul insists that he has not acted unjustly (the literal sense of the verb *adikeō*). The verb "ruin" refers here to corrupting others through false teaching. In fact, Paul will accuse the intruding missionaries of doing this very thing (11:3). For his part, the Apostle has been consistently clear that his proclamation of the †gospel, through word and deed, openly manifests the truth (4:2). We will discover later that he has been accused of taking advantage of, or defrauding, the Corinthians in the matter of the collection (12:16–18). Paul categorically denies such behavior. In short, he makes clear that the community has no reason to distrust their founding †apostle.

7:3   Lest the Corinthians think he is putting them on the defensive, Paul quickly explains, **I do not say this in condemnation**. His intention in verse 2 is to promote reconciliation, not to enter into polemics. Paul goes on to restate his love for the community: **you are in our hearts**. This repeats what he stated in 6:11, where he described his heart as enlarged out of love for them. He makes this point even more poignant when he asserts that the Corinthians are so deeply fixed in his heart that they would **die together and live together**. The latter phrase was a common way of expressing deep, abiding friendship in the ancient world (see 2 Sam 15:21).[12]

Most commentators suggest that, by employing this expression, Paul intends to convey such a friendship with the community. I propose that he means something

12. See Furnish, *II Corinthians*, 367, for references to nonbiblical examples of this formula.

more. The word order—die then live—is, at first glance, peculiar. But notice how it recalls the dynamic of Jesus' death and resurrection. Paul grounds his intimate friendship with the Corinthians in the mystery of Christ's love and in the power of God to give life (4:6–7). Through his ministry enacted in self-giving love, Paul participates in the "dying of Jesus," through which God brings life to the community (4:10–12; see 5:15). Moreover, he looks forward to the resurrection of the dead when God will bring them together into the divine presence (4:14).[13]

Paul then offers to the Corinthians two examples of his love for them. First, **7:4** he reiterates that he speaks to them with frankness and candor. The NAB's **I have great confidence in you** does not capture the proper sense of the word *parrēsia*. This is the same term Paul used in 3:12, where he declared that, as a minister of the new covenant, he conducts himself *boldly*. As was the case there, he now insists that he deals forthrightly with the community; indeed, his teaching and exhortations in 6:14–7:1 are a perfect example of such frankness. Paul's candor is a reflection of his love for them. It is therefore preferable to translate the first part of verse 4: "I can speak with the greatest frankness to you" (NJB).

Second, Paul has **great pride in** the Corinthians. He explains that, in the midst of his **affliction**, he has been **filled with encouragement** and is **overflowing with joy all the more**.[14] Observe that he sounds forth themes from the opening blessing (1:3–7), where he revealed that God brings him encouragement in the midst of afflictions. In the following passage Paul will recount how, in a time of great personal anguish, God encouraged him with the return of Titus, who reported that the community responded favorably to the †tearful letter. This news brings great joy to Paul, as he learns that the Corinthian church acted in a way that makes him proud. What is important to appreciate concerning verse 4 is that Paul communicates his love for the Corinthians by expressing his pride in them. He thereby gives the community another reason to be reconciled to him.

Reflection and Application (7:2–4)

Paul's pastoral wisdom. Paul's words in verses 3–4 reveal profound pastoral insight. He sincerely communicates great depth of love and warmth toward

13. See Jan Lambrecht, *Second Corinthians*, SP (Collegeville, MN: Liturgical Press, 1999), 126–27. He argues that Paul "points to the future life of which the actual Christian life already is an anticipation" (127).

14. The NJB most accurately conveys the content and flow of Paul's thought in v. 4: "I can speak with the greatest frankness to you; and I can speak with the greatest pride about you: in all our hardship, I am filled with encouragement and overflowing with joy."

those to whom he is ministering. He also expresses his pride and confidence in them. Paul thereby provides a good example for parents, adult leaders of youth, mentors, bishops and pastors, religious superiors—in short, for those in positions of leadership who must inevitably deal with strained relationships. When a healthy foundation of love and right conduct has been laid, expressing these things can go a long way toward rebuilding the relationship, as do affirmations of pride and confidence in those being ministered to.

Theology in relation to spirituality and ministry. We have now reached the conclusion of Paul's extended explanation of his way of being an apostle. Second Corinthians 2:14–7:4 is a treasure trove of important theological themes: [†]new covenant, the restoration of humanity in God's [†]image, suffering, resurrection, Jesus' sacrificial and redemptive death, God's reconciling the world to himself, the revelation of God's righteousness. The Apostle reveals his capacity to think theologically in a profound and inspired manner.

But theology, which St. Anselm aptly described as "faith seeking understanding," was not an end in itself for Paul. As important as it is to know and understand what God has brought about through Christ's life, death, and resurrection, it is even more important that *theology should lead to transformed lives.* This is what we can learn from Paul. As much as anyone, he appreciated the role the Holy Spirit plays in the ongoing drama of salvation. In his lengthy treatise on apostleship, what he conveys most eloquently is a spirituality understood as life in and empowered by the Holy Spirit. The Spirit of faithfulness propelled Paul to embody in his ministry the gospel he preached about Jesus the [†]Messiah. It is one thing to talk about God's love and Jesus' faithfulness; it is quite another thing to participate in the ongoing revelation of God's righteousness by incarnating Christ's self-giving love. It is one thing to talk about God's work of reconciliation; it is quite another to strive to facilitate reconciliation in the face of misunderstanding and pain. It is no accident that Paul's majestic, theologically rich discourse on the new covenant ministry climaxes in his reaching out in love to the Corinthians.

Looking Back, Once More

2 Corinthians 7:5–16

Following his lengthy treatment on the nature and integrity of his apostolic ministry (2:14–7:4), Paul picks up the rehearsal of recent events he left hanging at 2:13. He recounts his reunion with Titus and his joy at hearing the latter's report about the Corinthians' positive reception of the †tearful letter (7:5–7). Responding to their repentance, Paul now declares the community innocent concerning what happened during the painful visit (7:8–13a). He concludes by expressing his confidence in them (7:13b–16).

Joyful Reunion with Titus (7:5–7)

---

[5]For even when we came into Macedonia, our flesh had no rest, but we were afflicted in every way—external conflicts, internal fears. [6]But God, who encourages the downcast, encouraged us by the arrival of Titus, [7]and not only by his arrival but also by the encouragement with which he was encouraged in regard to you, as he told us of your yearning, your lament, your zeal for me, so that I rejoiced even more.

OT: Ps 102:13–23; 138:1–8; Isa 49:13–22
NT: Matt 11:28–30; Luke 1:52; 1 Thess 3:6–10; James 1:9

Recall that Paul interrupted his rehearsal of recent events (1:15–2:13) at the very point where the Corinthians' interest and curiosity were at their peak: they were left wondering how he reacted to Titus's report of their favorable response to his †tearful letter. He now conveys his reaction of great joy at the encouragement he received from Titus and the community, encouragement he insists is a gift from God.

7:5–6   Paul left a promising missionary opportunity in †Troas because he had not heard from Titus (2:12–13). Titus was the trusted envoy who had been sent to deliver the tearful letter and to gauge the Corinthians' response. Paul now informs the community that **when** he **came into Macedonia**, his **flesh had no rest**. His anxiety was so great that he sought to meet Titus along the way in order to get the news more quickly.[1] Notice that he employs the term "flesh" here to convey human existence as weak and vulnerable. Indeed, Paul immediately describes himself as **afflicted in every way** (see 4:8–9; 6:4–10), afflictions he succinctly summarizes as **external conflicts, internal fears**. What does he mean by external "conflicts," or literally, "battles"? Paul uses the Greek term figuratively to indicate quarrels or controversies (2 Tim 2:23; Titus 3:9; see James 4:1). Thus he refers here to disputes with others—whether with non-Christians (see Acts 16:16–17:15 for the opposition he encountered during his first visit to †Macedonia) or with Christians who opposed him (see, e.g., Phil 3:2, 18–19) or with both. What is meant by "internal fears"? In addition to his anxiety as he awaited news from Titus—anxiety over whether the tearful letter had produced the intended effect—Paul was worried about the safety of his envoy, as traveling was always a precarious enterprise. It is also easy to imagine that he engaged in some second-guessing over what he had written.

Paul then reports that he was **encouraged . . . by the arrival of Titus**. The word *parousia* means both "arrival" and "presence." Paul, who was so anxious to meet up with his envoy, received consolation not only from Titus's arrival but also from his companionship. What is most striking about Paul's report is that he attributes this gift of encouragement to **God**. In his opening prayer he blessed God as "the Father of compassion and God of all encouragement, who encourages us in our every affliction" (1:3–4). Paul now offers another example of how God has encouraged him in the midst of affliction (see 1:8–11). Note that he describes God as the one **who encourages the downcast** (*tapeinous*). This description is an allusion to Isa 49:13, at the end of the second Isaian servant song (Isa 49:1–13). We saw in 6:2 how Paul applies this song as God's personal encouragement to him in his ministry to the †Gentiles. That God brings consolation to the *tapeinoi* (the "lowly," "humble") recalls what Paul intimated in 4:13, where he reads the †Septuagint version of Ps 116 as a summary of the story of Jesus: just as God raised and exalted Christ, who "humbled (*etapeinōsen*) himself" and was obedient

1. See stage 5 under Historical Context in the introduction.

God and the "Lowly"

BIBLICAL BACKGROUND

The Psalms in particular express God's special love and concern for the lowly and humble. In the following citations, the italicized words are rendered *tapeinos* (plural *tapeinoi*) in the †Septuagint. The Lord secures justice "for the orphan and *oppressed*" (Ps 10:18). God saves "*humble* people" while he brings low the haughty (18:28; see Prov 3:34). The Lord is close to the brokenhearted and "saves *those* whose spirit is *crushed*" (Ps 34:18). God is called upon to defend "the lowly and fatherless" and to render justice to "*the afflicted* and needy" (82:3). He heeds "the plea of *the lowly*" and does not scorn their prayer (102:18). Although the Lord is exalted, he "cares for *the lowly*" and knows the proud from afar (138:6).

Tellingly, in one of the messianic oracles found in the prophet Isaiah, the "shoot" from "the stump of Jesse" is described as judging "*the poor* with justice" and as deciding "aright for the land's *afflicted*" (Isa 11:4). Jesus the †Messiah—who is Emmanuel, "God-with-us," in fulfillment of another Isaian prophecy (Matt 1:23; Isa 7:14)—incarnated in his ministry God's mercy and care for the lowly, even in the midst of his agony on the cross (see Luke 23:42–43, where Jesus responds to the plea of the repentant criminal crucified beside him).

unto death (see Phil 2:8), so will he raise those who conduct themselves after the manner of Jesus.[2] The allusion to Isa 49:13 also echoes a theme found in Mary's Magnificat, that God has "lifted up the lowly" (Luke 1:52; see James 1:9).

Paul goes on to explain that God **not only** encouraged him by the **arrival** and presence of Titus, **but also** by what his envoy reported about the Corinthians. We learn that Titus himself received **encouragement** from the community's response to the tearful letter. Notice Paul's pastoral subtlety as he names the Corinthians themselves as instruments of God's encouragement (by referring to the encouragement **with which** Titus **was encouraged in regard to** the community). They would be pleased to have the Apostle acknowledge them in this manner. And Titus shares this encouragement with Paul, describing to him the community's **yearning, lament,** and **zeal** for him. The Corinthians' "yearning," or great longing, is their desire to see him again in person (see also 1 Thess 3:6). Their "lament," or wailing, expresses their regret at remaining silent after the incident with the wrongdoer during the painful visit. Their "zeal" is seen in the action they subsequently took in punishing this person (see 2 Cor 2:6). In hearing how the community had responded to the tearful letter, Paul **rejoiced**

7:7

---

2. See the exegesis of 4:13–15, above.

even more. The Corinthians' longing for him and their sorrow over what had happened reveal that they *are* heeding the way of the †gospel. Thus we can see why he stated in 7:4 that, in the midst of his affliction, he is "filled with encouragement" and is "overflowing with joy all the more."

Reflection and Application (7:5–7)

Finding God in all things. The spirituality of St. Ignatius of Loyola is founded on a simple principle, namely, that God can be found in all things. God is assuredly encountered in a special way in the liturgical proclamation of Scripture and in the celebration of the sacraments. But Ignatius insisted that human experience is also filled with religious significance. Through the practice of a daily examination of consciousness—a review of key moments in one's day—a person can become adept at recognizing the presence of God in his or her daily encounters and activities. Paul's bold statement in verse 6 reveals such adeptness. What might look to an outsider as simply the reunion of two friends was, for him, a manifestation of *God's* gift of encouragement. The more we are aware of God's presence in our lives, the more grateful we become—and the more we desire to praise and serve him at every moment and in every circumstance.

Allowing others to bring good news to us. One important corollary of finding God in all things is that God works in and through the people around us. We are undoubtedly familiar with the story of Doubting Thomas (John 20:19–29). In my opinion, the tragedy of the story is not Thomas's difficulty in believing that Jesus was raised from the dead. The real tragedy is that, for one whole week(!), he refused to accept the good news his fellow apostles were trying to convey to him. People in ministry are more used to giving than to receiving. But no minister is exempt from the need to receive support and encouragement from others—not even St. Paul! To be sure, our only unfailing support is God. But just as those apostles whom Thomas had seen cowering in fear behind locked doors had a stupendous gift to offer him, so we might be surprised by the ways and the people through whom God offers us support. Am I open enough to see them? Am I humble enough to accept them?

The Tearful Letter, Once More (7:8–13a)

8For even if I saddened you by my letter, I do not regret it; and if I did regret it ([for] I see that that letter saddened you, if only for a while), 9I rejoice now, not because you were saddened, but because you were saddened into repentance; for you were saddened in a godly way, so that you did not suffer loss in anything because of us. ¹⁰For godly sorrow produces a salutary repentance without regret, but worldly sorrow produces death. ¹¹For behold what earnestness this godly sorrow has produced for you, as well as readiness for a defense, and indignation, and fear, and yearning, and zeal, and punishment. In every way you have shown yourselves to be innocent in the matter. ¹²So then even though I wrote to you, it was not on account of the one who did the wrong, or on account of the one who suffered the wrong, but in order that your concern for us might be made plain to you in the sight of God. ¹³For this reason we are encouraged.

OT: 2 Sam 12:1–25; Ps 32; 51; Jon 3
NT: Luke 5:1–11; 18:9–14; 23:39–43; James 4:7–10
Catechism: contrition, 1451–54; satisfaction and penance, 1434–39, 1459–60

Paul brings up once more the †tearful letter. He rejoices because it produced in the Corinthians a change of heart according to God's will. He then acknowledges the fruit of their repentance: their increased zeal for him and their taking action against the community member who had offended him.

Earlier in the letter (1:23–2:4), Paul explained why he wrote a letter with **7:8–9** "anguish of heart" and "many tears"—a letter that is no longer extant—in the aftermath of his painful visit. There he insisted that his motivation in writing was to convey his love for the Corinthians. Paul now discusses his thoughts about this **letter** in light of its effect on the community. He recognizes that the Corinthians were **saddened** by its contents—probably because he poignantly expressed to them how the incident with "the one who did the wrong" (7:12) affected him and how disappointed he was at their not coming to his defense.³ Note the prevalence of the words "sadden" and "sorrow" here and in the following verses. Although the community was saddened, Paul candidly informs them that he does **not regret** sending the letter, for reasons that will become clear. Nevertheless, he concedes that, for a while, he **did regret** sending it. This second instance of the verb "regret" is in the imperfect tense, signifying ongoing action in the past. Paul probably refers here to his anxiety as he awaited Titus's return, wondering whether or not his words had been too strong. He also acknowledges for a second time that his letter **saddened** the Corinthians, **if only for a while**. By admitting his temporary regret over sending the letter

---

3. Like many other commentators, I hypothesize that "the one who did the wrong" (v. 12) had slandered Paul and called his apostolic authority into question. See stage 4 under Historical Context in the introduction.

St. John Chrysostom and Five Ways of Repentance

Near the end of his homily "On the Power of Man to Resist the Devil"—the second of three homilies he delivered concerning the powers of demons—St. John Chrysostom set forth five ways of repentance. The first way is the honest acknowledgement and confession of one's own sins. This way is salutary because the one who condemns his or her own sins is "less inclined to fall into them again" (2.6). Chrysostom exhorts his listeners to arouse their inner accuser, that is, their conscience, in order to avoid having an accuser at the Lord's judgment seat. The second way of repentance involves the refusal to hold grudges, even against one's enemies, and the commitment to forgive others. In offering this way, Chrysostom cites Matt 6:14: "If you forgive others their transgressions, your heavenly Father will forgive you." The third way is "fervent and diligent prayer . . . from the bottom of the heart" (2.6). This way is effective because God, the recipient of such heartfelt prayer, is merciful and compassionate. The fourth way of repentance is almsgiving. In showing kindness and generosity to others, one opens oneself to receive God's forgiveness. The fifth way is to conduct oneself with humility and modesty. According to Chrysostom, these five ways of repentance are like medicines that effectively treat the self-inflicted wounds of sin (2.6).

and by recognizing the sorrow it caused, he shows his sensitivity and concern for the community.

Notwithstanding his ambivalence about writing the tearful letter, Paul declares that he **now** "rejoices." Lest there be any misunderstanding about why he is filled with joy, he clarifies that it is *not* **because** the Corinthians **were saddened**, or distressed, by the letter's contents. Paul does not take satisfaction in their pain. Rather, he rejoices because their sorrow has led to **repentance**.

The word for repentance, *metanoia*, means, literally, "a change of mind," although more than just thinking is involved. The repentance, or contrition, referred to here involves "a genuine acknowledgement of wrongdoing, coupled with the humble resolve to change one's behavior."[4] Authentic *metanoia* is therefore manifested in changed behavior. That *metanoia* is essential for Christian life is evident from Jesus' use of the verbal form of this word in his opening

4. Victor Paul Furnish, *II Corinthians: A New Translation with Introduction and Commentary*, AB 32A (New York: Doubleday, 1984), 387. The NEB and REB aptly translate *metanoia* as "change of heart."

proclamation: "The kingdom of God is at hand. Repent [*metanoeite*], and believe in the gospel" (Mark 1:15).

Paul goes on to remark that the community was **saddened in a godly way**. The phrase "in a godly way" signifies "according to the will of God."[5] Because the Corinthians were saddened in this manner, Paul assures them that they **did not suffer loss in anything because of** him. Even though his letter caused them distress, it was the catalyst that led to authentic repentance. The real loss would have occurred if they had rejected him, the one who had brought the ⁺gospel and God's gift of reconciliation to them.

Paul sets forth an important distinction—the distinction between **godly sor-** **7:10** **row** and **worldly sorrow**. On the one hand, "godly sorrow"—the sorrow that is according to God's will—is rooted in the recognition that our sinful thoughts, words, actions, and omissions offend God, adversely affect others, and hurt ourselves. In short, it comprehends the truth about sin. Godly sorrow **produces** authentic **repentance** (*metanoia*), that is, both inner sorrow and the resolve to amend one's life. Paul reveals that the fruit of such repentance is "salvation" (the NAB's **salutary** comes from the Latin word meaning "salvation").[6] Salvation refers primarily to the fullness of life with God, that is, to eternal life. It also signifies the fruit of the ministry of reconciliation in the present: human relationships that are restored and at peace. Paul adds, with great understatement, that such repentance leading to salvation is **without regret**.

On the other hand, "worldly sorrow"—literally, sorrow "according to the world"—is grounded in a worldview that refuses to acknowledge the presence and power of God. Worldly sorrow is self-centered and does not lead to a change of heart or behavior. It is the regret felt, for example, when ill-gotten gains are lost, when one is prevented from engaging in sinful pursuits, or when one's immoral activity is brought to light. As Chrysostom astutely observed, such sorrow often leads to the thirst for revenge.[7] Paul concludes by asserting that worldly sorrow **produces death**, referring to the "death" of wallowing in anger and bitterness in the present—and, even more, to eternal death.

Paul goes on to emphasize the fruits **produced** by the Corinthians' **godly** **7:11** **sorrow**. He lists seven attitudes and actions that show forth the genuineness of their repentance. Their sevenfold response reveals that the community has understood the wrongness of their silence following the affront to Christ Jesus' ambassador by one of their own members. Paul first acknowledges their

---

5. The NIV's "as God intended" captures well the sense of *kata theon*.

6. The NAB's "salutary repentance" does not do justice to the phrase *metanoia eis sōtēria*. The RSV and NRSV's "repentance that leads to salvation" better captures Paul's meaning.

7. *Homilies on 2 Corinthians* 15.2.

earnestness to amend the situation. As we will see, this term—which can signify an eager commitment to other people as well as to religious obligations—will play an important role in his appeal for generosity in the collection.[8] Second, he lists their **readiness for a defense**, a reference to their clarifying that they were neither in agreement with the slander nor in league with the wrongdoer. Third, Paul recognizes their **indignation**, their righteous anger at their own silence and at the action of the guilty party. Fourth, he names the **fear** they felt as they reflected on their failure to take action. In fact, such fear is an expression of the "fear of the Lord" (see 5:11; 7:1), because they realized they had endangered their relationship with the †apostle whom God had sent to them with the †gospel. Fifth and sixth, Paul lists their **yearning** and **zeal**, the same terms used in verse 7 to indicate their strong desire to see him again and their renewed commitment to him.

Finally, Paul refers to the Corinthians' **punishment** of the wrongdoer. This action—which probably entailed ostracizing the wrongdoer from the community—expressed their zeal for Paul and their desire to address what had happened. Although most commentators surmise that he demanded such punishment in his tearful letter, I am of the opinion that the Corinthians acted of their own accord.[9] In either case, he now shows his appreciation to the community for their renewed commitment to him.

Moreover, Paul declares the Corinthians' innocence: **In every way you have shown yourselves to be innocent in the matter**. At first glance, it might seem odd that he would pronounce the community's innocence. Has he not just rejoiced in their recognition of wrongdoing? Paul's statement here must be understood at two levels. At one level, he expresses his awareness that the offense against him was committed by only one individual; that is, he now knows that the wrongdoer's words did not reflect the opinion of the entire community. Thus the Corinthians are in fact innocent of the actual slander. At another level, Paul's declaration serves as an absolution of the community. Although they did not perpetrate the slander, their silence rendered them complicit in the wrongdoing. Paul's tearful letter made this clear to them and evoked their "lament" (v. 7) and subsequent repentance. Given their dramatic expression of contrition, he now extends his forgiveness. Notice that in doing so he again puts into practice the ministry of reconciliation he proclaims, just as he did when he exhorted the Corinthians to receive back and confirm their love for the punished party (2:5–10).

8. Paul employs the noun *spoudē* or its adjective form *spoudaios* in 8:7, 8, 16, 17, 22.
9. See my explanation in the exegesis of 2:5–11, above.

Paul next explains his reason for writing the tearful letter. In claiming that it was neither **on account of the one who did the wrong** (i.e., the wrongdoer) nor **on account of the one who suffered the wrong** (i.e., Paul), he is not denying he wrote about his own pain over the slanderer's words. The Apostle employs here a Hebraic mode of expression by which a comparison is conveyed through contrast.[10] Thus he states that, *more than* these secondary purposes, his primary purpose involved the Corinthians themselves: **in order that your concern for us might be made plain to you in the sight of God.** That is, Paul desired that the members of the community recognize their "concern," or eagerness, for him through the actions described in verse 11. Their recommitment to their founding apostle bears testimony to their own deepening commitment to live according to the gospel. This is what Paul wants the community to understand. His expressed purpose thus manifests his love for the Corinthians (see 2:4).

Indeed, there is no greater expression of love than assisting others to grow in their Christian commitment. And because the community has responded favorably to the tearful letter, Paul reiterates at the beginning of verse 13 that he is **encouraged**. Here he uses the †divine passive, indicating that, through the words and actions of the Corinthians and Titus, he has received encouragement *from God*, the one "who encourages the downcast" (v. 6).

Reflection and Application (7:8–13a)

The importance of contrition. Paul's teaching about "godly sorrow" that produces repentance unto salvation (vv. 9–10) invites us to consider the importance of contrition in our spiritual lives. Contrition was defined by the Council of Trent as "sorrow of the soul and detestation for the sin committed, together with the resolution not to sin again."[11] While all sincere contrition involves the hatred of sin, the motives for contrition can vary. One motive is the fear of suffering punishment for sin, especially the pains of hell. While it is true that Jesus' preaching focused on the power of love in God's kingdom, nevertheless he also taught, "I shall show you whom to fear. Be afraid of the one"—God—"who after killing has the power to cast into Gehenna" (Luke 12:5; see Matt 10:28; 25:31–46). The contrition motivated by the fear of eternal punishment is called "imperfect contrition." It is imperfect in comparison with "perfect contrition,"

---

10. As explained by Alfred Plummer, *A Critical and Exegetical Commentary on the Second Epistle of St. Paul to the Corinthians*, ICC (Edinburgh: T&T Clark, 1915), 224. For example, Hosea 6:6—"For it is love that I desire, not sacrifice"—does not obviate the call for sacrifice but rather emphasizes the importance of love. See also 1 Cor 1:17.

11. As quoted in the Catechism, 1451.

the contrition motivated by love for God. That is, perfect contrition expresses sorrow at having offended the one who is all good, all faithful, and all loving. Contrition is one of the three acts of the penitent—along with the confession of sins and penance (see below)—that are necessary to celebrate the Sacrament of Reconciliation.

An effective way to inculcate true contrition is to examine one's conscience every day and to express sorrow for one's sins through the prayer called the "Act of Contrition." This prayer expresses both imperfect contrition ("I detest all my sins because I dread the loss of heaven and the pains of hell") and perfect contrition ("I detest all my sins because they offend you, my God, who are all good and deserving of all my love"). Authentic contrition not only looks back at our sins with sorrow but also compels us more and more, with God's †grace, to avoid sin in the future.

Penance and practicing the faith. Paul teaches that genuine *metanoia* is manifested in changed behavior. As mentioned above, penance is an essential part of celebrating the Sacrament of Reconciliation. This involves more than seeking to redress those whom we have wronged, which justice requires; it also entails engaging in activities that strengthen our ability to avoid sin and help us walk more in the way of Christ. Because penance is of great help in heeding the ongoing call to conversion, it can be a salutary feature of our practice of the faith.

Three traditional forms of doing penance are prayer, fasting, and almsgiving (see Matt 6:1–6, 16–18). Through prayer we open ourselves to God's love for us and commit ourselves to doing his will in our daily lives (as we pray "thy kingdom come" in the Lord's Prayer). Through fasting we purify ourselves and also become more sensitive to the needs of others, thereby stoking our "hunger and thirst for righteousness" (Matt 5:6). Through almsgiving we respond to those needs and align ourselves with the goodness and generosity of God. These are but a few of the ways by which we can practice becoming better Christians.

Paul's Confidence in the Corinthians (7:13b–16)

And besides our encouragement, we rejoice even more because of the joy of Titus, since his spirit has been refreshed by all of you. [14]For if I have boasted to him about you, I was not put to shame. No, just as everything we said to you was true, so our boasting before Titus proved to be the truth. [15]And his heart goes out to you all the more, as he remembers the

obedience of all of you, when you received him with fear and trembling.
¹⁶I rejoice, because I have confidence in you in every respect.

OT: Ps 2:11
NT: Mark 5:25–34; Phil 2:12–18

Paul informs the Corinthians about Titus's joy occasioned by their reception of him and the letter he bore. He then confides that he had previously boasted to Titus about them, and this boasting has now been vindicated. He concludes by reiterating his own joy and by expressing his complete confidence in the community.

After restating the **encouragement** he has received, Paul turns the Corin-   7:13b–14
thians' attention to his envoy Titus. He rejoices **even more because of the joy of Titus**. Titus has not only conveyed to Paul the community's favorable response to the †tearful letter, he has also expressed his own joy at what has taken place in Corinth. Observe that it is Titus's **spirit** that **has been refreshed**. We saw in 2:12–13 that the spirit is the interior place of contact with the Spirit of God. Paul thus suggests here what he made explicit concerning himself in verse 6, namely, that it is *God* who has brought refreshment to Titus through the reaction of **all** the Corinthians. What are we to make of Paul's reference to "all," especially in light of the fact that the present letter has given several hints that not everyone is fully reconciled with him? To be sure, the vast majority seems to have sided with their founding †apostle (2:6). The use of "all," in my opinion, suggests that Paul wants to accentuate the community's positive response to the tearful letter and that he subtly exhorts those who still have doubts about him to come on board with the rest.

Paul reveals to the Corinthians that prior to sending Titus with the tearful letter he had **boasted** to his envoy about them. This revelation is surprising, given what had transpired during his painful visit. At that moment, it might have seemed as if Paul had little to boast about concerning the community. As we saw in the analysis of 1:12–14, however, the positive sense of †boasting refers ultimately to what has been accomplished by God's †grace. Thus Paul in all likelihood communicated to Titus his confidence in what God had done—and would *continue* to do—in and through the Corinthians. And because the community has now responded to Titus's visit with godly sorrow and a renewed zeal for Paul, the latter can now declare that he **was not put to shame**. The Corinthians' actions have justified his boasting. The Corinthians would not only be glad to hear about Paul's vindication on their account, they would also be thrilled to learn that he has boasted about them to others. We once again see the Apostle's keen pastoral skills.

Moreover, notice how Paul now takes the occasion to restate a theme that has been prominent since 1:18: the veracity of his word. He insists that **everything** he **said to** the community **was true**. "Everything" refers to his initial proclamation as well as to all the teaching and pastoral advice he has imparted in his previous visits and letters. And **just as** his proclamation, teaching, and exhortations have been grounded in the truth, so has his **boasting before Titus proved to be the truth**.

7:15–16   Paul goes on to highlight Titus's great love for the Corinthians. He reports that his envoy's **heart goes out to** them. For "heart" Paul uses the same word, *splanchna*, he employed in 6:12 (there translated "affections"). This term refers to the seat of the emotions, especially to compassion and love. Just as Paul's heart is enlarged with love for the community (6:11), so is Titus's. The latter's love is inflamed as **he remembers the obedience** they manifested when he came to them with the tearful letter. To what does the Corinthians' obedience refer and to whom was it rendered? An important clue is given by the phrase **with fear and trembling**. In the Old Testament this phrase signifies the proper human response before God's power and majesty.[12] Paul employs the same phrase in Phil 2:12, where he encourages the Philippians to work out their salvation "with fear and trembling." This exhortation follows immediately upon the famous Christ hymn (Phil 2:6–11) that portrays Jesus' obedience unto death. Just as Jesus' obedience was rendered to God, so Paul exhorts the Philippians to obey the one who is at work in them both to will and to work for his good purpose (Phil 2:13).[13] Returning to verse 15: when Titus arrived in Corinth bearing the letter from Paul, the community recognized that they were hearing from God's emissaries (2 Cor 5:20) and ministers (6:4). In the end, the Corinthians responded to God's will for them by allowing their godly sorrow to manifest itself in repentance and renewed zeal for their spiritual father.

Finally, **I rejoice**—Paul once more expresses his great joy in the community. He concludes by declaring his **confidence in** them **in every respect**. Paul's joy and confidence result from the Corinthians' response to his sending Titus with the tearful letter. Not only has the community received Titus (v. 13), they have also heeded God's call (v. 15) by renewing their zeal for Paul (vv. 7, 11) and by repenting of their silence when one of their members was insolent toward

12. See, e.g., Exod 15:16; Ps 2:11; Isa 19:16. In Mark 5:33 the healing power of Jesus evokes a similar response.

13. Paul's initial missionary visit to Corinth was also with "fear and much trembling" (1 Cor 2:3) as he continued to heed God's call to him after his less than fruitful evangelization in Athens (see Acts 17:15–34).

him (vv. 9–10). In doing so they have vindicated his boasting to Titus about them (v. 14).

Why does Paul go out of his way to effusively express his joy and confidence in the Corinthians at this point in the letter? His earlier rehearsal of events (1:15–2:13) was an attempt to clear the air about recent misunderstandings concerning his change in travel plans and his decision, in the aftermath of the painful incident, to write a letter instead of returning to them. He then interrupted this account of past events to offer a lengthy discourse that explained his way of being an apostle (2:14–7:4). Recall that this explanation climaxed in Paul's appeal to the Corinthians to open their hearts to him (6:11–13; 7:2–4).

Now, in picking up where he left off at 2:13, he desires to aid the process of reconciliation between the community and himself. He wants the Corinthians to run with the momentum that Titus's mission has set in motion. Although the community has repented and expressed their zeal to see Paul again, there are lingering questions and doubts about him due in large part to the intruding missionaries. He thus expresses his joy and confidence in the Corinthians and praises them for their response to his tearful letter in the hope that their initial gestures toward reconciliation will mature into full reconciliation with him.

In 7:5–16 Paul also lays the groundwork for the remainder of the letter. He is now ready to appeal to the Corinthians to resume their participation in the collection he is taking up for the church in Jerusalem (8:1–9:15). In the aftermath of the painful visit, their participation grounded to a halt. Paul's reconciliation with the community is a necessary prelude to his asking for their generous contribution to a project that is, as we will see, a manifestation of God's work of reconciling Jews and †Gentiles. Indeed, Paul wants the Corinthians to know Titus's great love and enthusiasm for them because Paul is about to send him back to Corinth to facilitate their contribution.

In addition, Paul expresses his joy and confidence in the community with an eye toward 10:1–12:21, where he will take on the intruding missionaries. The Apostle has not only set forth the characteristics of an authentic minister of God. He has also made clear that he loves the Corinthians and has their best interests at heart. They should thus choose to listen to him rather than heed these "superapostles" (11:5; 12:11).

Reflection and Application (7:13b–16)

Pointing out the positive. Paul's expression of joy and confidence in the fledgling church in Corinth shows great pastoral sensitivity. One of the difficult challenges in ministry is to help people live the gospel more radically, which can entail exhorting them to ongoing conversion. Calling people to leave behind harmful patterns of behavior is hard, both for ministers, who understandably hesitate to call for correction, and for those being challenged. Paul shows that, when doing so, it helps to point out what others are doing well. People tend to receive criticism better when their good qualities are also acknowledged. Similarly, people are inclined to show more openness to challenge when their present efforts are appreciated. A glance at Paul's letters reveals that he is adept at pointing out the positive when exhorting others (e.g., 1 Thess 4:10–12). His strategy of pointing out the positive is a good example for parents, teachers, religious superiors, and others in leadership positions whose responsibility includes calling those under their charge to growth and improvement.

Collection for the Jerusalem Church (1): Participating in the Work of Grace

2 Corinthians 8:1–24

Now that Paul has cleared the air of past misunderstandings (1:15–2:13), has set forth his way of being an †apostle (2:14–7:4), and has communicated both his great joy over the Corinthians' favorable response to the †tearful letter and his confidence in them (7:5–16), he turns to the issue of the collection for the church in Jerusalem (8:1–9:15). He begins by raising the example of the Macedonians' enthusiasm and generosity (8:1–7). After setting forth the supreme example of Jesus' "gracious act," Paul appeals to the community to resume their participation in the collection (8:8–15). He then tells them that he is sending Titus, along with two brothers, to Corinth to facilitate their contribution (8:16–24).

God's Grace at Work among the Macedonians (8:1–7)

¹We want you to know, brothers, of the grace of God that has been given to the churches of Macedonia, ²for in a severe test of affliction, the abundance of their joy and their profound poverty overflowed in a wealth of generosity on their part. ³For according to their means, I can testify, and beyond their means, spontaneously, ⁴they begged us insistently for the favor of taking part in the service to the holy ones, ⁵and this, not as we expected, but they gave themselves first to the Lord and to us through the will of God, ⁶so that we urged Titus that, as he had already begun, he should also complete for you this gracious act also. ⁷Now as you excel in

Origins and Significance of the Collection — BIBLICAL BACKGROUND

Paul's collection for the poor in the Jerusalem church began with a request by Peter, James, and John at the conclusion of the Council of Jerusalem (Gal 2:1–10; see Acts 15:1–21). This early, important gathering of apostles and other church leaders confirmed Paul's ministry of proclaiming the †gospel and establishing churches among the †Gentiles without requiring circumcision. According to Gal 2:10, the only request made of Paul was to gather funds for the poor in Jerusalem, something he "was eager to do." Several factors brought about dire poverty in the Jerusalem church—among them: drought and famine; heavy taxation, imposed both by Rome and by Jewish authorities; and the constant addition of Jewish converts, some of whom may have been shunned socially and economically, and thereby impoverished, because they chose to be baptized.

We learn from 1 Cor 16:1–4 how Paul went about expediting the collection. He encouraged every person in his largely Gentile churches to set aside money each week according to each one's earnings. These contributions were to be collected and taken to Jerusalem by representatives chosen from the various communities. Later on, he decided to accompany the group himself (Rom 15:25–28).

In Paul's view, the collection was more than an act of charity. He reasoned that Gentile converts to Christianity were indebted to the Jerusalem church because the latter had shared spiritual blessings with them. It was thus a matter of justice that the Gentile churches now share their material blessings with the poor in Jerusalem (Rom 15:27). Moreover, the collection became a means to symbolically express the unity (*koinōnia*) of the Church, understood as the one body of Christ in which there is "neither Jew nor Greek" (Gal 3:28; Col 3:11). Paul also viewed the collection as an expression of "the ministry of reconciliation" (2 Cor 5:18).

---

every respect, in faith, discourse, knowledge, all earnestness, and in the love we have for you, may you excel in this gracious act also.

OT: Ps 34; 41:2–4; 72:1–14; Sir 3:29–4:10
NT: Gal 2:10; Eph 2:11–22; Phil 2:1–11; James 2:15–16

Paul begins his appeal by informing the Corinthians of the Macedonians' manner of participating in the collection. The latter, despite suffering affliction and poverty, have given generously—even beyond their means. Paul highlights as exemplary the Macedonians' initiative and the gift of their very selves in response to God's grace. He then informs the Corinthians that Titus is returning to complete the work previously begun among them and exhorts them to excel in their own contribution.

Paul's opening words—**We want you to know, brothers**—are typical of the way he introduces a topic of special importance (see 1 Cor 12:1; 15:1; Gal 1:11). As was the case in 1:8, "brothers" is an inclusive term. Paul's use of familial language here is significant for two reasons: first, he emphasizes his own intimacy with the Corinthians; second, he sets the stage for their regarding members of *other* churches as their brothers and sisters in the Lord. Paul wants the community to know about **the grace of God that has been given to the churches of Macedonia**. The reference to the "†grace" of God marks the first of ten occurrences of the word *charis* in 8:1–9:15. God's grace denotes his gift of love, the love made known most dramatically in the sending of his Son (John 3:16) and in the gift of the Spirit in our hearts (Rom 5:5). Grace thus signifies that God holds nothing back in reaching out to us in love. The participle rendered "has been given" is in the perfect tense, which indicates that something happened in the past that continues to have effects in the present. The communities founded and nurtured by Paul in the Roman province of †Macedonia—†Philippi, †Thessalonica, and (possibly) †Beroea (Acts 16:11–17:15)—have received "God's gift of enablement."[1] This gift now empowers the Macedonian Christians to hold nothing back in participating in the work of the collection, as the following verses make clear.

8:1

Paul then describes how the gift of grace given to the Macedonians has been manifested. Although they have endured **a severe test** (*dokimē*) **of affliction**, their communities are marked by an **abundance** of joy. In addition, their **profound poverty** has **overflowed in a wealth of generosity**. That "joy" arises in spite of "affliction" and that "generosity" springs from "poverty" can only be explained by the workings of God's grace (6:10). What was the affliction suffered by the Macedonians? In all likelihood, Paul alludes to the persecution and social ostracism they have endured on account of their faith.[2] Such persecution and ostracism, moreover, may very well account for their profound poverty. Nevertheless, Paul declares that the Macedonians have experienced the empowerment of God, who "encourages us in our every affliction" (1:4). This divine assistance accounts for their joy, which is a distinguishing mark of those who live in accord with the way of God (1:24). In fact, Paul accents the notion of obedience to God in a way that is not immediately apparent in

8:2

---

1. Murray J. Harris, *Second Epistle to the Corinthians*, NIGTC (Grand Rapids: Eerdmans, 2005), 560.
2. See Phil 1:29–30; 1 Thess 1:6; 2:14; 3:3–4; 2 Thess 1:4–7.

Paul's Use of *Charis* in 2 Corinthians 8–9

BIBLICAL BACKGROUND

One of the distinguishing characteristics of 2 Cor 8:1–9:15 is Paul's tenfold use of *charis*, usually translated "grace" (see 1:2, 12; 4:15; 6:1; 12:9; 13:13). In its most basic sense, *charis* refers to an expression of favor or kindness. It can also refer to the goodwill of the giver as well as to the gratitude of the receiver. For Paul, however, *charis* refers first and foremost to God's redemptive love as manifested in the life, ministry, death, and resurrection of Jesus and in the bestowal of the Holy Spirit.

No English translation renders every instance of *charis* as "grace" in 8:1–9:15. That is because in these chapters Paul employs the term with richness and nuance. The NAB captures this richness as follows:

"grace" (of God, 8:1)
"favor" (of participating, 8:4)
"gracious act" (i.e., the collection, 8:6)
"gracious act" (i.e., the collection, 8:7)
"gracious act" (of Christ Jesus, 8:9)
"thanks" (to God, 8:16)
"gracious work" (i.e., the collection, 8:19)
"grace" (God's blessing, 9:8)
"grace" (of God, 9:14)
"thanks" (to God, 9:15)

Although Paul's main objective here is to motivate the Corinthians to be generous in giving to the collection, he also provides a beautiful theology of grace that begins with God's gift and returns full circle in thanksgiving rendered to him.

---

the NAB's translation. The term rendered "generosity" is *haplotēs*, which most fundamentally signifies "singleness of mind and heart" (see 1:12). Here it refers to the Macedonians' unwavering commitment to follow the way of God, as the reference to "the will of God" in verse 5 makes clear. In this case God's grace has inspired and enabled their generosity that will assist and bring encouragement to others who are in dire need (see 1:4).

8:3–5   Paul goes on to **testify** to the magnanimous generosity of the Macedonian churches: not only have they contributed **according to their means**; they have given **beyond their means**. The Macedonians have responded to the needs of the Jerusalem church, even placing them before their own needs (see Phil 2:3–4). And they have done so freely, as signified by the word rendered **spon-**

taneously by the NAB, which means, literally, "self-chosen."[3] Paul emphasizes their initiative in verse 4: **they begged us insistently for the favor of taking part** in the collection. The word translated "favor" is *charis*. He thereby signifies that the Macedonian communities strongly desired to participate in a divine work that will give life to others, so much so that they regarded the opportunity to do so as a favor.

Paul refers to the collection as **the service** (*diakonia*) **to the holy ones.**[4] He has previously employed *diakonia* in describing the "ministry" of the †new covenant (2 Cor 3:7–11) and the "ministry" of reconciliation (5:18). By using the same term here, Paul suggests that the collection for the Jerusalem church is part of the work of reconciliation that characterizes the new covenant ministry, the ministry set in motion through the outpouring of the Spirit. The gift from predominantly †Gentile churches to Jewish Christians in Jerusalem will dramatically symbolize how God, through the cross of Jesus, has broken down the long-standing enmity between Jews and Gentiles. Through Christ, God has reconciled both groups to himself and has created a single body, the Church, in which Jews and Gentiles can live together in peace (Eph 2:14–16). This is ultimately the reason the Apostle attaches such importance to the collection for "the poor among the holy ones in Jerusalem" (Rom 15:26).

Paul makes clear that, as generous as the Macedonians' contribution is, they have done something even more significant—**they gave themselves first to the Lord**. It is noteworthy that Paul applies the expression "give oneself" to Christ in Gal 1:4. There he refers to Jesus as the one "who gave himself for our sins . . . in accord with the will of our God and Father." Thus, in saying that the Macedonians "gave themselves," Paul suggests that they participate in Jesus' self-giving for the sake of others in obedience to God's will. Indeed, he accents their *self*-giving by placing the reflexive pronoun, "self," in the prominent first position: literally, "themselves they gave . . ." Notice that the Macedonians have given themselves "to the Lord," that is, they have placed themselves in service of Christ Jesus. And because they have done so, they have placed themselves in service to Paul (as indicated by **to us**), who is Christ's ambassador (2 Cor 5:20) and coworker (6:1) **through the will of God** (see 1:1).[5]

Why does Paul begin his appeal to the Corinthians by referring to the example of the Macedonian churches in verses 1–5? He wants the former to emulate the latter. Paul highlights the Macedonians' joy and singleness of heart (v. 2),

---

3. The RSV translates *authairetos* "of their own free will"; the NEB and REB render it "on their own initiative."

4. See the exegesis of 1:1–2, above, for the reference to Christians as "holy ones."

5. See Ralph P. Martin, *2 Corinthians*, WBC (Waco: Word, 1986), 255.

the profound generosity by which they gave beyond what might be regarded as surplus (v. 3), their freedom and initiative (v. 4), and, most of all, their gift of themselves (v. 5). Paul wants the Corinthians, like the Macedonians, to recognize the collection for what it is—a work of God. These verses also allow him to broach the issue of the collection gently and indirectly. Such sensitivity is necessary because, as we will see momentarily, the Corinthians have not yet followed through on their initial commitment to participate.

8:6–7 In light of the Macedonians' generous contribution in response to God's grace, Paul begins to focus his attention on Corinth's participation. He informs the community that he has **urged Titus** to resume his work of facilitating their donation. We learn that Titus **had already begun** this work among the Corinthians. When did he do so? Scholars are divided. In my opinion, the best reading of the evidence is that before his mission of delivering the †tearful letter Titus had visited the Corinthians to help them follow through on the directions Paul had given in 1 Cor 16:1–4 (see 2 Cor 12:18). It was likely during this visit that Titus earned the trust and admiration of the Corinthians. Paul's painful second visit and the ensuing misunderstandings brought the Corinthians' participation to a halt. But now that he and the community are well along the path toward reconciliation, he exhorts Titus to help them **complete . . . this gracious act**. Paul uses *charis* yet again, here to signify the collection itself, suggesting that he regards the collection as a conduit of God's grace.

Finally, Paul appeals directly to the Corinthians. He acknowledges the ways in which they already **excel: in faith, discourse, knowledge, all earnestness, and in the love we have for you.**

Fig. 9. Before founding the church in Corinth, Paul had founded churches in Thessalonica and Philippi. Paul praises the Philippians in particular for their generosity (Phil 4:15-16). (*St. Paul Preaching to the Thessalonians* by Gustave Doré, in *The Doré Bible Illustrations*, Dover)

Felix Just, SJ/ catholic-resources.org/Art/Dore.htm

The community's "faith," "discourse," and "knowledge" are gifts conferred by the Holy Spirit (e.g., 1 Cor 1:5; 12:8–9). Their "earnestness" alludes to 7:11–12, where he recounted their concern and zeal for him. Implicit here is that, just as they responded favorably to his tearful letter, so they should heed his appeal for the collection.

The last item on the list is especially persuasive. Paul reminds the community of his "love" for them—and not only *his* love. Because he has brought the †gospel to Corinth, he has been the means through which "the love of Christ" (5:14) has been bestowed on them. Note Paul's strategy here. He reminds the Corinthians of the ways they have been generously blessed by God. It is on this basis that he exhorts the community to **excel in this gracious act also**. Once again Paul refers to the collection itself as *charis*. Indeed, his "point is that the receipt of *charis* should lead to the giving of *charis*; grace received should prompt grace given"[6]—a point he will return to in 9:6–10.

Reflection and Application (8:1–7)

Self-offering to God. Paul's admiration for the Macedonians reaches its apex when he recounts how they gave *themselves* to the Lord (v. 5). It is easy to offer some of my time, some of my talents, some of my possessions to God, for example, by sharing them with others. However, Paul teaches that while such giving has merit it falls short of the most appropriate offering each one of us is called to make to God, namely, all that I think and do and say—in short, my entire self.

The daily offering to God of one's prayers, works, joys, and sufferings is an efficacious way to deepen one's self-offering to him, especially when offered in conjunction with Jesus' self-offering celebrated in the Eucharist (as is done in the daily offering of the Apostleship of Prayer, a pious Catholic association that promotes devotion to the Sacred Heart). Such a daily offering to God is essential for the growth of all Christians, ministers and laity alike, and offers a way of enacting in our own lives what Paul is talking about. Indeed, it is a practical way for laypersons to grow in their call "to make the Church present and fruitful in those places and circumstances where it is only through them that she can become the salt of the earth" (*Lumen Gentium* 33).

The grittiness of grace. Paul makes a bold move when he refers to the collection itself as *charis* (vv. 6–7). To be sure, his purpose is not to reduce grace to dollars and cents. Even so, his exhortation cautions us not to overspiritualize

---

6. Harris, *Second Epistle to the Corinthians*, 575. I have transliterated Harris's use of the Greek.

the life of grace. The empowerment of God's Spirit takes place in the arena of flesh-and-blood human existence. Moreover, the gifts of the Spirit, including generosity (Gal 5:22), are to be enacted for the benefit of others within their nitty-gritty circumstances. As St. James teaches, "If a brother or sister has nothing to wear and has no food for the day, and one of you says to them, 'Go in peace, keep warm, and eat well,' but you do not give them the necessities of the body, what good is it?" (James 2:15–16).

Participating in Messiah Jesus' "Gracious Act" (8:8–15)

⁸I say this not by way of command, but to test the genuineness of your love by your concern for others. ⁹For you know the gracious act of our Lord Jesus Christ, that for your sake he became poor although he was rich, so that by his poverty you might become rich. ¹⁰And I am giving counsel in this matter, for it is appropriate for you who began not only to act but to act willingly last year: ¹¹complete it now, so that your eager willingness may be matched by your completion of it out of what you have. ¹²For if the eagerness is there, it is acceptable according to what one has, not according to what one does not have; ¹³not that others should have relief while you are burdened, but that as a matter of equality ¹⁴your surplus at the present time should supply their needs, so that their surplus may also supply your needs, that there may be equality. ¹⁵As it is written:

> "Whoever had much did not have more,
> And whoever had little did not have less."

OT: Exod 16; Sir 7:32–36; 29:10–13
NT: Mark 12:41–44; Acts 2:44–45; 4:34–37; Phil 2:6–11
Catechism: collection at Mass, 1351; sharing of material and spiritual goods, 2833
Lectionary: Mass for those suffering from hunger or famine

Paul cites the ultimate example of self-giving love, "the gracious act of our Lord Jesus Christ," to motivate the Corinthians to generosity. He advises them to complete their contribution to the collection as a sign of the genuineness of their love; they are to give willingly in accordance with their means. He then explains God's design of "equality" of material blessings among his people.

8:8–9   Paul makes clear at the outset that, in exhorting the community to be generous in giving to the collection, he is not issuing an order: **I say this not by way of command**. It would be inappropriate, not to mention contradictory, for him to demand a free-will offering. Besides, he has made clear that he does not "lord it over" their faith (1:24). Nevertheless, he does regard the collection as a "test" for the Corinthians; that is, by the collection, he tests **the genuineness of** their **love**. Paul uses the verb *dokimazō* for "test." As we saw in 2:9, the *dokim-* word group pertains to testing, including the testing of character. There he challenged the community to prove their obedience to God's will by forgiving and receiving back the person who had offended him during the painful visit. By doing so, they would reaffirm their love for the offender. Now Paul calls on the Corinthians to attend to the genuineness of their love for the poor in the Jerusalem church. The collection is a means for them to show that, through the power of Jesus' love, they no longer live for themselves but for others (see 5:14–15). Moreover, he gives them a standard by which they can test the quality of their love—the earnestness of the Macedonians who, despite their poverty, have given magnanimously (vv. 2–3).[7]

Paul then provides the Corinthians with the example of self-giving love par excellence, the **gracious act** (*charis*) **of our Lord Jesus Christ**. Because he is speaking of the collection, he employs economic categories to set forth, in shorthand, the story and character of Jesus: **for your sake he became poor although he was rich, so that by his poverty you might become rich**. Exegetes rightly point to Phil 2:6–11 as the best commentary on this verse.[8] Christ's wealth signifies his glorious, heavenly existence. The reference to his becoming poor points, in the first place, to the incarnation, to his "coming in human likeness" (Phil 2:7). In addition, it alludes to his earthly way of living, marked by humility and by obedience to the Father's will, expressed most dramatically in his self-offering on the cross (Phil 2:8). It is through Christ's poverty, through his becoming a human being and through his revelation of God's love for us, that we "become rich."

Our wealth is thus *spiritual* wealth, as Paul has made clear throughout the letter by his references to our empowerment by the Spirit (e.g., 1:21–22; 3:2–3; 3:18; 4:13). Moreover, this spiritual wealth will be fully realized in the gift of eternal life (5:1–10).[9] Paul highlights Jesus' benefaction to the Corinthians by placing the phrase "for your sake" in the prominent first position: "for your sake he became poor." The Apostle thereby presents the community with the supreme

---

7. The NAB's **by your concern for others** does not capture the sense of *dia tēs heterōn spoudēs*. The NRSV's "testing the genuineness of your love against the earnestness of others" is preferable. Paul will qualify this heroic standard in vv. 11–12.

8. See my comments on Phil 2:6–11 in the exegesis of 4:1–6 and 4:13–15, above.

9. See Chrysostom, *Homilies on 2 Corinthians* 17.1: "By riches, Paul means the knowledge of godliness, the cleansing away of sins, justification, sanctification, the countless good things which God bestowed upon us and which he intends to bestow" (quoted from Gerald Bray, ed., *1–2 Corinthians*, ACCS [Downers Grove, IL: InterVarsity, 1999], 272).

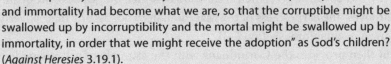

Sts. Irenaeus and Athanasius on the "Divine Exchange"

LIVING TRADITION

The Church Fathers waxed eloquent on the marvelous "divine exchange" Paul refers to in 2 Cor 8:9. For example, St. Irenaeus taught that "he who was the Son of God" became flesh in order that human beings, enslaved by disobedience and death, might receive adoption as children of God. Thus Irenaeus employed the language of corruptibility and mortality on one hand, and of incorruptibility and immortality on the other: "How could we be joined to incorruptibility and immortality unless, first of all, incorruptibility and immortality had become what we are, so that the corruptible might be swallowed up by incorruptibility and the mortal might be swallowed up by immortality, in order that we might receive the adoption" as God's children? (*Against Heresies* 3.19.1).

St. Athanasius captured well the two aspects of Jesus' becoming poor for our enrichment—the incarnation and his self-offering in love for us. Referring to the incarnation, Athanasius explained that the word of God, looking down on the wretchedness of human beings entrapped by ever-increasing wickedness, was "moved with compassion" and "took to himself a body, a human body even as our own." Furthermore, as one who became truly human, Christ "surrendered his body to death . . . and offered it to the Father. He did this out of pure love for us" so that through his death we might have life (*On the Incarnation* 2.8).

motivation for giving generously: Christ has held nothing back in showing God's love for them. He also reminds them of the source of their empowerment: just as God's *charis* has enabled the Macedonians' response (v. 1), so does the *charis* "of our Lord Jesus Christ" make the Corinthians' generosity possible.

8:10–12   Having set forth the preeminent example of Jesus' self-giving love, Paul proceeds with his appeal. In these verses he writes as the Corinthians' spiritual father (6:13), as one who is **giving counsel** concerning what is **appropriate**. Notice that he acknowledges that the Corinthians already began gathering funds for the collection **last year**. Paul's manner of expressing this may seem unusual: **you who began not only to act but to act willingly**. Normally, we would expect the notion of willing something to precede a reference to acting on it. But Paul shows great pastoral sensitivity here. He realizes that the community has not fully followed through on their initial enthusiasm to contribute. Thus he homes in on their original willingness rather than on their failure to follow through (so far).

Moreover, Paul is going to emphasize—as we will see in verse 12 and later in 9:7—that one's motivation in giving is more important in God's eyes than the actual amount given (see Mark 12:41–44). Even so, willingness *is* most authentically expressed in action, and so he advises the Corinthians to **complete** their contribution **now**. He wants their **eager willingness** to **be matched by** the **completion of** their donation.

Paul then explains his principle for contributing to the collection, what might be called the principle of proportionality. He exhorts the community to give willingly **out of what** they **have**.[10] Although Paul has praised the Macedonians for giving "*beyond* their means" (v. 3), he clarifies that such extraordinary generosity is not normative. He probably also has an eye out here for the poorer members of the church in Corinth who might fear that their gift would be too small; thus he adds **not according to what one does not have**. What Paul seeks above all is the Corinthians' **eagerness**, their zeal and readiness to participate in Jesus' self-giving way of life. If each member of the community demonstrates such eagerness **according to**—that is, in proportion to—**what one has**, their contribution will be an **acceptable** offering to God. In short, Paul's advice to Christians is to honestly assess what they can gladly and generously donate to alleviate the needs of others.

Paul goes on to lay a foundation for the principle of proportionality. In these verses he refers to the ideal of **equality**, or "balance." Paul first clarifies what the collection is **not** intended to produce: **that others should have relief while you are burdened**. In other words, he does not aim to render assistance for the poor in Jerusalem at the expense of impoverishing the Corinthians. Rather, Paul desires that there be "equality."[11] He then spells out the ideal of "equality": **your surplus at the present time should supply their needs, so that their surplus may also supply your needs**. Paul's vision of the Church bears some resemblance to the portrait of the Jerusalem church about twenty-five years earlier in Acts 2:44–45 and 4:34–37. There the wealthier members are described as having placed their possessions at the disposal of the community so that the needs of all could be met. The Corinthians are currently in a position to render financial assistance to that same Jerusalem church. In the future the situation might well be reversed, and the Corinthians would then be beneficiaries.

What Paul insists on is the responsibility to offer assistance within the larger Church—**that there may be equality**. Although his concern here is primarily economic, he elsewhere declares that the predominantly †Gentile churches, such

8:13–15

---

10. The NJB's "so far as your resources permit" aptly conveys Paul's meaning here.
11. The NIV expresses Paul's meaning well: "but that there might be equality."

as the one in Corinth, have already been the recipients of spiritual blessings from the Jerusalem church (see Rom 15:27), the mother of all the churches. We will see in 9:14 how the Jerusalem church will assist in extending even further spiritual benefits to the Corinthians.

Paul supplies divine warrant for the principle of equality in verse 15 by citing two lines from Scripture, indicated by the phrase **as it is written**. The lines are from Exod 16:18: **"Whoever had much did not have more, / And whoever had little did not have less."** The context of these lines is the story of God's gift of manna to the Israelites in the wilderness (Exod 16:1–36). Moses commanded the people to gather their daily portion of sustenance as God miraculously provided it for his people six days a week (a double supply was given before the Sabbath). No matter how much or how little each person gathered, there was sufficient daily manna for all. But some of the Israelites attempted to hoard this food rather than trust in their daily allowance. Those who hoarded, however, found that their extra food rotted (Exod 16:19–20).

Why does Paul allude to this story? In addition to providing divine sanction for the principle of equality employed in verses 13–14, he indicates that God now calls his people, who are empowered by the Holy Spirit, to implement through generous self-giving his plan of equitable sustenance for all. That is, Christians are to enact the divine will concerning the just distribution of material goods. Moreover, Paul implicitly admonishes the Corinthians not to hoard their resources. The Exodus passage warns that hoarding an abundance of goods does not assure that one will have more for oneself,[12] a warning that Jesus himself issued with his parable of the rich fool (Luke 12:16–21).

Reflection and Application (8:8–15)

Principles of stewardship. I have yet to meet a minister who likes to address his or her congregation about money. Asking for money—whether for the upkeep of the parish, for the maintenance of schools and religious education programs, for missions, or for special projects and emergency needs—makes most of us feel uncomfortable. Paul's delicate manner of raising the issue of the collection indicates that he himself did not find the task easy. Nevertheless, he provides several important principles of stewardship in verses 8–15 that can help both ministers and parishioners frame their way of thinking about financial contributions.

---

12. See Frank J. Matera, *II Corinthians: A Commentary*, NTL (Louisville: Westminster John Knox, 2003), 193.

The first principle pertains to the fundamental motivation for any act of donating resources: Christ Jesus has *already* enriched us immeasurably by offering himself in love on the cross. What is the appropriate response to such self-giving love? Surely one aspect of our response is to share our material resources to help build up the Church, the body of Christ. The second principle follows from this: what makes an offering acceptable to God is the "eager willingness" that accompanies the gift. This phrase is Paul's way of referring to a true desire to participate in Christ's self-giving way of life. As Jesus' comment concerning the widow's contribution to the temple treasury indicates (Mark 12:41–44), God measures the value of our gift on the basis of what is in our heart, not on the amount given.

The third principle is that of proportionality: each one of us is called to give according to our means. Although Paul applauds the Macedonians for giving beyond their means, the norm for giving entails the responsible assessment of our resources. To be sure, we can too easily err on the side of tending to the feathering of our own nest. That is why the fourth principle—God's plan for the equitable distribution of resources—contains an implicit warning: hoarding resources, especially when others are in need, works against the divine plan and, ultimately, leads one to ruin. Jesus himself cautioned: "What profit is there for one to gain the whole world and forfeit his life?" (Mark 8:36).

Implementing God's plan for equality. Paul's teaching on the principle of equality in verses 13–15 is challenging, especially for Christians who live in more prosperous circumstances. As individuals and parishes, it is important for us to reflect seriously on our responsibility for meeting the material needs of others, especially of those who live far from us. Mass media and instant forms of communication make us aware daily of the plight of millions of people: victims of entrenched poverty, of the ravages of war, of famine and other natural disasters. Contributing to organizations like Caritas Internationalis and Catholic Relief Services is a concrete way to respond to human need. So too is the growing practice of parishes and dioceses entering into relationships with sister parishes and sister dioceses in impoverished parts of the world.

Economic Justice for All. In 1986 the U.S. Catholic Bishops issued an important pastoral letter titled *Economic Justice for All.* This letter brought the rich resources of Catholic social teaching to bear on justice issues in the United States economy. Among other things, the bishops argued that the dignity of the human person should serve as the key criterion for every economic institution and decision, that participation in the economic life of society is the right of all peoples, and that society has a special obligation to the poor and vulnerable. The bishops' agenda was undoubtedly shaped by their view of the divine plan of equality as revealed in 2 Cor 8:13–15. They courageously and responsibly carried out their mission to proclaim how God's word affects people in their real life circumstances. Indeed, all Catholics, ordained and lay, would do well to immerse themselves in the teachings of *Economic Justice for All*.

Offering my "willing eagerness." Paul's statement in verse 12—that if a person is eager and willing to give, the gift is acceptable to God "according to what one has, not according to what one does not have"—is not limited to financial contributions. Those in pastoral ministry can become discouraged by their limited time, energy, and talents. Some can be haunted by perfectionist tendencies. Paul's reminder that God does not expect us to give what we do not have can be consoling and freeing. What we are capable of offering, and what we are called to offer, is our "willing eagerness."

Commendation for Titus and Two Brothers (8:16–24)

¹⁶But thanks be to God who put the same concern for you into the heart of Titus, ¹⁷for he not only welcomed our appeal but, since he is very concerned, he has gone to you of his own accord. ¹⁸With him we have sent the brother who is praised in all the churches for his preaching of the gospel. ¹⁹And not only that, but he has also been appointed our traveling companion by the churches in this gracious work administered by us for the glory of the Lord [himself] and for the expression of our eagerness. ²⁰This we desire to avoid, that anyone blame us about this lavish gift administered by us, ²¹for we are concerned for what is honorable not only in the sight of the Lord but also in the sight of others. ²²And with them we have sent our brother whom we often tested in many ways and found earnest, but who is now much more earnest because of his great confidence in you. ²³As for Titus, he is my partner and co-worker for you; as for our brothers, they are apostles of the churches, the glory of Christ. ²⁴So give proof before the churches of your love and of our boasting about you to them.

OT: Ps 26; 37:5–6; 112:5–6; Prov 3:3–4
NT: Acts 18:24–28; Rom 15:7–13; 16:1–2; 3 John 5–8

In order to facilitate the Corinthians' contribution to the collection, Paul announces that he is sending Titus and two "brothers" to Corinth. He commends them to the community and exhorts the church to receive his emissaries and to heed their directives. He also makes clear that the administration of the monies collected is transparent and above reproach.

Paul opens his commendation with a note of gratitude: **thanks** (*charis*) **be**   **8:16–17**
to God. Observe that he employs yet another sense of *charis*, the sense of thanksgiving (see 2:14; 9:15). Paul highlights, once again, God's role in initiating and enabling the work of the collection. It is God who has **put**, or "given," **concern for** the Corinthians **into the heart of Titus**. The one who gives the Spirit in the hearts of Christians (1:21–22; see 5:5) has now inspired "concern," or eagerness, in the heart of Titus.

This is the **same** concern—that is, the same love—that Paul himself has for the community (6:11). His pastoral skills are evident as he emphasizes that he and Titus are concerned, first and foremost, with the Corinthians themselves, not with their money or ability to give (12:14). He then explains how Titus's concern has manifested itself. Titus **welcomed** Paul's **appeal** (v. 6) to return to Corinth to help the community complete their contribution. Titus needed little prompting; his love for the Corinthians is so strong—**he is very concerned**—that he is coming to them **of his own accord** (the same term used in verse 3 to describe the Macedonians' initiative to "spontaneously" participate in the collection).

It is worth pausing a moment to make explicit something that lies implicit in 2 Cor 8, for Paul hints at an important feature of Christian †anthropology. In verses 1–3 he suggests that God's †grace (*charis*) has borne fruit in the generosity freely offered by the Macedonians. In verses 16–17 he intimates that God's gift of "concern" in Titus's heart has moved the latter to freely return to Corinth. What Paul implies in these passages is the catalyzing role that grace plays in the empowerment of human freedom. Indeed, it is when we submit ourselves to the Spirit's promptings to obey God's will that we are most free. That is why he claimed earlier, in 3:17, that "where the Spirit of the Lord is, there is freedom."

In addition to sending Titus, Paul announces that he is sending another   **8:18–19**
brother,[13] a fellow Christian who has been designated to participate in the work of the collection. He commends this "brother" to the Corinthians as one **who is praised in all the churches** because of his work for the †gospel. This brother, who is left unnamed (see below for a possible reason why), has earned a sterling reputation among the Christian communities in †Macedonia for his commitment to living and serving the gospel.[14] Paul explains that this brother

---

13. In vv. 17 ("has gone"), 18 ("have sent"), and 22 ("have sent"), Paul uses the †epistolary aorist, which ought to be translated into the *present* tense in English (see the exegesis of 2:5–11 above).

14. While the NAB interprets the Greek phrase *en tō euangeliō* (literally, "in the gospel") as **preaching of the gospel**, it is better to interpret the phrase more generally (e.g., "work for the gospel").

has also been appointed our traveling companion by the churches in this gracious work administered by us. In saying this, Paul makes clear that the Macedonian churches have actively taken part in choosing this emissary.

Indeed, Paul's wording suggests that, although he takes responsibility for sending the brother, it is the Macedonians who have put him forward to participate in the administration of the collection, which is referred to once more as *charis* ("gracious work"). Apparently the brother will be part of the group that takes the combined contributions of the Pauline churches to Jerusalem after the Corinthians make their gift. Why does Paul go to such pains to describe the Macedonians' role in appointing the brother? In the first place, the brother will represent their participation in the collection.[15] More importantly, Paul is concerned about the propriety of how the monies are collected and transported (as we will see in vv. 20–21). The brother provides an independent witness to the administration of the collection.

At the end of verse 19, Paul offers more clues as to how he views the collection. The verb translated "administered" is *diakoneō*, the verbal form of *diakonia* ("ministry"). Recall from verse 4 that Paul refers to the collection itself as *diakonia*, thereby meaning that it is part of the †new covenant ministry of reconciliation (3:7–11; 5:18). The aid given by †Gentile Christians to their Jewish counterparts in Jerusalem serves as a symbol of God's work of reconciling all peoples to himself and to one another (see Eph 2:14–16). For this reason, the collection is **for the glory of the Lord**. That is, the generous contribution from the Gentiles is an act of praise that gives glory to God (see Rom 15:7). The collection is also an **expression of** Paul's **eagerness** to participate as a minister of God's work of reconciliation (5:18–19).

8:20–22   Paul states what, through his careful administration of the collection, he desires **to avoid**: namely, **that anyone blame us about this lavish gift administered by us**. By using the term "lavish gift," he indicates that he expects the total amount of the collection to be substantial. Just as Paul was concerned in 6:3 to insist that there is nothing blameworthy in his ministry, so now he wants the Corinthians to be assured that his administration of a sizable amount of money is above reproach. We saw in 7:2 that one of the accusations against him was that he was taking advantage of the community, a charge he will vehemently deny in 12:16–18. Next, Paul states in positive terms what he wishes to accomplish: he is **concerned for what is honorable not only in the sight of the Lord but also in the sight of others**. Here he adapts the wording of Prov 3:4 in order to

---

15. Paul indicates in 9:4 that other Macedonians will also be involved in taking the collection to Jerusalem.

explain his manner of organizing the collection. As with all things, he acts as one who is always in the sight of God (2 Cor 1:23; 2:17). In addition, because of the potential for suspicion regarding the collection, Paul conducts himself with complete transparency before others. In doing so, he teaches that both one's actions and the way they appear to others are morally significant.

Having asserted the integrity of the gathering and administration of the collection, Paul goes on to commend a second unnamed **brother** he is sending to Corinth. The fact that he refers to him as **our** brother may indicate that this "brother" comes from Paul's own network of laborers for the gospel (although we learn in v. 23 that this second brother is also to be regarded as sent by the Macedonian churches). In any event, Paul informs the community that he has **often tested** (*dokimazō*) this brother and can vouch for his character, which is marked by earnestness. In fact, he claims that the second brother **is now much more earnest because of his great confidence in you**—perhaps because Titus has informed him about what has recently transpired in Corinth. We might wonder why Paul does not provide the names of the men he is sending along with Titus. This omission has led to much scholarly speculation. In my opinion, the simplest and most plausible reason is that he leaves it to Titus—whom the Corinthians *already* know—to introduce them by name when the three arrive in Corinth carrying the letter we call "Second Corinthians."

Paul summarizes his commendation of Titus and the two unnamed broth-   **8:23–24** ers. He makes clear that **Titus** is in charge of the delegation. Not only does he list Titus first but he also refers to him as his **partner and coworker** for the Corinthians. Paul regards Titus as a trusted companion and fellow laborer in ministering to the church in Corinth. Titus's prior work there attests to his skills and commitment. Paul commends the **brothers** as "emissaries," or "delegates" (*apostoloi*), of the churches.[16] As Titus will directly represent Paul when he comes to Corinth, the two brothers will represent the Macedonian churches in their support for the Apostle.

Notice that Paul commends these brothers as **the glory of Christ**: What does he intend by this description? Recall from the analysis of 1:20–22 that the Spirit empowers Christians to become the Amen, which was Paul's shorthand way of describing how Christians walk in the way of Jesus' "yes" in obedience to the will of God. Such faithfulness, as we saw there, is "for glory." Similarly, Paul alludes in 3:18 to the power of the Spirit to transform us into the likeness of "the

---

16. Given Paul's typical use of the term †apostle—as one who, like himself, has seen the risen Lord and been commissioned to exercise a distinctive position of leadership—it is preferable not to render *apostoloi* in v. 23 as **apostles**. The translations of the NJB ("emissaries"), NIV ("representatives"), and REB ("delegates") convey better Paul's meaning here.

glory of Christ" (4:4). Therefore, in calling the brothers "the glory of Christ," he signifies that they conduct themselves in fidelity to God's will after the manner of Jesus, thereby reflecting the glory of his self-giving way of life.

Paul concludes with an exhortation, urging the Corinthians to **give proof** of their **love**. Because the brothers represent the churches of Macedonia, the Corinthians' actions will, in effect, be witnessed by these congregations (this is the sense of **before the churches**). Once again, Paul challenges the Corinthians to attend to their character, here in terms of love.[17] How will the community publicly demonstrate its love? In the first place, by welcoming Titus and the brothers; and even more, by being generous in giving freely to the collection that these emissaries are coming to facilitate (v. 8). Paul also wants the Corinthians to "prove" his †**boasting** about them. We saw in 7:14 that he had earlier boasted to Titus about the community. In addition, Paul will reveal shortly (9:2) that he boasted about them to the Macedonians. He now wants the Corinthians to demonstrate that his high estimation of them is warranted.

Reflection and Application (8:16–24)

Transparency in ministry and administration. Paul's concern for blamelessness and for what is honorable before others in verses 20–21 might appear, at first glance, to contradict his criticism of those "who boast of external appearance" (5:12). But he is talking about something very different in the present passage. While Paul warns against placing too much stock in physical appearance, rhetorical eloquence, and the like, he insists that Christian ministry be conducted with complete integrity. Anything that leads to suspicion of wrongdoing undermines Christian ministry. If the minister's integrity is in doubt, the ministry suffers—and ultimately the recipients of the ministry suffer.

The importance of transparency in the handling of monetary affairs should be obvious. But the need for transparency extends much further. A tragic consequence of the sexual abuse crisis is the distrust, in some quarters, of bishops and other church administrators. One way to maintain trust is to conduct all affairs with as much openness as possible. Paul's criteria in verse 21 provide a perennially trustworthy measure for the behavior of ministers and administrators: we are to conduct ourselves at all times as if in the presence of God and the people to whom we minister.

---

17. Paul's use of *endeixis* and *endeiknymi* (together rendered "give proof") in v. 24 is synonymous with his use of *dokimē* and *dokimazō*—giving a test to ascertain one's character.

Collection for the Jerusalem Church (2): Theological Foundation and Fruits

2 Corinthians 9:1–15

Paul continues his appeal for the collection for the church in Jerusalem. He exhorts the Corinthians to have their contribution ready before he arrives so that it is truly given as a "blessing" (9:1–5). Paul affirms that God, the source of all blessings, can be counted on to provide the resources for the community's generosity (9:6–10). Finally, he describes the spiritual fruits of the collection, which culminates in praise and thanksgiving to God (9:11–15).

More Motivation to Be Generous (9:1–5)

---

¹Now about the service to the holy ones, it is superfluous for me to write to you, ²for I know your eagerness, about which I boast of you to the Macedonians, that Achaia has been ready since last year; and your zeal has stirred up most of them. ³Nonetheless, I sent the brothers so that our boast about you might not prove empty in this case, so that you might be ready, as I said, ⁴for fear that if any Macedonians come with me and find you not ready we might be put to shame (to say nothing of you) in this conviction. ⁵So I thought it necessary to encourage the brothers to go on ahead to you and arrange in advance for your promised gift, so that in this way it might be ready as a bountiful gift and not as an exaction.

OT: Sir 29:8–12
NT: 1 Cor 9:24–27; 12:31–13:13; Phil 3:17

Having commended Titus and the brothers (8:16–24), Paul makes explicit to the Corinthians that he is sending them to assist in completing the collection.

In doing so, he informs the community that he has boasted of their readiness to the Macedonians. He thus exhorts them now to follow through on their commitment.

9:1–2   Paul opens by acknowledging that it is **superfluous for** him **to write**—literally, "to go on writing"[1]—to the Corinthians about the collection. Once more he describes the collection as **the service** (*diakonia*) **to the holy ones** (8:4)—again meaning that it is part of the †new covenant ministry (*diakonia*) of reconciliation. By referring to the members of the Jerusalem church as "holy ones"—the same title he used of the Christians in Corinth and throughout †Achaia (1:1)—he points to the solidarity of all the members of the body of Christ. Paul explains why it is "superfluous" to continue writing: he already knows the Corinthians' **eagerness**, to which he referred in 8:10–11. He thus again acknowledges the community's genuine desire to participate in Christ Jesus' self-giving way of life. Paul confesses that their eagerness has been the subject of his "boast" **to the Macedonians.** Indeed, he sets forth the content of his †boasting: **Achaia has been ready since last year.**[2] Paul then reveals to the Corinthians that it was *their* **zeal** that **stirred up** many Macedonians to respond generously to the collection. Just as he now holds up the Macedonians as an example for the Corinthians (8:1–5), he previously held up the Corinthians' zeal to the Macedonians to inspire the latter's generosity.

The revelation that Paul has boasted to the Macedonians about the Corinthians' zeal for the collection raises questions. Did he overestimate or, even worse, misrepresent the Corinthians' response to the collection when he boasted to the Macedonians? Is he playing one group against the other, thereby setting up a competition between rivals? In my opinion, the answer to these questions is an emphatic no! Paul's reference to the Corinthians' being "ready since last year" points to something real. They were truly eager to participate (8:10–11). It was this eagerness that he reported to the Macedonians and that, we now learn, inspired them to participate generously.[3] But the painful visit and its aftermath created much misunderstanding between Paul and the Corinthians. One of the consequences was that the Corinthians stopped gathering monies for the collection—a decision that may have been abetted by questions raised

---

1. Following Jan Lambrecht, SJ (*2 Corinthians*, SP [Collegeville, MN: Liturgical Press, 1999], 149), who reads *to graphein* ("to write") as indicating that Paul here *continues* his line of thought from 8:1–24.

2. Recall that this letter is written to the church in Corinth as well as to all the Christians in †Achaia (1:1).

3. The NIV captures well Paul's meaning in v. 2: "For I know your eagerness to help, and I have been boasting about it to the Macedonians, telling them that since last year you in Achaia were ready to give; and your enthusiasm has stirred most of them to action."

by the rival missionaries about Paul's motives and integrity. Now that he and the Corinthians are on the way toward full reconciliation, he seeks their renewed participation in the collection. As we saw in 8:1–5, one way the Apostle seeks to motivate the community is to lift up the Macedonians' magnanimity as a model to follow.

Although at one level it is superfluous to continue writing about the collec-   9:3–4
tion, **nonetheless** Paul indicates that at another level he must do so, because the Corinthians have not followed through on their initial eagerness. For this reason he is sending **the brothers** to them.[4] The "brothers" refers to Titus and the other two emissaries Paul has just commended (8:16–24). They are coming to ensure that Paul's **boast about** the community **might not prove empty** (*kenōthē*). Just as he earlier cautioned the Corinthians not to receive God's gift of reconciliation "in vain" (*eis kenon*; 6:1), so now he exhorts them to let their eagerness bear fruit in generosity. While it may appear that Paul is concerned here with his own reputation, his purpose is to serve the community's just desire to be and be known as the kind of people who do what they say and finish what they start. To this end, he dispatches the brothers to Corinth to assist them so they are **ready** with their contribution before he arrives.

Paul then alludes to his pending visit, along with some **Macedonians**. In all likelihood these Macedonians will be part of the entourage that will take the collection to Jerusalem. He expresses his **fear** that, upon their arrival, they will discover that the Corinthians are **not ready**. Such a situation would **put** both Paul and the Corinthian community **to shame**. He would be put to shame because his public boasting would have proven to be false; they would be put to shame because they would have failed to follow through on what they began (see Luke 14:28–30). Notice that, although Paul refuses to set up a competition with the Macedonians as between rivals, he does resort to appealing to the community's reputation (see the Reflection and Application, below).

Paul concludes this section by telling the community that he **thought it**   9:5
necessary to encourage the brothers to go on ahead to you and arrange in
advance for your promised gift. Although it has been implicit all along, here he makes explicit the brothers' "mission" of facilitating the Corinthians' completion of the collection before he arrives. Once more, Paul reminds the community of the commitment they have already made when they had "promised" to participate. He now refers to their pending contribution as a "gift" (*eulogia*). The word *eulogia* in Scripture typically means a "blessing" or "benefit" bestowed by God (e.g., Eph 1:3). Just as Paul's use of *charis* for the collection connects

---

4. It is better to render **sent** as an †epistolary aorist.

it to God's self-giving love, so does his use of *eulogia*. That is, the collection will ultimately be *God's* blessing on the church of Jerusalem; the Corinthians, Macedonians, and others have the privilege of being channels of God's †grace. Paul explains why he desires the community to have their gift **ready** before he visits. He wants it to be bestowed **as a bountiful gift** (again, *eulogia*) and **not as an exaction** (*pleonexia*). The term *pleonexia* signifies, literally, "seeking more" for oneself and is usually rendered as "greed."

Paul is distinguishing here between two attitudes toward giving. He wants the Corinthians to give freely and generously in the spirit of a true blessing. What he discourages is their giving sparsely and grudgingly because they are overly concerned with their own self-enrichment. In fact, Paul's use of *pleonexia* echoes 8:15, where he alluded to the warning against hoarding implicit in Exod 16:18. In the end, what he seeks to avoid is a last minute pro forma offering by the community.[5]

Reflection and Application (9:1–5)

Proper method of motivation. Paul's appeal to the examples of the Macedonians' generosity (8:1–5) and the Corinthians' eagerness (9:2) are not intended, in my opinion, to set up a rivalry between them. Such a move would not only be unseemly for what is to be a free participation in the working of God's grace; it would also fly in the face of Paul's dogged commitment to break down divisions and rivalries in his communities (Rom 12:1–15:13). What, then, is he trying to accomplish? Paul's strategy is to encourage *friendly imitation* among fellow members of the body of Christ. He seeks to inculcate striving for excellence through mutual inspiration and help. His method to motivate excellence, which is the same method employed by good office managers, principals, and administrators, is one that pastors and other Christian leaders can emulate.

Having said this, it must be acknowledged that there are dangers in Paul's strategy. One is that setting up friendly competition can easily devolve into a destructive kind of rivalry. Another is that it can turn people's focus inward rather than outward. Paul's ultimate desire is to get the Corinthians to set their sights on Christ and the needs of the Jerusalem church. His attempt to inculcate friendly imitation is a means to do so. The danger is that the means can easily become the end, that is, "Let's win the competition." A third pitfall involves the issue of shame (v. 4). While a sense of shame is appropriate to feel when one

---

5. The NIV—"Then it will be ready as a generous gift, not as one grudgingly given"—conveys Paul's intent here.

is guilty of sin or wrongdoing, it is rarely, if ever, an appropriate motivational technique to persuade someone to perform a good deed. The Apostle's appeal to the †honor–shame mentality of his culture is not a strategy to be adopted today.

Tension with Jesus' teaching? At first glance, Paul's making public the Macedonians' and Corinthians' contributions, or intentions to contribute, seems to be at odds with Jesus' teaching that, when giving alms, "do not let your left hand know what your right is doing" (Matt 6:3). The tension is more apparent than real, however. Notice that Paul speaks of the contribution of *entire* communities. Presumably, he expects individuals to be discretely humble when contributing, in accord with Jesus' teaching (1 Cor 16:2). Nevertheless, as the work of an entire church, it is appropriate for them to let their light shine before others, so long as the purpose is that others "may see your good deeds and glorify your heavenly Father" (Matt 5:16). Indeed, this is what Paul intimates at the climax of 8:1–9:15.

God's Generosity and Bountiful Sowing (9:6–10)

---

⁶Consider this: whoever sows sparingly will also reap sparingly, and whoever sows bountifully will also reap bountifully. ⁷Each must do as already determined, without sadness or compulsion, for God loves a cheerful giver. ⁸Moreover, God is able to make every grace abundant for you, so that in all things, always having all you need, you may have an abundance for every good work. ⁹As it is written:

> "He scatters abroad, he gives to the poor;
>   his righteousness endures forever."

¹⁰The one who supplies seed to the sower and bread for food will supply and multiply your seed and increase the harvest of your righteousness.

OT: Ps 111–12; Prov 22:9; Isa 55:10–11
NT: Matt 5:43–48; Luke 6:38; Rom 12:6–8; 1 Tim 6:17–19
Lectionary: Mass for productive land

Paul makes one final appeal to the Corinthians to be generous in giving to the collection. He reminds the community that God, who is the source of all blessings, can be trusted to provide them with the wherewithal to share with others.

       Paul offers proverbial wisdom from the realm of agriculture: **whoever sows sparingly will also reap sparingly, and whoever sows bountifully will also reap bountifully**.[6] The proverb serves to encourage the Corinthians to be generous in their sowing, that is, in their contribution. The adverb "bountifully" translates the phrase *ep' eulogiais*, literally, "on the basis of blessings." This phrase connects verse 6 with the notion of *eulogia* in verse 5. Paul thereby intimates that, because the community has been richly blessed by God, they can give a blessing in turn through their generosity to the poor members of the church in Jerusalem. The following verses will make this intimation explicit. What is the bountiful harvest that the Corinthians can expect from their generous sowing? According to verses 8–11, God will continue to bless them abundantly in order to supply their own needs and to assist others. In addition, according to verse 14 the Jerusalem church, the recipients of their generosity, will offer prayers for them and long for them with affection.

While the focus in verse 6 is on quantity in giving, Paul returns in verse 7 to the importance of proper motivation: **Each must do as already determined, without sadness or compulsion**. Note that, although the final gift will be a collective one, Paul desires that *each* member of the community participate. Each person is to contribute "without sadness," or regret. Sadness in giving is the mark of one who lets go only grudgingly (v. 5). Each person is also to contribute without "compulsion." Paul does not want the Corinthians' gift to be the result of force or pressure, whether from himself or his emissaries. To express his thought positively, he desires that the community's assistance to those in need be offered with freedom and joy (see Rom 12:8). He grounds this exhortation with an allusion to Prov 22:9: **God loves a cheerful giver**. Paul makes an interesting adaptation of the [†]Septuagint version of this proverb, replacing the verb "blesses" with "loves." He thus reveals that God has a special love for those whose cheerful giving reflects God's own munificence.[7]

       Paul goes on to make explicit the theological foundation of all human generosity: **God is able to make every grace abundant for you**. Ultimately, the collection rests on the *power* of God (the verb *dynateō*, "is able," carries the notion of power). Paul once again employs *charis* ("[†]grace"), now to indicate what God makes abundant for the Corinthians. What precisely does *charis*, God's gift of abundance, refer to here? At one level, it signifies spiritual blessings. Just as God's grace inspired the Macedonians' generosity (2 Cor 8:1), so

---

6. See Prov 11:24, 26; 22:8; Job 4:8; Sir 7:3. There are numerous parallels in Greco-Roman philosophical and moral texts as well.

7. Murray J. Harris, *The Second Epistle to the Corinthians*, NIGTC (Grand Rapids: Eerdmans, 2005), 636.

Almsgiving in the Old Testament

Almsgiving—the practice of extending special help to the poor and needy—is found throughout the Old Testament. As the Israelites were poised to enter the promised land, Moses exhorted them with words that foreshadow those of Paul in 2 Cor 9:7: "When you give" to a kinsman in need, "give freely and not with ill will" (Deut 15:10). The prophetic literature is filled with admonitions to care for the needy. Indeed, Isaiah suggested that it is by tending to the needs of the poor that one's own prayer is heard (Isa 58:4–7).

The Wisdom literature contains many exhortations to render assistance to the poor. Kindness to the poor brings happiness to the giver (Prov 14:21) and, more importantly, glorifies God (14:31). Almsgiving is in accord with the divine commands, resulting in greater "profit" than gold and saving one from every evil (Sir 29:8–12). It can atone for sins (Sir 3:29; see Tob 12:9).

The theme of almsgiving is especially prominent in the book of Tobit. Tobit encourages his son, Tobias, to give without hesitation to the poor. God keeps his face turned toward those who do not turn their face away from the poor. Almsgiving is a "worthy offering" to God. Those who are generous to the needy store up treasure and are saved from death (Tob 4:7–11). While prayer and fasting are pious practices, almsgiving accompanied by righteousness is even better (12:8).

Jesus teaches the practice of almsgiving. While he warns against giving for the sake of self-exaltation and public recognition (Matt 6:1–4), he makes it clear that final judgment is based in large part on one's care for the poor—or lack thereof (25:31–46).

---

now he gives spiritual impetus to the Corinthians. At another level, it indicates material sufficiency, not only to meet their own needs but also to reach out and help others. God gives material resources in order that they be shared—as is clear from Paul's statement that God has so provided for the members of the community that they **always** have **all** they **need**.

The word rendered "need" means "self-sufficiency." This word was commonly used in Paul's time by Stoic and Cynic philosophers to signify the ideal of being self-sufficient so that one was not dependent on others for support or happiness. Paul turns this ideal of *self*-sufficiency upside down. He insists that any sufficiency is a gift from *God* (Phil 4:11–13), bestowed in order to enable us to reach out to other people, not to enable us to withdraw in independence from them. Indeed, he makes clear that God's gift of **abundance** to the community is for the purpose of **good work**; in this case, to participate in the collection.

St. Maximus the Confessor on Imitating God's Generosity

St. Maximus the Confessor, a seventh century monk and theologian, commented that almsgiving is a special way to express love for both God and neighbor. Such love is incompatible with clinging to one's money; rather, it is expressed "in God-like fashion" by distributing money, "giving to each one in need" (*Chapters on Charity* 1.23). The person who gives alms is to do so "in imitation of God." That is, in giving to those who are in need one "does not distinguish between evil and good, just and unjust, concerning bodily needs, but distributes to all in proportion to their need" (1.24). In doing so, one follows the way of the "heavenly Father" as Jesus describes in Matt 5:45.

Paul then grounds his theological claim with a citation from Scripture, citing the Greek text of Ps 112:9: **"He scatters abroad, he gives to the poor; / his righteousness endures forever."**[8] In all likelihood, Paul selects this passage because it links the agricultural metaphor from verse 6 with giving to the poor. In order to fully appreciate Paul's meaning here, the reader must understand that Ps 111—which is about God—and Ps 112—which is about a just person— function together. That is, the protagonists in both psalms are described as being merciful and compassionate, as generously providing sustenance for others, and as having righteousness that endures forever. The order of the psalms suggests that the just person mirrors God's goodness to others because he or she is empowered by God to do so: "God is the true origin of human compassion and . . . his righteousness is the true source of our righteousness."[9] Paul thus cites Ps 112:9 in order to give scriptural warrant to his statement in verse 8 that it is God who inspires our compassion and gives us resources so that we can respond generously to others' needs. If the Corinthians respond to the Apostle's appeal to be generous, they will participate in the ongoing revelation of God's "righteousness" (see 2 Cor 5:21). Through their faithfulness to God, expressed in self-giving love after the manner of Jesus (8:9), they will manifest his goodness and love.

Finally, Paul reiterates in verse 10 the theological point made in verse 8. He now refers to God as **the one who supplies seed to the sower and bread for**

8. Ps 112 in English translations is Ps 111 in the †Septuagint.
9. Dieter Georgi, *Remembering the Poor: The History of Paul's Collection for Jerusalem* (Nashville: Abingdon, 1992), 99.

food. These words are an allusion to Isa 55:10–11, a text that proclaims the power and efficacy of God's word. Just as snow and rain do not return to the heavens until they have watered the earth, making it fruitful, so God's word does not return to him without accomplishing its purpose. Paul adapts this principle of the effective power of God's word in a more specific sense. He wants the Corinthians to appreciate that God **will supply and multiply** their **seed**, that is, God will continue to bestow ample material resources on them.[10]

Paul's point is that the community can trust in God to provide for them. They do not need to hoard their resources but can give generously to those in need. Paul suggests that, if they do so, they will be channels through whom God's blessings produce their intended effect, namely, to bring life and sustenance to others. By trusting in God's continued provision to them and by sharing generously what they presently have, the community will allow God to **increase the harvest of** their **righteousness**. Paul once again points to the synergism between God's righteousness and that of the Corinthians—the righteousness that is expressed in self-giving love (2 Cor 5:21). Not only will the harvest be reaped by the recipients of their generosity, the following passage (9:11–15) indicates how even more fruits will be realized.

Reflection and Application (9:6–10)

God's generous provision. In the first entry under Reflection and Application (8:8–15), I listed several principles of stewardship in Paul's appeal for the collection. In verses 8–10 he supplies the theological underpinning of any act of charity. It is *God* who gives us the inspiration and the material resources to share with others. Therefore, when we give to others, we are fundamentally imparting what has been entrusted to us as a gift. The more we recognize that all we have—indeed, all we are—comes from God's goodness, the more we will be inclined to share what we have with others. Paul's teaching about God in these verses inculcates two virtues: *gratitude* for the many ways we have been blessed, and *trust* in God to continue to provide us with what we need and what he wants us to share with others.

The importance of almsgiving. I recall one time handing cash to a man who asked for a fairly sizable amount. He had given a heartrending account of a family emergency that required him to immediately catch a bus to another city. The very next day I happened to run into him again. Caught in his deceit, he responded by becoming belligerent with me. Such experiences can leave us

10. The RSV's "[God] will supply and multiply your resources" conveys well Paul's sense.

In the Liturgy

Second Corinthians 9:6–10 is proclaimed on the Feast of St. Lawrence (August 10). A deacon (*diakonos*) of the church of Rome in the middle of the third century, Lawrence regularly distributed alms to the poor and needy Christians at a time when Christianity was outlawed. On August 6, 258, Pope (Saint) Sixtus II was beheaded along with six deacons by decree of the emperor Valerian. The emperor also ordered that all the Roman church's material wealth and documents be confiscated. Lawrence, who was now the highest ranking churchman, was commanded to appear for his execution four days later and to bring with him whatever had been entrusted to him by the pope. In the short time he had left, Lawrence courageously dispersed the church's resources to the poor and sick. When he arrived for his execution, Lawrence brought with him a crowd of sick, crippled, and destitute Christians and declared that these were truly the "wealth" of the Church. His martyrdom illustrates that "bountiful sowing" entails more than financial generosity; it ultimately calls us to offer our very lives in service (*diakonia*) to God and his people.

jaded when it comes to responding to requests for help. Nevertheless, Paul's teaching—and the entire biblical tradition—insists that we are called to render assistance to the poor and needy. Jesus' identification with the hungry, thirsty, stranger, naked, sick, and imprisoned (Matt 25:31–46) warns us against hastily dismissing those who present themselves as destitute.

The Fruits of Generosity (9:11–15)

[11]You are being enriched in every way for all generosity, which through us produces thanksgiving to God, [12]for the administration of this public service is not only supplying the needs of the holy ones but is also overflowing in many acts of thanksgiving to God. [13]Through the evidence of this service, you are glorifying God for your obedient confession of the gospel of Christ and the generosity of your contribution to them and to all others, [14]while in prayer on your behalf they long for you, because of the surpassing grace of God upon you. [15]Thanks be to God for his indescribable gift!

OT: Tob 4:7–11; 12:6–10; Sir 3:29–4:10
NT: Luke 16:9; Rom 15:7–13; Eph 3:20–21
Catechism: types of prayer, 2626–43
Lectionary: Mass for those suffering from hunger or famine

Paul concludes his lengthy exhortation on the collection by setting forth the fruits it will bear. In addition to supplying material relief for the poor Christians in Jerusalem, it will evoke their offering of praise and thanksgiving to God—as well as their prayers for the church in Corinth. The Corinthians themselves, moreover, will glorify God through their generosity and their tangible expression of the unity of the Church.

Before turning to the spiritual fruits of the collection, Paul summarizes the preceding passage: **You are being enriched in every way for all generosity**. **9:11–12** He uses the passive of "enrich" to indicate that it is *God* who provides for the Corinthians (another instance of the †divine passive—see 3:16, 18; 7:13). God generously enriches the community for their *haplotēs*, which the NAB appropriately renders "generosity." Paul also intends a further nuance. He has been highlighting God's loving provision (9:8–10) and the divine plan of equality (8:13–15). Recall that the fundamental meaning of *haplotēs* is singleness of mind and heart (1:12; 8:2). Paul thus indicates that God is richly blessing the Corinthians so that they can dedicate themselves with single-hearted devotion to the divine will—in this case, by contributing generously.

Paul then introduces the topic of the next few verses, namely, the fruits to be expected from the collection. He states that **through us**—through himself, his emissaries, and those who will form the entourage to Jerusalem—the collection **produces thanksgiving to God**. Paul's great faith is evident from the fact that he employs the present tense here and throughout the remainder of the passage. That is, he writes as if the collection were already completed and its fruits were already being reaped. In doing so, he expresses his confidence in God's power to bring the work to completion.[11]

Paul employs worship imagery to describe the collection and its fruit. The NAB's translation—**the administration of this public service**—does not capture the rich liturgical sense of this phrase. The Greek word for "administration" here is *diakonia*—we have already discussed the significance of referring to the collection with this term (see 8:4; 9:1). "Public service" renders the Greek term *leitourgia*, which also denotes worship activity. In fact, the English word *liturgy* derives from it. Elsewhere Paul draws on this liturgical sense by referring to his self-giving way of life as "a sacrificial *service*" (Phil 2:17) and by calling himself a "minister" (*leitourgos*) in "the priestly service of the gospel" (Rom 15:16).

Here Paul understands the collection as tantamount to an act of worship. He does so because, in addition to **supplying the needs of the holy ones** in

---

11. See Victor Paul Furnish, *II Corinthians: A New Translation with Introduction and Commentary*, AB 32A (New York: Doubleday, 1984), 450.

the Jerusalem church, it will overflow **in many acts of thanksgiving to God**. The recipients will praise and thank *God* as the source of their blessings (see James 1:17). As significant as facilitating human relief is for Paul, the fruit of rendering thanksgiving to God is even more important.[12] Indeed, his concern for praise and thanks to God is evident in this letter (1:11; 2:14; 4:15; 8:16) and throughout his correspondence.[13]

9:13–15   In addition to the Jerusalem Christians' thanksgiving to God, Paul informs the Corinthians that their participation in the collection will give glory to God. Once more, he reveals to the community that the collection (*diakonia*, **service**) is a "test"[14] of their character and their appropriation of the †gospel (8:8, 24). On what basis will they pass the test and thereby glorify God? In the first place, by their **obedient confession of the gospel of Christ**. The Corinthians will demonstrate their obedience to God[15] by putting into practice the gospel imperative to offer relief to those in need (Luke 6:38; Matt 5:42; see also Rom 12:13). Generous assistance to others, in the spirit of Jesus' self-giving love, is an eloquent "confession of the gospel." So too is the commitment to participate in Christ's work of reconciling Jewish and †Gentile disciples to God and to one another (Eph 2:14–16). Recall that for Paul the collection serves to symbolize this reconciliation. Hence the second basis for **glorifying God** is **the generosity** (*haplotēs*) **of your contribution**.

While this rendering captures the economic aspect of the Corinthians' prospective gift, it does not convey the deeper, spiritual significance that Paul's phraseology attaches to it. As just mentioned in the treatment of verse 11, *haplotēs* refers to single-minded commitment to God's will. The word for "contribution" here is *koinōnia*, which means, fundamentally, "fellowship" or "communion."[16] Paul thereby indicates that God is glorified when we commit ourselves to promoting the *koinōnia*, or communion, of the larger Church. He explains that the Corinthians' generosity in contributing will glorify God because it will "confess" in action the gospel and embody God's gift of reconciliation.

12. See Harris, *Second Epistle to the Corinthians*, 650. At the heart of the Greek word for thanksgiving—*eucharistia*—is the word *charis*.

13. See, e.g., Rom 11:36; 14:1; 15:7; 16:27; 1 Cor 10:31; Gal 1:5; Eph 1:6, 12–14; 3:21; 5:20; Phil 1:11; 2:11; 4:20; Col 3:17; 1 Thess 5:18; 2 Tim 4:18.

14. As the RSV rightly translates *dokimē*, rendered by the NAB as **evidence**.

15. The NEB captures Paul's nuance of obedience rendered *to God* in v. 13—"For through the proof which this affords, many will give honour to God when they see how humbly you obey him and how faithfully you confess the gospel of Christ." See the exegesis of 2:5–11, above, for another "test" (*dokimē*) that pertains to obedience to God.

16. The NJB aptly translates *koinōnia* as "fellowship."

Paul lists yet another fruit of the collection: the members of the church in Jerusalem will offer **prayer** on the Corinthians' **behalf**. We saw at the beginning of the letter how much Paul values the power of intercessory prayer (1:11). Such prayer is a manifestation of trust in the power of God, of love for fellow Christians, and of solidarity in the Church. Moreover, the recipients of the collection will **long for** the Corinthians. They will be so grateful for the gift that they will desire to meet their donors to offer thanks and establish ties of affection. In other words, the collection will foster greater love and communion among the members of the body of Christ.

Notice that, at the end the verse, Paul names the underlying reason for the Jerusalem church's prayers and heartfelt yearning: **because of the surpassing grace** (*charis*) **of God upon** the Corinthians. The Jerusalem Christians will recognize that it is God's "†grace" that energizes the Christians in Corinth. Paul thus ends the lengthy appeal for the collection on the same note with which he began. Just as the Macedonians' magnanimity was rooted in the action of God's grace among them, the Corinthians' generosity will be so grounded.

Because God is the driving force behind the collection, Paul concludes with an exclamation of gratitude: **Thanks** (*charis*) **be to God for his indescribable gift!** Fittingly, he employs *charis*, "thanks," one last time as he brings 8:1–9:15 full circle. What began with God's self-giving love returns to him in a chorus of gratitude. Paul offers here yet another clue that he understands the collection within the context of redemption. The reason for gratitude is God's "indescribable gift." When Paul uses *dōrea* ("gift") elsewhere, he indicates God's work of redemption accomplished through Christ Jesus (Rom 5:15, 17; Eph 3:7; 4:7). The Apostle therefore offers thanksgiving to God first and foremost for the gift of salvation, the gift of reconciliation effected through the death and resurrection of Christ. He believes—and wants the Corinthians to appreciate—that the collection is an expression of this divine *dōrea*.

Reflection and Application (9:11–15)

Seeing through the mundane. We earlier reflected on how Paul's use of liturgical language and imagery invites us to think about the transforming power of liturgy in our lives (see the Reflection and Application on 2:14–17). We have also considered how Christ's redemptive death has given us new lenses through which to view one another (see the Reflection and Application on 5:14–17). Paul's use of liturgical language to describe the collection in verses 12–13 encourages us to use the lens of faith to see the full reality of what might otherwise be regarded as mere practical responses to need. For example, collections for foreign missions and disaster victims are in truth ways of participating in God's work of reconciliation. As such, they can inspire generosity and encourage Christians to think more concretely about what it means that the Church is "one, holy, catholic, and apostolic."

Even more fundamentally, Paul's use of liturgical language inspires us to reconsider seemingly ordinary duties in a spiritual light. This is what the saints have always excelled at—doing the ordinary tasks of life extraordinarily well *as service to God*. Christian life is an extension of the grace of the liturgy into these mundane tasks.

Paul's theology of grace. Throughout the exegesis of 8:1–9:15, I have highlighted the different ways Paul uses the word *charis*. It is worth summarizing his treatment because, although these chapters are fundamentally an appeal to raise money, they also provide a theology of grace that transcends the particular circumstances of the collection for the church in Jerusalem in the mid-50s AD.

Paul uses *charis* in six different, albeit interrelated ways. First and most fundamentally, *charis* refers in 8:9 to God's self-giving love made manifest in the incarnation, life, death, and resurrection of Jesus the †Messiah. Second, in 8:1 and 9:14 Paul refers to *charis* in the sense of the conferral of grace in human hearts, a conferral that empowers and guides human actions. Third, he uses *charis* in 8:4 to signify the favor granted to participate in good works. That is, he indicates that the invitation to partake in a divinely inspired enterprise is "grace." Fourth, Paul calls such an enterprise itself *charis* in 8:6–7 and 8:19; thus any work that extends God's saving love to others is *charis*. Fifth, in 9:8 *charis* refers to the material resources bestowed by God to carry out a particular work. Finally, Paul utilizes *charis* in 8:16 and 9:15 to indicate the thanksgiving offered to God for the blessings received through the ministrations of those who are inspired by God. In short, *charis* begins with God and eventually returns full circle to his praise and honor.

"Battling" on Behalf of God

2 Corinthians 10:1–18

Having cleared up misunderstandings between the Corinthians and himself (1:12–7:16) and having enlisted the community to participate in the collection (8:1–9:15), Paul turns his attention to the intruding missionaries. He has alluded to them several times already (2:17; 3:1; 4:2; 5:12). Now, as Paul prepares for his third visit to Corinth, he distinguishes his manner of being an †apostle from the values and behaviors of these interlopers. It might appear that he spends an inordinate amount of time talking and even bragging about himself in chapters 10–13. However, Paul's strategy is to help the Corinthians understand that his comportment embodies the †gospel. To reject him is tantamount to rejecting the gospel itself.

Paul begins by presenting himself as a soldier in God's army in the battle to bring about Christlike obedience within the community (10:1–6). He explains that his God-given authority is for building up the Corinthians (10:7–11). Finally, he sets forth what constitutes proper missionary †boasting (10:12–18). All the while, Paul contrasts himself with the intruding missionaries.

The Humble Warrior (10:1–6)

---

¹Now I myself, Paul, urge you through the gentleness and clemency of Christ, I who am humble when face to face with you, but brave toward you when absent, ²I beg you that, when present, I may not have to be brave with that confidence with which I intend to act boldly against some

who consider us as acting according to the flesh. ³For, although we are in the flesh, we do not battle according to the flesh, ⁴for the weapons of our battle are not of flesh but are enormously powerful, capable of destroying fortresses. We destroy arguments ⁵and every pretension raising itself against the knowledge of God, and take every thought captive in obedience to Christ, ⁶and we are ready to punish every disobedience, once your obedience is complete.

OT: Ps 48; Prov 21:22; Isa 59:16–21
NT: Matt 5:38–48; 11:28–30; 21:1–5; Rom 13:12; Eph 6:11–17; 1 Thess 5:8

Paul sets the entire discussion against the backdrop of Jesus' gentleness and clemency. After alluding to criticism raised against him, Paul points to his upcoming visit and makes clear his intent to act boldly if needed. He employs the imagery of siege warfare to convey how the power of the †gospel defeats false ideas and pretensions.

10:1–2   The emphatic self-identification with which the section begins—**Now I myself, Paul, urge you**—signifies the importance and urgency of what follows (see Gal 5:2). Paul grabs the Corinthians' attention by asserting his apostolic authority. He makes his appeal[1] **through the gentleness and clemency of Christ**. In grounding his appeal with reference to Jesus, Paul indicates that Christ is the source of his authority, and he highlights particular aspects of Jesus' character that are pertinent to the discussion that follows.

What precisely is meant by the "gentleness" (*prautēs*) and "clemency" (*epieikeia*) of Christ? The word *prautēs* connotes being kind, gentle, and modest toward other people; in one's relationship with God, it means reverent submission to his will. Jesus invited people to learn from him because he is "gentle" (*praus*) and humble of heart (Matt 11:29). Moreover, in the days before his passion, he entered Jerusalem as a "meek" (*praus*) king riding on a beast of burden, not on a war horse (Matt 21:5). Both in his teachings and actions, Jesus chose to exercise power and authority in a spirit of gentleness and humility (see 1 Cor 4:21, where Paul aspires to the same ideal). The term *epieikeia* indicates forbearance, which is how Paul uses it elsewhere.[2] Jesus' forbearance was most evident in his teaching to love one's enemies (Matt 5:38–48; Luke 6:27–36), in his nonretaliation during the passion, and in his prayer to God to forgive those who put him to death (Luke 23:34).

1. The verb rendered "urge" by the NAB, *parakaleō*, also means "appeal" (as in the NIV and NRSV).
2. See Phil 4:5; 1 Tim 3:3; Titus 3:2. In all three instances, Paul uses the adjectival form *epieikēs*. The NJB aptly translates *epieikeia* in v. 1 as "forbearance."

Paul draws attention to Jesus' character here for three reasons. First and most importantly, he aligns himself with Christ's gentleness and clemency in his role as father of the community (2 Cor 12:14–15). When Paul announces his third visit to Corinth (12:14; 13:1), he will communicate his preference to exercise his authority in a spirit of gentleness. Second, Christ's meekness and forbearance are in contrast to the values and behaviors of the intruding missionaries that Paul criticizes throughout chapters 10–12. As we will see momentarily, humility is a hallmark of Jesus' followers. Third, Paul holds up Christ's gentleness and clemency for the sake of the Corinthians. He wants them to emulate these characteristics, to live peaceably with him and with one another (13:11).

Paul alludes to criticism that has been leveled against him by some in the community, likely abetted by the intruding missionaries. They criticize him for acting in two different ways: on the one hand, he seems **humble**, or lowly (*tapeinos*), **when face to face with** the Corinthians, in other words when he is with them in person; on the other hand, he comes off as **brave**, or "bold," **toward** them **when he is absent**.[3] The accusation of boldness is probably made in reference to the †tearful letter he wrote after the painful visit (2:3–4; 7:8). The criticism that he is lowly most likely refers to a combination of the following: Paul abruptly left Corinth after the painful incident rather than directly confront the wrongdoer; he works with his own hands to support himself (11:7)[4]—something the other missionaries do not do; and he conducts himself, in general, as a "slave" to the community (4:5). Paul is also accused of acting **according to the flesh**. Recall from the treatment of 1:12 that "†fleshly" behavior refers to that which is not divinely influenced or empowered. He is thus regarded by some as timid and servile, only able to muster courage from the safety of distance.

Paul counters these "charges" in verse 2. He points to his coming visit—referred to by the phrase **when present**—and warns that, if necessary, he intends **to act boldly against** those who are giving a false characterization of him and his ministry. Paul makes clear that he can and will exercise tough love with those who persist in sin (13:2; see 1 Cor 4:21). Nevertheless, his preference is to act with the gentleness and clemency of Jesus. Hence Paul begs the Corinthians—at least those who are criticizing him—to change their ways and to see that his comportment proclaims the gospel.

Implicit here is that they recognize the truth about Paul's being "humble" (*tapeinos*). While humility was not at all considered a virtue in the ancient world, Paul insists that, rightly understood, it is an essential part of living out the gospel.

---

3. The NEB and REB add a parenthetical "(you say)" to convey that the words here are not Paul's.
4. According to Acts 18:3, Paul worked as a tent maker when he first came to Corinth.

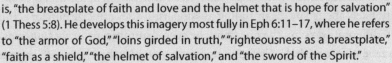

The Old Testament Background to Paul's War Imagery

BIBLICAL BACKGROUND

Paul's use of battle imagery draws on the Old Testament. The prophet Isaiah portrays God as putting on "justice as his breastplate," salvation "as the helmet on his head," "garments of vengeance," and "a mantle of zeal" (59:17). Thus armed, God goes forth as redeemer of those who turn from sin and battles their enemies. Paul adapts this imagery in exhorting Christians to ward off any forces that draw them away from following Christ. He encourages his communities to "put on the armor of light" (Rom 13:12), that is, "the breastplate of faith and love and the helmet that is hope for salvation" (1 Thess 5:8). He develops this imagery most fully in Eph 6:11–17, where he refers to "the armor of God," "loins girded in truth," "righteousness as a breastplate," "faith as a shield," "the helmet of salvation," and "the sword of the Spirit."

Paul's use of siege warfare (see below) in 2 Cor 10:4–6 may also allude to Prov 21:22: "The wise man storms a city of the mighty, / and overthrows the stronghold in which it trusts." The wisdom he girds himself with, against "the wisdom of the world," is that of the gospel of the crucified and risen †Messiah. Paul has come to appreciate that "the foolishness of God is wiser than human wisdom, and the weakness of God is stronger than human strength" (1 Cor 1:18–25). Armed with the wisdom and strength that come from the gospel he has been commissioned to proclaim, the Apostle destroys the "fortresses" of godless ideologies, of arguments against Christian faith and morality, and of the power of sin that holds people in bondage.

Indeed, Jesus' love for us was most dramatically demonstrated when "he humbled (*tapeinoō*) himself, becoming obedient to death" (Phil 2:8). We saw in 7:6 Paul's conviction that God encourages the lowly, or "downcast" (*tapeinoi*). The critics *are* correct when they characterize Paul as humble; they are wrong when they fail to recognize that his humility is patterned after Christ. Such humility is, in all actuality, an instrument of *power*, as he will proceed to show.

10:3–6   Paul acknowledges that he is **in the flesh**, that is, he shares like everyone else in the human condition. However, he insists, he does **not battle according to the flesh**, in ways deprived of God's power.[5] Rather, Paul explains, his **weapons** are **enormously powerful, capable of destroying fortresses**. The NAB's "enormously powerful" translates a phrase that is better rendered

---

5. As Victor Paul Furnish remarks, Paul is "in the world" but does not act "according to worldly standards" (*II Corinthians: A New Translation with Introduction and Commentary*, AB 32A [New York: Doubleday, 1984], 461). See Rom 12:1–2; 1 Cor 7:29–31; Phil 3:19–20.

"powerful because of God." That is, Paul's use of battle imagery serves to highlight *God's* power. It might seem surprising that the Apostle speaks about battles and weapons immediately after invoking Jesus' gentleness and forbearance. But with this juxtaposition Paul captures the paradox of how God's power is made known. Above all, God's power has been revealed in Jesus' death on the cross. Through this climactic expression of Jesus' humble, self-giving love, the powers of sin and death were defeated (Rom 5:12–21; 1 Cor 1:18–25).

Moreover, God's power *continues* to be manifested "in earthen vessels" like Paul (2 Cor 4:7), through the preaching of the gospel. Thus the "weapons of righteousness" (6:7), which he now describes himself as wielding, are in actuality the loving, self-giving way of life that eloquently proclaims the good news concerning what God has done through Christ. These weapons include the authority to refute what is contrary to the gospel and to punish those who persist in wrongdoing (12:20; 13:2).

Paul continues the battle metaphor as he sets forth the threefold progression of siege warfare (vv. 4–6). The first stage of siege warfare is to destroy the opponent's bulwarks and fortifications. Thus, as a soldier in God's army, Paul attacks and destroys **arguments and every pretension raising itself against the knowledge of God**. As we noted in 4:6 and 6:6, "the knowledge of God" refers to the gospel, to what God has revealed through the life, death, and resurrection of Christ. Paul's point here is similar to one he made in an earlier letter to the Corinthians: "For since in the wisdom of God the world did not come to know God through wisdom, it was the will of God through the foolishness of the proclamation to save those who have faith" (1 Cor 1:21). The true gospel, proclaimed by Christians through word and deed, reveals the emptiness of any theology that does not take full account of the power of the cross. The gospel makes manifest the harmful consequences of setting one's mind on "the things of the flesh" (Rom 8:5–8). It also deflates all forms of arrogance. Indeed, we will see throughout chapters 10–12 that much of what Paul condemns in the intruding missionaries is their haughtiness and self-importance, which reflect an erroneous understanding of the gospel.

The second stage of siege warfare is to take captives. Hence Paul states in verse 5 that he takes **every thought** (*noēma*) **captive in obedience to Christ**. Earlier in the letter, he asserted that "the god of this age has blinded the minds (*noēmata*) of the unbelievers" (4:4). This remark helps us interpret Paul's imagery here. He envisions his work of proclaiming the gospel as a type of rescue operation—and, in doing so, he adapts the notion of taking captives, turning

Siege Warfare in the Ancient World

Siege warfare is the military strategy of surrounding and weakening a walled city to the point of its surrender or destruction. This tactic was used with devastating effect by the Assyrians and Babylonians in Old Testament times. The siege first entailed cutting off the city's water and food supplies and means of communication. It involved building siege walls or earthen mounds that protected the attackers. Sometimes the attacking army attempted to weaken the foundation of the city walls. When a city was deemed sufficiently weakened—or if it refused to surrender—the attackers employed battering rams to knock down the gates or vulnerable parts of the wall. They also used primitive machinery to hurl fire and stones, and ladders so heavily armored soldiers could storm over the walls. Once inside, the attacking army usually set the city on fire. Those who were not killed were taken captive.

Second Kings 25 describes the siege of Jerusalem by Nebuchadnezzar, King of Babylon, that culminated in the destruction of the temple in 586 BC. In New Testament times, the Romans engaged in siege warfare against Jerusalem, a siege that ended with the burning of the rebuilt temple and city in AD 70. In fact, Jesus alludes to this in Luke 21:20 ("When you see Jerusalem surrounded by armies . . .").

---

it into something positive for those so "captured."[6] That is, he seeks to bring his hearers into the light of "the knowledge of the glory of God on the face of [Jesus] Christ" (4:6). While Paul refers here to "thoughts," his real concern is for the *persons* who hold them. His assumed logic is that people must correctly understand the gospel if they are to live by it.

What then does Paul mean by taking captives in "obedience to Christ" (*hypakoē tou Christou*)? Elsewhere I have argued—on the basis of both grammatical considerations and Paul's typical usage—for rendering this phrase as "Christ-like obedience."[7] Paul desires to inculcate the total commitment of mind and will *to God* after the manner of Jesus' "yes" to God (1:19). With reference to the Corinthians, we have seen that he seeks their obedience to God in reaffirming their love for the wrongdoer (2:8–9) and in giving generously to the collection (9:13). He now seeks their obedience to God in their rejection of the intruding missionaries. As a slave of God on behalf of the Corinthians

6. For a similar interpretation, see Frank J. Matera, *II Corinthians: A Commentary*, NTL (Louisville: Westminster John Knox, 2003), 224.

7. Thomas D. Stegman, *The Character of Jesus: The Linchpin to Paul's Argument in 2 Corinthians*, AnBib 158 (Rome: Pontifical Biblical Institute, 2005), 129–37.

(2:14; 4:5), Paul knows the paradox that captivity to God leads to actual liberty (Rom 6:16–18). It is only in submitting ourselves to the life-giving way of God that we find true freedom from selfishness and sinful desires.

The third stage of siege warfare is to deal with the fomenters of rebellion. Thus Paul declares in verse 6 that he stands **ready to punish every disobedience, once your obedience is complete**. As we have just observed, he wants the community to express its obedience by rejecting the interlopers and their misunderstanding of the gospel. This is his primary objective. When Paul is satisfied that at least the majority of the Corinthians have fully declared their obedience to God, he will turn his attention to those within the community who are following the intruding missionaries. What kind of punishment does Paul have in mind for them? He does not say, although 1 Cor 5:4–5 might provide a clue. There he calls for the excommunication of a man living in grave sin, with the hope that the man is shocked into repentance so that "his spirit may be saved on the day of the Lord." In any event, the Apostle makes clear that he intends to "act boldly" (v. 2) if he is forced to.

Reflection and Application (10:1–6)

Warfare imagery. Paul's employment of the siege metaphor is rhetorically powerful. It can also strike us as jarring, especially given the prevalence of violence and war in our world today. Indeed, we are only too aware of the tendency, seen more and more, to appeal to religion to justify the use of violent force against others. So how can we interpret verses 3–6 in a life-giving manner? First, it is essential to observe that Paul's primary point is to make manifest the power of *God* to overcome all that opposes the coming of his kingdom. Second, it is important to keep in mind that he is talking here about spiritual and intellectual warfare against Satan and mistaken ideas about God. He is not speaking about warfare against human beings. The spiritual life *does* involve engaging in battle against forces that seek to draw us away from living the gospel. Equipped with "the armor of God" (Eph 6:11–17), we can be confident of victory because Christ himself has already defeated the power of Satan (Mark 3:27).

The need to act boldly. It may be helpful here to review the Reflection and Application on 1:23–2:4. Pastors, teachers, administrators, parents, and other leaders do well to reflect on whether their own comportment and leadership style reflect Jesus' gentle and clement way of exercising authority. However, verses 2–6 also make clear that it is necessary, at times, to employ a sterner pastoral attitude. When confronted with arrogance, error, or disobedience, those in authority have to act with sufficient boldness to correct and, if necessary, discipline the persons in question. While gentleness and clemency are necessary for ministering in the name of Christ, they may not be sufficient by themselves.

The importance of theology. Paul's concern for "arguments" and "thoughts" (vv. 4–5) reveals the critical importance in the Christian life of what a person thinks. We need to have a correct understanding of who God is, what it means to be created in his image, and what Christian discipleship entails. For the Apostle, theology is not just an academic exercise. Its ultimate purpose is to transform lives. We will have occasion to return to this topic when treating 11:1–6 in the following chapter.

Authority to Build Up (10:7–11)

⁷Look at what confronts you. Whoever is confident of belonging to Christ should consider that as he belongs to Christ, so do we. ⁸And even if I should boast a little too much of our authority, which the Lord gave for building you up and not for tearing you down, I shall not be put to shame. ⁹May I not seem as one frightening you through letters. ¹⁰For someone will say, "His letters are severe and forceful, but his bodily presence is weak, and his speech contemptible." ¹¹Such a person must understand that what we are in word through letters when absent, that we also are in action when present.

OT: Isa 57:14–15; 62:10–12; Jer 1:1–10; 18:1–10
NT: 1 Cor 2:4–5; 3:9–10; 2 Tim 4:1–5

Paul challenges the Corinthians to consider that their very existence as a Christian community attests to the authority given to him by Christ. He explains that his authority is for building up, not tearing down. He then responds to criticism about the severity of his letters and the unimpressive way he presents himself in person. Against his critics—the intruding missionaries and some in the community—Paul insists that his character and comportment are consistent with one another.

10:7   Paul makes an impassioned appeal: **Look at what confronts you.**[8] What does he want the Corinthians to consider? First, he wants them to appreciate that he **belongs to Christ.** The Greek phrase rendered by the NAB as "belongs

8. Paul indicates emphasis by putting the verb "look" (*blepete*) in the prominent end position; more literally, "At that which confronts you—look!"

to Christ" has a more specific connotation here than simply being a member of the Christian community. Paul uses it as a synonym for being an †apostle or "minister of Christ" (see 11:13, 23). In the background is the intruding missionaries' claim of being **confident of belonging to Christ**, that is, their claim that Christ has commissioned them to be missionaries for him. For the time being and for argument's sake, Paul grants their self-assessment, although he will vehemently dispute it in 11:13–15. His point is that, if these "belong to Christ," so much more does he. Indeed, as verse 8 will suggest, the very existence of the church in Corinth attests to his apostleship (3:2–3). Therefore, if the Corinthians look at what is right before their eyes[9]—that is, if they consider how God has worked among them through their founding apostle—they should readily recognize that, if anyone has the claim to "belong to Christ," it is Paul.

Paul broaches the issue of the **authority** that **the Lord gave** to him **for building** the community **up**. Observe his unease in talking about himself: **even if I should boast a little too much**. The reason for his unease will become clear in the ensuing paragraphs of the letter. The reference to †boasting foreshadows a theme that recurs throughout 10:12–12:13. By speaking of the authority given to him by God through Christ "for building up" the Corinthians, Paul reminds them that it was he who laid the foundation of God's "building" when he came to Corinth proclaiming the †gospel (1 Cor 3:9–10). Paul's "building up" the community refers to all the labor he has since expended to promote their well-being. Because love drives his "building up" (1 Cor 8:1), he is confident that he **shall not be put to shame** when he appears before the judgment seat of Christ (2 Cor 5:10).

10:8

The imagery of building up likewise evokes the call of the prophet Jeremiah. When God empowered Jeremiah to proclaim his word, he gave him authority "to root up and to tear down" as well as "to build and to plant" (Jer 1:10). It is striking that, in reporting his encounter with the risen Jesus on the road to Damascus—the encounter that constituted his apostolic calling—Paul employs the language of Jeremiah's call (Gal 1:15–16; see Jer 1:5). Thus he also alludes here to his original call from the Lord, which is the basis of all his missionary activity.

Unlike Jeremiah, however, Paul's authority is *solely* for building people up and not for tearing them down. He thus implies a critical difference between himself and the intruding missionaries. While everything he does, including destroying arguments and pretensions (v. 5), is for the edification of his spiritual children, the interlopers' teaching, he will soon suggest, will lead to the community's destruction (11:3–4).

9. This is how the RSV and NRSV translate the beginning of v. 7.

Verse 9 is notoriously difficult to interpret in terms of its grammar and purpose in Paul's argument. In my opinion, the NAB's choice to render it as a type of imperative—**May I not seem as one frightening you through letters**—is the best solution.[10] In referring to letters he has previously written to the Corinthians, Paul takes up the criticism leveled against him that he alluded to in verse 1. Before setting forth and responding to the actual criticism, he wants the community to understand that, because all of his actions are geared toward building them up, they should not be frightened by anything he writes to them. Rather, they should trust that he always has their best interests at heart.

Various people—likely the intruding missionaries and some members of the Corinthian church—are criticizing both the way Paul writes when absent and the way he conducts himself when present. On the one hand, his critics say, **his letters are severe and forceful**. While these adjectives can be taken in a positive sense (e.g., as "rhetorically powerful"), Paul's awareness in verse 9 that he is accused of frightening the community indicates that "severe" and "forceful" are intended negatively (e.g., as "tyrannical and violent"). In all likelihood, the content of the †tearful letter is in the background here, but certain passages from the letter we call †canonical First Corinthians are also susceptible to such an interpretation (e.g., 1 Cor 4:19–21; 5:3–5). In short, he is criticized for striking fear—but only from a safe distance (2 Cor 10:1).

On the other hand, Paul's detractors comment, **his bodily presence is weak, and his speech contemptible**. Interestingly, he will shortly acknowledge that he is not a speaker trained in eloquence (11:6). But Paul has also insisted that, when he first came to Corinth, he chose not to use polished words when preaching the gospel. Why? In order to manifest that Christian faith rests "not on human wisdom but on the power of God" (1 Cor 2:4–5). The criticism of Paul's physical presence and bearing probably stems from his second visit to Corinth and, more specifically, to the incident with the wrongdoer (2 Cor 2:5; 7:12). His decision at that time to leave Corinth and write a letter from afar was interpreted by some as timidity, if not cowardice. In addition, the criticism of Paul's weak bodily presence might refer to the perception in certain quarters that, because he engaged in manual labor to support himself, his posture and bearing are too blue collar for their tastes.[11]

Paul wants those who hold such opinions to **understand** that what he is **in word through letters when absent** so also he is **in action when present**. But

10. Similarly, the REB renders v. 9: "So you must not think of me as one who tries to scare you by the letters he writes."
11. See Furnish, *II Corinthians*, 479.

what does this mean? Not that Paul intends, from now on, to soften the tone of his letters, nor that he is now committed to enhancing his physical appearance and honing his speaking abilities. Rather, his meaning is that *everything* he does for the Corinthians—whether via letters or in their presence—is for their edification and good. Why? Because his divinely given commission is to build them up. In other words, Paul insists that his character and conduct are utterly consistent at all times: whether he has been forced to challenge and chastise them in his letters; or whether he has embodied a more humble way of being in their presence, in imitation of Christ's gentleness (10:1). All is in service of the Apostle's proclamation of the gospel.

Reflection and Application (10:7–11)

Authority for building up. Paul understands the raison d'être of God-given authority as building others up. Such an understanding challenges all of us who hold positions of authority as pastors, chaplains, teachers, mentors, youth ministers, or parents. The words "edify" and "edification" come from the Latin translation for "building up" (as in v. 8). Those who are in positions of authority are called to be "edifiers," people whose values, attitudes, words, and deeds are constructive, for example, by laying a foundation in teaching, assisting, and forming others and then building on this foundation with encouragement and, if needed, positive correction. This is challenging work. We know how a single demeaning comment or insensitive act can undermine dozens of kind words and deeds. One way to examine my conscience as one who holds authority is to ask myself: How constructive were my words and deeds today?

The authority to build others up involves more, however, than growing in self-awareness of the effects of our speech and actions. It also calls for a lasting commitment to *love* those who are in our charge. Such love requires much patience, faithfulness, and the dedication to support and encourage. Even when challenge and discipline are required, we must take care not to act out of a feeling of superiority, anger, or vindictiveness.

It also helps to remember that each one of us is under the authority of another—ultimately, under the authority of our loving God. And it is useful to recall the beneficial ways we ourselves have been built up so that we can share those ways with others—or, conversely, avoid those ways that involve the harmful exercise of authority. Paul's teaching here reminds us that authority is given for *service.* In doing so, he echoes Jesus' teaching (e.g., Mark 10:42–44; John 13:12–17).

Paul's personal limitations. In the exegesis of verse 10 above, I have offered typical reasons commentators give to explain the criticism of Paul's bodily presence and speech. More generally, we can say that he appeared to be someone whose personal presence when speaking was not very powerful, despite his knowledge and spiritual authority. Ministers today can take consolation in this. All of us have our personal limitations. Rather than focus on them, we can—like Paul—trust in the power of God to proclaim the gospel as he has called us to do.

Proper Missionary Boasting (10:12–18)

[12]Not that we dare to class or compare ourselves with some of those who recommend themselves. But when they measure themselves by one another and compare themselves with one another, they are without understanding. [13]But we will not boast beyond measure but will keep to the limits God has apportioned us, namely, to reach even to you. [14]For we are not overreaching ourselves, as though we did not reach you; we indeed first came to you with the gospel of Christ. [15]We are not boasting beyond measure, in other people's labors; yet our hope is that, as your faith increases, our influence among you may be greatly enlarged, within our proper limits, [16]so that we may preach the gospel even beyond you, not boasting of work already done in another's sphere. [17]"Whoever boasts, should boast in the Lord." [18]For it is not the one who recommends himself who is approved, but the one whom the Lord recommends.

OT: Isa 26:12; Jer 9:22–23
NT: Acts 26:12–20; Rom 15:14–21; 1 Cor 1:31; 3:5–9

Recall Paul's unease about †boasting in verse 8. We now learn that the intruding missionaries engage in competitive self-commendation as they boastfully measure themselves and their accomplishments against one another. Paul insists that he boasts only within proper limits, for he boasts only in what God accomplishes through him. What matters ultimately is not †*self*-commendation but the commendation that comes from the Lord.

10:12   Paul begins on an ironic note. Having declared that he will act boldly against the Corinthians if necessary (vv. 2, 6, 11), he confesses that there is one thing he does *not* **dare** to do:[12] **to class or compare** himself **with some of those who recommend themselves.** Once again he draws on the notion of self-commendation

12. The same verb, *tolmaō*, is found in v. 2 ("act boldly") and here in v. 12 ("dare").

(see 3:1; 4:2; 5:12; 6:4), here with the emphasis on the *self*.[13] He then clarifies
what he means by the negative sense of self-commendation by referring to the
interlopers' practice: they **measure themselves by one another and compare
themselves with one another**. It appears that the intruding missionaries compete
with one another in promoting themselves, in taking pride in their credentials
and accomplishments, and in denigrating others—including Paul. He, on the
contrary, does not "dare" to partake in such activity, because it is futile and
dangerously wrongheaded.

The point is that the intruders, in measuring and comparing themselves
with one another, do not take into account the most important standard of all,
namely, *God*. It is God who provides an external criterion—indeed, the only
legitimate criterion—for all self-commendation. As Paul will make clear in the
following verses, he boasts only insofar as he is an instrument through whom
God is working to bring salvation through the proclamation of the †gospel. In
setting themselves up as the sole measure of success and in failing to appreciate
that God provides the true criterion for boasting, the interlopers demonstrate
they are without understanding.

Paul now takes up the notion of "measuring" (*metreō*). He insists that, un-   **10:13–14**
like the intruding missionaries, he **will not boast beyond measure** (*ametra*).
Rather, he is committed to **keep to the limits God has apportioned** to him.
The NAB's "limits" renders succinctly a phrase difficult to translate, *to metron
tou kanonos* (literally, "the measure of the standard"). What does Paul mean by
keeping to the *metron* that God—literally "the God of measure"[14]—has assigned

---

13. See the sidebar "Paul's Use of Self-Commendation in 2 Corinthians" on p. 233.

14. English translations fail—with the exception of the NIV's alternative translation in a footnote—to
capture Paul's description of God as "the God of measure" (*ho theos metrou*) in v. 13.

to him? In my opinion, he refers here to the simple historical fact that it was he who preached the gospel in Corinth before anyone else did, as the end of verse 13 suggests—**to reach even to you.** He reminds the Corinthians that it was he who **first came to** them **with the gospel of Christ.** Looking back at his missionary work in Corinth from the perspective of faith, Paul sees the providential hand of God operating through his founding the church there. Hence his "boasting"—by which he means giving witness to what *God* has done through him—is warranted. Paul is **not overreaching** himself, either in his missionary work or in his "boasting." In both instances, he remains within the "limits" apportioned to him by God. Implicit here is his criticism that the interlopers are overreaching themselves in their claims.

10:15–16   Paul reiterates that he is **not boasting beyond measure** (*ametra*). By adding that he does not boast **in other people's labors**, he suggests that this is precisely what the intruding missionaries are doing—taking credit for the work God has already done through Paul. He expresses his **hope** that, as the Corinthians' **faith increases**, his **influence among** them **may be greatly enlarged.** Paul's "influence" refers to his way of proclaiming the gospel, both in word and in self-giving love. His hope is that the community will grow in their faith because of his influence. This hope echoes what he said in 3:2–3, where he encouraged the Corinthians to grow in obedience to God, after the manner of Jesus' "yes," and thereby become a visible "letter about Christ" (my translation) for others to "read." Here Paul desires that they mature in faith so that he can move on to other missionary endeavors, as he makes plain—**so that we may preach the gospel even beyond you.**

We know from his letter to the Romans, written from Corinth shortly after penning 2 Corinthians, that he intended to go to Spain after taking the collection to the church in Jerusalem. In Paul's mind, Spain represented the western end of the world, and his God-given task is "to proclaim the gospel not where Christ has already been named, so that I do not build on another's foundation" (Rom 15:20). Because his call is to "plant" the gospel (1 Cor 3:6) where it has not been heard, he does not engage in **boasting of work already done in another's sphere.** Paul thus conveys two things in verses 15–16: first, he expresses his hope that the Corinthians grow in faith so that he can move on to other missionary fields; second, he intimates that the interlopers have no real basis for boasting because they have encroached on the work God granted him to do in Corinth.

Before proceeding, it is important to note that, in addition to explaining that he boasts only within the limits set for him by God, Paul is also laying a foundation in verses 13–16 for the "fool's boast" that follows (11:1–12:13). While he will acknowledge the danger of engaging in extended boasting on account of the intruders, here he sets the stage for his claim that, ultimately, his boasting is not unfounded.

Paul now explicitly sets forth the principle of legitimate boasting: **"Whoever** **10:17–18** **boasts, should boast in the Lord."** As he did in an earlier letter to the Corinthians (1 Cor 1:31), he alludes to Jer 9:22–23. Human boasting that claims anything beyond what God has accomplished in Christ Jesus (Rom 5:11) is groundless and therefore pointless.[15] Paul explains that **it is not the one who** commends **himself who is approved**. Rather, it is **the one whom the Lord** commends who is truly "approved." The intruding missionaries have completely failed to understand the way of God (v. 12). Instead of promoting themselves, they should be giving glory to God. And instead of worrying about what other people think of them, they ought to be concerned with how God regards them.

Now precisely what kind of person does the Lord commend? Paul offers a clue by using the word *dokimos* ("approved"). We have seen that this term pertains to the issue of proven character (2:9; 8:8; 9:13). Recall that Paul has set this discussion in the context of Jesus' gentleness and forbearance (10:1). Recall too the reference to Christ's obedience in 10:5. These references to Jesus' character strongly suggest that the person commended by God is the one who takes on his Son's character. Those who take on Jesus' character can legitimately boast because their "labors" and "work" (vv. 15–16) are empowered by God. The Apostle's forthcoming critique of the interlopers will be that their behavior and words are contrary to what Christ embodied.

Reflection and Application (10:12–18)

Turf wars. At first glance, it may appear as if Paul is engaging in a ministerial turf war, for he is indignant that other missionaries have encroached on his work in Corinth. His concern, however, is not to selfishly protect his own foundation, as if it were entirely his own work, not to be shared in by others. In fact, Paul demonstrates in 1 Cor 3:5–9 that he recognized and valued Apollos's contributions to the growth of the church in Corinth. And as he explains in verse 16, Paul wants the Corinthians to mature in their faith so that he can move on to

15. Most commentators take the referent of "Lord" in vv. 17–18 to be Christ. Passages like Rom 5:11 indicate, however, that God may be the ultimate referent. Indeed, v. 13, above, speaks of what *God* has apportioned to Paul. In the end, the meaning in vv. 17–18 is the same whether the Father or Christ is the intended referent.

other missionary work. Rather, the concern he expresses in this passage is that the intruders are exercising a malevolent effect on his spiritual children.

With this clarification in mind, Paul's words in verses 12–18 challenge us not to overidentify ourselves with the fruits of our ministerial labors. Some pastors and ministers have a difficult time being open to new assignments. At times this is because they are presently experiencing great success. Resistance to move on can also be grounded in the fear that, upon leaving their present work to others, their decisions and accomplishments will be undone by those who succeed them. Paul's words remind us that, ultimately, it is *God's* mission, not our own, that we are called to serve. They also challenge us to grow in our affection for and trust in one another so that we view one another as coworkers, not as competitors, in God's mission field.

The dangers of competitive comparison. The prevalence of "†boasting" language in 2 Corinthians can be off-putting. It is important to appreciate that, in the †honor–shame mentality of the culture, boasting of one's accomplishments was typical, especially in a competitive city like Corinth. Paul only engaged in boasting—in the qualified sense, explained above—because other missionaries were boasting falsely and had to be refuted.

While the negative type of boasting is largely frowned on today, the practice of measuring oneself against others is alive and well. As Paul recognized, this practice is futile and even harmful. More times than not, when people compare themselves with others, even if only in their own minds, they tend to sell themselves short, thinking that others have more going for them. Such thinking can lead to envy and self-pity. It can also lead, paradoxically, to the negative *self*-commendation that Paul refers to. The need to assert oneself over against others (e.g., "At least I am better than *him*") is often an attempt to compensate for self-doubt and low self-esteem. The Apostle teaches a better, healthier way. In recognizing that God is the one who bestows gifts upon all for building up the body of Christ, we can rejoice in our own gifts—as well as those of others.

Paul vs. the "Superapostles"

2 Corinthians 11:1–15

Having broached the topic of the intruding missionaries, their criticisms of him, and their competitive and boastful ways (10:1–18), Paul dubs them "superapostles" and seeks to convince the Corinthians that his manner of being an †apostle, not theirs, authentically proclaims Christ (11:1–12:13). Paul begins by expressing fatherly concern for the community as he conveys his fear that they are being led astray (11:1–6). Next he explains why he refuses to take financial remuneration from the Corinthians (11:7–11). Then he makes clear why it is dangerous to heed the interlopers (11:12–15).

Paul's Fatherly Concern for the Corinthians (11:1–6)

> ¹If only you would put up with a little foolishness from me! Please put up with me. ²For I am jealous of you with the jealousy of God, since I betrothed you to one husband to present you as a chaste virgin to Christ. ³But I am afraid that, as the serpent deceived Eve by his cunning, your thoughts may be corrupted from a sincere [and pure] commitment to Christ. ⁴For if someone comes and preaches another Jesus than the one we preached, or if you receive a different spirit from the one you received or a different gospel from the one you accepted, you put up with it well enough. ⁵For I think that I am not in any way inferior to these "superapostles." ⁶Even if I am untrained in speaking, I am not so in knowledge; in every way we have made this plain to you in all things.

OT: Gen 3:1–7; Isa 54:1–8; 62:1–5; Hosea 2:16–25
NT: Matt 25:1–13; Mark 2:19–20; Eph 5:21–33; Rev 19:6–8; 21:1–7
Catechism: Church as the bride of Christ, 796; spousal character of the human vocation, 505

Paul wants the Corinthians to give him a hearing, just as they are listening to and observing the intruding missionaries, whom he derisively terms "superapostles." As the Corinthians' spiritual father, he expresses his fear that the community is being deceived and led to follow, in effect, another Jesus. Although he may not be a trained speaker, he insists that he imparts true knowledge, the †gospel itself.

11:1   Paul exhorts the Corinthians to bear with him in what follows: **If only you would put up with a little foolishness from me! Please put up with me.** He is about to embark on a rhetorical tour de force. Because at least some members of the community are mesmerized by the self-promotion of the interlopers, Paul deems it necessary to play their game. This is what he foreshadows by the phrase "a little foolishness." As we will see in 11:16–12:13, Paul engages in †boasting in his own heritage, sufferings, and ministerial accomplishments. In the course of his boast, however, he will make it abundantly clear that he regards such bragging as foolish.[1] At this point, however, Paul simply requests that the Corinthians "put up with" him. In doing so, he offers a subtle rebuke for their having "put up with" the interlopers (see 11:4, 19–20).

11:2   Paul offers a powerful reason why the community should put up with him. It is he who has **betrothed** them **to one husband to present** them **as a chaste virgin to Christ**. In order to appreciate Paul's meaning here, we must know something about Jewish marriage practices at that time. The act of betrothal was legally binding in a way that engagement in our society is not.[2] Once it was agreed that a woman was betrothed to a man for marriage, it was her father's legal responsibility to safeguard her virginity until the time when she left her parents' house to move in with her husband—usually a period of one year. Notice that Paul refers to himself once again as the spiritual father of the Corinthians (1 Cor 4:15; 2 Cor 6:13; 12:14–15). In founding the church in Corinth, he betrothed the community to Christ as their "husband." It is now Paul's obligation to protect the Corinthians from paramours and other suitors so that he can present them "as a chaste virgin to Christ." The consummation of this marriage will take place when the risen Lord returns in glory.

As their spiritual father, Paul is **jealous of** the community **with the jealousy of God**. Just as God's covenant loyalty to his people manifested itself in "jealousy"—that is, in his zealous care for Israel and adamant insistence that

---

1. Paul uses the language of foolishness throughout this part of the letter: "foolishness" (*aphrosynē*) in 11:1, 17, 21; and "fool" (*aphrōn*) in 11:16 (twice), 19; 12:6, 11.
2. See Matt 1:18–19, where Mary is described as being betrothed to Joseph but not living with him, and where Joseph is portrayed as having decided to "divorce" her until learning that she was pregnant by the power of the Holy Spirit.

Marriage Imagery and God's Covenant Love for His People

BIBLICAL BACKGROUND

Paul's use of marriage imagery in 2 Cor 11:2 has its roots in the writings of the prophets. In particular, Isaiah, Jeremiah, Ezekiel, and Hosea portrayed God's special, covenantal union with his chosen people Israel as a marriage. For example, through Isaiah God proclaimed to Israel: "As a young man marries a virgin, / your Builder shall marry you; / And as a bridegroom rejoices in his bride / so shall your God rejoice in you" (62:5; see Isa 54:5–6; Hosea 2:18, 21–22). This image of marriage served to convey God's intimacy with and fidelity to Israel, as well as to remind his people that they belonged exclusively to him. When Israel abandoned God's way and turned to serve the idols of other nations, the prophets accused them of spiritual adultery (e.g., Jer 3; Ezek 16). Nevertheless the prophets also made clear that God stood ready to receive his people back if they recommitted themselves to him (e.g., Hosea 2).

In calling people to heed his proclamation of God's kingdom, Jesus presented himself as the bridegroom (Mark 2:19–20). Christians are to be faithful to their betrothal to Christ as they await the "wedding feast" that will be celebrated at his return in glory (Matt 25:1–13). Paul refers to the Church as the bride of Christ who has been sanctified and cleansed so that Christ "might present to himself the church in splendor, without spot or wrinkle or any such thing, that she might be holy and without blemish" (Eph 5:23–27). The New Testament reaches its climax in a song of victory: "Let us rejoice and be glad / and give him glory. / For the wedding day of the Lamb has come, / and his bride has made herself ready" (Rev 19:7). The Church is the "new Jerusalem, coming down out of heaven from God, prepared as a bride adorned for her husband" (Rev 21:2).

his people avoid idolatry—so Paul is "jealous" for the Corinthians. He strives to protect them from all harmful influences and to keep them loyal to Christ, who loves the Church with the ardor and fidelity of a spouse (Eph 5:21–33).

11:3–4 Because of his fatherly concern for the Corinthians, Paul expresses his fear that the intruding missionaries are leading them away from their commitment to Jesus. Just **as the serpent deceived Eve by his cunning,** so Paul is **afraid** that the community's **thoughts may be corrupted from a sincere [and pure][3] commitment to Christ**. He alludes here to the story told in Gen 3, where Eve succumbed to the wiles of the serpent and ate the fruit of the tree from which she and Adam had been forbidden to eat. Most

3. The words "and pure" are placed in brackets because there is some textual evidence that they may have been added to the original text. I read them as belonging to Paul's original letter.

commentators interpret this verse in a straightforward manner. Following his introduction of the marriage metaphor in verse 2, Paul warns the Corinthians not to be "seduced" by the interlopers' teaching and behavior. Whereas he has insisted that he does not act deceitfully (*en panourgia*) or falsify God's word (4:2), they are instruments of Satan's "cunning" (*panourgia*), as 11:13–15 will make clear.[4]

This traditional interpretation of verse 3, while correct, misses a subtle point. An alternate translation that, in my opinion, reflects the Greek more accurately is: "I am afraid that . . . your thoughts may be corrupted from the single-heartedness and the purity that is *in* Christ." Elsewhere I have argued at length that Paul refers here to two attributes of Jesus, his single-hearted devotion (*haplotēs*) to God and his innocent purity.[5] Why does Paul bring up these two qualities? Note that what he is concerned about at this point is the community's "thoughts" (*noēmata*).

The issue seems to be their proper understanding of the gospel—including who Jesus is—an understanding that is essential for their proper comportment. Paul wants the Corinthians to understand the truth about the †Messiah, whose manner of life was marked by his unequivocal commitment to obey God's will and by his innocence and self-giving love. Just as Paul seeks to rescue thoughts to bring about Christlike obedience (10:5), so now he attempts to safeguard the community's understanding of Jesus so that they can walk in the way of Jesus' single-hearted devotion to God and purity of life. In doing so, they will be prepared for the "wedding feast" (Matt 25:10) with Christ and avoid the sin of Eve (and Adam) that, ultimately, was disobedience to God.

This interpretation is supported by the reference to people who "come and preach" **another Jesus than the one** Paul **preached**.[6] He proclaimed "the Son of God, Jesus Christ," whose "yes" to God was the fulfillment of all the divine promises (1:19–20). But what can be said about this "other Jesus" preached by the intruding missionaries? Recall that for Paul the gospel is proclaimed most eloquently by one's way of life. Based on their arrogance and self-serving behavior (see 11:20), it is probable that the interlopers downplayed the challenging message of the cross—the culmination of Jesus' loving, humble, self-giving way of life that revealed God's love for us.

4. For the identification of the serpent in Gen 3 with the devil, see Wis 2:24. See Rev 12:9 and 20:2 for identifying the ancient serpent with Satan.

5. Thomas D. Stegman, *The Character of Jesus: The Linchpin to Paul's Argument in 2 Corinthians*, AnBib 158 (Rome: Pontifical Biblical Institute, 2005), 196–205.

6. Although Paul refers to "someone" in v. 4, this is a representative figure for those whom he will call "superapostles" in v. 5.

John Paul II on Fidelity to the Truth of the Gospel

LIVING TRADITION

In his first encyclical, *Redemptor Hominis* (*Redeemer of Man*), issued in 1979, Pope John Paul II explained what is at stake in understanding the truth about Jesus. On the one hand, "in Christ and through Christ God has revealed himself fully to humankind and has definitively drawn close to it." On the other hand, "in Christ and through Christ" human beings have "obtained full consciousness of their dignity, of the heights to which they are raised, of the surpassing worth of their own humanity, and of the meaning of their existence" (11). John Paul reminded the Church that, just as "the only Son" was completely faithful to revealing God's word, so "the same fidelity must be a constitutive quality of the Church's faith" when she is teaching it (19).

In doing so, the missionaries likely failed to communicate clearly that Christians are called to embrace Jesus' self-offering to God, in which life and victory come through self-giving and suffering. Paul makes clear that if the Corinthians have welcomed these missionaries and their way of proclaiming the gospel, they are in danger of having **accepted** a **different gospel** and of having **received** a **different spirit**. In warning them against accepting, or submitting to, the intruders, Paul reminds the community that *he* is the one with whom they should "put up" (v. 1). The Apostle thereby tries to awaken them to heed "the gospel of God" (11:7) which he proclaimed to them in word and action, through which they have been anointed with God's Spirit (1:21–22).

Paul gives another reason why the Corinthians should put up with him. He **11:5–6** is **not in any way inferior to these** intruding missionaries, whom he now calls **"superapostles."** Paul uses this term sarcastically. It refers, in all likelihood, to the inflated view the interlopers have of themselves and to the way they have presented themselves to the community (see, for instance, the issue of recommendation letters in 3:1). Paul insists that, although he is **untrained in speaking**, he is **not so in knowledge**. We saw in 10:10 that the "superapostles" and their supporters criticized his speech as contemptible. The issue seems to be whether or not Paul was a professional speaker, one who had received an orator's specialized training. Some, if not all, of the intruders probably were so trained and had impressed the Corinthians with their rhetorical skills. Paul acknowledges that he lacks such training. But this is not to say that he could not effectively communicate the gospel. Nor does it imply that he lacked rhetorical ability.[7] But Paul is concerned with substance over style. And the substance of his "knowledge" is the gospel itself (4:6; 6:6), which he has made **plain to** the community **in every way** and **in all things**—through his verbal proclamation and through his embodiment of Jesus' self-giving love (2:14–15; 4:5).

Reflection and Application (11:1–6)

Intimacy with Christ. Paul's image of the Church as the bride of Christ Jesus is rich and evocative. It refers both to the Church as a whole and to her individual members. Most fundamentally, the marriage imagery connotes intimacy. All Christians are invited to grow in intimate union with Jesus—especially through regular prayer, *lectio divina*, and participation in the liturgical and sacramental life of the Church. Marriage also implies exclusivity. We are thus called to grow in giving over our lives more and more to Christ. This can be a painful process as we become aware of values, interests, habits, and relationships that compete with our single-hearted devotion to him.

Intimacy with Christ therefore calls us to constant vigilance and conversion. It does not, however, draw us away from other people or from living in the world—although some may receive a call to a monastic kind of withdrawal from society. Rather, it transforms families, religious communities, and parishes by empowering us to love one another as Christ loves us. Intimacy with Jesus also enables us to live out our vocations and chosen paths with great zeal and integrity, and to expand the horizons of our concern for those most in need.

The importance of a proper Christology. Intimacy with Jesus is also important because it inculcates a more profound knowledge of who he is. Getting to know the beloved and growing in love go hand in hand, as any happily married couple can attest. Sustained intimacy with Christ—fostered by prayerful reflection on his life as revealed in Scripture and by frequent reception of the Eucharist— leads to a greater understanding of who he is.

Second Corinthians is a wonderful resource for contemplating the character of Jesus. Paul leads us to reflect on Christ's faithfulness and obedience to God (1:18–20; 4:13; 10:5), his graciousness and generosity (8:9), his gentleness and forbearance (10:1), his innocent purity and single-hearted devotion to God (11:3; see 5:21), and his love that manifested itself most dramatically in his dying "for all" (5:14–15). Such knowledge is crucial for Christians because each one of us is called to be *alter Christus*, "another Christ," for others. Apparently the

---

7. Paul's "fool's boast" in 11:21b–12:13 offers evidence of his written rhetorical skills.

superapostles were so enamored of status and human admiration that they failed to embody Jesus' humility and self-giving love. We must all examine ourselves and ask, Am I susceptible to the same shortcoming?

Preaching the Gospel Gratis (11:7–11)

---

[7]Did I make a mistake when I humbled myself so that you might be exalted, because I preached the gospel of God to you without charge? [8]I plundered other churches by accepting from them in order to minister to you. [9]And when I was with you and in need, I did not burden anyone, for the brothers who came from Macedonia supplied my needs. So I refrained and will refrain from burdening you in any way. [10]By the truth of Christ in me, this boast of mine shall not be silenced in the regions of Achaia. [11]And why? Because I do not love you? God knows I do!

OT: Ps 26
NT: Matt 10:8; Acts 20:33–35; 1 Thess 2:5–12; 2 Thess 3:7–9
Catechism: Swearing oaths, 2154

Paul now takes up the issue of financial support as he defends his practice of not taking remuneration for his ministry. He assures the community that he acts after the self-giving manner of Jesus and insists that his actions are grounded in his love for them.

Paul begins this section on an ironic note, asking whether he committed a sin[8] **when** he **humbled** himself **so that** the Corinthians **might be exalted**. In what particular way did he humble himself for their sake? He **preached the gospel of God** to them **without charge**. Recall from 10:1 that Paul acknowledged that he was "humble," or "lowly" (*tapeinos*), when he was in Corinth. There we saw that one of the issues is that he supports himself by manual labor—most likely by tent making, an occupation that required much output to eke out a living (Acts 18:3; 1 Cor 4:12). Although he, like any other evangelist, has the right to be supported financially (1 Cor 9:3–14; 1 Tim 5:18), Paul refuses to be a burden to the communities to whom he ministers (1 Thess 2:5–12; 2 Thess 3:7–9; see Acts 20:33–35). Paul is convinced that, because God's act of reconciling the world to himself through Christ is a free gift (*dōrea*; see Rom 5:17), he ought to proclaim the "gospel of God" to people "without charge" (*dōrean*). In this

11:7

---

8. The NAB's **Did I make a mistake** does not fully capture the Greek text, which reads, literally, "Did I commit a sin . . . ?" (as rendered by the RSV and NRSV). At the end of the fool's boast Paul will ask, ironically, for forgiveness (12:13).

he echoes Jesus' words in Matt 10:8: "Without cost (*dōrean*) you have received; without cost (*dōrean*) you are to give."

It is significant that Paul uses the phrase *tapeinoō* plus the reflexive pronoun ("humble oneself") only one other time, in Phil 2:8, where he describes *Jesus* as having "humbled himself, becoming obedient to death." Paul thus aligns himself with Christ's self-giving and makes clear that his own self-giving is for the sake of the Corinthians (2 Cor 4:12): that they "might be exalted." Through his ministry of proclaiming the good news, the community has been "raised from the death of heathen sins to the life of righteousness."[9] We can now better appreciate Paul's claim in 6:10 that, although he is poor, he enriches many. In doing so, he obviously does not commit sin.

Before proceeding in the analysis, it is helpful to pause and note two important social and cultural forces in the background of Paul's dealings with the Corinthians. One is the low esteem and value those with education, financial resources, and power attributed to manual labor. Paul's practice of supporting himself by tent making was regarded as demeaning by some in the community, and in all likelihood by the superapostles. By his work he is thought to be demeaning himself and, by association, the Corinthian community whose †apostle he is.

A second cultural factor, one at the center of the Greco-Roman social fabric, involves the relationship between †patrons and †clients. One way this relationship played out was in the patronage those who were wealthy extended to teachers, artists, and philosophers. Such sponsorship brought honor to the wealthy as patrons. Naturally, their extension of friendship in the form of financial support was also attractive to the recipients. But reception of patronage came at a price, because the recipient became a client, one who was obliged to respond to the patron's whims and wishes. Paul's practice of refusing benefaction from those to whom he ministered protected him from becoming beholden to anyone, thereby enabling him to retain apostolic freedom—freedom to relate equally to rich and poor, and to challenge and correct when necessary.

But from the perspective of those wealthy Corinthian Christians who sought to be his patron, Paul's refusal looked like a rejection of their offer of friendship. What made the situation worse, in all probability, was that the superapostles gladly received such patronage. For them it was a mark of pride to have their status and work recognized by patrons. In Paul's eyes this was tantamount to exploitation (see 11:20); the interlopers were "trading on" God's word (2:17).

9. Alfred Plummer, *A Critical and Exegetical Commentary on the Second Epistle of St. Paul to the Corinthians*, ICC (Edinburgh: T&T Clark, 1915), 303.

Further complicating matters, the Corinthians have learned that, while in Corinth, Paul received financial support from the Macedonians (as vv. 8–9 will make clear). Thus it seems to some in the community in Corinth that he operates under a double standard: he refuses the Corinthians' patronage while accepting help from other churches. Is Paul playing favorites? The inconsistency, however, is more apparent than real. While it is true that he does not accept direct remuneration from those to whom he presently proclaims the †gospel, he is willing to receive support from *other* churches in his missionary endeavors. In fact, the church in †Philippi has helped Paul as he worked in †Thessalonica as well as in Corinth (Phil 4:15–16).[10] Receiving such assistance allows him to spend more time in the work of evangelization and in caring for the churches; it also allows Christian communities to participate in the work of evangelization. Finally, as if the situation were not already complex enough, we will see in 12:16–18 that Paul is accused of using the collection for the church in Jerusalem as a subterfuge to line his own pockets, an accusation the superapostles likely promoted.

This background helps explain the tone and content of the remainder of the passage. Paul informs the Corinthians that he has **plundered other churches by accepting** assistance **from them**. Here he draws on the military imagery of 10:3–6. Paul does not mean to suggest that he coerces others into giving. By using the imagery of plundering, he makes the point that he is not a client beholden to the wishes of his benefactors.[11] Notice too that he insists that funds from other churches are used for the purpose of *ministry* (*diakonia*)—in the present case, to minister to the church in Corinth.

11:8–9

Paul acknowledges that certain **brothers who came from †Macedonia supplied his needs** when he was ministering in Corinth and was **in need**. It seems that this contribution to his support has only recently been discovered and that he needs to explain why he accepted help from the Macedonians while refusing it from the Corinthians.[12] Paul explains that he **did not** want to **burden anyone**. He is determined to proclaim the gospel "without charge" and to offer his communities an example of working hard (2 Thess 3:7–9). Because he refuses to be a financial liability to the people to whom he is ministering, he declares to the Corinthians that he has **refrained and will refrain from burdening** them **in any way**.

10. Paul expresses his desire in 1 Cor 16:6 and 2 Cor 1:16 that the Corinthians help him in other ventures he will undertake (see "send me on my way"). Compare Rom 15:24, where he seeks the Roman church's assistance for his planned mission to Spain.

11. See Victor Paul Furnish, *II Corinthians: A New Translation with Introduction and Commentary*, AB 32A (New York: Doubleday, 1984), 508.

12. At first glance, this would seem to call into question Paul's claim to be transparent. But it may be that his motive for keeping silent about the Macedonians' support was that he wanted to avoid conflict and misunderstanding, the very things that did in fact result.

11:10   Paul announces that his **boast** will **not be silenced in the regions of Achaia**, that is, in the lands surrounding Corinth, the capital of the Roman province of †Achaia. He is about to embark, beginning in 11:16, on what is known as the "fool's boast." Here he foreshadows both the ironic tone of that †boasting as well as its ultimate content. About what does Paul boast throughout Achaia? That he is not a financial burden to the church in Corinth (1 Cor 9:15)!

     We will see below (v. 12) that part of Paul's motive here is to contrast his way of ministering with that of the superapostles. But the beginning of verse 10—**By the truth of Christ in me**—is crucial to his meaning. This phrase operates, at one level, as an oath formula;[13] that is, he swears that his boast will be heard. At a deeper and more profound level, Paul explains why he is able to boast: Jesus' "truth" (*alētheia*) dwells in him. In other words, because "the Spirit of Christ" is within him (Rom 8:9), bestowing on him "the mind of Christ" (1 Cor 2:16), Paul is inspired to embody Jesus' self-giving way of life in his commitment to proclaim the gospel gratis, even if it means having to support himself by manual labor. Therefore his boast is, in reality, a "boasting in the Lord" (2 Cor 10:17).

11:11   Having declared his intention to boast, Paul reassures the Corinthians of his love for them. We have seen that in some quarters his refusal to take financial support from members of the community might be interpreted as a rejection of their friendship. (This is the sense of **why? Because I do not love you?**) He now makes clear that his motivation is love. Just as Jesus' manner of living, which culminated in his death on the cross, was an expression of his love (5:14), so is Paul's commitment to minister to the Corinthians without taking financial remuneration from them. Indeed, he will soon emphasize that, as their spiritual father, it is he who should "spend" and "be utterly spent" for his children, not vice versa. Hence he desires not what they have but rather their commitment to Christ—and, by extension, to himself (12:15). Paul concludes by appealing to God's omniscience. Although some in the community might not understand, he claims that **God knows** the love that underpins all his dealings with the Corinthians, including his refusal to take financial support from them.

Reflection and Application (11:7–11)

Ministerial recompense. It is important to point out that Paul's standard of preaching the gospel gratis goes beyond Jesus' teaching in Luke 10:7 that the laborer for the gospel "deserves his payment." To be sure, Paul himself recognizes

---

13. Paul uses various forms of oath formulas throughout 2 Cor: 1:18, 23; 2:10; 11:11, 31. See the sidebar on p. 59 on the issue of oaths.

this (1 Cor 9:14). While few ministers today would, or could, hold themselves to his standard, nevertheless all of us can benefit from reflecting on what this standard presumes.

In the first place, Paul takes seriously Jesus' instruction to his disciples, "Without cost you have received; without cost you are to give" (Matt 10:8). We are challenged to recall that the vocation to ministry is itself a gift from God and that it is to be exercised, as far as possible, as a gift to others. To regard oneself primarily as a professional, that is, with the emphasis on one's status, job title, and salary level, is foreign to the Apostle's concept of ministry.

In the second place, Paul recognizes that true recompense for ministry comes from God and is manifested in the peace and joy experienced in serving the divine will. This recompense is what Jesus refers to when he says that doing the Father's will is what gives him life (John 4:34). While other forms of recompense are important—including material and emotional support—Paul reminds ministers that our true and lasting reward is God himself.

Preserving freedom and avoiding conflicts of interest. Paul's guiding principle regarding financial support—accepting support from churches only insofar as it aids his ministry elsewhere—might seem overly complex, if not arbitrary. But there is real wisdom in his policy. To preserve one's freedom in preaching the gospel with integrity, it is important to avoid all conflicts of interest, both real and perceived. While it is necessary to raise funds for ministry, it is crucial to keep at the forefront the reason why monies are raised: for service (*diakonia*) to others. Benefactors are thus to be exhorted to give freely—not seeking undue control, power, or influence—out of the goodness of their hearts (see 9:7). The work of proclaiming the gospel should never be compromised out of fear that the rich and powerful might withhold contributions if they do not like what they hear.

Deceiving Appearances (11:12–15)

[12]And what I do I will continue to do, in order to end this pretext of those who seek a pretext for being regarded as we are in the mission of which they boast. [13]For such people are false apostles, deceitful workers, who masquerade as apostles of Christ. [14]And no wonder, for even Satan masquerades as an angel of light. [15]So it is not strange that his ministers also masquerade as ministers of righteousness. Their end will correspond to their deeds.

OT: Ezek 34:1–16
NT: Matt 7:15–20; 1 Pet 5:1–5

Paul insists that he will continue to refrain from taking recompense from the Corinthians because he wants to highlight an important difference between himself and the superapostles. He warns the Corinthians that the intruders are not serving God's plan; rather, they are aiding the cause of Satan.

11:12   Paul picks up his insistence that he **will continue** his practice of preaching the †gospel gratis. He explains that he wants to "cut the ground from under"[14] the **pretext** of the superapostles. Here Paul turns the intruders' game of comparison against them. They want to be **regarded as** he is **in the mission** at Corinth; that is, they want to be considered as equal to him, if not superior. But Paul intimates that the superapostles, who apparently **boast** that they are receiving the honor of †patronage, rather than being content to accept basic sustenance for their labors (in the spirit of Luke 10:7), are mere †clients to the wealthy in the community. They certainly are not embodying the humility and self-giving manner of Jesus, "of the Christ who became poor that others might be enriched."[15] Paul's preaching the gospel gratis is one way of accentuating the difference between himself and the self-serving interlopers.

11:13–15   Paul characterizes the superapostles with harsh terms. If in 10:7 he granted for the sake of argument that they, like him, "belong to Christ," he no longer grants this premise. He now refers to the intruders as **false apostles** and **deceitful workers** who disguise themselves or **masquerade as apostles of Christ**. To be sure, more than seeking patronage and status is in the background here. Paul makes these serious charges because the interlopers have encroached on his God-given mission in Corinth (10:15–16) to the detriment of the Church—in contrast to ministers like Timothy, Titus, and Apollos, who have served the community's good. The superapostles have upset the Corinthians by calling into question Paul's credentials and manner of being an †apostle. Their conduct and words betray that they preach "another Jesus" and "a different gospel" (11:4). While they "boast of external appearance" (5:12), in reality they have acted deceitfully and falsified God's word (4:2; see 2:17). In short, they have undermined what God has charged Paul to do in Corinth.

This undermining of *God's* work explains the invective in verses 14–15. Paul exclaims that it is **no wonder** that the superapostles masquerade as emissaries of Jesus because **even Satan masquerades as an angel of light**. Here he draws on extrabiblical Jewish writings and traditions about Satan appearing to Eve in the guise of an angel or messenger from God.[16] Paul states that **it is not strange**

---

14. This phrase—found in the NIV, NJB, NEB, and REB—better captures Paul's sense than the NAB's **end**.

15. Furnish, *II Corinthians*, 509.

16. See, e.g., ibid., 494–95, for citations.

that Satan's **ministers also masquerade as ministers of righteousness**. He thus dramatically sets forth to the Corinthians why it is dangerous to heed the intruders: in undermining his missionary work in Corinth, they are doing the work of Satan. In my opinion, Paul is not accusing the superapostles of choosing to side with Satan. They may sincerely believe themselves to be "ministers of Christ" (11:23). But by calling Paul's divinely given authority into question— thereby alienating the Corinthians from their spiritual father—and in failing to embody the character of Jesus while acting in his name, they unwittingly aid and abet the work of Satan.

Recall Paul's earlier caution to the community to be wary of Satan's purposes and to avoid being taken advantage of by him (2:11). Authentic "ministers of righteousness," true ministers of the †new covenant (3:6, 9), are marked by their walking in Christ's loving, self-giving way of life by which they participate in the ongoing revelation of God's righteousness (5:21); they serve the gospel by courageously proclaiming its truths. Finally, the Apostle makes clear that for serving Satan's purposes the interlopers will face harsh judgment (5:10): **their end will correspond to their deeds**.

Reflection and Application (11:12–15)

High stakes and the danger of demonizing others. Paul's passionate language illustrates the high stakes involved in the work of evangelization. Because the gospel is the source of salvation, its proper proclamation and embodiment are truly a matter of life and death. Paul's strong wording here reflects this reality. Sadly, people who think they are doing God's work can actually undermine that work if they do not operate in a Christlike way or if they weaken or damage the ministry of a person to whom God has entrusted primary responsibility. This is a point on which each of us can examine ourselves.

At the same time, we have to be very cautious about demonizing others. The rhetoric of many religious enthusiasts today too easily devolves into casting aspersions on one's enemies—even to the point of calling them children or agents of Satan. While it is necessary for church leaders to condemn aberrant teachings and practices, it is important to do so in a spirit of love. Our passage here should be read in the context of the larger corpus of Paul's writings. Indeed, in Rom 12:14 the Apostle echoes Jesus' teaching about loving one's enemies and blessing one's persecutors (Matt 5:44; Luke 6:27–28).

Foolish Boasting

2 Corinthians 11:16–33

Paul continues to distinguish his way of being a minister of Christ from that of the superapostles by engaging in boasting that he acknowledges is foolish (11:16–21a). He sets forth his apostolic pedigree and credentials—the latter are the sufferings he endures for proclaiming the †gospel (11:21b–29). Paul's boast reaches an initial climax when he turns a coveted badge of courage and honor, known as the "wall crown," completely on its head (11:30–33). Throughout his boast he employs irony and rhetorical flourish to make clear that what he ultimately boasts of is his weakness.

Playing the Fool's Role (11:16–21a)

---

¹⁶I repeat, no one should consider me foolish; but if you do, accept me as a fool, so that I too may boast a little. ¹⁷What I am saying I am not saying according to the Lord but as in foolishness, in this boastful state. ¹⁸Since many boast according to the flesh, I too will boast. ¹⁹For you gladly put up with fools, since you are wise yourselves. ²⁰For you put up with it if someone enslaves you, or devours you, or gets the better of you, or puts on airs, or slaps you in the face. ²¹To my shame I say that we were too weak!

OT: Ps 14
NT: 1 Cor 1:18–25; 2:6–16; 3:18–23

Although he regrets having to do so, Paul asks the Corinthians to hear him out as he embarks on a boast resembling that of the superapostles. He makes clear, however, that such †boasting is foolish, not "according to the Lord." He uses powerful irony to jolt the community out of their attraction to the intruders.

St. Ignatius on Being Regarded as a Fool for Christ

In the *Spiritual Exercises* (165–67), St. Ignatius of Loyola delineates three modes of humility. The first mode consists of the commitment to be faithful to God in all things and to never consent to do anything that would disrupt one's relationship with God (i.e., serious sin). The second mode goes deeper, as one decides to adopt an attitude of indifference to riches or poverty, to good or bad health, etc. What matters most is responding to God's call in whatever circumstances he leads us. The third mode, which encompasses the first two, goes even deeper. Here one desires and chooses to align oneself with Jesus in his poverty, humility, and rejection, even to the point of being accounted "worthless and a fool" for the sake of Christ (see 1 Cor 4:10). Paul was willing to play the role of fool for the Corinthians because, as will become clear in the remainder of his boast, he was fully committed to following Jesus with the most radical form of humility.

Paul picks up what he introduced in 11:1–4, namely, his request that the Corinthians put up with some foolishness from him. But first he insists that, in principle, **no one should consider** him **foolish**. As "an †apostle of Christ Jesus by the will of God" (1:1), Paul is a conveyer of God's wisdom (1 Cor 2:7). Nevertheless, he recognizes that some in the community *do* regard him as foolish, because he refuses to take remuneration from them, does not speak in a sophisticated manner, embraces suffering as part of his vocation, and places himself at the service of those in his care (2 Cor 4:5). In light of their criticism, Paul asks the community to **accept** him **as a fool,** because he has decided to play the superapostles at their own game (see 10:12). He **too** wants to **boast a little**. Unlike the intruders, however, he recognizes the foolishness of boasting.

11:16

Paul offers some parenthetical remarks.[1] He acknowledges that his "boasting-project"[2] is not **according to the Lord** (*kata kyrion*). Recall that Paul has insisted that the only legitimate boasting is "in the Lord" (10:17; 1 Cor 1:31). What he is about to do now is **as in foolishness**. Paul does not want to engage in boasting in the likeness of the superapostles; it is unsavory to him. Then why does he do so? Paul explains that it is necessary **since many boast according to the**

11:17–18

---

1. The RSV appropriately places these two verses within parentheses.
2. This is how Margaret E. Thrall aptly translates the phrase rendered **boastful state** by the NAB (*A Critical and Exegetical Commentary on the Second Epistle to the Corinthians*, ICC, 2 vols. [Edinburgh: T&T Clark, 1994–2000], 2:709).

flesh. "Many" refers to the intruding missionaries. The phrase "according to the †flesh" (*kata sarka*) signifies—as we have seen in 1:17; 5:16; and 10:2–3—a manner of doing things that lacks divine inspiration and empowerment. It is the opposite of acting "according to the Lord."

More specifically, Paul has intimated that the interlopers boast in "external appearance" (5:12), such as physical appearance and eloquence (10:10); and, as we will see, they apparently brag about their pedigree, heroic exploits, and dramatic religious experiences (11:22–12:10). But to boast of such things is foolish if one accepts Jesus' scale of values. To be sure, Paul is not here condoning the logic so often used by adolescents: "Everyone else is doing it. Why can't I?" Rather, he recognizes that some of the Corinthians have been deceived by the boasting of the superapostles (11:3). He therefore informs the community that he **too will boast**—but only in order to counter the boasting of the intruders.

But notice here that Paul hedges a bit: he refuses to say that his boast will be "according to the flesh." Although he recognizes the foolishness of boasting about himself, his boasting is eventually going to focus on his *weakness*. Why? Because through it Jesus' power is made manifest (12:9). Hence his boasting is, ultimately, not "according to the flesh."

11:19   After these parenthetical remarks, Paul returns to his request that the Corinthians put up with him (11:1) and accept him as a "fool" (v. 16) in his project of boasting. They should do so because they already **gladly put up with fools**, a reference to the way they welcome the superapostles. Paul then refers to the supposed wisdom of the community: **since you are wise yourselves**. He obviously does not intend to praise them for their wisdom and tolerance. Rather, he writes in an ironic tone in order to awaken them to the reality of what they have submitted themselves to in receiving the ministrations of the intruders (as the next verse makes dramatically clear). In putting up with the intruders— and in calling the Apostle and his ministry into question—the members of the community are acting foolishly.

11:20   Paul characterizes the superapostles' conduct toward the Corinthians by saying that they act as overlords over the members of the community (**if someone enslaves you**). Paul, conversely, refuses to "lord it over" (1:24) the Corinthians, choosing instead to serve them as their "slave" (4:5). The interlopers "devour," or exploit, the community—in all likelihood a reference to taking, perhaps even demanding, financial support.[3] Paul, by contrast, refuses to be a burden

---

3. The verb *katesthiō* ("devour," "exploit") appears in Mark 12:40, where Jesus condemns the scribes for "devouring" the houses of widows, i.e., for taking financial advantage of vulnerable members of society.

to them (11:9). The superapostles get **the better of**, that is, take advantage of the Corinthians. Paul, however, steadfastly denies ever having used the community for his personal advantage (7:2; 12:16–18). The rivals put **on airs** by acting haughtily and promoting themselves. Paul chooses a different way, that of lowering himself so that the community might be "exalted" (11:7). Finally, the intruders slap the Corinthians **in the face**, a metaphorical expression that summarizes how they abuse the Corinthians. Paul, on the contrary, serves as a protective (11:2) and loving (12:14–15) spiritual father to the community. The rhetorical force of verse 20 is to shock the Corinthians into seeing the deleterious consequences of putting up with the intruding missionaries, who in actuality tyrannize over the community.

Paul continues his ironic tone as he confesses, to his "**shame**," that he has been **too weak** to conduct himself as the superapostles do. If his loving service elicits the criticism that he is "weak," he could not agree more. Of course, this is not something that Paul is ashamed of. His being "weak" here means that he has refrained from using his authority for his own benefit. To exercise self-control in the use of one's powers is, in actuality, an act of strength. The reference to weakness introduces a key theme that he will develop in the course of his "fool's speech" (11:29–30; 12:5, 9–10). It is weakness—understood in Paul's sense of the term—that will become the object of his boasting.

11:21a

Reflection and Application (11:16–21a)

A risky strategy. The fact that Paul takes several verses (11:1–21a) to lead up to his boast (11:21b–12:10) is a strong indicator of his distaste for the undertaking. Why, then, does he choose to go through with his boast, a decision that leaves him vulnerable to the same criticism he levels against the superapostles? St. Ignatius of Loyola taught that sometimes it is necessary to enter the other person's door before you can bring him or her through your own door. In this case, Paul realizes that some of the Corinthians have been mesmerized by the manner and content of the intruding missionaries' boasting. He decides to play their game—that is, to go through another's door—by offering his own boast. But Paul's intent is to lead the Corinthians—perhaps the interlopers too—through his own door by showing that the only thing worth boasting about is what the Lord empowers. While the Apostle *can* in truth boast about many things, he considers them as nothing in comparison with "gain[ing] Christ and be[ing] found in him" (Phil 3:8–9).

Apostolic Hardships (11:21b–29)

But what anyone dares to boast of (I am speaking in foolishness) I also dare. [22]Are they Hebrews? So am I. Are they Israelites? So am I. Are they descendants of Abraham? So am I. [23]Are they ministers of Christ? (I am talking like an insane person.) I am still more, with far greater labors, far more imprisonments, far worse beatings, and numerous brushes with death. [24]Five times at the hands of the Jews I received forty lashes minus one. [25]Three times I was beaten with rods, once I was stoned, three times I was shipwrecked, I passed a night and a day on the deep; [26]on frequent journeys, in dangers from rivers, dangers from robbers, dangers from my own race, dangers from Gentiles, dangers in the city, dangers in the wilderness, dangers at sea, dangers among false brothers; [27]in toil and hardship, through many sleepless nights, through hunger and thirst, through frequent fastings, through cold and exposure. [28]And apart from these things, there is the daily pressure upon me of my anxiety for all the churches. [29]Who is weak, and I am not weak? Who is led to sin, and I am not indignant?

OT: Isa 50:4–11
NT: Acts 14:19–20; 16:16–40; 27:39–44; 1 Cor 8:7–13; Gal 4:19–20

Paul begins his boast. While insisting that he has the same Jewish heritage as the intruding missionaries, he claims to be a superior minister of Christ. Whereas the superapostles seem to focus on achievements, Paul—though his own apostolic works are greater—highlights his participation in the sufferings of Jesus. These sufferings include the constant pressure and anxiety he feels as spiritual father of the churches he has founded.

11:21b   Recall that, in verse 21a, Paul ironically confessed his "shame" for not conducting himself in the exploitative manner of the superapostles. Now he declares his readiness to boast like them: **what anyone dares to boast of . . . I also dare**. His use of the verb "dare" echoes his threat in 10:2 that, if necessary, he will "act boldly." The threat to the spiritual well-being of the Corinthians is reason enough for Paul to act with boldness. Nevertheless, as his parenthetical remark—**I am speaking in foolishness**—reveals, he realizes that boasting exclusively about one's pedigree and accomplishments is folly.

11:22   Paul begins by comparing his ethnic pedigree and religious heritage with that of the superapostles, who apparently take great pride in these matters. He asks three rhetorical questions to which he replies in each case, **So am I**. Although all three questions pertain to Jewish identity, they are arranged in order of ascending importance.[4] The term **Hebrews** refers here, in all likelihood, to bloodlines and, perhaps, to the ability to speak Hebrew or Aramaic. Most scholars think that Paul is claiming that, like the intruding missionaries, he is a pure-blooded Jew, born of two Jewish parents. The word **Israelites** highlights the notion of being members of God's chosen people, with all the privileges this entailed (see Rom 9:4–5), including the covenants, law, and temple worship. Similarly, the phrase **descendants of Abraham** (literally, "seed of Abraham") points to being recipients of the divine promises made to the great patriarch and father in faith (Gen 12:3; 15:5; 17:2), promises that have now been fulfilled in Jesus the †Messiah (2 Cor 1:20).[5] Thus Paul insists that the superapostles do not surpass him in regard to Jewishness.

At first glance, it might strike us as strange that Paul underscores his Jewish identity, especially given that Christianity and Judaism are, in our own time, two distinct religions. However, it is important to appreciate that, even after his encounter with the risen Lord and his call to proclaim the †gospel to the †Gentiles, Paul still considered himself a Jew. He regarded his Jewish heritage an immense gift of God and saw in Jesus the fulfillment of everything God had promised to the Jews. Moreover, he saw Jews along with Gentiles as essential to the constitution of the Church (Eph 2:14–18).

It is in connection with Jesus—specifically, with being **ministers** (*diakonoi*) **of**   **11:23**
Christ—that Paul differentiates himself from the superapostles. In response to their claim to be Christ's special envoys, he insists that he is **still more** (*hyper*); that is, he is more "super" than the superapostles (*hyperlian apostoloi*) themselves! In saying this, Paul once again acknowledges, parenthetically, how foolish such †boasting is: **I am talking like an insane person.** Yet he forges ahead with his boast because of what is at stake, namely, the spiritual well-being of the Corinthians. In what ways is he superior to the intruding missionaries? In all likelihood, they were boasting of their accomplishments and exploits. Notice, however, that Paul does not—as in truth he could—enumerate the churches he has founded or the converts he has made or the miracles he has worked. Instead, as he did when he legitimized his earlier claim to be a servant (*diakonos*) of God (6:4), he lists various sufferings and hardships as the authenticating marks of a servant of Christ.

Paul's †hardship catalog in verses 23–29 is the third such list in this letter (4:8–9; 6:4–10; see 12:10) and the most detailed.[6] The second half of verse 23

---

4. See Frank J. Matera, *II Corinthians: A Commentary*, NTL (Louisville: Westminster John Knox, 2003), 263.

5. See Gal 3:16, where Paul argues that Christ is Abraham's descendant or seed to whom the promises pointed; and Gal 3:29, where he reveals that all those who are "of Christ" are Abraham's true descendants.

6. See the sidebar "Paul's Use of 'Hardship Catalogs'" on p. 152.

Paul's Adaptation of the Achievement Lists

BIBLICAL BACKGROUND

Paul's use of the first person singular pronoun and of precise enumeration in 2 Cor 11:24–25 has formal parallels with the so-called "achievement lists" in the Greco-Roman world. The most famous of such lists is "The Deeds of the Divine Augustus" (*Res Gestae Divi Augusti*) published after the emperor's death in AD 14. This funerary inscription lists Augustus's political offices and accomplishments, his military victories, his benefactions for various peoples, and the numerous honors that had been accorded him. Two examples from this list provide a sense of what they were like: "I was twenty-one times saluted as emperor"; and "Twice I received triumphal ovations" following military victories. Because this list was made public throughout the Roman Empire, it is quite possible that the Apostle was familiar with it.

Paul adapts the "achievement list" for his own purposes. He does not seek to promote his own achievements and greatness. Rather, he lists the various times he has encountered the threat of death in the course of preaching the gospel in order to reveal the power of God at work in him (1:9–10; 4:7–11; 6:9).

---

serves, in effect, as the heading of this third catalog. Rather than focus on his accomplishments, Paul emphasizes his multitudinous missionary **labors,** including arduous travel and preaching and working day and night. He also highlights several **imprisonments**[7] and **beatings**, which often went hand in hand (e.g., Acts 16:22–24). In addition, Paul refers to **numerous brushes with death** (see Rom 8:36; 1 Cor 15:32; 2 Cor 1:8–10). Labors and sufferings are not disconnected topics. In giving himself generously, tirelessly, and fearlessly to his vocation, Paul has frequently encountered fierce opposition and even the threat of death. Unlike the superapostles, he is adamant that an essential authenticating mark of a "minister of Christ" is sharing in Christ's sufferings (1:5).

11:24–25 Paul lists his "numerous brushes with death." He relates that he **received forty lashes minus one** on **five** different occasions. Flogging was the punishment meted out by the synagogue (**at the hands of the Jews**; see Matt 10:17; 23:34), and he received the maximum punishment each time.[8] In all likelihood, he was punished for his teaching that the Gentiles did not need to adopt the Mosaic law upon becoming Christians. That the Apostle was subject to this synagogue discipline testifies to his ongoing Jewish identity. Paul states that **three times** he

---

7. According to *1 Clement* 5.16 (written ca. AD 96), Paul was imprisoned seven times.
8. See Deut 25:2–3. While forty lashes was the maximum penalty, it became common to administer thirty-nine to avoid miscounting (and thus exceeding what the law allowed).

was beaten with rods, an official Roman punishment (Acts 16:22; see 1 Thess 2:2). Why did he draw the ire of Roman magistrates? His preaching that Jesus Christ is the "Lord" (Phil 2:11; 2 Cor 4:5) would have provoked strong reactions from those who regarded the Roman Emperor as the one to whom people's devotion was due.

Paul next refers to a time when he **was stoned** (see Acts 14:19), an incident akin to a mob lynching, which he obviously survived. He then reports that **three times** he **was shipwrecked**. Seafaring was notoriously dangerous and, because his means were limited, the ships he boarded were likely not well suited for passenger safety. In fact, on one occasion, he spent a harrowing twenty-four hour period (**a night and a day**) **on the deep**, clutching desperately to a piece of wreckage while waiting to be rescued.

The references to sea journeys lead Paul to recount the various **dangers** he   **11:26** endured on account of his **frequent journeys** by land.[9] He repeats the word "dangers" eight times in order to convey the constant reality of perils and threats in his ministry. First, he lists two common hazards to land travelers: **rivers** and **robbers**. In a time when bridges were relatively rare, river-crossings could be treacherous at any time, and especially in the springtime when there was flooding. While the Roman legions sought to make the main highways safe, bandits were still a menace to travelers, especially those who traveled alone or in small groups.

Paul then alludes to the violent opposition he received for preaching the gospel, opposition from both Jews (**my own race**) and **Gentiles**. Paul probably encountered opposition from Jews because his ministry drew Gentile †Godfearers away from the synagogue (see, e.g., Acts 14:1–7; 17:1–9). His ministry also provoked vehement hostility from some Gentiles, including those whose economic opportunities suffered because of conversions to Christianity (e.g., Acts 16:16–21; 19:23–41). Paul reports that he has experienced "dangers" *everywhere* his ministry has taken him, whether **in the city** or in deserted places (**the wilderness**) or **at sea**. Nowhere was he immune from threats.

Finally and climactically, Paul mentions the "dangers" he has encountered from **false brothers**. These were fellow Christians—including the superapostles—who undermined the work of the gospel (see Gal 2:4). Hence the list of dangers concludes on a poignant note, as the danger here involves undercutting and damaging the work of the Spirit.

Paul turns to hardships he imposes on himself in his commitment to proclaim   **11:27** the gospel free of charge. The opening phrase, **in toil and hardship**, introduces

9. The Greek word *hodoiporia* refers specifically to land travel. The NEB and REB convey this as follows: "I have been constantly on the road."

the sufferings that follow. As in 6:5, he refers to the manual labor he undertakes so as not to burden the communities to whom he ministers. Because of this commitment, Paul often forgoes sleep (**many sleepless nights**) as well as eating and drinking (**hunger and thirst**). In all likelihood, there were times when his preaching during the day prevented him from fulfilling the work orders he had accepted, thus requiring him to labor into the night. At other times he availed himself of opportunities to preach and teach in the evenings after a long day of wearying toil. Moreover, because he devotes himself first and foremost to proclaiming the good news, Paul's manual labors are barely sufficient to cover the basic necessities of food, clothing, and shelter. Thus he is susceptible to being "many times without food"[10] and to **cold and exposure**. His meager resources would also have left him vulnerable to the elements in his travels. In contrast to the self-promoting superapostles, he accentuates self-giving and sacrifice as distinguishing characteristics of a minister (*diakonos*) of Christ Jesus.

11:28–29   Having listed the sufferings imposed on him (vv. 24–26) and those he imposes on himself (v. 27), Paul describes the emotional toll his pastoral responsibilities have taken on him. The constant need to encourage, teach, correct, and rebuke his fledgling churches creates an intense **daily pressure upon** him. Like parents who worry about children, Paul experiences constant **anxiety for all the churches** he has founded. Once again, he conveys to the Corinthians that he is their spiritual father, who has their best interests at heart (11:2–3). Implicit is that the intruding missionaries do not have such loving concern for them. Paul illustrates his anxiety by referring to his concern for the **weak**—those Christians who suffer scruples of conscience over various issues (see Rom 14:1–2; 1 Cor 8:9–11). He is so sensitive to the "weak" that he puts himself in their shoes, so to speak (1 Cor 9:22), in order to help them. What Paul does at all costs is to avoid their being **led to sin** (1 Cor 8:13—the Greek literally means "cause to stumble"). When others in the community cause the weak to stumble, he becomes **indignant**. In this, Paul shows the same compassionate zeal that Jesus manifested on behalf of the "little ones" (Mark 9:42) and demonstrates his own teaching that if one member of the body of Christ suffers, the whole body suffers (1 Cor 12:26).

Recall that, in the process of introducing his "fool's boast" in verses 16–21a, Paul employed an obvious ironic tone (e.g., confessing his "shame" that he was "too weak" to exploit the Corinthians). His tone has subtly changed in verses 21b–29. Although he continues to use irony, he is perfectly serious about what

---

10. While the word *nēsteiai* can mean **fastings** (as in the NAB), it refers more fundamentally to deprivation of food. I employ the phraseology of Victor Paul Furnish, *II Corinthians: A New Translation with Introduction and Commentary*, AB 32A (New York: Doubleday, 1984), 512.

he claims here, namely, that he has suffered many toils and hardships as a minister of Christ. The irony lies in the fact that Paul's purpose in these verses is neither to show forth his own power to endure such sufferings nor to prove his stoic demeanor in the face of adversity. Rather, in contrast to the "†fleshly" boasting of the superapostles—bragging about great exploits and accomplishments (see 12:12)—Paul stresses his participation in the sufferings of Christ. Therein lies his claim to glory.

Reflection and Application (11:21b–29)

Preaching the gospel heedless of the cost. In every age the Church needs men and women who are willing to suffer hardship and humiliation for the sake of the gospel. Fortunately, Paul's example has been followed through the centuries. The gospel has been planted in all parts of the world by courageous missionaries who endured much suffering in order to bring Christ to others. One such missionary was the French Jesuit, Isaac Jogues (1607–46), who labored in the regions around the Great Lakes in North America. Despite having suffered enslavement and torture, including the mutilation of some of his fingers, St. Isaac insisted on returning to work among the Native Americans, a commitment that led to his martyrdom. Heroic missionary work amid grave dangers continues even to our day, for instance, in the underground Catholic Church in China.

While not all of us are called to undertake dangerous missionary work, we are all called to proclaim and work for the gospel, heedless of the cost. Advocating for justice and peace, for sharing economic resources, and for the rights of the oppressed and impoverished can evoke virulent opposition from powerful forces. It behooves all of us to ask ourselves, How willing am I to suffer for the sake of the gospel?

Paul's Crowning Achievement (11:30–33)

[30]If I must boast, I will boast of the things that show my weakness. [31]The God and Father of the Lord Jesus knows, he who is blessed forever, that I do not lie. [32]At Damascus, the governor under King Aretas guarded the city of Damascus, in order to seize me, [33]but I was lowered in a basket through a window in the wall and escaped his hands.

OT: Wis 5:15–16
NT: 2 Tim 4:6–8; Rev 2:10

Paul's boast now takes a decided turn as he declares that he will boast only of his weakness. He provides a dramatically humiliating example of weakness—his ignominious escape from the city of †Damascus. In relating this event, he parodies a famous military honor known as the "wall crown." The tone of irony, so striking in verses 16–21a but less obvious in verses 21b–29, now becomes evident once again.

11:30   Verse 30 functions as a transitional verse, looking both backward and forward. It looks back in that Paul, as he intimated in verse 18, feels he **must boast**. We saw that he feels compelled to play the superapostles at their own game of †boasting because some of the Corinthians have been dazzled by their claims. However, as his †hardship list in verses 23–29 suggests, he is in fact subverting the game. This becomes explicit when Paul announces that he **will boast of the things that show** his **weakness**. In doing so, he sets the agenda for the remainder of his boast. Although he can truthfully boast about many things, he steadfastly commits himself to boasting only about his weaknesses (12:5, 9–10). Indeed, the catalog of sufferings serves to introduce this point, as God has continued both to deliver his servant from brushes with death and to work wonders through his self-giving ministry.

11:31   Paul swears an oath: **the God and Father of the Lord Jesus knows, he who is blessed forever, that I do not lie**. As he did in 11:11, Paul appeals to God's knowledge to guarantee the truth of what he is saying. And as he did in 1:3, he blesses God, the one who has revealed himself as the Father of Jesus. Why does Paul use such a formal oath[11] at this point? In the first place, he wants the Corinthians to take seriously the paradoxical declaration that he will boast only of "the things that show my weakness." Moreover, Paul is about to make two audacious claims: his missionary work provoked the animosity of a king or, at least, that of a governor (vv. 32–33) and he was temporarily taken up into paradise (12:1–6). Although his ultimate purpose in relating these claims is ironic, he desires that the community recognize that he is telling the truth—something he accuses the superapostles of not doing (4:2; 11:3, 13–15).

11:32–33   Paul recounts a dramatic instance of his weakness: he narrowly and awkwardly escaped the clutches of **the governor under King Aretas** while **at Damascus**. Although it is impossible to reconstruct precisely what happened, some background information will assist in understanding Paul's point. "King Aretas" is Aretas IV, who ruled over the Arab kingdom of Nabatea from 9 BC to about AD 40. This kingdom encompassed present-day Jordan and southern Syria. Aretas is connected tangentially to the story of John the Baptist. Aretas's

---

11. See the sidebar on oaths on p. 59.

daughter was married to Herod Antipas, who later divorced her in order to marry his brother's wife, Herodias. When John denounced Herod for this act, Herod imprisoned him and eventually had him put to death (Mark 6:14–29). Scholars debate the question of the actual political influence Aretas wielded over the city of Damascus at the time of the incident to which Paul refers.[12] His language suggests, minimally, that the **governor** served at Aretas's behest.

What had Paul done to cause the governor to "guard"—we can picture soldiers posted at the city gates—**the city of Damascus, in order to seize** him? One possibility is that he provoked the enmity of Aretas by bringing the †gospel to his kingdom shortly after encountering the risen Christ on his way to Damascus. Another possibility is that his evangelistic efforts within the city itself stirred up opposition, with the result that the local official in charge of maintaining public order sought to detain him as a troublemaker.[13]

In any event, Paul relates that he **was lowered in a basket through a window in the wall and escaped** the governor's **hands**. Because the city gates were being guarded, he had to be secreted out of Damascus through an opening in the wall of the city.[14] The basket was a braided, flexible container that could transport sizable items. That Paul was helpless, needing the aid of others, is indicated by his use of the passive voice ("was lowered"). He thus unapologetically presents a pathetic image of himself, a grown man, being lowered like a baby in a basket in order to escape danger.

Most commentators interpret verses 32–33 as an extreme example of Paul's "weakness." However, there is probably more going on here. At this time there was a well-known Roman military honor called the *corona muralis* ("wall crown"). It consisted of an actual crown—made of gold and fashioned in the likeness of a fortified defense wall—that was awarded to the first soldier who successfully scaled the wall of an enemy city during a siege. Paul turns this convention on its head.[15] Unlike the powerful, daring soldier who climbs up and enters the opponents' stronghold, the Apostle portrays himself as a helpless figure who is *lowered* in order to escape the fray. Paul's point is that he is a

---

12. Damascus was under Roman rule. However, the emperor Caligula (AD 37–41) granted territorial control to certain †client kings in the east. Jerome Murphy-O'Connor estimates the date of the event recounted here at AD 37 (see Murphy-O'Connor, *Paul: A Critical Life* [New York: Oxford University Press, 1996], 7).

13. According to Acts 9:23–25, which narrates the same event, the opposition in Damascus against Paul came from certain Jews in the city.

14. See Josh 2:15, where Rahab similarly assisted the Israelite spies in their escape from Jericho. Her house is described as "built into the city wall," and she "let them down through the window with a rope."

15. This interpretation was first proposed by Edwin A. Judge, "The Conflict of Educational Aims in New Testament Thought," *Journal of Christian Education* 9 (1966): 32–45.

Fig. 10. The Kisan Gate, said to be the site of Paul's escape from Damascus.

different kind of "soldier" (10:3–6). While he does wield powerful "weapons" (6:7), they are those of the gospel of a crucified and risen †Messiah; that is, they are manifested by wielding the sword of God's word (Eph 6:17; Heb 4:12) and by embodying the self-giving love of Jesus. Paul therefore holds out as his "crowning achievement" his commitment to courageously proclaim the gospel and his following the way of Christ. This is the path to attain the only crown worth pursuing, "the crown of righteousness . . . , which the Lord, the just judge, will award" (2 Tim 4:8).

Reflection and Application (11:30–33)

Turning cultural values upside down. Paul's adaptation of the "wall crown" is a vivid example of how life in the kingdom of God operates under a different calculus of values than that of the prevailing culture. The "evangelical counsels"— poverty, chastity, and obedience—lived by consecrated religious similarly point to the countercultural impetus of the call to follow Christ. In a society that accumulates wealth, greedily consumes resources, and thinks more is better, the radically simple life of vowed religious men and women sounds a jarringly different note. In a culture that glamorizes sex appeal, condones easy sexual relations, and is lax about relational commitments, celibate chastity strikes an uncomfortable chord. And in an ethos that values self-sufficiency, pride, and the drive to succeed at the expense of others, the ideal of obedience to higher religious authority rings out a challenging tone.

The call to bear witness to the countercultural values of the gospel does not belong exclusively to vowed religious, however. Their life is a reminder that *all* Christians are summoned to live the values of the kingdom of God, not least those contained in the Beatitudes (Matt 5:3–10).

Power in Weakness

2 Corinthians 12:1–13

Having set forth his Jewish pedigree and apostolic credentials, especially his suffering for the sake of the †gospel, and having illustrated his weakness by subverting the coveted wall crown, Paul continues his fool's boast. Referring to a revelation he received upon being transported into Paradise, he intimates that such private, ecstatic experiences are not the proper subject of boasting (12:1–7a). Rather, he chooses once again to boast of his weakness, this time concerning a "thorn in the flesh" he received in the aftermath of his revelatory experience. Paul's boast reaches its climax with the risen Lord's revelation that power is made perfect in weakness (12:7b–10). He concludes by reiterating that he is in no way inferior to the superapostles (12:11–13).

Boasting of Visions and Revelations (12:1–7a)

[1] I must boast; not that it is profitable, but I will go on to visions and revelations of the Lord. [2] I know someone in Christ who, fourteen years ago (whether in the body or out of the body I do not know, God knows), was caught up to the third heaven. [3] And I know that this person (whether in the body or out of the body I do not know, God knows) [4] was caught up into Paradise and heard ineffable things, which no one may utter. [5] About this person I will boast, but about myself I will not boast, except about my weaknesses. [6] Although if I should wish to boast, I would not be foolish, for I would be telling the truth. But I refrain, so that no one may think

264

**more of me than what he sees in me or hears from me ⁷because of the
abundance of the revelations.**

OT: Gen 28:10–15
NT: Acts 18:9–10; 22:17–21; Gal 1:12

Paul turns to the subject of visions and revelations. While he makes clear
that he has been blessed with ecstatic experiences from God, he subtly chides
those who boast about private spiritual encounters. He once again insists on
†boasting about his weaknesses.

As in 11:30, Paul asserts that he **must boast.** The success of the boastful su-   **12:1**
perapostles in capturing the hearts of at least some of the Corinthians has forced
him to engage in boasting, something he finds distasteful. Paul again suggests
the futility of boasting by remarking, **not that it is profitable.** Nevertheless,
he proceeds to **go on to visions and revelations.** "Visions" and "revelations"
should be understood as a hendiadys, the use of two words to express a single
reality—in this case, revelatory experiences that have both visual and audible
features.[1] Paul qualifies these "visions and revelations" with the phrase **of the
Lord.** In doing so, he suggests that the Lord Jesus is the source of these profound spiritual experiences and that their content concerns things about Jesus
himself. Why does Paul boast about visions and revelations? In all likelihood,
it is because the superapostles are making much of their ecstatic experiences
and, perhaps, are questioning whether he has had any.

Paul offers a dramatic instance of special revelation from the Lord. That he   **12:2–4**
recounts only one revelatory experience does not mean he did not have others; indeed, he refers in verse 7 to the "abundance" of revelations he received.
His reason for focusing on this particular one will become clear as the passage
unfolds.

There are several noteworthy features of Paul's description. One is that he
narrates the event in the third person: **I know someone in Christ who.**[2] As the
passage unfolds, it becomes apparent that Paul is referring to himself. Why, then,
does he use the third person? Such an intimate, spiritual experience is best kept
to oneself. He really does not want to talk about it with others but feels compelled
to do so because of the interlopers' boasting. Paul thus uses the third person out

---

1. See Jan Lambrecht, SJ, *2 Corinthians*, SP (Collegeville, MN: Liturgical Press, 1999), 200. Acts
recounts several visions Paul had up to this point in his ministry, including one that involved the risen
Lord (18:9–10; see also 22:17–21). Paul himself refers in Gal 1:12; 2:2; and Eph 3:3 to "revelations" he
received.
2. The phrase "in Christ" here signifies one who has been baptized and is a member of the body
of Christ.

St. Teresa of Jesus and Mystical Experiences

LIVING TRADITION

The great Spanish Carmelite nun and reformer, St. Teresa of Jesus (1515–82), was blessed with many mystical encounters with God. Her writings describe her spiritual experiences and teach the way of prayer. In her autobiography, Teresa set forth four states of prayer, beginning with discursive meditation. The states progress through quiet and contemplative prayer—marked more and more by passivity on the part of the person praying—to union with God. In discussing the fourth state of prayer, she portrayed her experience of rapture into the hands of God in terms that recall Paul's sense of being caught up in 2 Cor 12:2–4: "It comes, generally, as a shock, quick and sharp, . . . and you see and feel it as a cloud, or as a powerful eagle ascending and bearing you on its wings. I repeat: you see and feel yourself transported, you know not where" (*Life* 20.3–4).[a] Teresa also expressed her sense of wonder in the aftermath of such experiences in a way that echoes the Apostle: "It has happened to me on occasion, when this prayer was over, to be so beside myself that I did not know whether I had been dreaming" (*Life* 19.2). On such occasions, the gift of tears and the great courage she felt confirmed the reality of her mystical experience.

a. St. Teresa did not give a title to her autobiography; rather, she bracketed the book with the monogram "J. H. S." in honor of the holy name of Jesus.

of modesty. It also serves to convey something of the mysterious, extraordinary, and transcendent quality of the experience, a quality that is also suggested by his uncertainty, expressed in verses 2–3, about whether the experience took place **in the body or out of the body**. It is possible that Paul was aware of being away from his body while, at the same time, having certain physical sensations.[3] In any event, he insists that **God knows** what happened. As in 11:11 and 11:31, Paul appeals to God's knowledge to uphold the truth of what he is saying.

The mysterious, extraordinary, and transcendent quality of his experience is also suggested by the twofold use of the verb **was caught up** (vv. 2, 4). The same verb is used in 1 Thess 4:17 to describe how believers, both living and dead, "will be caught up," or snatched up, in the clouds to meet the Lord at his coming in glory. It conveys a sense of suddenness and surprise. Note too the passive voice of the verb. This is an instance of the †divine passive, which puts

3. The extrabiblical *1 Enoch* 71:1–5 (cited by Margaret E. Thrall, *A Critical and Exegetical Commentary on the Second Epistle to the Corinthians*, ICC, 2 vols. [Edinburgh: T&T Clark, 1994–2000], 2:787) may shed light on this peculiar phenomenon. Enoch is described on one hand as being carried off in spirit into the heavens, and on the other hand as having his hand taken by an angel.

Levels of Heaven and Paradise in Jewish Writings

BIBLICAL BACKGROUND

Paul's reference to being transported to "the third heaven" seems to suggest that he believed that heaven consists of multiple levels. A few passages in the Old Testament can be read as implying at least two levels in heaven. For example, Deut 10:14 proclaims that "the heavens, even the highest heavens, belong to the LORD" (see also, e.g., 1 Kings 8:27). However, it is in extrabiblical writings much closer to the time of Paul that we find more elaborate speculation about heaven. The earliest manuscripts of the *Testament of Levi* (chaps. 2–3) speak of three levels of heaven, as Paul does here. A more common description, found in later writings, is seven levels of heaven (e.g., *2 Enoch* [J] 3–21). What is common to these heavenly schemas is that God dwells in glory in the highest of the levels.

The word *Paradise* derives from a Persian word for a walled garden. The †Septuagint uses this term to translate the "garden" of Eden where God placed Adam and Eve (Gen 2:8). By Paul's time, Paradise had come to be understood by many Jews in an †eschatological sense, referring to a place where the righteous deceased reside, a place hidden at the present that will appear at the end of history when God will definitively set all things right. It is often described as resembling the original Garden of Eden (e.g., *2 Enoch* 8). This is similar to how Paradise is used in the New Testament (Rev 2:7; see also Luke 23:43).

---

the accent on God's initiative and activity rather than on any action of Paul, who was merely the recipient of the revelation.

Yet another striking feature of Paul's description of his revelatory experience is that he gives it a precise date, **fourteen years ago**—hence, sometime in the early 40s. Note that this date is several years after his initial encounter with the risen Christ (Gal 1:11–16; see Acts 9; 22; 26), which most scholars date to the early 30s, and nearly a decade before he first set foot in Corinth. In fact, it is difficult, if not impossible, to identify the experience described in verses 2–4 with any of Paul's visions or revelations known from his writings or from Acts of the Apostles. Why is this significant? Paul is just now revealing to the Corinthians an event from long ago, something he had ample time to have told them about in his prior visits and writings. This shows that he has been circumspect in talking about his special prayer experiences, experiences he regards as divine gifts and not as badges of personal honor. Unlike the superapostles, he has not made it his practice to boast of such things. In addition, his admission here adds to the evidence that "the †apostle to the †Gentiles was also a visionary,"[4] one for whom such experiences were not uncommon.

Paul declares that he was transported **to the third heaven**, a place he then identifies as **Paradise**. He thus intimates that he was temporarily taken up by God to the highest place in heaven, where the divine glory dwells. Given that Paul referred in verse 1 to "visions and revelations" of the Lord Jesus, does he suggest here that he was set in the presence of the glorified Christ? Perhaps, although he does not register what he saw. Instead, he reports that he **heard ineffable things, which no one may utter**. These "unutterable utterances"— surmised by some commentators to be angelic praises or revelations of divine mysteries—were beyond what human language could convey. What is more, even if he were able, the Apostle states, he is not permitted to do so.[5]

What is the effect of Paul's cryptic description of his ecstatic experience? At one level, he reveals—albeit with great reluctance—to those Corinthians impressed by the boasting of the superapostles that he too has in fact been the recipient of visions and revelations. At a deeper and more ironic level, he criticizes the interlopers for boasting about such spiritual experiences. There is a certain playfulness with which Paul recounts his journey to the third heaven: he is not certain how he was taken up, he does not report what he saw, and he cannot repeat what he heard.[6] He thereby suggests that, while this mysterious experience was important to him personally, it did not provide him with information he could use in his ministry. It is certainly not reason to boast about himself. Rather, he implies a critique of the intruding missionaries: "If their experience was the same as Paul's, it contributed nothing to their ministry. If it was something about which they could talk, it was less ineffable than his!"[7]

12:5   Paul now concludes his use of the third person pronoun in talking about himself: **About this person I will boast**. He can boast about what happened fourteen years ago because he has clearly explained that it was ultimately *God's* doing. Hence he is, in actuality, boasting "in the Lord" (10:17). Paul then returns to his preferred manner of boasting, the one he expressed in

4. Frank J. Matera, *II Corinthians: A Commentary*, NTL (Louisville: Westminster John Knox, 2003), 279.

5. The JB captures well Paul's meaning in v. 4: "and heard things which must not and cannot be put into human language." The phrase "unutterable utterances," taken from Plummer (*A Critical and Exegetical Commentary on the Second Epistle of St. Paul to the Corinthians*, ICC [Edinburgh: T&T Clark, 1915], 337), cleverly conveys the wordplay in Greek (*arrēta rhēmata*).

6. See Victor Paul Furnish, *II Corinthians: A New Translation with Introduction and Commentary*, AB 32A (New York: Doubleday, 1984).

7. Jerome Murphy-O'Connor, *Paul: A Critical Life* (New York: Oxford University Press, 1996), 320.

11:30: I will not boast, except about my weaknesses. There he recounted his harrowing, ignominious escape from †Damascus. In the following passage (vv. 7b–10) he will reveal another form of weakness, the "thorn in the flesh" with which he was inflicted in order to keep him from becoming overly proud because of the visions and revelations granted to him.

Paul makes one last comment about his ecstatic experience. Were he **to boast**   12:6–7a
about it, he **would not be foolish** because he **would be telling the truth.** But he chooses to **refrain** from boasting about his spiritual experiences because he does not want people to focus on **the abundance of the revelations** (v. 7a). In the final analysis, these are deeply personal experiences. What Paul desires is to be regarded solely on the basis of what one **sees in** him **or hears from** him. Rather than being highly thought of because of his mystical encounters with God, he wants the Corinthians to focus on how he lives and what he says (see Phil 4:9). What does Paul preach? The good news that Jesus Christ is Lord. How does he comport himself? As a slave whose self-giving love is modeled on Jesus (2 Cor 4:5). It is solely the proclamation of the †gospel—verbal and embodied—that the community is to heed, not the reports about unverifiable spiritual encounters.

Reflection and Application (12:1–7a)

Paul's priority. Our passage is illuminated by Paul's response to a situation that had arisen earlier in Corinth. Some members of the community who had received the gift of tongues were being disruptive in the liturgical assembly (1 Cor 12–14). These disruptive members were apparently not only giving free rein to their audible but incomprehensible utterances, they also took much pride in the gift bestowed on them. To be sure, the problem was not with the charism of tongues per se—it *is* a gift from the Spirit (1 Cor 12:10)—but its appropriate reception and exercise.

Paul's response to this earlier situation is relevant to our passage, where some in Corinth are placing much stock in mystical experiences, at least in those of the superapostles. Just as he now reveals that he has been the recipient of mystical revelations, so in 1 Cor 14:18 he acknowledges that he speaks in tongues. But he also goes on to insist that "in the church I would rather speak five words with my mind, so as to instruct others also, than ten thousand words in a tongue" (1 Cor 14:19). That is, within the context of the community's worship, Paul prioritizes teaching over tongues because others can benefit from teaching, whereas un-interpreted tongues are, in effect, a personal experience of prayer (1 Cor 14:2, 4). In doing so, he insists that the fundamental call of all Christians is to build up the body of Christ. This is what Paul wants the Corinthians to see in him in 2 Cor 12:6. His purpose is not to denigrate or stifle spiritual experiences or the life of prayer; nevertheless, he consistently directs his spiritual children to focus on the fruit of self-giving love (e.g., 1 Cor 13:4–7) produced by the Spirit.

Paul's Thorn and the Lord's Sufficient Grace (12:7b–10)

Therefore, that I might not become too elated, a thorn in the flesh was given to me, an angel of Satan, to beat me, to keep me from being too elated. [8]Three times I begged the Lord about this, that it might leave me, [9]but he said to me, "My grace is sufficient for you, for power is made perfect in weakness." I will rather boast most gladly of my weaknesses, in order that the power of Christ may dwell with me. [10]Therefore, I am content with weaknesses, insults, hardships, persecutions, and constraints, for the sake of Christ; for when I am weak, then I am strong.

OT: 1 Kings 19:1–8; Ps 31:10–17
NT: Mark 14:32–42; Gal 2:20
Catechism: God's omnipotence, 268–71; the mystery of God's "apparent powerlessness," 272–74
Lectionary: Mass for the Sick

We arrive at the climax of Paul's boast, as he explains why he has decided to boast only about his weaknesses. After referring to a painful "thorn in the flesh" given to him to prevent him from becoming overly proud, he tells the Corinthians that he fervently prayed for its removal. Paul then reveals the risen Lord's answer to that prayer: "My grace is sufficient for you, for power is made perfect in weakness." Buoyed with this promise, he has resolved to be content with weaknesses and hardships, knowing that the power of Christ is at work in him.

12:7b Paul discloses the main reason for recounting the revelatory experience from fourteen years ago. It is the *aftermath* of that experience that has had lasting significance for him. God did something **to keep** him **from being too elated** at receiving such a wondrous revelation of the Lord Jesus. Paul reports that **a thorn in the flesh was given to** him. That God is the subject of this action is signified by the use of the [†]divine passive "was given" (see 12:2, 4). The word "flesh" is used here "in the broad sense of physical life." Thus the "thorn" caused Paul "serious and ongoing annoyance in his life."[8]

What precisely is this thorn with which Paul is afflicted? Much scholarly attention has been devoted to this question. In general, three interpretations

8. Matera, *II Corinthians*, 283.

have been offered. First, it is argued that Paul suffered sexual temptations, an interpretation that is often based on the Latin Vulgate translation, *stimulus carnis*. While this interpretation was at one time widespread, it is rarely set forth today. Second, since the time of Chrysostom, it has been suggested that the thorn refers to those who opposed Paul in his ministry of proclaiming the †gospel and founding churches, such as the superapostles. Third, it is thought that he suffered some physical malady, such as headaches, fevers, or problems with his eyes (see Gal 4:13–14; 6:11). This line of interpretation is widely accepted today.

It is impossible to determine with certitude what Paul means. Perhaps the Corinthians already know what he is referring to; or maybe he intends to be vague. In any event, he describes the thorn as **an angel**, or messenger, **of Satan** who continually "beats" and buffets him. Paul's point is that God has permitted Satan's "angel" to afflict him in order to keep him from becoming overly proud.

Paul's pain and distress are apparent, as he informs the Corinthians that he **begged the Lord about this**—that is, about the thorn—**that it might leave** him. Evidently, he did not immediately perceive the divine initiative behind his affliction. Or it may be that, if he did, he was not initially ready to accept that this was God's will for him.[9] Paul's begging **three times** to be relieved of his affliction echoes Jesus' threefold prayer in Gethsemane, on the night before he died, that the cup of suffering be taken from him (Mark 14:36). Jesus' prayer in the garden concluded with the petition to God the Father: "not what I will but what you will." Similarly, Paul has now committed himself to aligning his will with the divine will, as revealed to him in verse 9. But before examining the divine response, it is worthwhile to observe that his prayer in verse 8 is directed to the risen Lord Jesus, who granted him "visions and revelations" (v. 1). For the most part, prayer in the New Testament is directed to God the Father (e.g., 2 Cor 1:3; 2:14). However, from the earliest times in the Church, prayers were also offered to the Lord Jesus (e.g., Acts 7:59–60; 9:10–17; 22:19; 1 Cor 1:2; 16:22). In fact, the New Testament ends with the prayer "Come, Lord Jesus!" (Rev 22:20).

12:8

The response to Paul's prayer is: **"My grace is sufficient for you, for power is made perfect in weakness."** There is no divine intervention to relieve Paul from his suffering. Rather, the risen Lord promises him the gift of "†grace." The use of the perfect tense verb **said** (literally, "he has said") signifies that Christ's promise of grace made in a revelation to Paul several years before has enduring value. What he needs most, grace—the gift of divine life imparted to him at his baptism and the divine power that commissioned him to be an †apostle—is what the Lord *continues* to offer to him. And this grace is "sufficient" because,

12:9

9. Ibid., 284.

paradoxically, the mysterious divine "power" (*dynamis*) accomplishes its purpose in the arena of weakness.

The most dramatic example of this paradox is Jesus himself, who "was crucified out of weakness, but . . . lives by the power of God" (13:4). Through the cross God has broken the power of sin and death, bringing about not only the resurrection of Jesus but also the possibility of newness of life for all people. Paul himself has become an example of divine power accomplishing its purpose through weakness. As he stated so eloquently in 4:7–15, though a mere earthen vessel, he is sustained by the divine power through sufferings and hardships and is empowered to walk in the way of Jesus' self-giving love, thereby bringing life to others. This same gift is available to all Christians who entrust themselves to the workings of God's power.

We finally reach the pinnacle of Paul's entire boast in the second half of verse 9. Having heard the risen Lord's response to his prayer, Paul settles on a different course of action, indicated by the conjunction "consequently" (not translated by the NAB). As a consequence of the Lord's word to him about divine grace in human weakness, **rather** than praying for the thorn's removal, Paul resolves to **boast most gladly of** his **weaknesses**. Paul has shed the use of irony here. He is perfectly serious about this boast because it serves an essential purpose: **in order that the power of Christ may dwell with me**. It is important to note that Paul is *not* saying that †boasting of his weaknesses in and of itself activates the "power of Christ"; grace is a divine gift, not subject to human manipulation.

Instead, Paul's wording here suggests two things. First, he chooses to draw attention to his weaknesses rather than to things like his religious heritage and apostolic accomplishments, because he wants others to recognize that it is Jesus who is working through him. Boasting about his weaknesses is, paradoxically, a way of boasting about the Lord (see 10:17). Second, Paul intimates that boasting of one's weaknesses is valuable for one's spiritual life. The more we are aware of our personal inadequacies, the more inclined we are to turn in prayer to the risen Lord and open ourselves to the grace he generously offers. When we open ourselves to the power of this grace, we can say, along with the Apostle, that it is no longer we who live, but Christ who dwells in us, empowering us to lovingly give ourselves for the sake of others (Gal 2:20).[10]

12:10   Paul concludes by setting forth his attitude and self-understanding in light of the Lord's response to his prayer. He insists that he is **content with weaknesses, insults, hardships, persecutions, and constraints** insofar as these are suffered

---

10. The verb "dwell" in v. 9 is *episkēnoō* (literally, "pitch a tent upon"), a compound form of the verb used in John 1:14 to express the mystery that the eternal Word took flesh and *dwelled* among us.

for the sake of Christ. Once again, Paul offers a †hardship list (see 4:8–9; 6:4–10; 11:23–29), albeit an abbreviated version. The only new element introduced here is "insults," which he may have added in light of the recent slanders against him.

Paul then expresses in succinct fashion how he has appropriated the Lord's words to him: **when I am weak, then I am strong**. These words have become, in effect, his apostolic way of proceeding. Granted that "his bodily presence is weak, and his speech contemptible" (10:10), nevertheless, by grace he has been called to be an apostle, and this grace "has not been ineffective" (1 Cor 15:10). Granted that he suffers many persecutions and hardships in his work of proclaiming the gospel (e.g., 2 Cor 4:8–9), nevertheless, by the divine power he continues to be protected and strengthened to persevere (e.g., 6:9). And granted that he conducts himself as a slave, offering himself in loving service to others (4:5), it is *through* such humble self-sacrifice that the power of Christ is made manifest. Others might regard him as weak and foolish, but "the weakness of God is stronger than human strength" (1 Cor 1:25). Paul thereby continues to distinguish his way of being an apostle from that of the intruding missionaries. He wants the Corinthians to understand that he, not the superapostles, faithfully sets forth the gospel, as he relies solely on the power of Christ. Implicit is that the community should reject the ways of the interlopers.

Reflection and Application (12:7b–10)

Willingness to listen in prayer. This passage offers us an intimate look into Paul's prayer life, as he shares with the Corinthians his intense prayer to be relieved of suffering. On the one hand, the fact that he prayed three times in hope of relief confirms that it is good and right to pray this way. On the other hand, it is necessary to do so with an underlying surrender to God's will. The Catechism teaches that "even the most intense prayers do not always obtain the healing of all illnesses" (1508). In fact, in the case of Paul, he was led to understand that in his sufferings he was "filling up what is lacking in the afflictions of Christ on behalf of his body, which is the church" (Col 1:24). The Apostle could only come to such understanding because he was willing to *listen* as he prayed. As important as petitionary prayer is, it is essential that we grow in our willingness and ability to listen to God (see the second entry under the Reflection and Application on 4:16–18). It is instructive to note that in Greek the word for "obey" means, literally, "listen under." This suggests that humble attentiveness in prayer leads not only to knowledge of God's will but also to the power to make it our own.

273

Turning to God in our need. Most of us can recall an occasion when we found ourselves with a task or problem that seemed well beyond our resources. At such times it is tempting to become discouraged and debilitated by focusing on our shortcomings. However, I personally have found solace and help by acknowledging to God my weakness and therefore my utter dependence on his help to do what needed to be done. In turning to God, I recalled his promise that his power is made perfect in weakness. I have entrusted myself to God to make his promise effective in my circumstances— and he has! As in Paul's case, our weakness can become the occasion of God's working through us.

Conclusion of the Fool's Boast (12:11–13)

¹¹I have been foolish. You compelled me, for I ought to have been commended by you. For I am in no way inferior to these "superapostles," even though I am nothing. ¹²The signs of an apostle were performed among you with all endurance, signs and wonders, and mighty deeds. ¹³In what way were you less privileged than the rest of the churches, except that on my part I did not burden you? Forgive me this wrong!

OT: Dan 6:26–28
NT: 1 Cor 2:4; Gal 3:5; 1 Thess 1:5; Heb 2:1–4

Paul brings the fool's boast to its conclusion. After briefly reproving the Corinthians for not coming to his defense, he reminds them that he is not inferior to the superapostles in any respect: *all* the "signs of an †apostle" have been made manifest to them through his ministry. Throughout these verses he reminds the community of major points of difference between himself and the intruding missionaries.

12:11–12   Having reluctantly engaged in extended †boasting, Paul pauses and looks back. He acknowledges that he feels **foolish** for having boasted, even if he has made clear how his boasting differs from that of the superapostles. But Paul has been **compelled** to boast by the Corinthians. It is *they*[11] who should have **commended** him when he was under attack by the interlopers. Earlier Paul reminded the community that their very existence as a church, which came into being through his missionary activity, was his "recommendation letter" (3:2–3). As a sign of their gratitude, the Corinthians should have defended Paul

11. Paul twice uses the personal pronoun "you" (*hymeis; hymōn*) in v. 11 for emphasis.

when the intruding missionaries criticized him. Indeed, he insists once more (see 11:5) that he is **in no way inferior to these "superapostles."** But lest he be understood as promoting himself, Paul concedes that he is **nothing**. That is, his qualification for being a minister of the †new covenant "comes from God" (3:5); he is an apostle only by God's †grace (1 Cor 15:9–10).

Paul reminds the Corinthians of **the signs of an apostle** that they witnessed during his ministry among them. These "signs" are certain marks that authenticate one as truly sent by God.[12] Paul delineates these marks as **signs, wonders**, and **mighty deeds**. These terms refer to the working of miracles—most likely healings and exorcisms—from three different vantage points. As "signs" they point beyond themselves to their source of authentication, that is, to God; as "wonders" they evoke astonishment and awe; and as "mighty deeds" they signal that it is divine power that is at work.[13] These miracles accompany Paul's proclamation of the †gospel in his ministry of founding churches (1 Cor 2:4; Gal 3:5; 1 Thess 1:5). While he is normally reticent about such powerful works, Acts of the Apostles recounts several miracles worked through his hands.[14] It is therefore evident that his apostolic labors were regularly attended by miracle-working powers.

Even though Paul reminds the Corinthians of the miracles they witnessed in his ministry, he makes clear that it is ultimately *God* who works such wonders. Once again (2 Cor 12:2, 4, 7), he employs the †divine passive—**were performed**—to indicate that God is the doer. Elsewhere Paul makes this point explicit: "I will not dare to speak of anything except what Christ has accomplished through me to lead the †Gentiles to obedience by word and deed, by the power of signs and wonders, by the power of the Spirit" (Rom 15:18–19). Whereas the superapostles glory in such mighty deeds, Paul directs the glory and credit to the one to whom they belong—God. Moreover, *before* listing "signs and wonders, and mighty deeds," notice that he identifies another authenticating mark of an apostle: he has ministered to the community **with all endurance**. Recall that he set "endurance" at the head of his †hardship list in 6:4–10, a list enumerating his credentials as a minister of reconciliation in the new covenant. Paul thereby suggests that, while God does in fact work healings and exorcisms through him, God does so in the context of Paul's walking in the way of Jesus' suffering and self-giving love (see 11:23b–29). Thus, once again, the Apostle implicitly contrasts himself with the intruding missionaries.

---

12. The NJB conveys well Paul's meaning in v. 12: "the marks characteristic of a true apostle."

13. See Murray J. Harris, *The Second Epistle to the Corinthians*, NIGTC (Grand Rapids: Eerdmans, 2005), 839.

14. Acts 14:8–10; 16:16–18; 19:11–12; 20:7–12; 28:1–9. Moreover, in Acts 15:12 Paul describes "the signs and wonders" worked during his and Barnabas's missionary labors among the †Gentiles.

Paul concludes by reiterating one more point of contrast as he challenges the Corinthians to take stock of his ministry to them. By asking them **in what way** they **were less privileged than the rest of the churches**, he wants them to realize they have not been deprived of anything essential through his pastoral care for them. Paul has held nothing back in his ministry. The only sense in which he has "deprived" them is that he has refused to **burden** them. This is a reference to his declining to take remuneration from the community (11:9). We have seen that Paul steadfastly refuses to do so because he is committed to preaching the gospel gratis. While the superapostles gladly receive, perhaps even require, payment from the Corinthians—and do so as a badge of honor—he humbles himself in imitation of Jesus (11:7; see Phil 2:8).

Paul ends the entire boast on the same ironic note he began. His request of the community to **forgive** him **this wrong**—his proclaiming the gospel without charge—evokes the question he asked in 11:7: has he committed a sin in thus conducting himself? On the contrary, the preceding verses have made it abundantly clear that, if anything, it is the Corinthians who have wronged Paul and who ought to beg him for forgiveness!

Reflection and Application (12:11–13)

What constitutes true power. Acts of the Apostles portrays Paul as a great miracle worker. Through the power of God, he heals a man crippled from birth (14:8–10), casts out an evil spirit from a slave girl (16:16–18), and even brings a young man back from death (20:7–12)—to name but some of the miracles attributed to him. It is striking, however, that in his own writings Paul merely alludes to such wonder-working. Not that he denies such dramatic manifestations of the divine power at work in him. But he chooses to highlight another aspect of this power, namely, that it enables him, a mere earthen vessel, to imitate Jesus in his suffering and his loving, self-giving way of life (2 Cor 4:7–15). This is the insight he has appropriated from the risen Lord's revelation to him that "power is made perfect in weakness" (12:9). We too can be instruments of God's power by imitating the Apostle's commitment to love and serve others even when we encounter misunderstanding and opposition. In doing so, we may very well discover God's working signs and wonders and mighty deeds through us.

Announcing His Third Visit

2 Corinthians 12:14–13:4

Following his lengthy attempt to convince the Corinthians to heed him, their founding †apostle, rather than the intruding missionaries (10:1–12:13), Paul announces his third visit to Corinth. He takes up once more the vexing issue of financial remuneration as he expresses his love for the community and steadfastly denies having taken advantage of them (12:14–18). Next, he expresses his fear that, upon arriving in Corinth, he will find among them divisive behavior and lack of repentance for sexual immorality (12:19–21). Finally, he warns the Corinthians that he will take strong action against those who remain in sin and responds to a direct challenge to offer proof that Christ speaks in him (13:1–4).

Paul's Love for the Corinthians (12:14–18)

¹⁴Now I am ready to come to you this third time. And I will not be a burden, for I want not what is yours, but you. Children ought not to save for their parents, but parents for their children. ¹⁵I will most gladly spend and be utterly spent for your sakes. If I love you more, am I to be loved less? ¹⁶But granted that I myself did not burden you, yet I was crafty and got the better of you by deceit. ¹⁷Did I take advantage of you through any of those I sent to you? ¹⁸I urged Titus to go and sent the brother with him. Did Titus take advantage of you? Did we not walk in the same spirit? And in the same steps?

OT: Isa 49:15
NT: Luke 13:34; 1 Cor 4:14–21; 1 Thess 2:7–12

Paul informs the Corinthians that he is coming to visit. He cautions them that he will continue his practice of not taking financial support from them. In doing so, Paul insists that he acts out of love as their spiritual father. He then strongly denies an accusation that he has defrauded the community through his representatives in the work of the collection.

12:14   While Paul has been hinting at an impending visit to Corinth (10:1–2, 10–11), he now explicitly declares that he is **ready to come** for a **third time**. In addition to the founding visit (1 Cor 2:1–5; Acts 18:1–18), he made an emergency trip to Corinth that he later described as "painful" (2 Cor 2:1), one that ended prematurely after a nasty encounter with one of the community's members.[1] Why does Paul now plan to visit the Corinthians again? In part, he desires to follow through on his plans, made some time prior, to spend an extended period of time with them (1 Cor 16:6–7). He also intends to pick up their contribution to the collection for the church in Jerusalem (2 Cor 8:1–9:15). Moreover, Paul wants to see whether the Corinthians have distanced themselves from the superapostles (10:1–12:13) and whether those members he previously warned have repented of their sinful ways (12:20–13:2). Ultimately, he hopes to deepen the reconciliation between himself and the community that the †tearful letter and Titus's mediation have helped set in motion (7:5–16).

Paul next takes up the issue of financial remuneration from verse 13. There he referred to his practice of not receiving direct payment from the Corinthians for his ministry to them (see also 11:7–12). Here he makes clear his intention to *continue* this practice when he arrives in Corinth: he **will not be a burden** to the community. As we have seen, some of the Corinthians regard his refusal to accept payment as a rejection of their offer of friendship (11:7). Paul sees the situation differently. He is committed to proclaiming the †gospel without charge. In his mind, this is a concrete expression of Jesus' self-giving love (11:11).

Moreover, Paul refuses to enter into a †patron–client relationship that would compromise his freedom to challenge his benefactors. He is not the community's client; he is their spiritual father who regards them as beloved children (1 Cor 4:14–15; 2 Cor 6:13; 11:2). As their father in faith, he is interested in their spiritual well-being, not in their possessions or money. This is what he means when he tells them, **I want not what is yours, but you**. We should probably also see here a jab at the superapostles, whom he implicitly accuses of not having the Corinthians' best interests at heart.

Paul explains that it is the role of **parents** to **save** up **for their children**, not vice versa. The Greek verb for "save," or "lay up" (*thēsaurizō*), in this context

1. See stage 4 under Historical Context in the introduction.

connotes setting aside an inheritance for one's heirs.[2] The "treasure" (*thēsauros*) that Paul as spiritual father shares with the community is the gospel (4:7). Once again, he intimates that he has a special role as their father in faith—something the superapostles cannot claim.

Paul expresses the extent of his love for the Corinthians: **I will most gladly spend and be utterly spent for your sakes**, literally, "for your souls." He employs the verbs "spend" and "be utterly spent" metaphorically to signify that he holds nothing back from the community in his ministry to them: he lavishly expends his time, talents, energy—even his very life (4:12; see Phil 2:17). That Paul is mainly concerned to nurture their *spiritual* well-being is evident from his use of *psychē*, "soul," in the phrase rendered by the NAB as "for your sakes."[3] His wording offers a succinct summary of his living in the pattern of Jesus' self-sacrificial love. Recall from the analysis of 4:10–12 that Paul refers to this love from two vantage points. First, from the vantage point of Jesus, who "gave himself" (note the active verb) in love for our sake (Gal 2:20; Eph 5:2). Second, from the vantage point of the Father, whose love for us is so great that he handed Jesus over for our sins (Rom 8:32); from this perspective, it can be said that Jesus "was handed over" (passive verb) for our sake (Rom 4:25; 1 Cor 11:23).

12:15

Similarly, Paul willingly expends himself on behalf of those to whom he ministers. He also suggests by his use of the passive "be utterly spent" that he has entrusted himself into God's hands to carry out God's will; indeed, he is "an †apostle of Christ Jesus by the will of God" (2 Cor 1:1). After conveying his self-giving love to the Corinthians, Paul poignantly asks them: **If I love you more, am I to be loved less?** It seems the more he loves them, as, for example, by refusing to burden them, the less he is loved in return. But notice that by employing a rhetorical question, he deftly leaves the door open for the community to reciprocate his love.[4]

Paul has raised the issue of financial remuneration because his refusal to take payment from the Corinthians has been interpreted by some in the community as indicating his lack of love for them. Now he reveals that there is another reason for bringing up the subject, namely, suspicions concerning fraud. Verse 16 suggests that, while everyone can agree that Paul **did not burden** the com-

12:16

---

2. See Victor Paul Furnish, *II Corinthians: A New Translation with Introduction and Commentary*, AB 32A (New York: Doubleday, 1984), 558. Elsewhere Paul reminds his communities that adult children have the "religious duty" to provide care for elderly parents (1 Tim 5:4, 8).

3. See Murray J. Harris, *Second Epistle to the Corinthians*, NIGTC (Grand Rapids: Eerdmans, 2005), 886.

4. See Ralph P. Martin, *2 Corinthians*, WBC (Waco: Word, 1986), 444.

munity by taking direct remuneration from them, nevertheless, some suspect that he has been **crafty** and gotten **the better of** them **by deceit**.[5] It seems that some have called into question the integrity of the collection for the Jerusalem church (8:1–9:15). Perhaps abetted by the superapostles, the insinuation is that, while Paul makes a big deal about proclaiming the gospel without charge, he sends delegates who solicit funds for a large collection of money—but will *all* the collected money go to those in need? Or is he somehow taking advantage of the Corinthians through this project?

12:17–18   We are in a better position to understand Paul's earlier adamant denials that he has ever acted deceitfully in his ministry (4:2) or taken advantage of anyone (7:2). He now responds to the accusation by asking a series of four rhetorical questions. The first two questions are worded in such a way as to expect the answer "No!" Paul asks, **Did I take advantage of you through any of those I sent to you?** He then clarifies that he **urged Titus to go**—a reference to Titus's first visit to Corinth when he began to facilitate the work of the collection (8:6, 10). We have seen that Titus earned the trust and admiration of the community; indeed, this was the reason Paul sent Titus with the †tearful letter. Because he is sure of Titus's reputation among the Corinthians, he confidently knows that his second question—**Did Titus take advantage of you?**—will be answered in the negative.

The next two questions are phrased so as to elicit the response "Yes, of course." The unstated presupposition is that Paul and his associates act in concert with one another, that is, his associates represent him fully in word and deed. As Titus acted with complete honesty in Corinth, the Apostle asserts, he himself has always conducted himself **in the same spirit** and **in the same steps**. The accusations against him are groundless. He is their spiritual father, who always has their best interests at heart.

Reflection and Application (12:14–18)

Parental love of ministers. We have seen that Paul presents himself as the Corinthians' spiritual father, their father in faith. In this role he tries to protect the community from harmful influences (11:2) and exhorts them to proper behavior (6:13). In a previous letter he intimated that, as their "father," he would come "with a rod"—that is, with the force of discipline—if they did not mend their ways (1 Cor 4:21). As we will see, Paul is about to issue a similar

---

5. The RSV, NRSV, NEB, and REB appropriately add a parenthetical "you say" to v. 16 to convey that the second half of the verse is an accusation made by some in the community.

threat. Such parental authority, however, is only legitimately and effectively exercised when it is grounded in love. This is especially true in connection with discipline.

Our passage sets a high standard for ministers, as Paul reveals his love for those for whom he exercises pastoral care. Elsewhere he describes his conduct among his spiritual children in intimate terms as a "nursing mother" who cares for her children with gentleness (1 Thess 2:7) and as a loving father who encourages his children toward growth (1 Thess 2:11–12). Like the Apostle, all ministers are called to grow in loving those God has put in their charge—willing to "gladly spend and be utterly spent" for their sake.

The Catholic priest as father. Paul's manner of exercising spiritual fatherhood is, at least in part, why Catholics refer to their priests as "Father." To be sure, Matt 23:9—where Jesus says, "Call no one on earth your father; you have but one Father in heaven"—is sometimes cited to object that this practice goes against biblical teaching. However, Jesus' words in Matt 23:9 are set in the context of criticizing religious leaders who seek titles of honor for their own self-aggrandizement. Paul's vision of spiritual fatherhood makes clear that the designation "father" for those who are honored with the title presumes the exercise of love and service.

Paul's Fears (12:19–21)

---

¹⁹Have you been thinking all along that we are defending ourselves before you? In the sight of God we are speaking in Christ, and all for building you up, beloved. ²⁰For I fear that when I come I may find you not such as I wish, and that you may find me not as you wish; that there may be rivalry, jealousy, fury, selfishness, slander, gossip, conceit, and disorder. ²¹I fear that when I come again my God may humiliate me before you, and I may have to mourn over many of those who sinned earlier and have not repented of the impurity, immorality, and licentiousness they practiced.

OT: Prov 6:16–19; Jer 7:8–10; Hosea 4:1–2
NT: Mark 7:21–23; Gal 5:19–21; Eph 5:3–5; 2 Tim 3:1–5; 1 Pet 4:1–5

Paul explains to the Corinthians that, as one who conducts himself as in the presence of God, he has been speaking to them "in Christ" for their benefit, not his own. He then expresses his fear that, upon his arrival in Corinth, he will find the community rent apart by divisive and destructive behavior. Moreover, Paul suspects that some who have been guilty of sexual immorality have not yet repented. Such failures will cause him much sorrow and force him to take decisive action against the guilty parties.

12:19 Paul anticipates a possible reaction to his letter. At least some of the Corinthians might be **thinking** that he has merely been **defending** himself **before** them, seeking only to justify himself in their eyes. Paul asserts, however, that this is not the case. Rather, he wants the Corinthians to understand two things. First, everything he does—including writing this letter—is undertaken as one who stands **in the sight of God**. Observe once again that Paul appeals to God as his witness (1:23) that he speaks to the community **in Christ**, as one sent by him to faithfully proclaim the †gospel (2:17). It is God who will judge his work, not the Corinthians (1 Cor 4:1–5). Second, Paul makes explicit that his writing has been aimed at **building** *them* **up**. His manner of expressing this in Greek gives special emphasis to **you** in the phrase "building you up." Indeed, it is for this purpose that Christ has given him apostolic authority (2 Cor 10:8).

Thus what might appear as self-defense—for example, Paul's explanations for changed travel plans (1:15–17) and for writing the †tearful letter (2:1–4), the lengthy exposition of his manner of being an †apostle (2:14–7:4), and his †boasting in reaction to that of the superapostles (11:1–12:13)—has been in service to the Corinthians to help them understand and appropriate the gospel. And by referring to the community as **beloved** (see 7:1), he reinforces his fundamental motive for writing, namely, love.

12:20 While Paul is committed to building up the Corinthians, he makes clear that he will not tolerate behavior that belies the identity of the Church as "sanctified by Christ Jesus, called to be holy" (1 Cor 1:2). He conveys his **fear** that, upon arriving in Corinth, he **may find** the community **not such as** he might **wish**. That is, he is afraid that he will encounter a situation marked by infighting and division—the antithesis of the Church's call to be the body of Christ, the recipients of God's gift of reconciliation. Paul lists eight vices he fears exist among the members of the Corinthian church. The first, **rivalry**, or quarreling, functions as the heading of the list. The second vice, **jealousy**, erodes relationships. The next six vices are given in the plural form to indicate several instances of the named behavior. Thus **fury** can be rendered "outbursts of anger." The fourth vice, **selfishness**, denotes factiousness and is aptly translated "personal rivalries."[6] The fifth and sixth vices, pertaining to speech, are "words of **slander** and **gossip**."[7] The last two are actions grounded in **conceit** that result in

---

6. As in the NEB and REB.

7. As rendered by Jan Lambrecht, SJ, *2 Corinthians*, SP (Collegeville, MN: Liturgical Press, 1999), 210.

Lists of Virtues and Vices

The listing of virtues to be attained and vices to be avoided was common in the Greco-Roman world of Paul's day. In particular, Stoic philosophers produced lists of virtues and vices. For the most part, moralists tended to stress virtues that pertain to an *individual's* moral development. The cardinal virtues—prudence, courage, temperance, and justice—formed the basis of virtue lists, which set forth various subdivisions and nuances of these four. Their opposites served as the starting points of vice lists.

The New Testament contains several lists of virtues and vices, especially in Paul's writings. Examples of virtue lists include Eph 4:2–3; Col 3:12; and 1 Tim 6:11. Vice lists can be found in Rom 13:13; Eph 5:3–5; and 2 Tim 3:2–4. Sometimes Paul offers lists of vices and virtues in succession, such as in Gal 5:19–23. In fact, Gal 5:19–21 closely resembles the list of vices found in 2 Cor 12:20–21. In both Paul focuses on what might be called *social* vices—attitudes and behaviors that break down communities—and on sexual immorality. The virtue list in Gal 5:22–23, by contrast, highlights qualities that promote community life and the well-being of others. The nine virtues listed there—love, joy, peace, patience, kindness, generosity, faithfulness, gentleness, and self-control—are, in effect, a character portrait of Jesus.

disorder. In all cases, Paul names ways that members of the community tear apart what God has brought together.

Given Paul's expression of full confidence in the Corinthians in 7:16, it is surprising to read about his fears here. Seeming inconsistencies like this have led some commentators to propose that the †canonical letter of 2 Corinthians is a compilation of one or more letters.[8] However, the inconsistency is more apparent than real. In 7:5–16 Paul was responding to the community's favorable response to the tearful letter he wrote in the aftermath of his painful second visit to Corinth. There he acknowledged the Corinthians' repentance and zeal for him, thereby facilitating the possibility of further reconciliation between himself and the community.

Here Paul refers to a more pervasive problem. The community in Corinth has engaged in quarreling and rivalries almost since its founding (see 1 Cor 1:11). The members of the church there had difficulties—as we can today—with letting go of values and ways of living that oppose the gospel. For instance, socioeconomic, ethnic, and gender differences divided the community; so too

8. See the section Literary Unity in the introduction.

St. John Chrysostom on Paul's Pastoral Sensitivity

LIVING
TRADITION

In a homily on 2 Cor 12:16–21, St. John Chrysostom highlighted Paul's pastoral sensitivity expressed in verse 21. Chrysostom commented that, at one level, Paul's being humiliated by God points to his anxiety over the situation in Corinth; he was anxious because his work there was for *God's* sake. At another level, Paul's reference to being humiliated is a sign of "apostolic virtue" and reveals the special mark of a teacher: "to empathize with the calamities of his disciples and to grieve over the wounds of those under his charge" (*Homilies on 2 Corinthians* 28.2). Chrysostom observed that Paul shows pastoral concern in that, while mourning over the failure of some in Corinth, he also reveals the way out of the morass of sin, namely, repentance.

did behavior grounded in cultural values of the time, such as cutthroat competitiveness and self-promotion manifested in boasting.[9] The superapostles very likely exacerbated these problems. Paul warns the community that if he finds such divisive behavior when he arrives in Corinth, they will **find** him **not as** they **wish**. Although he prefers to manifest "the gentleness and clemency of Christ" (2 Cor 10:1), he intimates that he will not hesitate to discipline those who persist in conduct detrimental to the well-being of the church.

12:21   Paul refers to another former way of behaving that some members of the Corinthian church have not left behind. He fears that he **may have to mourn over many of those who sinned earlier and have not repented**. He then lists three sins. The first, **impurity**, signifies sexual impurity in general. Paul continually had to remind his converts—especially those †Gentiles who were accustomed to laxity in sexual matters—that "God did not call us to impurity but to holiness" (1 Thess 4:7). This call to holiness excludes, for instance, indulging in lustful thoughts and looking at pornography. The second sin, **immorality**, is illicit sexual relations such as fornication and prostitution, in Paul's day sometimes associated with idolatry. The third sin, **licentiousness**, is unbridled debauchery. It seems that some of the Corinthians thought that life in the Spirit had nothing to say about what we do with our bodies (see, e.g., 1 Cor 5; 6:12–20; 10:14–22). Paul has consistently argued, on the contrary, that what we do with our bodies

---

9. See, e.g., 1 Cor 1:10–13; 3:1–4; 5:2; 8:1–2; 11:18–19. Harris provides a full list of passages in 1 Corinthians that provide evidence of the sins listed in 2 Cor 12:20 (see *Second Epistle to the Corinthians*, 900n48).

is of extreme importance because it is through our embodied existence that we manifest Christ to others (2 Cor 4:10–11). As will be made clear in 13:2, he will take appropriate action against those who have continued to engage in sexual immorality.

Paul makes a striking statement: **I fear that when I come again my God may humiliate me before you.** What does he mean by saying that *God* may humble him? The failure of members of the church in Corinth falls hard on Paul because his founding the church there was in response to God's call to him (10:13–16). His point here is not that God will humiliate him in order to punish him. Rather, "Paul is revealing his profound understanding of himself as God's coworker who endures everything for the sake of God. God humbles his coworkers by causing them to endure the insults and disobedience of others."[10] This is another way the Apostle enters more deeply into the mystery of suffering after the likeness of Jesus "on behalf of his body, which is the church" (Col 1:24).

Reflection and Application (12:19–21)

The witness of unity. Throughout his letters Paul encourages fellow Christians to live in unity with one another. Indeed, most of his specific exhortations promote unity. Why? One of the concrete manifestations of God's power at work in the gospel (Rom 1:16) is that it breaks down barriers that frequently alienate and divide people from one another, including barriers of race, ethnicity, socioeconomic differences, and gender (see Gal 3:28). For Paul it is tantamount to a miracle, a "new creation" (2 Cor 5:17), that the gospel brings together disparate people as brothers and sisters, adopted children of God through Christ. This is why the Apostle insists that the members of the churches he founded should strive to live in loving harmony with one another, seeking first the other's good. By doing so, they bear witness to what God has brought about through Christ Jesus and the outpouring of the Spirit.

But it is not just social differences that divide. So too do sins such as those Paul lists in verse 20. This list offers a concrete way of examining our commitment to unity—not just in our parishes, but also in our religious communities, in our families, at the workplace, and within our social circles. The sins Paul names there are, ultimately, manifestations of self-love and self-will. They are the opposite of what life in the Spirit empowers and rend apart the bonds of love that God creates. Working for unity calls each one of us to repent of our selfish

10. Frank J. Matera, *II Corinthians: A Commentary*, NTL (Louisville: Westminster John Knox, 2003), 300.

and conceited ways, of our acting out of jealousy and lashing out in anger, of our gossip and slander. Repentance, to be sure, is not sufficient in and of itself to bring about unity. Nevertheless, it is a necessary first step. Do we share Paul's passion to work for unity?

How Christ Speaks in Paul (13:1–4)

[1]This third time I am coming to you. "On the testimony of two or three witnesses a fact shall be established." [2]I warned those who sinned earlier and all the others, and I warn them now while absent, as I did when present on my second visit, that if I come again I will not be lenient, [3]since you are looking for proof of Christ speaking in me. He is not weak toward you but powerful in you. [4]For indeed he was crucified out of weakness, but he lives by the power of God. So also we are weak in him, but toward you we shall live with him by the power of God.

OT: Deut 19:15
NT: 1 Cor 1:22–25; 2:1–5; 11:1; Rev 1:5

Paul repeats his announcement that he is coming to Corinth for the third time. Citing a legal instruction from the book of Deuteronomy, he informs the community that he is now ready to take disciplinary action against those who persist in their sins. He indicates that he has been challenged by the Corinthians to prove that Christ speaks in him. While Paul is prepared to punish the guilty, he insists that his ultimate proof is that he conducts himself, through the power of the risen Jesus, in the way of Jesus' self-giving love.

13:1–2   As he did in 12:14, Paul notifies the Corinthians that he is **coming to** them for the **third time**. He follows this announcement with a quotation from Scripture: **"On the testimony of two or three witnesses a fact shall be established."** The text is Deut 19:15, a legal prescription that offered protection against inadequate or false testimony. According to this passage, two or more witnesses were required to convict a person of a crime.[11] Why does Paul cite this passage, and how does he appeal to its legal function? He reminds the community that he has already **warned those who sinned earlier and all the others** when he was **present on** his **second visit** to Corinth. The phrase "those who sinned earlier" refers to 12:21, that is, to those who have persisted in sexual immorality. The

11. The directive in Deut 19:15 is used in Matt 18:16 and 1 Tim 5:19; it is also alluded to in Mark 14:56; John 8:17; Heb 10:28; and 1 John 5:8.

phrase "all the others" points, in all probability, to those members of the community who are engaged in the types of divisive attitudes and behaviors listed in 12:20. In addition, Paul makes clear that he is *again* warning **them now while absent**, that is, as he writes.

What is the content of Paul's repeated warning? That if the Corinthians stubbornly remain in their sinful ways, he **will not be lenient**, literally, "will not spare." The time to repent and amend their ways is now (see 6:2). Up to this point Paul has sought to spare the community the rod of discipline. However, he will no longer do so if he finds members of the community persisting in actions that undermine the holiness of the Church, "the temple of the living God" (6:16). He will act definitively. Hence he cites Deut 19:15 to emphasize the gravity of his warning. In doing so, Paul employs the notion of witnesses figuratively. His warning on his second visit constitutes one "witness" against them; the present warning in conjunction with the upcoming third visit amounts to a second "witness."[12]

In addition to understanding "witnesses" in this figurative sense, I suggest that Paul's use of Deut 19:15 conveys a deeper level of meaning, one that rests on taking the literal meaning of two Greek words in the passage.[13] The word translated "witness" is *martys*, a term that can also denote one who bears witness at the cost of his or her life, that is, a martyr. The phrase rendered "on the testimony of" is, literally, "out of the *mouth* of."

At the most fundamental level, I propose that Paul is referring to Christ Jesus and to himself as *martyres*, witnesses. That is, he holds up Jesus as the first witness, the one whose entire life was marked by obedience to God's will (2 Cor 1:19–20). He bore witness to God's love for us by giving his life "for all" (5:14–15; John 3:16). Recall, moreover, that in 4:13 Paul interpreted the words of the Greek version of Ps 116:10 as the words of Jesus, thereby bearing witness to Jesus' faithfulness to God and to God's rescuing him from death.

Paul presents himself as a second witness. Indeed, he has portrayed himself throughout the letter as bearing witness by "always carrying in the body the dying of Jesus" (4:10), offering himself in self-giving love and enduring suffering for others because Christ dwells in him. What comes out of Paul's mouth is not only the proclamation "Jesus Christ is Lord" but also the words of his commitment to humbly serve the Corinthians in love (4:5), thereby embodying authentically what it means to "speak in Christ" (2:17; 12:19). He thus presents

---

12. This is how Chrysostom (*Homilies on 2 Corinthians* 29.1) understood Paul's meaning. The majority of commentators interpret Paul as referring to visits, warnings, or a combination thereof.

13. For a more detailed explanation of what follows, see Thomas D. Stegman, *The Character of Jesus: The Linchpin to Paul's Argument in 2 Corinthians*, AnBib 158 (Rome: Pontifical Biblical Institute, 2005), 369–75.

Jesus and himself to the community as two *martyres* who bear witness to complete faithfulness and obedience to God. Implicit here is the exhortation that the community is to emulate their example.

13:3–4   This interpretation is bolstered by the next verses and the paragraph that follows (vv. 5–9). Paul acknowledges that the Corinthians have challenged him to offer **proof** (*dokimē*) **of Christ speaking in** him. As we have seen (2:9; 8:8, 22; 9:13), *dokim-* terminology pertains to the testing of character; it also refers to the tried and true quality of character ascertained by such testing. In criticizing Paul for his humility (10:1; 11:7), for his unimpressive appearance and speaking abilities (10:10), and for his suffering and weaknesses (e.g., 11:23–33), some members of the community—likely abetted by the superapostles—have called his character into question. Is he really an instrument through whom Jesus reveals himself? Shouldn't a genuine †apostle demonstrate more impressive qualities than he does? Will he confront head on any disobedience or challenge to his authority—as some apparently have criticized him for not doing during his second visit? Paul assures the community that, through his ministry, Christ *is* **powerful** among them (**in you**). But he also wants them to appreciate *how* Christ's power will be operative through him and how Christ will continue to speak in him.

In verse 2, Paul has just made clear one way it will be evident that Christ speaks in him—through his apostolic authority to discipline those who have remained in their sinful ways. But he offers a further response to the Corinthians' challenge. In doing so, he seeks to correct their limited understanding of how divine power is manifested. Yes, it is revealed through "signs and wonders, and mighty deeds" (12:12). Yes, it is revealed, when necessary, through the exercise of authority to discipline. But, as Paul has been insisting all along, God's power also works through weakness (4:7; 6:4–5; 11:30; 12:9). This is what some of the Corinthians have failed to appreciate.

Paul thus sets forth Jesus as the prime example of the dynamic of divine-power-working-through-weakness. Indeed, he reminds the community that Christ **was crucified out of weakness**. What Paul means by this becomes clear when we recall how he has been using "weak" and "weakness" throughout chapters 10–12. These terms have connoted a way of appearing and behaving characterized by humility and gentleness, the antithesis of the arrogance and †boasting of the superapostles and their advocates. The terms have also signified a way of life marked by suffering and self-giving for the sake of others. Therefore, when Paul says that Jesus "was crucified out of weakness," he means that Christ's death on the cross was the culmination of his *entire* life that was poured out for the sake of others.

But the story of Jesus the †Messiah does not end in death. Rather, Jesus now **lives by the power of God**, a reference to God's raising him from the dead (4:14). This is the power that Paul has called "the life of Jesus" (4:10, 11), which is now at work in the Apostle and his ministry in Corinth.

Paul explains that this power enables him to participate in the character and story of Jesus to which he has just alluded. Notice that he concedes that he is **weak in** Christ. He thereby closely aligns himself with Jesus. Because of his intimate relationship with Christ—signified by the phrase "*in* him"—Paul shares in Jesus' "un-self-striving, self-negating, servant-like, God-centered" faithfulness.[14] He likewise participates in Christ's sufferings and offers his entire self, including his lack of impressive appearance and speaking skills, in service to Christ.

Paul goes on to say that, upon coming to Corinth, he will **live with** Jesus **by the power of God**. Moreover, this living with Jesus will be exercised **toward** the Corinthians. What does Paul mean here? He has already threatened to bring the rod of discipline (v. 2). But by referring to the story of Jesus and by aligning himself with Jesus' weakness, Paul is suggesting something more. He reminds the community once again that "the power of God" is at work through his self-giving love, his humble service, his suffering—in short, through his ministry as an earthen vessel (4:7).[15] He wants the community to understand that, while he can wield his God-given authority to take strong action against sinners, his way of being an apostle—the way marked by humility and self-giving—is also a manifestation that "Christ speaks in him." In fact, it is the manifestation par excellence.

Reflection and Application (13:1–4)

Fraternal correction. We have already considered the Church's vocation to holiness and the need for Christians to exercise mutual responsibility in living out this call (see the first entry under the Reflection and Application on 6:14–7:1). Our passage here invites us to consider that an essential aspect of mutual responsibility is fraternal correction. Fraternal correction refers to an individual admonishing a brother or sister in Christ who is engaged in sinful or harmful behavior. An act of charity, fraternal correction seeks the reformation of the other as well as his or her restoration within the community. It is not easy to

---

14. Timothy B. Savage, *Power through Weakness: Paul's Understanding of Christian Ministry in 2 Corinthians* (Cambridge: Cambridge University Press, 1996), 174–75.

15. The NIV successfully captures Paul's meaning here: "yet by God's power we will live with him to serve you." See also the NEB.

confront and challenge a person who is veering from the path of Christian life. It is much easier to complain about his or her faults to someone else. But Jesus calls us to exercise this kind of care for one another (Matt 18:15; see also Gal 6:1; James 5:19–20). While there is no guarantee that such an intervention will be well received—indeed, it is often met with scornful refusal—the price of not doing so is high. Was it the lack of fraternal correction within the Corinthian church that forced Paul to threaten a more severe form of punishment?

The proof of the pudding is in the eating. The Corinthians threw down the gauntlet before Paul by challenging him to prove that Christ speaks in him. The challenge was aimed at ascertaining whether he would stand up against those who were persisting in sinful behavior. In verse 2 the Apostle makes clear that he *is* willing to exercise the power of discipline. But he insists that the real proof that Christ speaks in us lies in something more profound and durable, not to mention, more difficult, namely, growing in our appropriation of Jesus' character, the character to which he has been alluding throughout the letter (see the second entry under the Reflection and Application on 11:1–6).

"Take on the Character of Jesus"

2 Corinthians 13:5–13

Having responded to the community's challenge to prove that "Christ speaks in him" (12:14–13:4), Paul now turns the challenge back on them. He admonishes the Corinthians to test themselves, to attend to whether or not they are growing in the way of faithfulness set forth by Jesus (13:5–10). He then offers a series of exhortations and concludes the letter with a solemn benediction (13:11–13).

Climactic Challenge (13:5–10)

⁵Examine yourselves to see whether you are living in faith. Test your-selves. Do you not realize that Jesus Christ is in you?—unless, of course, you fail the test. ⁶I hope you will discover that we have not failed. ⁷But we pray to God that you may not do evil, not that we may appear to have passed the test but that you may do what is right, even though we may seem to have failed. ⁸For we cannot do anything against the truth, but only for the truth. ⁹For we rejoice when we are weak but you are strong. What we pray for is your improvement.

¹⁰I am writing this while I am away, so that when I come I may not have to be severe in virtue of the authority that the Lord has given me to build up and not to tear down.

OT: Deut 30:15–20; Sir 15:15–17
NT: Rom 8:9–10, 29–30; 1 Cor 16:13–14; Gal 4:19–20

Paul challenges the Corinthians to examine themselves: Are they conducting themselves in the way of faith? He informs them that he is praying for them and reminds them one last time of his apostolic practice and authority.

13:5–6   Taking up the subject of character raised in 13:3–4, Paul issues a direct counterchallenge to the Corinthians to **examine** *themselves*.[1] That this self-examination pertains to character is clear from his reinforcement of the challenge: **Test yourselves**. Paul once again employs *dokim-* terminology, which we have seen involves the issue of character and its testing (2:9; 8:8, 22; 9:13; 13:3). In fact, he uses forms of *dokim-* terminology five times in verses 5–7.

In his challenge to the community, Paul makes clear what their test consists of: **to see whether you are living in faith**. The phrase translated by the NAB as "in faith" is literally "in *the* faith."[2] The inclusion of the definite article is significant because it indicates that he holds up a particular kind of faith as the standard for the community's test. What kind of faith does Paul refer to here? It is the "faith" or, better, the "faithfulness" alluded to in 13:4, namely *the faithfulness of Jesus*. Recall that Paul has just mentioned Christ's being "crucified out of weakness." This phrase is his shorthand for invoking Jesus' character, marked by humility and gentleness, and for his way of living, distinguished by self-giving and suffering for the sake of others. Jesus' character and manner of living, moreover, were undergirded by his obedience, his faithful "yes," to the Father's will (1:19–20). Recall too that in offering proof (*dokimē*) that Christ speaks in him, Paul has just insisted that, as one who lives with Jesus by the power of God, he conducts himself in the way of Jesus. Now, in verse 5, he exhorts the Corinthians to take on the character of Jesus, especially his faithfulness.

That this is the case is indicated by the rhetorical question: **Do you not realize that Jesus Christ is in you?** Paul's way of phrasing this question seeks to elicit the answer yes. But what, precisely, does "Christ is in you" mean? Paul uses the same phrase in Rom 8:10, where he describes what life in the Spirit involves. There the expression "Christ is in you" is the equivalent of saying "the Spirit of God dwells in you," the Spirit who has been identified as "the Spirit of Christ" (Rom 8:9). The rhetorical question in verse 5 serves, I suggest, to remind the community of the power of the Spirit of Christ already within them. Indeed, we have seen that this Spirit, whom Paul calls "the Spirit of faithfulness" (4:13, my translation), has already been bestowed on the Corinthians as a "first installment" in which they were both "anointed" (literally, "christed") and "sealed" (1:21–22).

Recall from the analysis of 1:21–22 that Paul indicated that God's gift empowers those who receive it to take on the character of Christ. This empowerment of

---

1. Paul indicates emphasis on self-testing by setting *heautous* (**yourselves**) in the prominent beginning position of v. 5.
2. The NIV, JB, and NJB appropriately insert the definite article before "faith."

John Paul II on Faith

In a speech at his weekly audience, Pope John Paul II reflected on the response of faith to the revelation of the incarnate Son of God. He set forth a description of faith that reflects Paul's teaching in 2 Corinthians, observing that faith consists in more than the adherence of the intellect to revealed truth; it also entails "a submission of the will and a gift of self to God revealing himself. It is a stance that involves one's entire existence" (General Audience, March 18, 1998). In the same address, the pontiff pointed out "the interior helps of the Holy Spirit" for the life of faith. Moreover, he insisted that faith spurs people "to true and deep consistency, which must be expressed in all aspects of a life modeled on that of Christ."

the Spirit is dynamic, for taking on the character of Jesus is an ongoing process. Paul refers to this ongoing empowerment in Gal 4:19, where he speaks to his spiritual children about "Christ be[ing] formed in you." It is important to point out that, in Gal 4:19, he employs the phrase "Christ . . . in you" in connection with being formed after the likeness of Jesus. Hence Paul's rhetorical question in verse 5 is an implicit exhortation to the community to grow more and more into the likeness—that is, into the "image"—of Christ (2 Cor 3:18).[3] The Corinthians can do so because the risen Christ dwells in them, individually and corporately (see, e.g., Matt 18:20; Col 1:17).

Continuing to home in on the issue of character, Paul adds: **unless, of course,** the Corinthians are "*not* tried and true," or "*not* genuine."[4] His strategy here is to send the community a wakeup call, to capture their attention and inspire the appropriate response: to be "in the faith." Paul expresses his **hope** in verse 6 that they **will discover that** *he* is "tried and true."[5] That is, he hopes that the Corinthians will understand what he has said in verses 3–4—that his humble service and self-giving love demonstrate his genuine apostolic character.

Paul informs the Corinthians that he prays **to God** for them—information he repeats at the end of verse 9. This notice ought not to be passed over too quickly. Just as he has asked the community to pray for him (1:11), so here he

13:7

---

3. Victor Paul Furnish captures well what Paul means by "faith" in v. 5: life "placed under the rule of Christ's love (5:14) . . . conducted according to the guidance of the Spirit" (*II Corinthians: A New Translation with Introduction and Commentary*, AB 32A [New York: Doubleday, 1984], 577).

4. These phrases capture better the meaning of *adokimos* here than the NAB's **fail the test**.

5. This phrase expresses positively what is expressed as, in effect, a double negative in the Greek text.

reveals that he holds them up before God in prayer. Such is part of his apostolic care for them. What is the content of Paul's prayer? That the Corinthians **may not do evil**, or, as he expresses this more positively, that they **may do what is right**. He explains that his ultimate concern is for *them* (see 12:19), not for his own vindication as one shown to be "proven" (*dokimos*).

In effect, Paul prays that all the members of the community embody the Amen (1:20), the faithful commitment to carry out God's will in their lives. This is what is meant by doing what is right or good (see Rom 12:2; 1 Thess 5:21). If the Corinthians succeed in this, especially in the manner of ridding themselves of divisive and sinful behavior, there will be no need for Paul to administer disciplinary punishment upon his arrival. In this sense he is happy to be regarded as having **failed** to exercise punitive power (see v. 3, where it is implied that, from the perspective of some in Corinth, he needs to prove his character by a demonstration of power).

13:8   Paul reminds the Corinthians one last time of his apostolic way of proceeding: he **cannot do anything against the truth, but only for the truth**. By "truth" he refers to what he has just suggested about "what is right," or "good," namely, doing the will of God.[6] More specifically, he refers to manifesting Jesus' faithfulness. Recall that in 4:2 Paul offered a positive commendation of himself by means of "the open declaration of the truth." As we saw there, this declaration of truth is another way of talking about the Spirit-empowered transformation into the image of Christ (3:18) manifested by incarnating Jesus' suffering and self-giving love (4:10–11). Similarly, Paul insisted in 11:10 that "the truth of Christ" is in him. Recall that there he explained that his practice of proclaiming the †gospel without charge is a concrete expression of his commitment to conduct himself after the manner of Jesus' humility and self-offering.

13:9   Paul states that he can **rejoice when** he is **weak**—when he offers himself freely to the Corinthians, not using his apostolic authority for self-aggrandizement, and when he suffers on account of Christ—because in doing so the Corinthians are made **strong**. Here he reiterates the point he made in 4:12, where he revealed that his ministry among them—one marked by "death," that is, by self-giving service—has brought "life" to them. The community is made "strong" in faith because Christ is acting through Paul. Indeed, it is through the power of the risen Jesus that he aligns himself with Jesus' manner of living, thereby embodying the gospel he has proclaimed to them. Paul then repeats his commitment to **pray** for the Corinthians. Now he

---

6. Paul uses "the truth" and "the good" as synonyms in Rom 2:8, 10.

prays for their **improvement**, or better, their "restoration," for their putting their ways right.[7]

Finally, Paul reiterates his purpose in **writing** (see 12:19): he wants the Corin-   **13:10**
thians to attend to their life "in the faith" and to mend their ways **so that when**
he comes he will **not have to be severe**. The warning about acting with severity
pertains specifically to his command to put an end to the divisive behavior and
sexual immorality in their midst. The Apostle concludes by reminding the community of **the authority that the Lord has given** him **to build up and not to
tear down** (10:8; 12:19). He does not want to act with severity. But if forced to
do so, he makes clear, it will be for the well-being of the church in Corinth.

It is important to add that, throughout the letter, Paul has made clear a
number of things the Corinthians need to do in order to manifest their living
"in the faith." He has called them to appreciate and accept his manner of being
an †apostle, and to deepen their reconciliation with him; to follow his lead and
offer forgiveness to the person who had offended him; to give freely and generously to the collection for the church in Jerusalem; and to reject the dangerous
influence of the superapostles and their criticisms of him.

Reflection and Application (13:5–10)

The importance of character formation. In the course of analyzing this letter, we
have seen that Paul challenges the Corinthians to various tests of character. He
regards his exhortation to forgive and receive back a fellow community member
as a test of their obedience (2:9): Will they obey God's call to participate in the
work of reconciliation inaugurated through the life, death, and resurrection of
Christ? Similarly, he considers the collection for the Jerusalem church to be a
test of their love: Will they respond with compassion and generosity to fellow
Christians in need (8:8)? Moreover, in challenging the Corinthians to reject
the superapostles and their opposition to him, Paul explains how he conforms
his life and ministry to the pattern of Jesus' humility and self-giving love (e.g.,
4:7–15; 11:23–33): Will the community pass the test to heed him rather than
the intruding missionaries? Will they recognize that "gentleness and clemency"
(10:1) are marks of an authentic ambassador of Christ? It therefore comes as
no surprise that, when we arrive at the climax of the body of the letter, he issues a final character test to the Corinthians: Are they truly making progress
in walking "in the faith"—in the way of Jesus' faithfulness to his Father's will,
the faithfulness that bore fruit in his self-giving love?

---

7. The NEB conveys well Paul's sense: "my whole prayer is that all may be put right with you."

Paul thus shows the importance of character formation for ministers, teachers, parents, and others who exercise positions of Christian leadership. What is needed is not just any character formation, but specifically formation in the values, attitudes, and behavioral patterns of Jesus himself. Paul's strategy in 2 Corinthians reveals that, before getting involved in the particulars of discerning what we should be doing, it is essential to be concerned with *what kind of people we are becoming.*

Final Exhortation and Benediction (13:11–13)

¹¹**Finally, brothers, rejoice. Mend your ways, encourage one another, agree with one another, live in peace, and the God of love and peace will be with you. ¹²Greet one another with a holy kiss. All the holy ones greet you.**

¹³**The grace of the Lord Jesus Christ and the love of God and the fellowship of the holy Spirit be with all of you.**

OT: Exod 34:4–9
NT: Matt 28:19–20; 1 Cor 12:4–6; Eph 4:4–6; 1 Thess 5:14–25; Titus 3:4–7
Catechism: the Trinity, 238–60
Lectionary: Trinity Sunday (Year A)

Paul concludes the letter with a series of brief exhortations to the Corinthians, assuring them of God's love and peace. He then calls the members of the community to greet one another with "a holy kiss." After extending greetings to them, he offers a threefold benediction.

13:11   Paul signals the transition to the ending of the letter with **Finally**. Significantly, he refers to the community as **brothers**, a term that includes *all* the members of the church in Corinth (i.e., as "brothers and sisters"—1:8 and 8:1). After his stern warning in 13:2, it is important for Paul to end on a note of affection and love. Although he is their founding †apostle and spiritual father, he is also their brother in the family of God.

Moreover, he reminds the Corinthians that they are brothers and sisters to one another, a reality that grounds the five exhortations that follow. First, Paul calls on them to **rejoice**. They are to rejoice in the good things God has done for them (see Phil 4:4; 1 Thess 5:16). They can also take joy in the fact that Paul rejoices in them and prays for them (2 Cor 13:9). Second, he summons the community to **mend** their **ways**, a shorthand exhortation to put an end to sexual immorality and divisive behavior (12:20–21) as well as to all the ways they have opposed Paul. The verb "mend" (*katartizō*) recalls their "restoration" (*katartisis*) for which he prays (13:9). Third, he exhorts them to **encourage one another**, an echo of the opening †blessing (1:3–7). As Paul has committed himself to encourage the Corinthians, so are they to help one another. Fourth, he urges them to **agree with one another**, literally, to "think the same" (see Phil 2:2). This does not mean to have the exact same thoughts or opinions about everything. It does mean their heeding the Spirit's bestowal of "the mind of Christ" (1 Cor 2:16; see Phil 2:5), inspiring them to live no longer for themselves (2 Cor 5:15) and to seek to be reconciled with one another. Fifth, he encourages them to **live in peace** (1 Thess 5:13), something they can do if they are truly committed to the work of reconciliation.[8]

Paul follows his five exhortations with a consoling promise—a promise that holds for all readers of this letter: **the God of love and peace will be with you**. Paul refers here to two divine attributes, love and peace, that are gifts God has bestowed on us. God's love was most dramatically demonstrated in his sending his Son to us while we were still sinners (Rom 5:8), and Jesus the †Messiah revealed this divine love by dying "for all" (2 Cor 5:14). Moreover, God's love has been poured into our hearts through the gift of the Spirit (Rom 5:5; 2 Cor 1:21–22). Concerning peace, God has conferred this gift on us by reconciling the world to himself through the death of Christ (Rom 5:10; 2 Cor 5:18). With his reference to "the God of love and peace," Paul reminds the community of what God has *already* done for them; therefore it is appropriate for them to "rejoice." With his use of a future tense verb, he suggests that God's love and peace *will be with* the Corinthians so that they will be empowered to mend their ways, encourage one another, be of one mind, and live in peace with one another.

Paul exhorts the members of the community to **greet one another with a holy kiss**. The "holy kiss" refers to the formal greeting of peace between members of the church. The kiss is holy because it takes place between those who are the "holy ones" (as later in this verse; see 1:1). Keep in mind that the Corinthians will hear this exhortation as they are assembled—perhaps at the eucharistic liturgy[9]—to listen to the letter as it is read aloud. While Paul regularly invited his communities to exchange the kiss of peace (Rom 16:16; 1 Cor 16:20; 1 Thess

13:12

---

8. Frank J. Matera (*II Corinthians: A Commentary*, NTL [Louisville: Westminster John Knox, 2003], 312–13) comments that the fifth imperative is a fitting finale to the series of exhortations because peace is the result of reconciliation. Indeed, it is an appropriate climactic sounding of the motif of reconciliation.

9. Evidence is not sufficient to determine whether the earliest church practiced the "holy kiss" at liturgical celebrations. The practice was established by the mid-second century. See Justin Martyr, *1 Apology* 65.

5:26), his exhortation here is particularly poignant because it dramatically reinforces his summons to reconciliation (see Luke 15:20).

He then sends greetings to the Corinthians from **all the holy ones**—minimally, a reference to the Christians in †Macedonia (i.e., in †Philippi or †Thessalonica or both) with whom he is staying as he dictates the letter; perhaps, more broadly, a reference to "all the churches of Christ" (Rom 16:16). The mention of other churches here is not accidental. Paul thereby reminds the community in Corinth that their reconciliation and growth in the Spirit are not for their sake alone. Others, such as the Jerusalem church, stand to benefit if the Corinthians heed the challenges of this letter. The Church is always more than an individual community of believers.

13:13   At long last, Paul brings the letter to a formal conclusion as he offers a solemn benediction: **The grace of the Lord Jesus Christ and the love of God and the fellowship of the holy Spirit be with all of you.** This closing blessing is particularly striking when compared with Paul's other concluding blessings. Typically, he ends his letters thus: "The †grace of the (or our) Lord Jesus (Christ) be with you."[10] The additions to this typical benediction in verse 13 are important on the level of theology and the level of Christian life. In terms of theology, the additions serve to remind the Corinthians of the chief theological concerns of the letter. Central to this final blessing is "the love of God." God's love for us is such that he holds nothing back from us in order that we might have the fullness of life.

As we just saw at the end of verse 11, God's love has been manifested in two supreme ways, both of which are signified here. First, God has sent his Son to save us from sin and death (5:18–21). Hence Paul refers to "the grace of our Lord Jesus Christ," the same phrase he employed in 8:9 to signify Jesus' self-giving love in becoming human and offering his life on the cross in obedience to the Father's will. Second, God has bestowed in our hearts the gift of the Holy Spirit[11] (1:22; 3:3) to purify and sanctify us, to make us his holy people (6:16). Hence Paul adds the reference to the Spirit.

In addition to its theological import, the solemn final blessing functions as a bulwark for life in the Church. The phrase "the fellowship (*koinōnia*) of the Holy Spirit" is, as one commentator aptly notes, "powerfully ambiguous."[12] It

---

10. See Rom 16:20; 1 Cor 16:23; Gal 6:18; Phil 4:23; 1 Thess 5:28; 2 Thess 3:18; Philem 25. Similarly, Eph 6:24 and 2 Tim 4:22. In the remaining letters (Col 4:18; 1 Tim 6:21; Titus 3:15), Paul concludes with "Grace be with you."

11. The RSV, NRSV, JB, NJB, and NIV all appropriately capitalize the word "Holy" in referring to the Spirit in v. 13.

12. J. Paul Sampley, "Second Letter to the Corinthians: Introduction, Commentary, and Reflections," in *The New Interpreter's Bible: A Commentary in Twelve Volumes*, ed. L. E. Keck et al. (Nashville: Abingdon, 2000), 11:179.

refers to the gift of the Spirit in us whereby each one of us is, literally, in close communion with God. In other words, it points to the intimacy God offers us through the Spirit's presence in our hearts. As we have seen at various points in the letter (e.g., 1:22; 3:2–3; 3:18; 4:13), the presence of the Spirit forms us more and more into the likeness of Jesus. In addition, the phrase signifies the fellowship among believers, among the "brothers and sisters" in God's family, that the Spirit creates and enables. This is particularly important for the Apostle, who has called the Corinthians to end divisions, in other words, to seek greater communion with one another. He has also invited them to foster the *koinōnia* of the larger Church through their selfless generosity (9:13). In both cases, they can do so through the Spirit's empowering them to walk in the way of Christ's self-giving love.

How fitting it is that the letter that began with a blessing (1:3–7) ends with a solemn benediction. Because Paul's second †canonical letter to the Corinthians has become part of the Church's Scripture, we too are included in these blessings. Through the careful study and appropriation of the rich content of this epistle, we can become a blessing to others. And in doing so, we give glory to the God named by Paul as one and triune—as the God who is the Father of love, the Lord Jesus Christ, and the Holy Spirit.

Reflection and Application (13:11–13)

Holy Trinity. The doctrine of God as one and triune took hundreds of years to be fully formulated. What Paul's writings reveal, at a remarkably early period—recall that he wrote 2 Corinthians only a quarter century after the death and resurrection of Christ—is an extraordinarily rich appreciation of what theologians call the "economic Trinity," that is, God revealed in his activity in history through the sending of his Son and the outpouring of his Spirit. One prominent Pauline scholar refers to Paul's benediction in 2 Cor 13:13 as "the most profound theological moment in the Pauline corpus."[13] The Apostle's blessing here contains in embryonic form the rich understanding of the Trinity formulated in the Church's great ecumenical councils.

Liturgical connections. Two elements from verses 11–13 have made their way into the Catholic Church's eucharistic celebration. The exchange of the kiss of peace takes place after the recitation of the Lord's Prayer, just before Holy Communion. Its location there is significant for two reasons. First, having

---

13. Gordon D. Fee, *God's Empowering Presence: The Holy Spirit in the Letters of Paul* (Peabody, MA: Hendrickson, 1994), 363.

In the Liturgy

The rich portrayal of God in 2 Cor 13:11–13 makes this passage an appropriate reading for the celebration of the solemnity of the Holy Trinity (Year A), where it is read along with Exod 34:4b–6, 8–9 and John 3:16–18. Paul's characterization of "the God of love and peace" is given greater texture by God's self-revelation to Moses in Exod 34:6: "The Lord, the Lord, a merciful and gracious God, slow to anger and rich in kindness and fidelity." While the gospel reading highlights God's love as manifested through his "giving his only Son" for the life of the world, Paul's reference to "the fellowship of the Holy Spirit" sheds light on how God accedes to Moses' request to "come along in our company," that is, to be present to God's people.

just finished praying in one voice to our Father, we are reminded that we are brothers and sisters in the family of God; thus we are to regard and treat one another as such. Second, as a sign of peace and reconciliation, we are challenged by this gesture to commit ourselves more earnestly to "the ministry of reconciliation" (5:18). Indeed, we can most authentically receive the body and blood of Christ only when we are fully reconciled with *all* of our brothers and sisters (see Matt 5:20–26).

In addition, Paul's solemn benediction has become the prayer greeting following the opening Sign of the Cross. We ought not to let our familiarity with its words prevent us from appropriating its profound content. As the Catechism teaches about the epiclesis, or invocation, of the Spirit:

> The epiclesis is also a prayer for the full effect of the assembly's communion with the mystery of Christ. "The grace of the Lord Jesus Christ and the love of God and the fellowship of the Holy Spirit" have to remain with us always and bear fruit beyond the Eucharistic celebration. The Church therefore asks the Father to send the Holy Spirit to make the lives of the faithful a living sacrifice to God by their spiritual transformation into the image of Christ, by concern for the Church's unity, and by taking part in her mission through the witness and service of charity. (Catechism, 1109; quoting 2 Cor 13:13)

A better summary of the spirituality of 2 Corinthians does not exist.

Suggested Resources

Introductions to Paul's Life, Writings, and Message

Gorman, Michael J. *Reading Paul*. Eugene, OR: Cascade, 2008. Gorman sets
forth eight of Paul's "big ideas" in a reliable and accessible manner.

Harrington, Daniel J. *Meeting St. Paul Today: Understanding the Man, His Mission, and His Message*. Chicago: Loyola, 2008. Harrington, a Jesuit priest,
provides an excellent introduction to Paul, his work, and his writings.

Martini, Carlo Maria. *The Gospel according to St. Paul: Meditations on His Life
and Letters*. Translated by M. Daigle-Williamson. Ijamsville, MD: The Word
among Us, 2008. Martini, a Jesuit and the retired archbishop of Milan, shares a
life's worth of profound biblical reflections on the life and writings of Paul.

Murphy-O'Connor, Jerome. *Paul: His Story*. New York: Oxford University Press,
2004. Murphy-O'Connor, a Dominican priest, presents a moving reconstruction of Paul's life and ministry.

Wright, N. T. *Paul: In Fresh Perspective*. Minneapolis: Fortress, 2005. Wright,
an Anglican bishop (Diocese of Durham), offers a helpful introduction to
key themes in Paul's writings as well as a brief systematic presentation of the
structures of his theology.

Background on Corinth

Murphy-O'Connor, Jerome. *St. Paul's Corinth: Texts and Archaeology*. 3rd rev.
and exp. ed. Collegeville, MN: Liturgical Press, 2002. Murphy-O'Connor

brings ancient Corinth to life through an exploration of literary and archaeological evidence.

Commentaries on 2 Corinthians

Furnish, Victor Paul. *II Corinthians: A New Translation with Introduction and Commentary*. AB 32A. New York: Doubleday, 1984. Although a generation old, Furnish's excellent commentary remains one of the most consulted.

Harris, Murray J. *The Second Epistle to the Corinthians*. NIGTC. Grand Rapids: Eerdmans, 2005. Harris's monumental, technical work contains several profound theological insights.

Matera, Frank J. *II Corinthians: A Commentary*. NTL. Louisville: Westminster John Knox, 2003. Matera, a priest of the Archdiocese of Hartford, offers an insightful yet accessible interpretation.

Sampley, J. Paul. "The Second Letter to the Corinthians: Introduction, Commentary, and Reflections." In Vol. 11 of *The New Interpreter's Bible: A Commentary in Twelve Volumes*, edited by L. E. Keck et al., 1–180. Nashville: Abingdon, 2000. Sampley's commentary includes helpful pastoral reflections following his exegetical comments.

Thrall, Margaret E. *A Critical and Exegetical Commentary on the Second Epistle to the Corinthians*. ICC. 2 vols. Edinburgh: T&T Clark, 1994–2000. Thrall's comprehensive work sets forth the fruits of a lifetime of study.

Pastoral Commentaries on 2 Corinthians

Barclay, William. *Letters to the Corinthians*. New Daily Study Bible. Louisville: Westminster John Knox, 2002. Barclay conveys well the theological and pastoral significance of Paul's writings.

Barnett, Paul. *The Message of 2 Corinthians: Power in Weakness*. Downers Grove, IL: InterVarsity, 1988. Barnett provides a reading that is sensitive to Paul's teaching and apostolic self-understanding.

Wright, N. T. *Paul for Everyone: 2 Corinthians*. Louisville: Westminster John Knox, 2004. The Anglican bishop supplies a fresh translation and offers brief, accessible commentary with thoughts on the text's relevance for today.

Theology of 2 Corinthians

Murphy-O'Connor, Jerome. *The Theology of the Second Letter to the Corinthians.* New Testament Theology. Cambridge: Cambridge University Press, 1991. Murphy-O'Connor offers an interpretation of the letter with an eye toward its theological content.

Spirituality of 2 Corinthians

Martini, Carlo Maria. *In the Thick of His Ministry.* Translated by D. Livingstone. Collegeville, MN: Liturgical Press, 1990. Martini proposes retreat reflections geared especially for ministers from selected texts from 2 Corinthians.

Glossary

Achaia: the Roman province of which Corinth was the capital. It consisted of roughly the southern half of present-day Greece. Paul brought the gospel to Achaia, first in Athens (Acts 17:15–34) and then in Corinth, where he founded a church (Acts 18:1–18).

Aegean Sea: the body of water (part of the Mediterranean Sea) between present-day Greece and Turkey. Paul crossed this sea on different occasions in his missionary work (e.g., Acts 18:18–19).

analogy of faith: as defined by the Catechism (114), "the coherence of the truths of faith among themselves and within the whole plan of Revelation."

anthropology: the study of human beings. According to Paul, human beings are composed of spirit (the dimension of human existence wherein the Holy Spirit communicates with and inspires people), soul, and body (1 Thess 5:23).

Antioch (in Pisidia): a city in the south-central part of present-day Turkey to which Paul along with Barnabas brought the gospel before his mission to Macedonia and Achaia (Acts 13:14–50).

apostle, apostleship: literally, "one who is sent." Paul uses the term to indicate two interrelated characteristics: (1) an apostle is one to whom the risen Christ has revealed himself (1 Cor 9:1; 15:8–9); and (2) an apostle is one commissioned by the risen Lord to proclaim the gospel (Gal 1:15–16; see Acts 9:15). Paul's commission was to preach Christ especially among the Gentiles. He understood apostleship to entail both verbal proclamation and living after the manner of Jesus' self-giving love (2 Cor 4:5).

ark of the covenant: the wooden chest that contained the two tablets on which were written the Ten Commandments. The covering of the ark was flanked by two cherubim that formed, in effect, a throne for God (Exod 25:10–22). Originally, the ark was placed in the meeting tent (Exod 40:20–21); later it was kept in the innermost sanctuary of the temple built by Solomon (1 Kings 8:1–11).

Asia: the Roman province of which Ephesus was the capital. It consisted of the western part of present-day Turkey.

Beliar: another name for Satan, the personification of evil and God's archenemy. The only occurrence of "Beliar" in the New Testament is 2 Cor 6:15.

Beroea: a town in the province of Macedonia to which Paul brought the gospel (Acts 17:10–13).

blessing: (in Hebrew, *berakah*) a typically Jewish form of prayer of praise to God, often used in liturgical settings. Paul uses this form of prayer in 2 Cor 1:3–7 and Eph 1:3–14. Other examples in the New Testament are Luke 1:68–79 (known as the *Benedictus*, the Latin word for "blessed") and 1 Pet 1:3–9.

boasting: a common phenomenon in the Greco-Roman world of Paul's time, reflecting the spirit of competition and self-promotion. For Paul there are two kinds of boasting, illegitimate and legitimate. Illegitimate boasting focuses on one's own self, for example, talents and accomplishments. Legitimate boasting puts the spotlight on what *God* is doing through people. Paul's rule on boasting is: "Whoever boasts, should boast in the Lord" (1 Cor 1:30; 2 Cor 10:17).

canonical: relating to an established rule or list; used to describe those writings that comprise the Bible because they set forth God's revelation.

captivity epistles: the letters Paul wrote while in prison: Ephesians, Philippians, Colossians, 2 Timothy, and Philemon.

client: see **patron–client relationship**.

***commend* oneself**: the positive form of self-commendation, indicated by the word order in which *self* comes last. Paul refers to it in 2 Cor 4:2 and 6:4. According to him, Christians "commend themselves" by conducting themselves after the manner of Jesus. Compare *self*-**commend**.

Damascus: the city in present-day Syria near where Paul received his call from the risen Lord to preach the gospel to the Gentiles (Acts 9:1–22; 22:1–21; 26:1–23; see Gal 1:15–17). Paul later narrowly escaped the clutches of the governor of this city (2 Cor 11:32–33).

divine passive: the use of the passive voice (e.g., "was caught up into Paradise," 2 Cor 12:4) to indicate that God is the doer of the action. This usage reflects Jewish reverence for God's name.

ecclesiology: the theological study of the Church.

Ephesus: the capital city of the Roman province of Asia, located on the west coast of present-day Turkey. Paul ministered there immediately after establishing the church in Corinth (Acts 18:19–20). A short time later Ephesus served as Paul's missionary base for over two years (Acts 19:1–41; see 1 Cor 16:8–9).

epistolary aorist: a literary convention in Greek in which the letter writer uses a past tense to describe an event that is happening as the author writes but will be past from the time perspective of the recipients of the letter. Paul uses this convention in 2 Cor 2:9; 8:17, 18, 22; and 9:3.

eschatological: referring to the end time and last things, for example, Christ's return in glory, the resurrection of the body, judgment, heaven, and hell.

expiatory: serving to make atonement. Paul understands Jesus' death on the cross as a sacrifice for the forgiveness of sins (e.g., Rom 3:25; 1 Cor 5:7; 2 Cor 5:21).

flesh: often used by Paul as the opposite of "Spirit." As such, it signifies that which derives from human beings, not influenced or empowered by God's Spirit (see Gal 5:16–26). Used in this sense, it refers to the condition of fallen humanity, opposed to God and God's way.

Gentile: a person who is not a Jew by race or religion. Paul's apostolic call was to proclaim the gospel to the Gentiles (Gal 1:16). He proclaimed that, through Christ, God is forming the Church from both Jews and Gentiles, "one new person in place of the two" (Eph 2:15; see Gal 3:28).

God-fearers: Gentile sympathizers to Judaism, whose contact with synagogues led to their knowledge of Jewish ways and Scriptures. The Roman centurion Cornelius was such a "God-fearing" Gentile (Acts 10:22).

gospel: the "good news" about the salvation God has brought about through the life, death, and resurrection of Jesus. For Paul this "good news"—including the very act of proclaiming it to others—"is the power of God for the salvation of everyone who believes" (Rom 1:16). Paul's understanding and use of the word *gospel* predates the writing of the four canonical Gospels (Matthew, Mark, Luke, and John).

grace: literally, a "favor" or "gift." For Paul it refers primarily to the gift of God's redeeming love revealed in the life, death, and resurrection of Jesus and in the bestowal of the Holy Spirit in human hearts.

hardship catalog, hardship list: a convention in Paul's time used by some philosophers to show that the endurance of sufferings proves one's wisdom, courage, and ability to rise above the vicissitudes of life. Paul adapts this convention. In setting forth the various sufferings he endures for the sake of Christ, Paul reveals that it is God's power that sustains him (2 Cor 4:8–9; 6:4–10; 11:23–29; 12:10).

honor–shame: the social value system in the world of Paul. It involved the issue of public reputation, which was equated with one's self-identity. A person experienced honor when his or her claim to self-worth was acknowledged by peers or by society at large. Shame resulted from the failure to obtain or maintain acknowledgement of one's claim to worth and honor.

Iconium: a city in the south-central part of present-day Turkey to which Paul along with Barnabas brought the gospel before his mission to Macedonia and Achaia (Acts 13:51–14:5).

image of God, divine image: theological concept signifying that human beings bear a resemblance to God by virtue of their being created in God's likeness (Gen 1:26–27). Paul taught that Christ is the image of God par excellence (2 Cor 4:4), the one who showed forth the glory and greatness of God through his self-giving love that culminated in his death on the cross. Now raised from the dead, Christ fully radiates God's glory. Empowered by the gift of the Holy Spirit, human beings can manifest God's glory in the present by embodying Jesus' character and manner of life (2 Cor 3:18).

intertextuality: a literary term referring to the use of an older text in such a way that its meaning is transformed within the context of a newer writing.

Judea: the area of the Holy Land surrounding Jerusalem. During the time of Paul's ministry, it was ruled by Roman governors called procurators.

Lystra: a city in the south-central part of present-day Turkey to which Paul along with Barnabas brought the gospel before his mission to Macedonia and Achaia (Acts 14:6–20).

Macedonia: the Roman province, including present-day northern Greece, into which Paul brought the gospel in response to a vision (Acts 16:9–10). Paul founded churches there in the cities of Philippi (Acts 16:11–40) and Thessalonica (Acts 17:1–9).

meeting tent: the sanctuary, housing the ark of the covenant, wherein Moses frequently communicated with God (Exod 33:7–11; 34:34–35). Its layout and construction are described in Exod 25–40.

Messiah: literally, the "anointed one"—translated into Greek as *Christos* ("Christ")—the figure from the line of David through whom God was expected to bring salvation to Israel. Paul proclaimed "the Son of God, Jesus Christ" as the fulfillment of all God's promises (2 Cor 1:19–20), the one through whom God has reconciled all people to himself (2 Cor 5:18). Raised from the dead, Jesus the Messiah now reigns as Lord (Rom 1:3–4).

Mosaic covenant: the covenant made between God and the people of Israel through the mediation of Moses (Exod 19–24). An important aspect of the covenant was the divine law given to Israel through which the people were instructed how to show forth God's holiness to the nations (see Lev 19:2). Paul came to understand that the law given to Israel served as a "disciplinarian" until the coming of Christ (Gal 3:23–25), the one to whom the law pointed and in whom it is fulfilled (Rom 10:4).

Mount Sinai: the place where God and Israel entered into a covenant relationship following the exodus from Egypt.

Neapolis: seaport town for Philippi, on the coast of the Aegean Sea. When Paul first brought the gospel to present-day Greece, he landed at Neapolis (Acts 16:11).

new Adam: a reference to Jesus, who revealed how human beings are intended by God to live in faithful obedience to God and in self-giving love for others. Through the disobedience of the first Adam, human beings fell under the enslaving powers of sin and death; now, through the obedience of Christ—the new Adam who was obedient to death (Phil 2:8)—have come the abundance of grace and the possibility of being made righteous for eternal life (Rom 5:12–21).

new covenant: what God has brought about through the life, death, and resurrection of Jesus and through the outpouring of the Holy Spirit. Paul was called to proclaim the gospel as a minister of the new covenant (2 Cor 3:4–6). Through belief in the gospel and the empowerment of the Spirit, the people of the new covenant—the Church—are able to "fulfill the law of Christ" (Gal 6:2), which is the law of love (Mark 12:28–34).

old covenant: the **Mosaic covenant**.

pagan: pertaining to polytheistic religion; often associated with sensuality and idolatry.

paschal mystery: Christ's life, suffering, death, resurrection, ascension, exaltation, and sending of the Holy Spirit, which as a whole reveal and accomplish God's work of redemption.

patron–client relationship: a type of social relationship prominent in Paul's world. The patron bestowed benefaction, usually financial support, on chosen recipients who were called clients. Such patronage brought honor to the benefactor from the client and gave him or her influence over the client, who was often beholden to the whims of the patron.

Pharisee: a member of a Jewish renewal movement, consisting mostly of lay members, who sought to purify Israel through rigorous observance of the Jewish law. Before his encounter with the risen Christ, Paul was a Pharisee (Phil 3:5) who had great zeal for his ancestral traditions (Gal 1:14).

Philippi: a city in the province of Macedonia where Paul founded a church, the first one he established in what is present-day Greece (Acts 16:12–40). A letter from Paul to the church in Philippi is part of the New Testament canon.

self-**commend**: the negative form of self-commendation, indicated by the word order in which *self* comes first. Paul refers to it in 2 Cor 3:1; 5:12; 10:12. According to him, *self*-commending is characterized by boasting of one's own accomplishments and seeking one's own glory; it often includes denigrating others. Compare **commend oneself**.

Septuagint: the Greek translation of the portions of the Old Testament that were originally written in Hebrew and Aramaic, along with other writings composed in Greek. Most Scripture quotations and allusions found in New Testament writings come from the Septuagint.

Son of David: a designation of Jesus denoting his identity as Messiah. The Messiah was expected to be a descendant of David (see, e.g., Luke 1:32–33; John 7:42; Rom 1:3–4).

soteriological: pertaining to God's work of salvation in Christ and its implications.

soteriology: the study of salvation, focusing in particular on the death and resurrection of Jesus as the salvific event in Christianity.

tearful letter: the letter, no longer extant, written by Paul to the Corinthians following his second, painful visit to the community. He refers to this letter in 2 Cor 2:4 and 7:8.

textual attestation: a scholarly term referring to what is found in the earliest and best manuscripts from which translations of the Bible are made.

Thessalonica: a city in the province of Macedonia where Paul founded a church (Acts 17:1–9). Two letters from Paul to the church there are part of the New Testament canon.

triumphal procession: an extravagant celebration of a great military victory, conducted in Rome. A parade honoring the victorious general and his army, it involved exhibiting the spoils of war—including the forced march of chained prisoners from the conquered forces, many of whom were then led to death. Paul uses this imagery in 2 Cor 2:14 and Col 2:15.

Troas: a seaport city on the Aegean Sea on the northwest coast of the province of Asia in present-day western Turkey. It was there that Paul saw the vision of a Macedonian that led to the proclamation of the gospel in present-day Greece (Acts 16:8–10). Later, Paul left behind a promising missionary venture in Troas in order to find Titus to hear how the Corinthians had responded to the tearful letter (2 Cor 2:12–13).

YHWH: the Israelite name for God, probably pronounced "Yahweh" (Exod 3:15). Over time Jews came to consider this name too sacred to pronounce aloud; thus when reading Scripture, pious Jews would say *Adonai*, that is, "Lord." The Septuagint rendered the sacred name as *kyrios* ("Lord"), a term that became one of the titles for Jesus.

Index of Pastoral Topics

This index indicates where topics that may be useful for evangelization, catechesis, apologetics, or other forms of pastoral ministry are mentioned in 2 Corinthians.

313

Index of Sidebars

N
THRACE
Thessalonica
Philippi
Thermaic Gulf
MACEDONIA
Troas
Aegean Sea
ASIA
Corinth
Athens
ACHAIA
Ephesus
Egnatian Way
0 25 50 mi
0 25 50 km